D0855356

PATRONS AND CLIENTS

Patrons and Clients

in Mediterranean Societies

edited by

Ernest Gellner
and John Waterbury

Duckworth

in association with the Center for Mediterranean Studies
of the American Universities Field Staff

First published in 1977 by
Gerald Duckworth and Co. Ltd.
43 Gloucester Crescent, London NW1
© Gerald Duckworth and Co. Ltd 1977

Library of Congress Cataloging in Publication Data

Main entry under title:

Patrons and clients.

  1. Patronage, Political – Addresses, essays,
lectures.   2. Patronage, Political – Mediterranean
region – Addresses, essays, lectures.   3. Mediterranean
region – Politics and government – Addresses,
essays, lectures.   I. Gellner, Ernest.
II. Waterbury, John.
JF274.P37   1977   329'.024'091822   77-4726
ISBN 0-910116-99-7 American Universities Field Staff

ISBN 7156 0941 6 (U.K.)
ISBN 0-910116-99-7 (U.S.A.)

Filmset by
Specialised Offset Services Ltd., Liverpool
and printed and bound in Great Britain by
Redwood Burn Limited, Trowbridge & Esher

For Kalman H. Silvert
1921-1976

CONTENTS

PREFACE

Most of the articles in this book were presented as papers at a Conference held under the patronage of the Center for Mediterranean Studies of the American Universities Field Staff in Rome, and were subsequently rewritten in the light of the discussions. The chapters by Sabri Sayari, Michael Attalides and Michael Johnson were added after the Conference. All contributions were written in English, with the exception of Bruno Etienne's, which was translated from the French by John Waterbury. The Editors wish to put on record their debt to E.A. Bayne, the director of the Center for Mediterranean Studies, and to his staff, as well as to the other participants who contributed significantly to the discussions: John Davis (University of Kent); Mohammed Guessous (Université Mohammed V, Rabat); John Hale (University of London); Joseph LaPalombara (Yale University); Jean Leca (Université de Grenoble); Serif Mardin (Bogaziçi University); Dennison Rusinow (AUFS); Kalman Silvert (Ford Foundation); Abdelqader Zghal (CERES, Tunis).

E.G.
J.W.

FOREWORD

This book is the distinguished product of a process that began one day in January of 1972 at the Center for Mediterranean Studies, an outpost of a group of American educational institutions which was founded in 1951 as the American Universities Field Staff. An independent, cooperative venture, the AUFS is directed by its member universities and financed by them and by educational foundations. It maintains a career corps of experienced scholar-observers resident on five continents who report on social and political developments abroad through a reports service, books, teaching, and a quarterly journal.

The four associates stationed in the Mediterranean region who guide the programme of the Center decided that day that an international, interdisciplinary inquiry into the changing forms of patronage in Mediterranean society had priority over many other explorations into the changing social characteristics of the region. For one thing, the diverse peoples of the basin were sharing several fundamental experiences. The pace of industrialisation, urbanisation and possibly secularisation had been speeded for all, north and south. These phenomena could be examined comparatively to advantage and provided the background to the suggested inquiry. The subject seemed to be a prerequisite, therefore, to much social and political analysis in the region.

The Center undertook the study, and a search for a chairman of the Seminar followed. The target was a leader whose experience encompassed the region, whose disciplinary interests were multiple and whose understanding of the contemporary Mediterranean social scene was wide and deep. There were few such persons with widely varying talents, but one eminent choice was available. Professor Ernest Gellner of the London School of Economics and Political Science readily comprehended the cultural complexities surrounding the subject and welcomed the theoretical challenges involved. He promptly organised a gathering of twenty-eight experts from twelve countries, a distinguished nucleus of those social scientists who might be termed 'Mediterraneanists', and they eagerly explored the inner relationships of a mosaic of societies for five days in November 1974.

This book has grown out of that Seminar, edited for a wide audience by Professor Gellner and the Field Staff's senior associate for the Islamic Mediterranean area, Professor John Waterbury. The Center for Mediterranean Studies is especially grateful to Professor Gellner for his labour of organisation and leadership in the project as well as to his able colleague, Dr. Waterbury. The book will be a major addition not only to a growing literature on the region as a single study area but to the social sciences in general. It is a most satisfactory conclusion to the Center's undertaking.

Moreover, its publication permits a friendly restatement of thanks from the Center and from its parent American Universities Field Staff to the Seminar participants and contributors. More privately, this remembrance is particularly focussed on the late Professor Kalman Hirsch Silvert, who died in June, 1976. He was not only a perceptive member of the Seminar, but an especially honoured associate and Director of Studies of the Field Staff from 1956 to 1968.

E.A. Bayne
Director
AUFS Center for Mediterranean Studies
Rome

CONTRIBUTORS

Michael Attalides, Social Research Centre, Nicosia

Jeremy Boissevain, Department of Social Anthropology, University of Amsterdam

Kenneth Brown, Department of Social Anthropology, University of Manchester

Bruno Etienne, Centre de Recherche et d'Etudes sur les Sociétés Méditerranéennes, Université d'Aix-en-Provence

Amina Farrag, anthropologist, Great Britain

Ernest Gellner, Department of Sociology, London School of Economics and Political Science

Michael Gilsenan, Department of Anthropology, University College London

Ghita Ionescu, Department of Government, University of Manchester

Michael Johnson, Department of the Politics of Developing Areas, University of Khartoum, Sudan

Samir Khalaf, Department of Anthropology, American University of Beirut

Peter Loizos, London School of Economics and Political Science

Sawsan El-Messiri, Department of Sociology, American University of Cairo

Clement Henry Moore, Department of Political Science, University of Michigan

Emrys Lloyd Peters, Department of Anthropology, University of Manchester

Amal Rassam, Department of Anthropology, Queen's College, City University of New York

Joaquin Romero-Maura, International Division, Williams and Glyn's Bank Ltd., London

Sabri Sayari, Department of Social Sciences, Bogaziçi University

James Scott, Department of Political Science, University of Wisconsin

Sydel Silverman, City University of New York Graduate School

John Waterbury, American Universities Field Staff Associate for the Islamic Mediterranean

Alex Weingrod, Department of Anthropology, Brandeis University

Alan Zuckerman, Department of Political Science, Brown University

Ernest Gellner

Patrons and clients

The terms *patron* and *client* have a variety of senses. In England, one often sees signs such as 'This car park is reserved for the use of patrons'. This does not mean that only men with political influence may leave their cars in the area indicated. Or again, the non-Philistine Left holds that the state should be a patron of the arts. By this they do not mean, however, that the police should wrest control of Sotheby's from the Mafia.

The kind of patronage which does concern us is a form of *power*. In part, it intrigues us because we disapprove of it. Why? It offends both our egalitarianism and our universalism. Patrons and clients are generally unequal. Patronage relations are highly specific. They fail to illustrate the principle that like cases should be treated alike.

Of course, we may be in error when we disapprove of it. Patronage may have its merits. We should keep an open mind when approaching the problem. But all the same, we may as well admit that the subject appeals to our political voyeurism. We like to observe a political relationship which we suspect of being illicit.

One might approach it by way of elimination, by saying what it is *not*.

Power in a well centralised and law-abiding bureaucracy is not a form of patronage. In as far as bureaucrats are selected for their posts by fair and public criteria, are constrained to observe impartial rules, are accountable for what they do, and can be removed from their positions without undue difficulty and in accordance with recognised procedures, they are not really patrons, even if they do exercise much power. It is only to the extent to which some or all of these features are lacking, that bureaucracies also become, as indeed they often do, a form of a patronage network.

The political organisation of a kinship-dominated society also is not really an instance of patronage. This may sound paradoxical, in as far as patronage often borrows the language of kinship, and also utilises the links of kin. Nevertheless, it seems to me that a genuine kinship society is antithetical to patronage. A genuine kinship society is one in which kin criteria are crucial for the definition of social groups and power relations. (Kinship is never the sole determinant of these things, but it can be the main one.)

Some of us hold that kinship societies in this sense did exist until very recently on the southern, Muslim shores of the Mediterranean. The issue is in dispute, for some hold that kinship was an idiom rather than a reality; that an idiom of patrilineal kinship covered a political reality which was closer to patronage. One reason why I find this difficult to accept is that, if we say that kinship was *always* an ideology rather than a reality, we deprive ourselves of any way of saying that in recent times, there has been a shift, owing to increased centralisation, from a reliance on kinsmen to a reliance on patrons. This seems to me one of the most conspicuous changes that occurred in erstwhile 'tribal' areas within living memory, and I am most loth to accept a theory which would deprive me of any terms in which to record this transformation.

If I am right in believing in the political primacy of kinship in some societies, then a form of organisation exists in which men look for their security to concentric groups of cousins, 'sons of paternal uncles'; they expect their support in feud or at the collective oath, and recognise the corresponding duty to provide such support. In such circumstances, the unsymmetrical relationship of patronage may be of secondary importance.

A point should be added: the terminology of patronage and clientage which we employ has its origin in the terms used for the incorporation of genealogically unrelated groups in a kin-defined system. Any kinship society is likely to possess devices and terms for such incorporation. A kinship society generally relies on some kind of rough balance between its component groups, and the accidents of demography will upset this balance unless culture can compensate for nature, and restore some equality in defiance of genealogy. But although such procedures have given us the language of patronage, they do not really exemplify what we now mean by patronage. They constitute a kind of complication within kinship systems, without modifying their principle.

Feudalism is also not a form of patronage, notwithstanding obvious similarities. Feudalism can be defined as a system which sharply differentiates between warriors and peasants, ascribing a different legal status to each; within which, furthermore, individual members of the warrior stratum autonomously control delimited territories, where they combine the performance of administrative, judicial and military functions; and a system which, moreover, is so organised that these local lords owe some measure of obedience to higher ones within a pyramid which, ideally, has a single man at its apex.

The exchange of labour, support, rent or tax in return for protection and access to land, leads to many features observed both in feudalism and in patronage relations. That is particularly so in the sphere of morals: a stress on the fidelity to persons rather than to principles, a cult of honour and loyalty, violence and virility. Nevertheless, it seems to me wrong to equate feudalism and patronage.

Under feudalism, these principles become open and avowed, and, in principle, unique and unambiguous. Each man, qua holder of this or that fief, is overtly committed to one lord (even if, notoriously, complex patterns of landholding led to weird asymmetries). These loyalties and inequalities have their rituals and sacraments, their ethic is codified and formalised, it is proudly proclaimed. The ethos and symbolism of the system have great glamour which, notoriously, often survives when the system itself has gone.

By contrast, it seems to me of the essence of a patronage system that, though no stranger to pride, it always belongs to some *pays réel* which is ambivalently conscious of not being the *pays légal*. Patronage may not always and necessarily be illegal or corrupt, and it does have its own pride and morality; but though it may despise the official morality as hypocritical, fraudulent, or effeminate, it nevertheless knows that it is not itself *the* official morality. Feudalism can constitute the Great Tradition of a society; patronage does not. Is patronage a feudalism manqué? or is feudalism patronage sanctified by ritual stability and overt recognition?

The market is not patronage either. Purely economic relations, as their critics like to remind us, can be unequal and brutal. But they are also, in as far as they are economic, impersonal. According to the critics, this is indeed their culminating sin. No doubt, very frequently, economic and political links go together. But when the economic relationship operates more or less on its own, we can speak of exploitation, but hardly of patronage. Ironically, the current ordinary English usage of the terms *patron* and *client* is applied in just such economic contexts. But here we must go counter to ordinary usage. We are not interested in the patterns of retail trade, in societies in which customers normally have no political links with their suppliers.

The liberal nightwatchman state, which is the political correlate of the market, is correspondingly distant from indulging in or promoting patronage. In as far as it lives up to its ideal of minimal interference, and merely holds the ring in an impartial manner, it also does not give rise to patronage relations.

Finally, it also seems to me that small, intimate societies should not be counted as systems of patronage. Such communities are of course familiar with long-term unsymmetrical relationships, in which incommensurate services and protection are exchanged and accompanied by feelings of loyalty without yet finding formal ratification in a ritual or code. Hence, in terms of the syndrome which I have been outlining, some of them at least might appear to qualify as patronage societies. Nevertheless, I feel reluctant to include them. 'Real' patronage seems to me to be a system, a style, a moral climate. In a small intimate society, quasi-patronal relations can hardly form a system, either in the sense of forming a larger network, or in the sense of being self-conscious. In larger societies, patronage proper is an ethos: people know that it is *a* way of doing things, amongst others.

Naturally, no one has a right to impose his definitions on others. I have attempted to circumscribe patronage in a way which on the one hand does some degree of justice to the existing associations of the term, and on the other may be of use in classifying and understanding concrete societies. Patronage is unsymmetrical, involving inequality of power; it tends to form an extended system; to be long-term, or at least not restricted to a single isolated transaction; to possess a distinctive ethos; and, whilst not always illegal or immoral, to stand outside the officially proclaimed formal morality of the society in question.

In some measure, this cluster of traits may be present almost everywhere, or at any rate is very common indeed. What makes a patronage society is not the sheer presence of this syndrome, but its prominent or dominant position, to the detriment of other principles of social organisation. Mediterranean societies clearly do have a patronage image. Is this justified? Is it the same kind of patronage throughout? What are its preconditions and consequences?

What favours the emergence of patronage? It is a form of power. Where power is effectively centralised, or on the other hand well-diffused, patronage is correspondingly less common. Hence segmentary societies with their wide dispersal of power, or effective centralised bureaucracies, or market economies with a restrained liberal state, are unpromising seedbeds of patronage. It is the incompletely centralised state, the defective market or the defective bureaucracy which would seem to favour it.

Incomplete centralisation may have at least two different forms: territorial or qualitative. A state may have but partial control of outlying geographical areas, and find it uneconomic to assert itself in them. It may then hand over power in them to individuals who in name may be its officials, but who in fact possess a local power-base, and who mediate between central requirements and local interests. Or again, a state may control its entire territory, but lack the technical resources to implement its will in some aspects of life, say the economy, or education, or medicine. This will then once again lead to the emergence of informal brokers-patrons, controlling benefits which cannot be distributed in accordance with the official rules. The failure to do this may arise from an excessively high level of aspiration, due to some international competition for prestige. For instance, if a state decrees a free national health service without possessing the required number of doctors, the inevitable consequence must be some informal brokerage in the dispensation of scarce but nominally free medical services.

Another unrealistic aspiration may be the requirement of national consensus, in one-party states addicted to the idea that some over-arching national ideal should command general loyalty. In such circumstances, patronage networks can become surrogate political parties, informal associations for the promotion of given viewpoints. In such societies, *factionalism* is held to be a major political sin. Such would-be parties are abused as political clientêles, followers of self-seeking politicians. We are used to the idea that personal followings may masquerade as ideological movements. We should also consider the contrary possibility – that on occasion, what appears as a personal following may cover an ideological movement.

The forms of power and vulnerability – which for John Waterbury seem the key to patronage – are legion, but some seem specially prone to generating patronage. A weak state, not quite weak enough to tolerate open and avowed feudalism, may yet encourage quasi-feudal exploitation in outlying rural areas. Then agricultural labour or produce may be exchanged for protection or, more brutally, may be the price of non-harrassment. A different kind of patronage arises when a modern or semi-modern state operates in an idiom as yet unintelligible to a large part of its population, who then need brokers (lawyers, politicians, or characteristically both of these at once) to obtain benefits or to avoid persecution. This may be combined with a situation in which the state is a large or the main employer, and brokers control access to employment.

It is also important to remember that insecurity and the consequent exchange of protection for benefits are not restricted to inaccessible rural areas. Long before the emergence of urban guerrillas or the collapse of control in some industrial cities, the state may have been unwilling or unable to impose its will in large urban settings. This again leads to the emergence of a characteristic urban 'protector', imposing control where it is not imposed from above.

Again, the weakness of the state, allowing the emergence of patrons, may have different forms. It has been said, for instance, that whereas the Lebanese state is an association of patrons, the Tunisian state is a machine for the making and unmaking of patrons. There may be a kind of spectrum, ranging from a state which is an association for the protection of a pre-existing patron class, via a state which plays off patrons against each other, to a state which creates and destroys them through temporary allocation of political positions.

Perhaps some aspects of life are more patronage-prone than others. Politics may indeed be such a sphere. Political benefits, such as security, life, or identification with a community, are almost incalculable, incommensurate, and long-term. It is not easy to put a price on them, to express them in terms of some natural currency. If they go, all else may go, including any neutral measures of value. And yet, life and its crises force us to make our choices, and to balance such imponderables against other considerations. Political allegiance may involve the promise of unconditional support in hypothetical situations of total conflict. By contrast, economic benefits are, at least ideally, calculable, noncommital and single-shot: hence an economic operation is isolable, and does not need to give rise to any permanent relationship. I buy at this price and sell at another, and neither vendor nor purchaser becomes a foe or friend, or even necessarily an acquaintance. By contrast, the long-term imponderables which are being 'exchanged' in a political relationship, ipso facto give a much deeper colouring to the links between the parties to the transaction. Hence politics may be patronage-prone, whereas economics are such only when they are politicised. Or again, it is plausible to suspect that patronage is only avoidable when relations are anonymous and specific, in a mass society; and that in an inevitably more intimate elite, where relations cannot be anonymous nor criteria universalistic, patronage must be endemic.

These problems have not been exhausted, let alone solved. But we like to think we have made a start.

Sydel Silverman

Patronage as myth

A large amount of social science energy has gone into efforts to define
'the phenomenon' of patronage and to describe the varying forms it
can take in different places and times. Rarely, however, has the debate
over definition engaged underlying differences in assumptions as to
the kind of phenomenon 'it' is. Are we talking about something 'out
there' in observable actions, something in the heads of our informants,
or an analytical scheme in our own heads? In my view, our failure to
recognise the differences among these stances and to treat them
separately has impeded the development of productive theories of
patronage and communication both within and across disciplines.

In the study of Mediterranean societies, the problem is
compounded by linguistic confusion. We need to be able to
distinguish the 'patron' of our theory from the *padrone* or *patrón* our
informants talk about. These may be one and the same, but they may
not be; we cannot know unless they have been defined separately at
the outset.

The problem is, firstly, a methodological one. On what grounds do
we identify patterns in our data and call them 'patronage'? Do we
look at behaviour and the effects of action, or do we ask people what
they think is happening and how they feel about it, or both? If we do
both, is this a matter of summing up diverse kinds of information, or
do we 'weight' them differently? And how do we handle discrepancies
in different kinds of information?

Beyond questions of method, there is the issue of the theoretical
status of ethos or value. The most common approach in studies of
patronage is to assume congruence between behaviour and value.
'The relationship has moral overtones'; the exchange of benefits is
'confirmed or rationalised by an ethos'; patronage forms a system of
hierarchies and networks which 'receive their recognition' in a certain
'moral climate'.* But can congruence be assumed in advance? Is the
congruence an artifact of our method – that is, are we defining the
patronage 'relationship' and the patronage 'ethos' each in terms of the
other? Our goal should be, rather, to discover the degree of actual

---

* Seminar Prospectus, 'Changing forms of patronage in Mediterranean society',
Center for Mediterranean Studies, Rome, November 25-30, 1974.

congruence and try to explain it. This raises the more general theoretical issue: where do we seek explanation? What causal models best account for the 'relationships' and 'moral climates' encompassed by the concept of patronage?

My concerns derive, of course, from dilemmas I have encountered in my own work. These dilemmas have led me to rephrase the questions I have been asking of my material. Although the avenues of inquiry have led backward into history more than forward into contemporary change, I think they have bearing on both the problems and the possibilities in the study of patronage.

My work has focused on Central Italy, particularly a small commune in the province of Perugia, which I have called Colleverde. In 1960 when I did my initial fieldwork there, the community's agricultural production – its economic base – was still organised within the *mezzadria* system, the share-farming pattern that had characterised much of Central Italy for centuries. The *mezzadria* contract bound a landlord and a peasant family into a series of reciprocal rights and obligations concerning the joint agricultural enterprise. Especially when the landlord lived locally – in the towns around which farms were dispersed – the relationship often extended to areas of life beyond the agrarian contract. The landlord-tenant relationship, almost by definition, followed a patron-client model, and the language for it merged with the language of patronage. Clearly, there was in Colleverde a concept of patronage – the idea of a *padrone* who had certain rights and obligations – that was meaningful to the people, and that continued to be expressed even as it confronted changes in the present. For all these reasons, my description of the traditional social and political structure of Colleverde placed a strong emphasis upon patronage, and I felt that the decline of patronage (of the traditional kind) marked a significant change of the contemporary period.

When I returned to Colleverde several years later, however, I began to see the matter in another light. The more I delved into historical evidence on the traditional patrons, the more I was struck by how limited was the actual extent of reciprocity; within relationships defined (by the natives) as patronage, the actual downward movement of goods or services was rarely very substantial. I could not easily quantify the exchanges, but what seemed clear to me was that whatever was the 'reality' of patron-client relationships in Colleverde, patronage was also a 'myth' – a set of assumptions and evaluations used by the people themselves. This is not to say that people were not aware of discrepancies between the myth and the reality of patronage; on the contrary, the language of patronage was often used ironically to point up such discrepancies. What all of this suggested to me was that the myth (or ideology or value) of patronage was a phenomenon different from the structure of relationships; that it would be incorrect to read off one of these phenomena from the other; and that the myth too was 'real' and had to be explained.

In approaching this problem, I found it useful to follow the distinction between 'etics' and 'emics' that has had considerable currency in anthropology during the past decade. The distinction is between two modes of analysis, two methodological strategies, and two kinds of phenomena that correspond to different definitions of culture.

Etics and emics

The opposition between 'etic' and 'emic' approaches to cultural analysis derives from linguistics, especially from the work of Kenneth Pike (see Pike 1954). It is drawn from the distinction between phonetics and phonemics. Phonetics is concerned with the description of articulatory behaviour as it can be detected by an observer, and with the classification of articulatory behaviour in ways that can be applied to all languages and agreed upon by a scientific community of observers. Phonemics, in contrast, is concerned with discovering those phonetic distinctions that are recognised as significant by the speakers of a language, and with classifying them so as to represent the patterns of a particular language. The 'cross-language' study of phonemics compares not articulatory events but the patterning of meaningful distinctions.

The analogy to cultural analysis developed in anthropology during the 1960s with the so-called 'new ethnography'. This approach revived the view of culture as cognitive processes and set itself the task of describing certain cultural domains (e.g., kinship, curing, and ethnobotany) in terms of the patterns of meaning – the significant distinctions – in a particular culture. The 'emicists' met with skepticism from other anthropologists who questioned the possibility of 'getting inside the natives' heads'. (Harris, 1964) The outcome of the debate between emicists and eticists was the recognition that both represent kinds of analysis which are complementary to each other but whose results are not isomorphic. Neither type of phenomenon can explain the other directly; neither can be reduced to other.

Etic analysis is concerned with phenomena that can be identified and studied independently of the natives' cultural judgment; emic analysis aims for an orderly and explicit representation of cognitive patterns (after Harris 1971:147). The difference is above all a matter of method, that is, (where) the analyst seeks verification. In etic analysis, the reference point for verification is the community of scientific observers; the usefulness of methods of observation and units of analysis depends upon their applicability to all cultures and all observers. In contrast, the adequacy of an emic analysis is judged by the responses of the natives themselves. This is not a matter of asking the natives to do the analysis or to evaluate it. Rather, the analyst tests his own representation against the natives' responses more or less the way a linguist would ask native speakers whether or not statements generated from his own model of the grammar constituted grammatical speech.

The etic/emic contrast is not the same thing as the contrast between the 'real' and the 'ideal' as these terms are usually used in anthropology. Etic analysis deals only with the way people actually behave, but emic analysis takes in more than ideals: it is concerned with cognitive patterning both of what is supposed to happen and of what does happen (which is not the same as what can be *observed* to happen). Thus, the emic study of patronage is not only what people think patrons are supposed to do. The more relevant questions would be, what does it mean to be a 'patron' and how is it *appropriate* for one to behave? Ideas about appropriateness might well include the expectation that patrons will often not do what they are supposed to; it may be expected, for example, that they will abuse their positions or exploit their clients while adopting the manners and language of paternalism. Such expectations cannot be taken as descriptions of real behaviour any more than can statements of ideals.

My basic point is that patronage ought to be studied both from an etic and an emic point of view, and that our ultimate aim should be to investigate how the etics and the emics of patronage may be related. To look at relationships between them requires that the two kinds of analysis be done independently. If one describes the behaviour of patrons and clients on the basis of what informants say, or alternatively if one describes ideas about patronage on the basis of one's inferences from behaviour, then one has relinquished the possibility of asking how ideas and behaviour are related, whether they conform or diverge, and why.

The etic study of patronage involves at least two kinds of tasks. First, there is the structural description of relationships and networks. What kinds of patron-client relationships are there in a society? (The operational questions are: what kinds of behaviours can be observed? what patterns do they fall into? what are the effects of each of these patterns?) What kinds of exchanges do they involve? 'Exchanges', in an etic sense, must be described independently of the values attached to the goods and services exchanged. Second, it is necessary to deal with patronage as a variable. What is the actual frequency, or density, of patron-client relationships? Most importantly, what is the quantifiable exchange of goods and services? In other words, what does the 'reciprocity' fundamental to so many patronage theories consist of in specific cases? (See Kaufman 1974:307-8.) This is the problem that needs to be addressed in answering the question raised by Dalton, 'How exactly are peasants "exploited"?' (Dalton 1974). We need not conclude, with Dalton, that since many kinds of people might be considered 'exploited' the concept is only a value judgment. 'Exploitation' can be measured; at some point an unequal exchange becomes something other than reciprocity.

The emic study of patronage involves questions of a different order. It is concerned with the ways people conceptualise, talk about, or rationalise behaviour – perhaps the behaviour that the social scientist identifies as patronage, but more particularly, behaviour that is defined as patronage (or something like it) in the native idiom. The more difficult part of the task lies in discovering implicit meanings and cognitive patterns. Difficult but not impossible. Methods have been developed for studying other cultural domains that might be adapted, and we have already learned something about the pitfalls; for instance, we know that we must expect as much individual variation in culturally patterned cognition as in culturally patterned behaviour. However, some emic phenomena are quite explicit. Many cultures in the Mediterranean have public ideologies or myths of patronage. Although they are voiced and believed by different people with different degrees of conviction, such ideologies have an existence of their own. Since they are readily accessible to study without probing deeply 'inside heads', this may be a useful place to begin.

The ideology of patronage in Colleverde

To say that there was a myth of patronage in traditional Colleverde (pre-World War II) is not to deny that patron-client relationships existed and were important, involving enduring relationships between individuals of unequal wealth or power and the asymmetrical exchanges of goods and services. The 'myth' refers to the fact that such relationships were surrounded by a rhetoric that magnified and distorted the real exchanges, while other relationships in which exchanges were minimal were couched in an idiom of patronage.

Most land in Colleverde was worked under the *mezzadria* system, and most household-heads were parties to *mezzadria* contracts either as landlords or peasants. The contract stipulated the contributions required of each party, the division of produce, and subsidiary rights and obligations on each side. For a number of reasons, the Central Italian *mezzadria* tended to create a more continuing and personalised relationship between landowner and cultivator than is often the case in sharecropping systems. A peasant family usually occupied the same farm for many years, sometimes for generations. The contract provided for both parties to contribute working capital and for both to participate in decision-making; the landlord was generally involved actively in operations, and there was necessarily a great deal of contact between the 'partners'. Furthermore, the contract stipulated other terms that furthered the tie between them. The landlord was obliged to assist the peasant family in times of crisis, and in times past he could control the peasant family's activities in many ways (prevent a son from leaving the farm, disapprove a marriage, prohibit unseemly behaviour, and so on). The peasant was required to provide the landowning family with certain prestations (such as poultry and eggs on various holidays) and certain personal services (such as cartage and laundry services). The broad outlines of the contract were quite uniform throughout the *mezzadria* area, though specific terms varied a great deal according to local custom and particular circumstances.

In its general form, the *mezzadria* relationship resembled that of patron and client. Yet a distinction must be made between those cases in which the exchange of goods and services was limited to the terms stipulated by formal contract, and those relationships that went beyond the contract (by implicit agreement of the parties) and that extended the tie into areas not directly related to the agricultural enterprise. A landlord might lend money or guarantee loans, find work for family members not needed on the farm, obtain medical services, give advice on matters of bureaucracy and law, intervene with the authorities in case of trouble, or in other ways provide a defence against emergencies or a buffer in contracts with the outside world. Such an extension of the *mezzadria* relationship could be occasional and of little consequence, or it could involve substantial exchanges and a wide variety of functions. From an etic point of view, patronage in Colleverde was a variable. In emic terms, however, all *mezzadria* contracts were phrased as patronage. The landlord was referred to and addressed as *padrone*. The personal relationship between the contractors and their two families used the idiom and manners of patronage – symbols of command and deference, protection and loyalty, concern and affection.

Patron-client relationships were also formed between lower-class persons other than *mezzadri* (peasant proprietors, labourers, and artisans) and members of the local upper class. Even more, however, the *idiom* of patronage was extended widely to interaction between unequals. The term *padrone* was often used as an honorific in addressing a social superior, and it was returned with terms of affection and concern (e.g., *coco mio*). Persons of high status would command services as their due (for instance, tell someone to run an errand) and bestow favours in the name of 'fondness' and 'generosity'.

Most importantly, the idiom of patronage was applied to persons who might be called public patrons: certain members of the local elite who were defined, and defined themselves, as protectors and benefactors of the community. According to the ideology, these persons bestowed material benefits, political advantages, and glory upon the community as a whole; they in turn were entitled to the obedience, respect, and loyalty of the community. This role was seen as a counterpart of the patron's identification with the community, as a devoted citizen of his native *paese*. His prestations were part of an obligation to glorify the community, assert its uniqueness, and defend its special identity.

The etics of public patronage involved a certain amount of material contribution, leadership in community activities, and political action or intervention on behalf of local interests. A large element of the 'services' attributed to public patrons, however, was intangible: they lent prestige and contributed rhetoric and sentiments. A landowner might sponsor a community festival; he would donate ritual objects or furnish a festive meal for the most active participants, but above all he lent his name to the event. A member of the local elite might act as patron to a community association, such as the band. He would offer advice, perhaps provide a room in his house for rehearsals, and contribute something toward the expenses of uniforms and instruments (though the major part of costs would be met by the members themselves and by payments they earned for performing). Again, the patron's most conspicuous function was to lend the prestige and unspecified 'protection' of his name. Examples of more substantial material contributions within the pattern of public patronage are furnished by cases in which individuals (particularly those without heirs) left legacies to support local charities or community services (such as subsidies for the salaries of administrative personnel or of a local doctor). However, the several cases that appear in the documents of three centuries were remarked upon so much as to suggest that such legacies were, in fact, uncommon.

Public patronage was extolled in official proclamations, on tombstone inscriptions, and in local folklore. For instance, in 1896 the communal council voted to name a street after a landowning family, citing particularly their efforts to obtain provincial funds for restoration of the town-hall and for local roads (including a road serving their own property, for which they 'generously donated' the land). The council paid tribute to the family:

The V., their cultivation coupled with a love for their native place second to none, consumed their considerable wealth for the good of the *paese* and for the public. ... To this family we owe projects for the community ... for which they spent substantial sums. ... They were always jealous custodians of the *paese* and of the progress of the sciences and the arts.

As was true of landlord-patronage, the rhetoric of public patronage exaggerated the actual downward movement of real goods and services. A 'myth' was perpetuated that was disproportionate with the etics of the situation. Why should this be so?

To some extent, the answer lies in the nature of local relationships. Clearly, the ideology of patronage underwrote the status and authority of the elite. It was particularly useful for landowners in the *mezzadria* system: it provided the terms of interaction between landlord and peasant, was a means for staving off challenges to the landlord's position, and in general contributed to the smooth functioning of the system. For the peasants and others of the non-elite, who knew all too well the discrepancies between myth and reality, there were other reasons for voicing the ideology. For them, it was a way of making claims on their landlords and other accessible persons of high status and power. The claim might pay off only occasionally and even then only in minute favours, but it cost little. It was an investment made in resources that the peasant had in ample supply: family labour, deference, and of course, talk. (Contributions of produce were mandated by the contract and were not at issue in the extension of a *mezzadria* relationship into a broader patron-client tie.) Moreover, the claim made through ideology did not necessarily exclude other avenues of action. Even at the time of my first fieldwork, it was quite common for peasants to deal with their landlords through the language and rituals appropriate to clients, while at the same time actively to support the Communists with votes, contributions, and participation in strikes.

Yet, the full significance of the ideology of patronage, and particularly the myth of public patronage, can be understood only by going beyond relationships between individuals to the structure of the community, and beyond the locality itself to its economic and political context. Looking at the history of Colleverde in this perspective, it is convenient to talk of four major phases. The first coincides with the age of the communes, from the twelfth to the early fourteenth centuries, and the period of the *signorie* (lordships) that followed. For most of this time Colleverde was held within the territory of the powerful city-state nearby. However, like many other small towns and *castelli*, its internal organisation replicated that of the urban communes and it attempted repeatedly to become autonomous. Given the multicentric political structure of the region, a degree of autonomy could be attained by alliance (or submission) to other cities or to the Pope or Emperor, and by playing off these different powers against each other.

The theme of autonomy recurs throughout Colleverdese history, and it can be detected in abortive form even to the present day. It is clear that it had an economic counterpart: it served the interests of the local landowning elite. From the communal period until the unification of Italy, autonomy meant that the community could remain outside the laws of the nearby city; for the landowners this meant maximum flexibility in selling their grain on the urban markets of the region. The quantity of surplus grain and other commodities varied over time, but this fundamental consideration did not. To achieve this autonomy, the local elite followed a twofold strategy: they tried to manipulate alliances and connections within the wider political sphere of the region; and they tried to maintain undisputed control over the local sphere.

A second phase begins with the consolidation of the Papal States in the sixteenth century. Colleverde's effective autonomy vis-à-vis the nearby city was strengthened, and it shared in the growing agricultural commerce of the region. At the same time, a process of colonisation of the countryside began, as peasant families were settled on the land on farms which they created and cultivated under *mezzadria* contracts. Town-landlord and peasant were drawn into ties based on the *mezzadria*, and the patronage role of the landlord was elaborated. The beginning of the nineteenth century marks a high point for the local landowning elite, economically and politically. They benefited from the population increase and agricultural revival of the late eighteenth century, and at least one family acquired substantial Church lands. They won favourable administrative status for Colleverde, first under the French in 1798 and then under the restored Papal regime. This time, too, saw lavish expressions of public patronage – in fact (for example, the construction of an elegant theatre by a consortium of nine local landowners) and, even more, in rhetoric.

In this succession of events, the myth of the public patron emerges not merely as an 'expression' of social relationships or as a 'moral climate', but as a part of political action. The manoeuvring of the local elite was accompanied by a rationale, which appears both explicitly and implicitly. On the one hand, the past glories and historical autonomy of Colleverde were cited. Thus, a local spokesman wrote in 1814:

Since this land has enjoyed privileges that have constituted it as almost a free and independent community, it would be overly oppressive if it became subject to an outside power other than Rome.

On the other hand, the continuing capacity of the community to govern itself was emphasised. This capacity was demonstrated – so the rationale went – by the persistence of communal institutions; by the 'quality and culture of the inhabitants' (' ... the major landowners, who are not restricted in finances due to the property which they have in abundance ... do not lack that culture, civilisation, and breeding which one sees in a city ...'); and by elite sponsorship of public amenities and a civilized way of life in the community.

A third phase is marked by the unification of Italy. New links with the outside afforded new opportunities for the local upper class, but unification also brought the stresses in the *mezzadria* system and challenges to the landlords' control. Their response was to widen the system of patronage by assuming positions of mediation between Colleverdesi and the nation-state (see Silverman 1965). At the same time, bureaucrats and professionals brought into the community were absorbed into the local elite. Knowledge of and connections with the national political system became the marks of successful patrons. However, concern with local identity remained strong, and if anything, increased. Under the banner of Colleverde, the elite sought both governmental aid and autonomy of action within the larger system, and they promoted the local activities, associations, and rituals that made for a vigorous community life.

Fundamental change in the role of the local elite and in the patterns of patronage came only after World War II. The *mezzadria* system began to break down; new forms of articulation with the national system developed; labour organisations, political parties, and intermediaries from within the bureaucracy and the Church replaced the traditional patrons. In this situation, the idiom of patronage has come to be restricted to specifically political contexts. For instance, it enters into expectations about how a mayor should behave and how political parties should operate, but it rarely appears in casual interaction today. At the same time, the ideology of patronage has become overtly polemical. The major political factions in the community (which are activated mainly by the Christian Democratic and Communist parties) express different assumptions about the value of patronage: the DC advocates refer to the benefits of vertical connections and the obligations that accompany power, while the Left challenges this view and appeals to an ideology of horizontal, class-based alliance.

We may return now to the question, why did the myth of the local patron persist in Colleverde? I think the ideology was fostered by the local elite partly because it served the strategy for achieving effective autonomy. The emphasis upon public patronage, in particular, formed part of a myth of 'community' that backed up claims to autonomy. Throughout early Colleverdese history, the symbols of local identity provided moral underpinnings for the assertion that 'Colleverde ought to be subject to no other authority than that of the Holy See itself'. National unity did not fundamentally alter the claim but rephrased it in terms of local interests within the nation. The themes of patriotism toward Italy and devotion to Colleverde – both entities expressed by the single term 'paese' – become mutually reinforcing. The 'community' was, in fact, the landowning class, who pursued their interests in the name of Colleverde. The projects of public patronage – but more, the language that celebrated them – served these interests by underlining the uniqueness and glory of the community. (The pattern was, of course, anything but unique to Colleverde. Each town constituted a local centre of its own and insisted upon its own uniqueness. Minute differences between one town and another were – and still are – magnified, while 'local traditions' were everywhere nurtured.)

To the extent that local identity could maintain the boundaries of the community, it also helped the elite to preserve their internal control. At the same time, a rationale for such control was provided by the myth of the patron – the local figure who looks after his own better than any outsider could.

The discussion thus far has emphasised patronage as it applied to landowners. However, the local patrons also included minor professionals, bureaucrats, and shopkeepers; typically, in fact, such occupations were combined with ownership of *mezzadria* farms. This phenomenon of urban or small-town bourgeois landownership is as old as the communes in Central Italy, and the paternalistic phrasing of relationships between these townsmen and the peasantry is probably almost as old. Yet after the unification, the local elites saw many newcomers, a result of the expansion of the bureaucracy and the national-level recruitment of professionals and administrators. In Colleverde, such new arrivals became the most conspicuous *padroni* and the most vigorous advocates of public patronage; they married into local landowning families and became strongly identified with the community. From the viewpoint of the Colleverdesi, the ideology of patronage was a means of drawing these high-status outsiders into local commitments. From *their* viewpoint, on the other hand, it was a way of building a local power-base. If the symbolic expression of localism contributed to maintaining community boundaries this too served them, for it enabled them to play a brokerage role between the relatively cut-off lower class and their own higher-level patrons and other connections outside.

In this exercise I have attempted to relate the emics of patronage to the etic history of Colleverde. I have looked only at explicit emic patterns, the public myths; historical data do not easily lend themselves to more subtle analysis of cognition. My purpose has been to show that the myths are not mirror images of social reality, nor in any direct way either expressions of or guidelines for the relationships that prevail in a society. I have tried to demonstrate, however, that they may form part of the strategies for social and political action, just as actual patron-client relationships may form part of such strategies. I think that carefully designed field studies can say a great deal more than this about the emics of patronage. Moreover, I think that developments in emic analysis now make possible a more dynamic perspective than has generally been the case in 'subjective' studies.

For one thing, the study of emics does not require that one assume uniformity of cognition or values within a society; on the contrary, the kinds and degree of disparity that exist, and the social regularities they are related to, should be one of the objectives of study. Similarly, there is no reason to suppose that societies are held together by consensus rather than conflict; one might well wish to inquire into the conditions under which emic differences may manifest themselves in conflict. Furthermore, such study need not be static; we should not assume that emic phenomena are timeless, either on theoretical or on methodological grounds.

Conclusion

The etic/emic distinction bears on a number of issues that have been raised in the study of patronage. For one thing, there has been some discussion as to whether patronage (as dealt with in the social science literature) refers 'merely' to folk concepts that anthropologists have encountered in certain local idioms, or whether it constitutes a powerful tool for the analysis of social or political structures. In fact, students of patronage do not always specify whether they are depicting folk concepts or social structure, and they often argue from one to the other. Patronage can be described both as idiom and as structure, but to confound these two endeavours impedes both.

The attempt to explain patronage by 'political culture' produces other kinds of etic/emic confusion. The concept of political culture itself merges the two dimensions; Almond and Verba, for example, define it as 'attitudinal and behavioural propensities' (1965:32). A more serious problem is that 'the' political culture tends to be treated as a substratum of values and predispositions that defies (or at least does not demand) explanation, yet has causal significance for etic phenomena. Powell, for instance, presents a careful account of how patron-client relationships can build up into larger-scale clientelist political systems, but in his conclusion he describes clientelism as an element of the political culture – itself left unexplained (Powell 1970).

Many approaches to patronage emphasise the 'moral content' of relationships; some, indeed, define patronage in such terms. Thus, John Davis sees patronage as 'political relationships in which inferiority is accepted and then defended by moral suasion' (Davis 1974), while Jeremy Boissevain speaks of 'a self-perpetuating system of belief and action grounded in the society's value system' (Boissevain 1966). The etic/emic contrast suggests that 'morality' ought to be studied as a problem in its own right, but that relationships must also be analysed quite apart from the meanings attributed to them.

The notion of morality, however, requires closer examination. There has sometimes been a tendency by political scientists using anthropological data to equate the norms operating in a patron-client relationship with a 'moral code'. The equation may be carried further: role expectations may be used to infer a moral economy, which is taken to mean a subjective perception of fairness and then merged with 'legitimacy' (see Scott 1974). In this way, a norm of reciprocity (which may mean only that certain exchanges occur regularly and that people act as if they expect them to continue) may be translated as 'moral expectations'; similarly, the fact of legitimacy (i.e., institutionalised power) may be translated as 'acceptance'. The relationship of morality to social norms, on the one hand, and to legitimacy, on the other, is questionable. But if moral codes are to be studied at all, they must be approached through methods carefully designed for the purpose. Such methods must be capable of recognising different kinds of 'morality'. As the case of Colleverde shows, an ideology of patronage does not imply moral consensus or a notion of equity any more than the absence of rebellion means that a political system is perceived as morally legitimate.

The point of the etic/emic distinction is neither to clutter up our literature with more jargon nor to assign a priority to studies of values or studies of behaviour. It is to remind us to set forth our concepts in such a way that we can investigate the interplay between values and behaviour, between belief and action.

REFERENCES

Almond, G.A. and S. Verba (1965) *The Civic Culture.* Boston and Toronto.

Boissevain, J. (1966) 'Patronage in Sicily', *Man* 1, 18-33.

Dalton, G. (1974) 'How exactly are peasants "exploited"?' *American Anthropologist* 76, 553-61.

Davis, J. (1974) 'Patronage.' Working paper for Seminar, 'Changing Forms of Patronage in Mediterranean Society', Center for Mediterranean Studies, Rome, Nov. 25-30, 1974.

Harris, M. (1964) *The Nature of Cultural Things.* New York.

Harris, M. (1971) *Culture, Man, and Nature.* New York.

Kaufman, R.R. (1974) 'The patron-client concept and macro-politics', *Comparative Studies in Society and History* 16, 284-308.

Pike, K. (1954) *Language in Relation to a Unified Theory of the Structure of Human Behaviour,* Vol. 1. Glendale, Calif., Summer Institute of Linguistics.

Powell, J.D. (1970) 'Peasant society and clientelist politics', *The American Political Science Review* 64, 411-25.

Scott, J.C. (1974) 'Legitimacy and patronage'. Working paper for Seminar, 'Changing Forms of Patronage in Mediterranean Society', Center for Mediterranean Studies, Rome, Nov. 25-30, 1974.

Silverman, S.F. (1965) 'Patronage and community-nation relationships in Central Italy', *Ethnology* 4, 172-89.

James Scott

Patronage or exploitation?

The terms 'patron' or 'patronage' are morally loaded. To take them at more or less face value is to accept a definition of role behaviour very much in accord with how elites would like to have things seem. How are we to know whether the vertical structures of deference that are called patron-client links are seen as legitimate or not? What is the difference between genuine protection and what we might call a protection racket? How are we to distinguish false deference from real deference, coercion from collaboration, forced compliance from legitimate power? These are serious empirical questions which cannot easily be addressed so long as the legitimacy of the patron is smuggled into the analysis by definition.

In this context, the essay which follows is an analytical inquiry into how patron-client structures of deference acquire or lose their moral force. I have intentionally confined the discussion to a theoretical level at the expense of ethnographic material from the Mediterranean. I hope, nonetheless, that the issues raised here will have some bearing on the many case studies assembled in this volume.

The discussion is limited in two respects. First, I focus exclusively on clientelism in agrarian class relations. Although some of the principles developed below would, I hope, be applicable to other forms of patron-client bonds, I make no such claim. The choice of rural class relations and, more particularly, of landlord-tenant exchange, is not entirely one of analytical convenience and interest. Throughout much of the Mediterranean world the relations between the tillers of land and its owners have represented the locus of livelihood and material well-being for a large share of the population. It goes without saying that this relationship has at the same time often embodied the most explosive class tensions.

Limiting the analysis to agrarian class relations implies a second restriction. I assume, in this context, that we are dealing with clients who live at or near the subsistence level and for whom tenancy or farm labour is the principal, if not sole, means of livelihood. This restriction is necessary to define a population whose welfare needs and social experience are coherent enough potentially to foster a common view of equity. At the same time, the argument is less applicable both to well-off clients or to those for whom tenancy or rural farm labour represent only a sideline employment.

With these points in mind, I contend that the irreducible minimum terms the peasant/client traditionally demands ('expects' is perhaps more appropriate) for his deference are physical security and a subsistence livelihood. This expectation is at the root of the peasantry's 'paternalist moral economy' – the basis of its conception of justice and equity. A breach of these minimum terms in the exchange relationship, if it occurs on a large scale, serves both to undermine the legitimacy of the patron class and to provide the peasantry with a moral basis for action against agrarian elites.[1]

The feelings of peasants, individually and collectively, about agrarian elites have an important objective dimension and are not simply a matter of consciousness or ideology. Peasants have some implicit notion of the balance of exchange – of what it costs them to get a patron's services – and any substantial objective change in that balance is likely to lead a corresponding change in the legitimacy of the exchange relationship. Although new ideas and values can undoubtedly influence the perceived cost and importance of certain services – especially in the long run – the claim here is that in many contexts, variations in the legitimacy of agrarian elites are traceable more to real shifts in the balance of exchange than to ideology or 'rising expectations'.

Distinguishing characteristics of patron-client ties

First, patron and client are not equals. The basis of exchange between them both arises from and reflects the disparity in their relative wealth, power, and status. A patron is most often in a position to supply goods and services unilaterally which the potential client and his family need for their survival and well-being (Blau 1964, 21-5).

While a client is hardly on an equal footing with his patron, neither is he entirely a pawn in a one-way relationship. If the patron could simply issue commands, he would have no reason to cultivate a clientele in the first place. His need for a personal following which can be mobilised on his behalf requires some level of reciprocity. Thus, patron-client exchange falls somewhere on the continuum between personal bonds joining equals and purely coercive bonds. Determining exactly where between these two poles a particular patron-client system should be placed, or in which direction it is moving, becomes an important empirical question in any attempt to gauge its legitimacy.

The second distinguishing feature of patron-client dyads is their diffuse, face-to-face, personal character as opposed to the explicit quality of impersonal contracts or of formal relations of authority. It is this diffuseness and wide range of reciprocity that is perhaps the most strongly traditional quality of patron-client bonds. The link between patron and client is a very flexible one in which the needs and resources of the partners, and, hence, the goods and services exchanged, may vary widely over time.

Elements of exchange

What follows is an attempt to describe the major categories of exchange in a way that illustrates something of the scope of reciprocity found in patron-client exchange.

Patron to client flows

1. *Basic means of subsistence.* This is the central core of the classical patron-client bond. In many agrarian settings this service boils down to the granting of access to land for cultivation and it may include the provision of seed, equipment, marketing services, technical advice, and so forth. In the case of office-based patronage, it may mean the provision of steady employment or opportunities for gain, thereby guaranteeing subsistence.

2. *Subsistence crisis insurance.* Typically, the patron is expected to be a friend in need. One of his most valued services is his willingness – and obligation – to give loans in time of economic distress, to help in case of sickness or accident, or to carry his client through the year following a poor harvest. As a generalised relief agency of first resort, the patron often guarantees a subsistence 'floor' for his clients by absorbing losses (in agriculture or income) which might otherwise jeopardise their livelihood.

3. *Protection.* The need for physical security was a central feature of the feudal bond in Europe. It is especially prominent in office-based patronage but common in land-based patronage as well. It is likely to include shielding the client both from private dangers (banditry, personal enemies) and from public dangers (soldiers, outside officials, courts, tax collectors).

4. *Brokerage and influence.* If the patron protects his clients from outside depredations, he also uses his power and influence to extract rewards from the outside for the benefit of his clients. Protection is his defensive role vis-à-vis the outside; brokerage is his aggressive role. The interests of patron and client coincide in relations with the outside since it is not a question of distribution of resources within the network but of wresting resources from the outside which increase the pool available for distribution among the following – and perhaps expanding the clientele.

Collective patron service

Internally, patrons are often responsible for many *collective economic functions* of the village. They may subsidise local charity and relief, donate land for communal use, support local public services (such as schools, small roads, and community buildings), host visiting officials, and sponsor village festivals and celebrations. Quite apart from providing tangible resources to the community, patrons in most stratified villages are seen to supply much of its *organisation and leadership*. That is, they may not only subsidise celebrations, small public works, and village marketing arrangements, but they also furnish the initiative and mobilising potential for these activities. Finally, the patrons collectively may be valued also for their capacity to mediate in disputes and preserve local order.

In dealing with the outside world, patrons may do together for the village what a particular patron is expected to do for his client. That is, they may *protect the community* from outside forces – whether the state or private marauders – and they may *advance the community's interests* by securing works and services, administrative favours, community loans, agricultral assistance, and so on.

Client to patron flows

Flows of goods and services from client to patron are particularly hard to characterise because a client is usually his patron's 'man' – and his services consist in lending his labour and talents to his patron's designs, whatever they might be. Some typical elements of this overall compliance include:

1. *Basic labour service*. An employer-employee relationship, though not at all of the impersonal contract kind, is at the core of the dependence nexus in most strong and durable patron-client bonds. The client contributes his labour and other specialised skills to the farm, office, or enterprise. Such services may range all the way from bearing arms as a member of the patron's band to daily manual labour in the patron's fields.

2. *Supplementary labour and goods*. Clients commonly provide several subsidiary services to their patron which become an anticipated part of the exchange. These may include supplying water and firewood to the patron's household, personal domestic services, food offerings, and so forth. Some of these services are substantial, some are mainly of symbolic value as expressions of deference, and, in more commercialised settings, some have been discontinued in lieu of cash equivalents.

3. *Promoting the patron's interests*. This catch-all category signifies the client's membership in his patron's faction and the contribution he is expected to make to the success of his leader and, indirectly, his own prosperity. A typical client protects his superior's reputation, acts as his eyes and ears, campaigns for him if he should stand for office, and generally uses his skills and resources to advance his patron over other patrons.

The legitimacy of dependence

A crucial question for rural class relations in patron-client systems is whether the relationship of dependence is seen by clients as primarily collaborative and legitimate or as primarily exploitative. Here the issues of compliance and legitimacy are analytically distinct.[2] By virtue of his control over critical goods and services which peasants need, the patron is often in a position to require compliance with many of his demands. Whether that compliance is accompanied with approval or disapproval, with legitimacy or simply with resignation, however, depends on the client's subjective evaluation of the relationship.

Accepting Barrington Moore's interpretation of exploitation as a more or less objective phenomenon, it may be possible, in a given agrarian context, to view changes in the legitimacy or approval given a class of patrons as largely a function of changes in the objective balance of goods and services changed individually and collectively between the strata.[3] The notion of balance is somewhat complex because we are dealing here with a balance within a context of unequal exchanges. The question, however, is not whether the exchange is lopsided, but rather *how* lopsided it is.[4]

For the client, the key element of evaluation is the ratio of services he receives to the services he provides. The greater the value of what he receives from his patron compared with the cost of what he must reciprocate, the more likely he is to see the bond as legitimate. For the patron, on the other hand, the level of satisfaction with the bond depends on the ratio of the value of his client's services to the costs of retaining him. The two ratios are not mirror images and the patron's gain is thus not necessarily the client's loss. For example, the opening of a new school may make it easier (less costly) for the patron to help his client's children get an education while not necessarily reducing the value of that service to clients. The patron's position is improved and the client's is not worsened. Under other circumstances, though, patron and client are at loggerheads; a landlord who previously took 50% of the harvest and now takes 60% of the same harvest is gaining at the direct expense of his client.

The concept of balance employed here is not directly quantifiable, but both the direction and approximate magnitude of change can often be ascertained. Once the kinds of services and their frequency or volume are specified in both directions, we have a rough picture of the existing balance. If the patron discontinues a service and the client's services remain unchanged, we know the balance has become less favourable for the client. If patrons demand more services from clients without doing more for the clients, we also know that clients are now worse off than before.[5]

Beyond changes in the nature and number of reciprocal services themselves, the cost of a given service may shift. In an era when wage labour opportunities are opening up, a patron's demand for free labour service from his clients may seem more onerous (costly) than before and hence affect the balance. The balance may be similarly altered by a change in the value of a given service. Thus, the value of physical protection was especially high in the chaos of the early feudal period in Western Europe but declined later as banditry and invasions subsided. Variations in the cost or value of a service can, in such cases, lead to a shift in the legitimacy of the exchange while the content of the exchange remains constant.

This conceptualisation of reciprocity runs into difficulty, of course, when we want to know *how much* of a shift has taken place and not merely its direction, and also when we try to gauge the net effect of changes which push the balance in different directions. Precise calibration is out of the question, but we can detect gross differences. When a patron, for example, ceases to give subsistence loans prior to harvest, we may be able to infer roughly how large an effect this will have on the balance of exchange from our appreciation of the scarcity of food at that season and from other historical evidence – including protest, banditry, and even starvation. With a series of changes it may similarly be possible to estimate both their net direction and something of their extent.

The *relational* quality of exchange requires emphasis. An analysis of changes in the legitimacy of agrarian elites thus necessarily focuses on changes in the exchange relationship and not on the position of the peasantry taken alone. Although shifts in the relationship and shifts in the peasantry's material well-being may often coincide, they may occasionally diverge as well. It is possible for peasants to experience an improvement in their standard of living – perhaps due to state assistance, high market prices, etc. – while, at the same time, their position in the balance of exchange with landowners is deteriorating as rentier owners revoke past services. A crisis in agrarian class relations may, in such instances, accompany an advance in peasant welfare. The opposite case, in which peasants are materially worse off but enjoy improved terms of trade with landowners, is also conceivable.[6] The test, then, is not the level of welfare but the terms of exchange and how they are shifting.

Any assessment of the balance of exchange must also consider, as peasants themselves do, the entire pattern of reciprocity. The more precommercial the context, the more likely it is that the exchange will involve a great variety of reciprocal services beyond the arrangements for cultivation and crop division. A patron's crisis help, influence, and protection may be more valuable in the peasant's estimation than a five or ten percent increase in the share of the crop he may retain. The disappearance of such services may thus jeopardise the legitimacy of agrarian elites even though landowners take less of the crop and peasant labour requirements are reduced.

The norm of reciprocity

Anthropologists, noting the importance of mutual exchange among peasants in such diverse contexts as Latin America, Europe, and Asia, have often been persuaded that reciprocity is the norm governing social relations among villagers. Between equals, such exchanges are largely self-regulating. One peasant assists another because he knows that only in this way can he elicit the services he himself will need later. Obligations are thus enforced not only by the sanctions of village opinion but also by the concrete reciprocal needs of cultivators. Much of the need for reciprocity is then inherent in the agricultural and ceremonial cycle. The point, for our purposes, is that the norm of equivalent or comparable exchange which serves as the basis for our notion of legitimacy in patron-client exchange is, at the same time, a widely shared moral sentiment within the 'little tradition'.

This brings us to the question of reciprocity between unequals. What is expected of those relatively wealthy villagers whose resources put them in an advantageous bargaining position? Almost without exception, judging from the anthropological literature, the position of well-off villagers is legitimised only to the extent that their resources are employed in ways which meet the broadly defined welfare needs of villagers (Phillips, Foster, Pitt-Rivers, Campbell, Barth, Wolf). Most studies repeatedly emphasise the informal social controls which tend to either redistribute the wealth or to impose specific obligations on its owners. The prosaic, even banal, character of these social controls belies their importance. Well-to-do villagers avoid malicious gossip only at the price of an exaggerated generosity. They are expected to sponsor more conspicuously lavish celebrations at weddings, to show greater charity to kin and neighbours, to sponsor local religious activity, and to take on more dependents and employees than the average household. The generosity enjoined on the rich is not without its compensations. It redounds to their growing prestige and serves to surround them with a grateful clientele which helps validate their position in the community.[7] It represents, in addition, a set of social debts which can be converted into goods and services if need be.

What is notable here is that the normative order of the village imposes certain standards of performance on its better-off members. There is a particular rule of reciprocity – a set of moral expectations – which applies to their exchanges with other villagers. Whether or not the wealthy actually live up to these minimal moral requirements of reciprocity is another question, but there can be little doubt that they exist. Their normative character is apparent in the reaction provoked by their violation. The principles involved are perhaps most clearly expressed in Julian Pitt-Rivers' analysis (1961) of an Andalusian village.

The idea that he who has must give to him who has not is not only a precept of religion, but a moral imperative of the pueblo. ... The successful patron, thanks to his wealth, acquires great prestige within the orbit of his influence and escapes, thereby, the condemnation which is reserved for *los ricos*.

The resentment [of *los ricos*] aims not so much at the existence of economic inequality as at the failure of the rich man to care for those who are less fortunate; at his lack of charity. It is not so much the system which is wrong, it is the rich who are evil.

Clearly, neither the power of the wealthy nor the dependency of others which it implies is self-justifying. Such power is condoned only insofar as its possessors conform to the standards of service and generosity expected of them. When they use their wealth in ways which villagers judge to be benign and protective, their status is reinforced and it becomes possible to speak of legitimacy and patronage.[8] When they use their power to violate local norms, they engender hatred and condemnation. They may still be able to have their way but their behaviour is no longer regarded as legitimate.

The normative process by which disparities in power are either legitimated or repudiated is hardly unique to peasant society. It is but a special case of a more general phenomenon. For any stratification system, the question arises: 'Why should some be placed above others?' It is largely by virtue of the contribution of the powerful to the welfare of the group that their power is legitimated and becomes authority. The difference between power that is validated and power that is endured thus rests on some shared conception of its just use.

Traditions and needs

If the legitimacy of the patron were merely a direct linear function of the balance of reciprocity, our task would be deceptively simple. The historical character of human expectations and the discontinuous character of human needs, however, make such an easy formula inconceivable. At least three major qualifications seem necessary if the analysis is to reflect more closely the complex relationship it addresses. In particular, the simple model outlined earlier overlooks (1) the effect of tradition on legitimacy; (2) the effect of sudden changes in the balance of reciprocity, and (3) the existence of physical and cultural thresholds beyond which the consequences for the client are dramatic.

Tradition and stable exchange

From the standpoint of the client there is obviously a difference between a stable, traditional patron-client relationship and one that is more impermanent and formless. Given similar balances of exchange, the more traditional is likely to be viewed as more legitimate. Its greater legitimacy seems to flow *not* simply from its antiquity but from the fact that its age represents, in effect, a higher probability that the implicit terms will be observed and that the flow of services will continue into the future. The client assumes that his patron will conform to at least the minimal traditions of service if he can and that local opinion and institutions will help to guarantee the observance of traditional terms. If the client then considers a traditional patron-client contract preferable to less traditional arrangements, his choice has some rational basis. Tradition represents legitimacy because it generally promises a higher level of performance according to expectations as well as greater durability and cultural sanction than less institutionalised forms of security.

Breaches of stable exchange

In stable agrarian settings, the power relationships between peasants and elites may have produced a norm of reciprocity – a standard package of reciprocal rights and obligations – that acquires a moral force of its own. The resulting norms, so long as they provide basic protection and security to clients, will be jealously defended against breaches which threaten the peasants' existing level of benefits. Sudden efforts to reset these norms will be seen as a violation of traditional obligations which patrons have historically assumed – a violation that serves as the moral rationale for peasant outrage. Thus any balance of exchange above a certain minimum is likely to take on legitimacy over time and *even small movements* away from the balance that reduce peasant benefits are likely to encounter a fierce resistance that invokes tradition on its behalf.

The right to subsistence

Living near the thin edge of subsistence, the capital concern of peasants is necessarily with the security of their food supply. That food supply is menaced, on the one hand, by a variety of more or less impersonal forces: the vagaries of weather, the quality of the soil, the existing level of techniques, the risk of illness, the availability of arable land. It is menaced, on the other hand, by a variety of social claims which are not impersonal: claims of rent, taxes, and debts. Even if the crop itself is sufficient for subsistence, the claims on it by others may make it insufficient.

Put starkly, the central economic preoccupation of low-income cultivators is to feed their household reliably. This preoccupation explains a great number of economic and social choices which would otherwise seem anomalous in the context of neoclassical economics. Unlike a capitalist enterprise which can be liquidated, the peasant household is a unit of consumption as well as a unit of production. The household begins with a more-or-less irreducible consumer demand, based on its size, which it must achieve to continue in existence. Thus peasant families which must feed themselves from small plots in overpopulated regions will, for example, work unimaginably hard and long for the smallest increments in production – well beyond the point at which a prudent capitalist would move on. Similarly, a land-poor peasant with a large family and no other labour outlets is rationally willing to pay huge rents, what Chayanov (1966) calls 'hunger rents', so long as the additional land will make even a small net addition to the family larder.

Above all, the ecological precariousness of peasant production impels most peasant households to follow what has been called the 'safety-first' principle (Roumasset 1971). In the choice of crops, seeds, and techniques of cultivation this simply means that the cultivator *prefers to minimise the probability of having a disaster rather than to maximise his average return*. That is, he does not gamble any more than he has to with his subsistence. He thus avoids taking risks that might raise his income if those risks increase the possibility of falling below the subsistence danger level. In one form or another, this risk avoidance principle has been noted by most economists who have studied low-income agriculture in the Third World (Behrman, p.236; Mellor 1969, p.214; Myint 1969, p.103; Joy 1969, pp.377-8). It finds expression in a preference for crops that can be eaten over crops which can be sold, a preference for stable yields over high risk crops, a tendency to try to spread risks, and a reluctance to upset stable subsistence routines which have proved adequate in the past. Safety-first does not imply that peasants are creatures of custom who never take risks. What it does imply is that there is a defensive perimeter around subsistence routines within which any unnecessary risks are avoided as potentially catastrophic.

Classically, the marginal tenant, sharecropper, or tied labourer has looked to his landlord for social insurance against periodic subsistence crises. For him the basic purpose of the patron-client contract, and therefore the cornerstone of its legitimacy, is the provision of basic social guarantees of subsistence and security. If and when the terms of trade deteriorate sufficiently to threaten these social rights which were the original basis for attachment and deference, one can anticipate that the bond will quickly lose its legitimacy. The patron may still be able to extract services from the client but clients will increasingly consider the relationship unjust and exploitative. Legitimacy, then, is not a linear function of the balance of exchange. Instead, there are certain thresholds for many clients below which the loss of legitimacy is swift and often complete. No doubt these thresholds have a cultural dimension since they depend on what is necessary for the satisfaction of minimum cultural decencies – e.g., caring for elderly parents, celebrating crucial rituals – but they also have an objective dimension – e.g., enough land to feed the family, subsistence help in case of sickness or accident, minimum physical protection against outsiders. A relationship of dependence that supplies these minimal guarantees will retain a core of legitimacy; one that abrogates them transgresses nearly universal standards of obligation.

The claim to basic social rights which might be termed the 'right to subsistence' or even the 'right to a living' is so widespread in traditional society that it all but constitutes the fundamental social morality of the traditional, precapitalist order. Where peasants have lived in largely unstratified communities, it can be seen as the implicit principle behind the social mechanisms of redistribution and reciprocity which tend to guarantee all villagers a livelihood. In more stratified peasant communities it finds expression in a set of shared norms and social pressures which prescribe a minimum level of performance for local patrons.

Many customary obligations of the traditional patron-client contract were considered subordinate to the basic claims of subsistence and protection. Thus during periods of crop failure or plague in feudal Europe the lord (and the ruler of the kingdom as well) was expected to forego a portion of his normal claims to dues and grain if payment would jeopardise his clients' rights to subsistence. A failure to make these allowances, either willfully or inadvertently, put tremendous strains on the legitimacy of patron demands (Mousnier 1970, pp. 305-48). Again and again, the popular paternalist view that the social order should guarantee a man and his family a subsistence is the key to many riots and uprisings in eighteenth- and nineteenth-century Europe – outbreaks which were legitimised in the popular mind by the failure of the ruling class to meet its fundamental obligation of providing for the minimum well-being of their subjects.

The right to subsistence in tenancy

The subsistence ethic may be applied to patron-client relations in tenancy. Whereas a 'surplus-value' view of exploitation in the Marxist tradition would lead us to believe that a landlord who took, on the average, twenty percent of the harvest would be seen as twice as exploitative as a landlord who appropriated only ten percent, the subsistence ethic implies that the absolute level of the claims may be less important than how they complicate or ease the tenant's problem of staying above the subsistence danger level. A high rent after a good crop, for example, may be experienced as less onerous than a low rent following a crop failure. The criteria of peasant judgment tend to be more sharply focused on what is left after the claim is met – whether it is sufficient for subsistence – than on the level of the claim *per se*.

To illustrate this, Figure 1 (overleaf) represents two hypothetical claims of peasant resources. Line A reproduces the tenant's crop yields, while the horizontal line at 80 units of grain indicates the subsistence danger level. Lines B and C then reflect two vastly different forms of extraction which may be thought of as varying forms of land rent or, for that matter, taxation.

Line B represents the impact on peasant subsistence of an unremittingly fixed rental claim. Year in and year out a steady twenty units of grain is taken from the yield; the effect is simply to retain the shape of the yield line but to lower it twenty units. The net remaining for consumption plunges not once but thirteen times below the danger

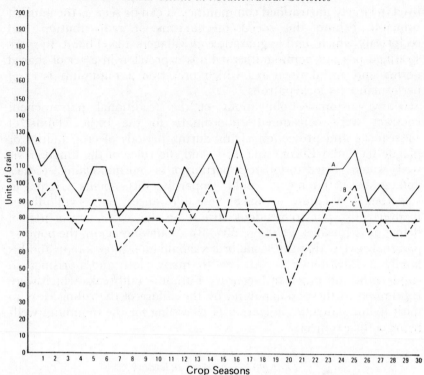

Crop Seasons

level. Its impact on peasant life is massive. The risks of yield fluctuations are, in this case, borne entirely by the cultivator – and at a level that is increasingly insupportable. By contrast, the landlord (or the state in the case of taxes) has stabilised his (its) income at the expense of the peasant household.

Line 'C' represents the polar opposite of a fixed claim. Each year grain is extracted in variable amounts that leave the peasant household five units above the subsistence danger line. On two occasions when the yield line falls below 85 units, this implies an actual subsidy to the peasant household to raise it back to that level. Here the qualitative changes in peasant life are enormously reduced as the subsistence crisis level is never reached. The central ligaments of peasant life remain intact. In this example, the risks of agriculture are borne by the landlord whose income fluctuates to steady the net resources available to the peasant household.

The key element in the peasant's evaluation of the extractions which are an inevitable part of his life is how they affect his 'right to subsistence'. This is not necessarily identical, by any means, with what might be called the *average* extraction of resources by agrarian elites. The *total* resources squeezed from a tenant under variable claim C – that stabilises his income – is actually, in this example, greater than under the fixed levy B. If we were to use, as the standard of exploitation, the average take of the landlord from the tenant – i.e., the average surplus value – then the stabilising claim would qualify as the most exploitative. Our argument, however, is that, given the subsistence precipice along which the typical peasant treads, the stabilising claim (though it may end by taking more) is less resented and is seen as less exploitative, inasmuch as it avoids the outcomes which peasants fear most.

Thus, the *manner* of exploitation makes all the difference. Who stabilises his income at whose expense *is* a critical question. Forms of 'exploitation' that tend to offer a built-in subsistence guarantee and which are, in this sense, adopted to the existential dilemma of peasant economics are, and are seen to be, much less damaging than claims which are heedless of minimum subsistence needs.[9]

The first question a peasant implicitly asks of a tenancy system is, 'Does this institution safeguard my minimal social rights; does it provide me a subsistence living regardless of what the land may yield this season?' In this context, land tenure systems can be located along a continuum according to how each distributes risks between the landowner and tenant. Table 1, below, compares the protective value of three simplified forms of tenure.

Table 1   Distribution of risk in tenancy systems[10]

Landlord Assumes Risk A	Risk Shared B	Tenant Assumes Risk C
e.g., Traditional (feudal) systems of subsistence insurance	e.g., Equal-shares sharecropping	e.g., Fixed-rent tenancy
— cultivator's minimal return fixed and guaranteed	— cultivator's return a fixed *share* of crop	— cultivator assumes risk and profit of cultivation
— landowner assumes risk and profit of cultivation	— landowner's return a fixed *share* of crop	— landowner's return fixed and guaranteed

The continuum essentially contrasts the extent to which a tenure system insulates cultivators from crop losses that might ruin them. Toward the 'A' end of the continuum the landlord ensures the tenant's livelihood while, at the 'C' end, the tenant, in effect, underwrites the landlord's income come what may. We assume, with good reason, that most low-income tenants will prefer arrangements which relieve them of risks which they can ill afford. This preference will be strongest where plots are small, yields highly variable, peasants quite poor, and where few alternative subsistence opportunities exist. It will be weaker where large tenancies, stable yields, a well-off peasantry, and ample outside economic opportunities greatly reduce the likelihood of ruin. The situation of most tenants in the Mediterranean world more closely approximates the first set of conditions.

The relative legitimacy of tenure systems that embody subsistence guarantees springs from the fact that the cultivator's needs are taken as the first claim on the harvest. His income is steadied and the risk of the enterprise is shifted to the shoulders of the landlord who is better able to absorb occasional losses. A full subsistence guarantee must, of course, go beyond the tenant's prior claim on the crop – for what if the total crop will not provide for his minimal needs? Thus, complete subsistence insurance implies a personal commitment of the landowner to the basic welfare needs of his tenant. The terms 'patron' and 'patronage' become applicable here inasmuch as the relationship is ultimately focused on the tenant's needs as a consumer and not on an impersonal economic bargain confined only to the disposition of the crop. In such arrangements, the cultivator is likely to be more than just a tenant; he is likely to be a 'client' tied to his landlord by bonds of deference.

In societies where most of the peasantry and lower class are not expected and do not expect to be part of the politically relevant public, the unwritten expectation that preserves these boundaries is that the elite, political class will assure a minimum level of subsistence and protection to the non-participant lower classes. At the centre of the system of patron-client reciprocity, then, is the exchange of deference and compliance by the client in return for the patron's provision of *minimal social rights*. When these guarantees break down, the structure of exclusion loses a key element of its legitimacy.

So long as the aggregate structure of patronage remains intact, the failure of a single patron does not call into question the domination of the patron class. Structural changes in the economy or state which bring about a widespread collapse of the social guarantees of patronage, however, may threaten the claim to ascendancy of the entire patron class. As the peasantry experiences a collective failure of the elite to meet what are seen as the social obligations of its position, its claim to that position will be increasingly unjustified.[11] The consequence, barring repression, may be a burst of peasant activity that simply aims at restoring the old balance of exchange or taking what is needed for subsistence, or it may be a more fundamental attack on the social hierarchy itself.

In understanding the peasant's view of the patron-client relationship, we do well to avoid seeing the peasant as either a fickle, cost-conscious bourgeois, with but fewer alternatives, or as a serf whose loyalty knows no bounds. We do far better to view the peasant as a cultivator who faces a set of continuing existential dilemmas over his economic and physical security which he is often poorly equipped to solve by himself or with other peasants. To the extent that someone of higher status is willing to assist and protect him, providing the cost is not prohibitive, a relationship of deference may develop that grows in its resilience and closeness as expectations about mutuality and assistance are met. The patron validates his friendship by helping the peasant at times of crisis. It is on that basis that trust and confidence grows; friendship and favour are, for the client, synonymous. When a relationship of patronage fails to protect the peasant, it not only leaves him worse off but it also represents a betrayal of the trust he had placed in a powerful friend.[12] Pitt-Rivers (1961, p.204) has noted how the system of patronage in Andalusia rested on performance.

Patronage is good when the patron is good, but like friendship upon which it is based it has two faces. It can either confirm the superiority of the *senorito* or it can be exploited by the rich man in order to obtain a nefarious advantage over poor people. It covers a range of relationships from noble protection of dependents in accordance with the moral solidarity of the pueblo to the scurrilous coercions of the later period of *caciquismo*. The system is, clearly, only to be judged good insofar as it ensures that people do not go hungry, that injustice is not gone. Where the majority of the community can look to the person in time of need, such a system reinforces the integration of the pueblo as a whole. Where those who enjoy the advantages of patronage are a minority, then they and their patrons are likely to be resented by the remainder.

The reverence in which the institution of patronage is held thus ultimately depends upon how well it helps peasants survive the recurrent crises of food supply, defense, and brokerage which mark their life. Its failure as an institution to serve these basic human needs must inevitably tarnish the claim to deference of those patrons who sit astride it.

Relative bargaining positions

A particular balance of exchange in patron-client relations reflects the relative bargaining positions of the two parties. One way of assessing the comparative bargaining strength of patron and client is to consider the client as both a buyer of scarce services and a seller of his favour and compliance, and then to ask what his market position is in terms of (1) his demand for the services of the patron and (2) his ability to pay (reciprocate) the supplier. As the discussion below indicates, the aggregate bargaining position of clients depends largely on structural factors such as the concentration of landholding, population growth, and the spread of state power.

1. Demand
The effective demand for patron services rests in part on whether there are alternative sources for such services. If there is unclaimed arable land, if the peasant can fall back on his kin group for protection and upon professional moneylenders for loans, the peasant's dependence on patrons is somewhat diminished. The more effective and numerous such alternative mechanisms are, the more they serve to establish a

baseline below which the terms of patron-client exchange cannot sink. The patron class as a whole thus competes against other social mechanisms for the provision of important needs.[13] For patron-controlled services, client demand will hinge primarily on how *vital* and *scarce* these services are. A man who can distribute jobs amidst widespread unemployment can drive a harder bargain with his clients than he could if jobs were plentiful.

2. *Ability to reciprocate*

A particular client with special religious, military, or agricultural skills may find himself in a better bargaining position than most. Collectively, however, the average position of clients vis-à-vis patrons depends on structural factors that either enhance or diminish the importance of creating personal following. A few of the major factors which have historically augmented the value of building a clientele are the need to assure a permanent and reliable labour force where cash wages are inadequate to the task, the need for a substantial supply of manpower to help defend the patron's domain, and the need for an electoral following to win control of local resources. In such circumstances, clients may anticipate a somewhat more favourable balance of exchange.

Assuming that a following is valuable, a shortage of potential clients will also benefit peasants. In most of Europe prior to the nineteenth century, there was an abundant supply of arable land to which clients could flee while the supply of labour was often scarce. But as population has grown and most good land been occupied, the rural client's bargaining position has been eroded.

We should not forget, however, the role of coercion in patron-client exchange. Many patrons, by virtue of their local power, are able to resort to coercion to improve their bargaining position – to require more from clients and provide less. To the extent that they do take advantage of their monopoly of resources and force to demand compliance, they are likely to lose legitimacy, though they may have the power to impose their will. The distinction here is essentially between a patron who protects his clients and one who organises essentially a 'protection racket' in which clients comply in order to be protected against their 'patron'. Clients can easily distinguish between real protection and extortion; the test for them is whether they would be better off without the patron's services. If such negative services outweigh any real benefits, the relationship is less a patron-client bond than a forced dependence which inspires no legitimacy.

It is not the aim of this essay to analyse the structural and political changes that are likely to affect the relative bargaining power of patrons and clients. It is important, however, to recognise that the term patron-client relationship is often used indiscriminately to refer to *any* relationship of personal dependence, regardless of how exploitative it may seem to the clients. A far better procedure, I have argued, would be to avoid the evaluative terms of 'patron' and 'client' and instead speak of relations of personal dependence between members of different classes. Then, the question of how equitable or exploitative they are becomes a matter for empirical analysis rather than a covert assumption. My contention has been that in most agrarian social orders it will be possible to characterise a balance of social exchange and to say whether it is becoming more or less onerous for the client. Furthermore, I would expect that any significant shift in the balance of exchange would be reflected in the legitimacy of the 'patron' class. When the core existential needs of a client class for subsistence security are violated, I would expect the client increasingly to view the relationship as one of forced compliance. An empirical analysis of these issues may well force us to modify the relationships which I have suggested. In any event, once we move away from the mystification of the term 'patron' to the empirical examination of class relationships over time and to the values and opinions of real actors, we will be operating for the first time on solid terrain.

NOTES

1. I am indebted to Barrington Moore, Jr.'s persuasive argument (Moore, 1966, pp.453-83) that exploitation is, for the most part, an objective relationship in which feelings of exploitation bear a relationship to the services an elite offers the peasantry in return for the surplus it extracts. His argument was advanced considerably by its successful application to Central Italy by Sydel F. Silverman (1970) in which the categories of exchange are carefully analysed. It is from Moore and Silverman, and from Peter Blau's theoretical work on exchange theory (1964) that my conceptualisation of agrarian relations is drawn. See also Arthur Stinchcombe's fine essay (1961-2) on rural class relations, particularly the portion on family-sized tenancy.
2. Empirically, of course, disapproving submission may be difficult to distinguish from approving submission if there are no means for the expression of discontent.
3. This is not to deny that norms of equity in the balance of exchange may vary from culture to culture. They most certainly do. For this reason it would be dangerous, in the absence of gross differences, to draw conclusions about the relative legitimacy of agrarian elites in two different cultural and historical settings on the basis of the comparative balance of exchange between elites and peasants in each setting. Within a *particular* cultural and historical context, however, *shifts* in the balance of exchange are likely to be reflected in shifts in the legitimacy with which subordination is viewed.
4. This remains the case so long as the clientele is linked individually to the patron. While his following *as a whole* may be important to the patron, any particular client is generally expendable. If the clientele dealt with the patron as a unit, of course, the situation would change.
5. These models, in fact, correspond roughly to two processes of agrarian change. The former is characteristic of a commercialising landowner class which reduces or terminates most services performed by the traditional aristocracy while continuing to squeeze the peasants. The latter resembles the efforts of a declining rural aristocracy to survive by exacting each and every feudal privilege while being unable to maintain, let alone raise, their services for their retainers.
6. Empirically this might occur in traditional settings when landowners provide rations to their peasant clients following a serious crop failure. Here a slight decline in material welfare might accompany improved class relations.

7.   We should also recall that where strong outside guarantees for wealth and position do not exist, the standing of local elites depends ultimately on the following they can muster in a showdown. There are thus very good reasons for local powerholders to build sizeable clienteles in such circumstances.

8.   It is worth noting that the voluntary grant of status to a member of a group is not simply a sign of approval but also a form of social control. The weaker members of the group confer status on the strong in part to persuade him to use his power for the benefit of the group rather than against it. See, on this point, Emerson (1962), pp. 39-41, and Tibaut and Kelley (1961), p. 231.

9.   This conclusion is in keeping with a substantial body of sociological evidence which suggests that an insecure poverty is far more explosive and painful than poverty alone. See, for example, Zeitlin (1966), Leggett (1964), Rimlinger (1960).

10. In this illustration we have focused primarily on the provisions for dividing the crop. A more accurate scheme for the distribution of risk would also have to include the distribution of production costs. If the landowner provides all equipment, seeds, plough animals, and other cash costs, he assumes this risk, while, if these costs are shifted to the tenant, the tenant then assumes an even greater risk than the arrangements for dividing the harvest would indicate. In addition, the labels 'sharecropping' and 'fixed-rent' are often only an indifferent guide to the actual tenancy relation. The traditional 'kasama' tenancy system in the Philippines, for example, nominally describes fifty-fifty sharecropping. In practice, however, owners in some areas often soften the terms considerably in poor years while, elsewhere, no mercy is shown. The key is the actual content of the relationship – the actual pattern of reciprocity – and not its formal terms.

11. There may be a further progression in consciousness here. The failure of a single patron undermines his claim to position but not that of the patron class. The failure of the patron class undermines its claim to position, but not necessarily the peasantry's faith in other potential patron classes (e.g., party bosses) who might perform according to expectations. Perhaps it is only the repeated failure of patronage as a system that saps the legitimacy of vertical patronage *per se* rather than the legitimacy of a particular patron class.

12. The amount of anger and moral indignation generated by such a failure probably depends upon how critical the services were and what alternatives the client has.

13. The vertical patron-client tie is but one of several social mechanisms that can provide important guarantees for peasants. One way of determining how significant patron-client structures are in a given context is to ask what proportion of the rural populace is tied to patrons. In practice, however, a peasant may rely simultaneously on his neighbours, his kin, village custom, a patron, and perhaps even the law for assistance and protection, and it is thus a matter of gauging the *relative* importance of patron-client ties. The social weight of rural patron-client bonds is, then, a function both of the proportion of the population that is covered by them and their relative importance in satisfying social needs for those who are covered.

REFERENCES

Barth, F. (1965) *Political Leadership among the Swat Pathans*. London School of Economics Monographs on Social Anthropology no.19, London.

Behrman, J.R. (1969) 'Supply response and modernization of peasant agriculture: A study of the major annual crops in Thailand', in C.B. Wharton (ed.), *Subsistence Agriculture and Economic Development*, Chicago.

Blau, P. (1964) *Exchange and Power in Social Life*. New York.

Campbell, J. (1964) *Honour, Family and Patronage*. Oxford.

Chayanov, A.V. (1966) *The Theory of Peasant Economy*, edited by D. Thorner, B. Kerblay and R.E.F. Smith. Homewood, Ill.

Emersón, R.M. (1962) 'Power-dependence relations', *American Sociological Review* 22 (1).

Foster, G. (1963) 'The dyadic contract in Tzintzuntzan: Patron-client relationship', *American Anthropologist* 65, 1280-94.

Joy, L. (1969) 'Diagnosis, prediction, and policy formation', in C.B. Wharton (ed.), *Subsistence Agriculture and Economic Development*, Chicago.

Leggett, J.C. (1964), 'Economic insecurity and working class consciousness', *American Sociological Review* 29 (2).

Mellor, J.W. (1969) 'The subsistence farmer in traditional economies' in C.B. Wharton (ed.), *Subsistence Agriculture and Economic Development*, Chicago.

Moore, B. Jr. (1966) *Social Origins of Dictatorship and Democracy*. Boston.

Mousnier, R. (1970) *Peasant Uprisings in Seventeenth-Century France, Russia and China* (translated by Brian Pearce). New York.

Myint, H. (1969) 'The peasant economics of today's underdeveloped areas', in C.B. Wharton (ed.), *Subsistence Agriculture and Economic Development*, Chicago.

Phillips, H. (1965) *The Peasant Personality*. Berkeley.

Pitt-Rivers, J. (1961) *The People of the Sierra*. Chicago.

Rimlinger, G. (1960) 'The legitimation of protest: A comparative study in labour history', *Comparative Studies in Society and History* 2 (3).

Roumasset, J. (1971) 'Risk and choice of technique for peasant agriculture: Safety first and rice production in the Philippines', Social Systems Research Institute, University of Wisconsin, Economic Development and International Economics 7118 (August).

Silverman, S.F. (1970) ' "Exploitation" in rural Central Italy: Structure and ideology in stratification study', *Comparative Studies in Society and History* 12, 32738.

Stinchcombe, A. (1961-2) 'Agricultural enterprise and rural class relations', *American Journal of Sociology* 67.

Thibaut, J.W. and H.H. Kelley (1961), *The Social Psychology of Groups*, New York.

Wolf, E. (1966) 'Kinship, friendship and patron-client relations', in M. Banton (ed.), *The Social Anthropology of Complex Societies*, New York.

Zeitlin, M. (1966) 'Economic insecurity and the attitudes of Cuban workers', *American Sociological Review* 31 (1).

Alex Weingrod

Patronage and power

I

What is meant by patronage? What is meant by power? These are both familiar terms, frequently and freely used in the literature of social science. They are, moreover, complex, 'freighted' concepts, each carrying varied meanings and open to diverse understandings. 'Power', for example, can be defined in terms of physical compulsion or in regard to control over prized resources, just as 'patronage' sometimes refers to interpersonal relations and at other times to a societal mode of organisation. What is more, in the hands of social anthropologists and political scientists these terms wander between a definitional specificity, on the one hand, and a kind of poetic metaphor, on the other. The main objective of what follows is to indicate in particular how the concept of power may be used in the analysis of patronage relationships.

There is an immediate, intuitive sense in which 'power' would seem to be crucial for the analysis of patronage. Patron-client relations are, if anything, characterised by inequalities in the status and power of the various actors, much as, on another level, clientele political systems can be distinguished from other types of political systems by the particular ways in which power is organised and distributed. To put it differently, since power is a fundamental feature of *all* political processes one expects to find an analysis of power at the centre of patronage studies, but, oddly enough, in many studies power has been at best a minor theme. Why this is so and how it handicaps our analysis will be considered in the latter portions of this article.

Patronage studies fall broadly into two clusters. There are, first of all, those studies of clientele politics undertaken by political scientists and sociologists. These are generally national-level or elite studies in which, among other interests, a major topic is to show how clientele systems are organised and how they 'articulate' with other broad features of the social system. Second, in studying political organisation in rural regions social anthropologists have often focussed upon the links between patrons and clients; here the concern has been to show, for example, ways in which landlords and tenants manipulate their ties in order to further their own interests. In addition, a third perspective may be added: patronage at either level may be conceived of in both processual and ceremonial terms, and attention will also be given to this type of analysis.

II

Patronage appears as the dominant mode of political organisation in many Mediterranean countries, and detailed studies of 'clientele politics' have been carried out in Southern Europe, North Africa and the Middle East.[1] What are the goals of these studies, and what is the place of concepts of power in the analyses?

'Political clientelism,' write Lemarchand and Legg, 'may be viewed as a more or less personalised, affective and reciprocal relationship between actors, or sets of actors, commanding unequal resources and involving mutually beneficial transactions that have political ramifications beyond the immediate sphere of dyadic relationships' (1972, pp. 51-2). This definition is a useful starting point; to paraphrase briefly, clientelism refers to a form of political organisation in which the links between leaders and followers are rooted in 'mutually beneficial transactions' and in which the ties are of a personal, enduring kind. A 'clientele' can therefore be distinguished from an interest group or an ideological movement, and its leaders can hence be labelled 'patrons' and their followers 'clients'. How does power enter into this formulation? The key phrase is 'commanding unequal resources': in a clientele system power accrues to those who control and therefore are able to allocate resources. Patrons are powerful since they can tap and distribute tangibles – government contracts, jobs, loans and the like – and it is through the shrewd investment of these resources that they may build and maintain their personal clientele. In principle, the greater the resources controlled the more powerful the patron.

This is illustrated in Waterbury's recent study (1970) of elite politics in Morocco. According to Waterbury the Moroccan political fabric is composed of a multitude of clienteles each seeking to 'create or corner a patrimony and then defend it' (p.73). At the national level these clienteles 'may include parties, unions, student groups, regional interests, prominent families, tribes, the officer corps, *'ulema* and *shurafa*. Often leading members of these groups will be high ranking government employees and ministers' (p.82). The King stands at the summit of this pyramid: 'the monarchy is the major distributor of spoils and patronage in Morocco, and it considers the entire elite as its clientele group. To maintain its following ... the palace manipulates its systems of rewards ... to great advantage' (pp. 142-3).

How does a concern with power enter into this analysis? Power is implicitly regarded as a measure of control over prized resources: the elite members – business entrepreneurs, army generals, government ministers, and so forth – are powerful since they have carved out areas in the economy or the public administration which can be used to reward their followers and consequently enrich their clientele. An example may suffice. Waterbury relates how, beginning in 1966, responsibility for agricultural development was moved from the Moroccan Ministry of Agriculture to the Ministry of Interior. In this process of shifting control over resources from one ministry to the next 'Agriculture has very little left with which to occupy itself, and will as a result have little appeal for elite factions looking for patronage. Conversely, Interior will have greatly augmented its control of patronage, and it is likely that some of this will see its way, as in the past, into the hands of the king's loyal administrators' (p.286). These latter officials, it is clear, will have become *more powerful* than their colleagues in the other ministries.

Control over resources is one meaning and measure of power. But there are others: in particular, power can also be conceived of in regard to decision-making. Relative influence in determining the outcome of decisions can be taken as a measure of power.

LaPalombara's study of national administration and politics in Italy provides an interesting case of patronage and power in decision-making. The author describes two types of relationship, *clientela* and *parentela*, which closely link specific interest groups with the Italian government bureaucracies. In the *clientela* pattern the bureaucracy becomes so closely linked with the interest group's objectives that it comes to serve the latter's purposes, while what distinguishes the *parentela* connection is the fact that these ties are mediated through the reigning political party.

The classic example of *clientela* is the intimate tie between Confindustria, the Italian industrialists association, and the Ministry of Commerce. One of LaPalombara's sources describes the relationship as follows (LaPalombara, 1964, p.268):

Confindustria is said to maintain strong and continual contacts with all of the directors and inspectors general within the Ministry. Most of these people are identified as personal friends – often of long standing – of functionaries within the Confederation and of some of Italy's leading industrialists. Because of this ... the Confederation does not feel that it has any serious problems concerning its ability to interact fruitfully with this particular branch of the national administrative system.

LaPalombara does not include specific, detailed cases in which this 'fruitful interaction' is described. In more general terms, however, he does show how the Ministry has become dependent upon Confindustria for data collecting; in effect, the ministry which is charged with regulating industries uses the data gathered by the industrialists themselves in making its decisions! Another of LaPalombara's sources remarks that 'once this step has been taken and the data – and recommendations – submitted, the ministry is unable really to evaluate their objectivity. As a result, the decision, while formally made by the bureaucracy (or the legislature), may in fact be the decision of the industrial confederation' (p.286).

With this example in mind we can return to the more general questions of power. It is clear that Confindustria's leaders can bring considerable power to bear in their negotiations with government administrators; their control over the collection and analysis of statistical data affords the industrialists great advantages in influencing government decisions. Of course, control over data-gathering is only one way in which a group can influence decision-making, and a thorough analysis would presumably reveal other tactics and strategies through which one party succeeds in having decisions conform to its own interest. The point to be emphasised is that this entire process can be analysed in terms of the relative power of the different contestants.

If power is a function of control over resources, then the central problem is to determine 'who controls what, when and how' within a national or a regional political system. Since resources are typically many and varied, studies are likely to discover that power is fragmented among a number of competing clienteles. Waterbury's study of the Moroccan elite makes this point, just as other analyses of clientele politics point to divided or contesting 'power groups' each based upon control over some resources. If we then ask, 'What gives coherence to such a national or regional system?', the answer may already appear obvious. Namely, coherence (or integration) is a result of a *balance of power* that arranges the otherwise fragmented groups into a system. The various clienteles aggregate power, but then competing groups also control resources and consequently they are able to neutralise or to 'balance' the clientele's potential. To put it differently: these are equilibrium systems of a kind, and the fragmentation of resources and power is a key to the balance.

The limitation of this formulation, I suggest, is that power tends to become almost a residual category – the emphasis is upon the organisation or internal composition of the clienteles rather than upon the use or exercise of power and its outcomes. Power is, as it were 'congealed' around some base of resources where it can become 'unbalanced' against other groups controlling other resources. To be sure, this conception highlights one dimension of the overall category of power, but by the same token it neglects others. Most important, the outcomes or consequences of the use of power in political life broadly, and more particularly in the organisation of clientele systems, is given short shrift. This is a theme that we will return to again.

The main problem faced in studies of power and decision-making is the *reverse* of the one just stated. Whereas in the 'balance of power' theory overall equilibrium or integration is emphasised while power is an underdeveloped motif, in studies of decision-making the uses of power are often described but they are not then linked to on-going social processes. To put it differently: although clientele studies often relate particular incidents or cases in which patrons influence decision-making, this use of power is not usually given sociological meaning. Instead, these cases are analysed in terms of the types of policies adopted or the rise and fall of particular patrons. In brief, studies that deal with decision-making and clienteles need to focus more clearly upon ways in which decisions relate to such fundamental social processes as cohesion, integration or schism.

III

What meanings have anthropologists given to the term patronage? How have concepts of power entered into the analysis of patron-client relations at the village or town level?

Classically, the patron-client pattern defines a situation of structured inequality in which a client is able to obtain political rights only through the intervention of his patron. To be sure, there is an element of reciprocity and exchange in the relationship – the clients supply economic services as well as support in times of crisis – but there is no doubt that clients are fully dependent upon their patron. Examples of this classic pattern include feudal Europe, the 'primitive states' of Central Africa, or Bedouin tribes and their dependents (Mair 1962, Ch.3, and Peters 1968).

Relationships of this type are no longer to be found anywhere in the Mediterranean. Nonetheless, anthropologists have continued to use these terms in describing certain features of political organisation in rural regions; the personalised links between landlords and their tenants in Calabria, or between villagers and aristocratic families in Spain, have been termed 'patron-client' relations. Inequality and reciprocity are also features of this second pattern – but these are based upon differences in wealth and local power, not differences in legal status, and the exchanges too include services or activities of a rather different kind.

How concepts of power enter into modern patron-client studies can best be seen by examining several instances of 'patronage behaviour' as these are described in anthropological analyses. A good place to begin is Jeremy Boissevain's article entitled 'Patronage in Sicily'. Boissevain opens his study by depicting three brief examples of patronage, and these can provide an empirical basis for our own analysis.

The first of these is the case of the student, Salvatore, who was in search of a special favour from a *Professore* in Palermo. Salvatore's immediate problem was to gain an introduction to the Professore. This he accomplished by first approaching a local small-town politician who owed him, Salvatore, a favour. The politician put Salvatore in touch with a cousin in Palermo, and the latter in turn contacted an assistant to the Professore who then arranged the appointment. Salvatore's favour was granted, and he, in exchange, promised to campaign for the Professore who was standing for election.

The second example of 'patronage' centres upon Calogero, who was anxious to be appointed to a post in a Sicilian municipality. Calogero succeeded in having his name proposed by the local town council, but he was concerned that his nomination be acted upon favourably by the provincial commission that screened and passed upon all candidates. He therefore contacted two prestigious acquaintances, the one being his former military commander, the other a lawyer whom he retained for a fee, and asked that they intervene on his behalf. These two discreetly contacted their acquaintances on the commission. Soon thereafter Calogero received the appointment.

Boissevain's third example is slightly more complicated. Professor Volpe suspected that a colleague of his was secretly blocking his son's entrance to the University as a means of bringing dishonour upon the Volpe family. He therefore arranged to have the colleague followed by 'clients' of his and of his brother, an 'important man' in Palermo. His suspicions aroused further, Professor Volpe's brother had a 'key decision-maker' contacted and their combined pressure was adequate to defeat the design of the enemy. Professor Volpe's son was accepted at the University. Some months later, moreover, the conflict between Professor Volpe and his colleague broke into the open when the colleague insulted the Professore. Volpe turned to an old family friend, a local *mafioso*, and the latter discreetly threatened the colleague with 'unpleasantness' unless he apologised. Soon thereafter the Professore received a written apology.

Judging from the data presented by Boissevain, patronage consists of mobilising various contacts in order to gain one's ends: clients search after a patron who agrees to press their particular interest. Locating the patron presents problems, but once the proper connections are made the clients' desires may be advanced. Exchanges are also expected (the student Salvatore promised to campaign for the Professore in the next election) – but these appear as a kind of 'deferred payment' to be collected in the future.

The theory that guides this analysis is straightforward: since in society all persons are arranged at different points on an overall stratification hierarchy, and also since they have differential access to the resources controlled by bureaucratically-organised groups (such as government agencies), it follows that informal social networks can become pathways through which persons arrive at decision-making points and thereby, if successful, gain their objectives. Thus, in the first case the student Salvatore arrived at his objective, gaining entrée to the Professore, by first approaching a local politician, just as Professor Volpe made certain that his son would be accepted at the University by manipulating social networks that brought him into contact with the 'key decision-maker'. In brief, according to this formulation, personal ties and social networks – friends, acquaintances and 'friends of friends' – are the essential substance of patronage.

Moreover, since from this perspective the critical problem is to make the proper connections, among the key actors are those persons who can make the contacts or pass the messages. In each case the person who is seeking a favour turns first to someone who presumably can connect them with those who make decisions. These intermediaries are, in other words, 'brokers' – they are specialists in bringing the more and the less powerful into contact.

Finally it should be clear that it is the 'clients' rather than the 'patrons' who appear at the centre of Boissevain's cases – the student Salvatore, Calogero the office seeker, and even Professor Volpe, are each clients in search of networks that will lead them to the more powerful decision-makers. How the clients calculate and then unfold their schemes is well-stated; but how those who make decisions or who grant favours behave, or what their calculations may be, is mentioned hardly at all. This absence is bound to distort the analysis since, at the least, the clients themselves may be responding to the patron's suggestions or manipulations. In short, this depiction turns out to be a kind of 'clients' view of the world'.

We can turn next to the problem of power. How does power enter into the analysis of patron-client relations?

To put it broadly, the behaviour described and analysed in these cases is more concerned with types of social ties than with the uses of power. Power is, at least implicitly, defined in terms of control over resources or in regard to decision-making; yet there is little behaviour in these episodes that develops these themes. The central characters are mainly shuttling about making contacts, and there is little systematic attention given to how power accumulates, or how it becomes dispersed, or the types of exchanges negotiated between the more and the less powerful. The one exception is the incident in which the *mafioso* threatens Professor Volpe's opponent; but this too is not spelled out or analysed systematically. Thus we may conclude that the uses of power is not a theme much elaborated in these studies.

Boissevain's research is by no means unusual in this regard – anthropological studies of patronage are in general more concerned with social networks and broker relations than with examining the organisation of power (Silverman 1965, Kenney 1966, Campbell 1964). How can this be explained?

This neglect of power, I suggest, arises from the fact that most anthropological studies of politics are not so much about how power is distributed and used as about social integration or social cohesion. This may seem to be contradictory (power, after all, is likely to be related to cohesion) and yet an inspection of recent studies will show this to be the case. To cite two examples from recent 'classics': the intellectual issues that lie behind the political analysis of fission and fusion among the Nuer, or the *mayu-dama* link in the Kachin Hills, have primarily to do with social integration and the maintenance of norms and social institutions. The study of politics has thus been reduced to an interest in familiar sociological issues.

Moreover, this orientation is also prominent in recent studies of complex societies; contemporary work in politics has focussed upon uncovering processes of social integration in societies that are highly differentiated and populous. For example, F.G. Bailey's attempt at reconceptualising the anthropological study of politics (in his *Stratagems and Spoils*) is also developed in terms of an overall theory of social integration. Thus it is no surprise to discover that studies of patronage emphasise brokers and types of social networks, and the neglect of power is the result of a long-term theoretical orientation in anthropology.

IV

Comparing studies of clientele politics with research in patron-client networks throws into relief certain contrasts between the two types of studies. One difference may be obvious: clientele studies place emphasis upon the elite patrons, whereas most anthropological studies adopt the clients' perspective, and as a result the issues raised and developed in these studies differ. Moreover, the substance of political clienteles is different from the patron-client ties described in the literature. Political clienteles are collections of supporters or hangers-on clustered around a leader-patron who is fully engaged in political activities, while the patron-client tie refers more to links and exchanges between clients and a patron who is well connected and therefore powerful. Stating it succinctly, clienteles are groups or 'quasi-groups', while patron-client relations are a feature of networks.

On the other hand, these studies share many themes in common. Most important for our present purposes is the fact that they are both *structural studies*: both types of analysis aim at depicting on-going social relationships as if they were systems, and they also observe how these systems 'function' to maintain the overall structure of the society. Patronage studies have, in other words, adopted the dominant theoretical framework of the past several decades.

It is possible, however, to consider clientele politics and patron-client links in different terms and at a different level of analysis. Namely, these relationships can also be conceptualised in processual terms, and, in addition, they can be thought of as ceremonial performances. What are the objectives of a processual study? By focusing upon particular events, such studies aim at abstracting underlying social processes that emerge from the interactions of persons who join together or who are brought together as they pursue their own goals or interests (Swartz et. al. 1966, intro.). To put it differently, this perspective focuses upon a kind of 'micropolitics' in which, over time, recurrent or characteristic social processes can be perceived.

Specifically in regard to patronage, processual studies may be able to show, for example, how the uses of power lead to new forms of social alignment, or dilemmas that recur in mobilising and sustaining blocs of supporters.

Julian Pitt-Rivers' description of a dispute over water-rights, as presented in his *The People of the Sierra*, can be useful in illustrating the potential rewards of a processual analysis. This particular episode is long and complicated (Pitt-Rivers devotes fourteen pages in his book to the details and analysis of the incident), and can be compressed as follows. The principal actor is Fernando Pinas, one of the two major political figures in the Spanish town of Alcala. Fernando, a bachelor and son of a tenant farmer, had risen rapidly in local society and was described as a 'wealthy miller and farmer, a syndical chief ... close friend of the mayor and a person of local consequence' (Pitt-Rivers 1961, p.141). One year Fernando sent workers to repair the major stream-bed that supplied water to his land and the adjoining land of Juanito, a small farmer who had no clear title to the land and he therefore complained bitterly; others supported Fernando, however, since the new channel meant more power for the grain and olive mills located below the watercourse. The next year Fernando moved again; but this time he proposed a major change in the downward flow of the stream so that it would provide even greater power for his own mill. In order to make these changes he had secretly entered into negotiations with Juanito and paid him a good price for his land. The difficulty, however, was that Curro, a second landowner, would lose water for irrigation, and, in addition, the millers further down in the valley feared that the changes would also adversely affect them.

Curro, who had formerly been an admirer of Fernando, protested and sought to organise opposition to the plan. Fernando offered to pay him compensation for the loss of water, but this Curro proudly refused; he would seek 'justice'. Curro appealed to several of his friends, but they failed to appear at his side. He asked the Mayor and the local Civil Guard to intervene, but their reply was that the issue could only be decided by the Hydrographic Commission in Seville. Finally, Curro approached Don Antonio, the rival of Fernando Pinas for leadership in Alcala, and asked him to intervene on his behalf. Don Antonio offered advice, but it soon became clear that he was not 'prepared to become involved in any way himself'. Finally Curro engaged a lawyer and brought suit against Fernando.

The case was tried in the local court. Fernando won the case, and Curro, the loser, was 'outraged, humiliated and ruined'. All the while Fernando had continued with his project of diverting the water, and soon the new system was in operation. Fernando did suffer some loss, however. It appears that he had not strictly observed the contract made between himself and Juanito, and in a later court action Fernando lost the case and was required to pay damages and court costs.

How can these data be interpreted in processual terms? What benefits can be gained from this type of analysis? The following 'patchwork' interpretation can be suggested. The events described by Pitt-Rivers illustrate a process of 'ebb and flow', or vulnerability, of power. The political field in Alcala was divided between two rival patrons, Don Antonio and Fernando Pinas, and their friends, supporters and clients. In recent years Fernando's power had grown at the expense of Don Antonio as well as other minor figures; his position would be enhanced still further if he could bully or otherwise persuade both Juanito and Curro into accepting his plans for diverting the stream. Juanito was bought-off temporarily, but Curro contested Fernando's claims. The latter's reputation was sufficient, however, to frighten Curro's erstwhile allies who deserted him; they were 'allies', not 'clients', and hence they owed him no allegiance. Don Antonio, Fernando's rival, also refused Curro's pleas for help – he may have wished that Fernando continue to involve himself in entanglements. Fernando appeared triumphant when the court ruled in his favour. Yet when he lost the subsequent case against Juanito the limits of his power – his 'vulnerability' – became apparent. Power might now flow in the direction of his rival.

Examining shifts in power is, of course, only a single facet of the overall phenomenon. Nonetheless, this brief interpretation can illustrate the potentiality of a processual analysis of patronage. Although the analysis is by no means complete, certain advantages can be indicated. First, in contrast with the cases examined earlier this analysis does concentrate upon power and its uses. This is an advantage since fresh topics and areas for study are suggested. For example, focusing upon the 'vulnerability' in power relationships raises new questions regarding how this process may be thwarted, or the social consequences of particular tactics and manoeuvres. Second, this mode of interpretation can be especially helpful in analysing patron-client relationships: since both patrons and clients are actors in the events analysed this focus need not be biased towards one or other, but instead provides a more comprehensive view.

Finally, patronage can also be thought of in much different terms. Encounters between patrons and clients, or among patrons themselves, are highly stylised, ritualised performances, and hence patronage relationships can also be conceptualised as ceremonies of a kind. This is perhaps what Campbell had in mind when he wrote that 'the role of the patron is to give benefits; that of the client is to honour the patron by accepting dependence' (Campbell 1964, p.259). To 'give honour' is to partake in a ceremonial offering, and hence patronage relationships can be conceptualised as a set of performances.

In these performances the various actors, patrons and clients, play particular roles, and their behaviour can be seen to contain a variety of meanings and 'messages'. Thus, for example, the encounters between Curro and Don Antonio, or Fernando Pinas and Juanito, might be analysed in terms of distinctive social rituals and etiquette. To cite another example, the Berber 'rebellion' described separately by both Gellner (1973) and Waterbury (1970) could be analysed as a series of performances in which the major actors were patrons of different rank. According to Gellner's interpretation, the local uprisings can be understood as a kind of 'signalling' behaviour in which men of power exhibit their comparative strength. Focusing upon the power dimensions of patronage hence enables us to expand the inquiry into the field of cultural performances as well.

ACKNOWLEDGMENTS

Many thanks are due to the following who read and commented on this article: Yael Atzmon, Shmuel Eisenstadt, Michael Gurevitch and Moshe Shokeid. Sheila Moser suggested valuable editorial changes.

NOTES

1. The illustrative materials presented here are all drawn from studies in the Mediterranean. Of course, concepts of power and patronage are not limited geographically to one world area, and data from other regions (such as Latin America) might also have been used. The material on the Mediterranean is rich and detailed, however, and it provides a particularly good basis for analysis and generalisation.

REFERENCES

Bailey, F.G. (1969) *Stratagems and Spoils.* New York, Shocken Books.
Boissevain, J. (1966) 'Patronage in Sicily', *Man* I, 8-33.
Campbell, J. (1964) *Honour, Family and Patronage.* Oxford.
Gellner, E. (1973) 'Patterns of rural rebellion in Morocco during the early years of independence', in E. Gellner and C. Micaud (eds), *Arabs and Berbers*, London.
Kenny, M. (1966) *Spanish Tapestry.* New York.
LaPalombara, J. (1964) *Interest Groups in Italian Politics.* Princeton.
Lemarchand, R. and Legg, K. (1972) 'Political clientelism and development: A preliminary analysis', *Comparative Politics* IV (January), 149-78.
Mair, L. (1962) *Primitive Government.* Harmondsworth.
Peters, E. (1968) 'The tied and the free', in J.G. Peristiany (ed.), *Contributions to Mediterranean Sociology.* Paris.
Pitt-Rivers, J. (1961) *People of the Sierra.* Chicago.
Silverman, S.F. (1965) 'Patronage and community-nation relationships in Central Italy', *Ethnology* IV, 172-89.
Swartz, M., V. Turner and A. Tuden (eds) (1966) *Political Anthropology.* Chicago.
Waterbury, J. (1970) *The Commander of the Faithful.* London.

J. Romero-Maura

Caciquismo as a political system

At the turn of the century, following their defeat in the Spanish-American War of 1898, Spaniards became introspective, and started looking, more often and more critically than before, into their political system. Most of those whose words can still be found said the system was defective, and that the ills were due to *'caciquismo'*, the boss-system, patronage networks, the misdeeds of political patrons (*caciques*) and of their clients.

Answers to why and how caciquismo had become so prominent and was so strong were diverse as were the views expressed as to the functional role of caciquismo. Caciques were said by some to be wealthy men who abused their wealth, and by others to be politically powerful men abusing their political strength. Many said caciquismo was engineered from the Ministry of the Interior and could be eliminated if its destruction were willed at the top; to others, it was the local man who was at the root of the matter. Depending on the analyst, too much or too little bureaucracy was seen as its cause. Backwardness of the economy and deep-rooted traditions were also at times seen as the main culprits. Caciquismo was said to have a socially distintegrative function; and there were some, even among those who loathed it, who affirmed on the contrary that, all other things being equal, caciquismo gave cohesion to the social body. And so on.

In the following pages I shall try first to show how the data related to a set of events and relationships constitutive of or related to caciquismo lend themselves to a coherent description once caciquismo is seen from a certain angle. For the sake of economy the bulk of the examples refer to Catalonia in the period from 1898 to 1909. However, data from my own research and from what I know from colleagues carrying out research in depth on other areas confirm – so far at least – that the description below can be said to refer to the data unearthed by them.

Spain was at that time governed by a Constitution which resembled the British system, on paper. In practice, the rotation of the two so-called 'Dynastic' parties – Conservatives and Liberals – was not assured by normal voting procedures. On the whole, people did not vote at all, regardless of what a cursory review of electoral data might suggest.[1] Deputies were returned by caciques, after negotiations between the latter and the government, and among party or factional leaders in the capital.

The country was organised since early in the nineteenth-century under a highly centralised administrative system. Civil Governors were the nearest thing to French *préfets*; i.e., authorities who held at the provincial level all the power of the State, whose delegates they were. Local authorities had very little independence, budgetary or otherwise. The Civil Governor was always a party man, belonging to the party which was in power. He was nominated as soon as the party took over the Cabinet, and his first mission was usually to 'prepare' the forthcoming election: indeed, the dissolution of Parliament was the Crown's privilege, and before a new election was called, the King brought in a Cabinet of the other dynastic party, which 'made' the election. No Cabinet ever lost an election – except once, when the incumbents tried to force results contrary to what the caciques and their factional leaders wanted.

A Civil Governor usually knew what sort of men he would find in the local constituencies. When one of them bothered to describe the caciques, the latter were portrayed much as they were in the *anti-caciquista* writings of the period: 'Here we have no selflessness, no discipline, no organisation. Everyone moves in pursuit of his own personal aims and all manner of personal passions are given priority over public and party interests' (González Seara 1966, p. 190). The local cacique tends to be 'obstinate, domineering, (is) accustomed to impose his will without argument' (Interior Ministry Archives 1905). 'The truth is that here we have no politicians, but a bunch of intriguers devoid of good faith and principles' (Maura Archives 1907).

Caciques were by no means always rich men. A local senator of Gerona refused throughout 1906 to pay taxes on a small mill he had, for the simple reason that he could not afford to do so. In Castillo de Haro, the break between the cacique and the villagers came when he flatly refused to accept a proposed reduction from Pts.8,000 to Pts.6,000 in the municipal budget – to all appearances because it would leave him destitute: the difference had originally been budgeted to cover the running costs of a non-existent hospital, and to help build at the village cemetery a chapel which nobody wanted. In Llagostera, the villagers complained that higher taxes were imposed on them than on their neighbours, and they offered the cacique a monthly pension of Pts.500 if he would retire from politics altogether (Romanones Archives). The cacique's hold on his area was thus not always, or even most often, that of a man who had key economic resources of his own. It could not be so, in a country where many areas simply had no very rich, no economically predominant landowners and employers.

The cacique who lacked such weapons, or who while having them refused to make use of them, had other levers of control. Civil Governors would experience it immediately upon arrival at their posts. Comas y Masferrer, the powerful Liberal cacique of Barcelona at the turn of the century, even had access to the secret cipher of the Ministry of the Interior, so that he did not have to entrust urgent and confidential electoral messages to the Governor. Just after taking over the Civil Governorship of Gerona in 1907, Moreno Churruca described the situation in the province under the previous, Liberal administration:

No one can imagine, unless he sees and experiences it, what Roure (the Liberal cacique there) meant when I first took over ... His influence pervaded the Provincial Court, the Tax Office, the Magistrates Court, the Provincial Authority's offices, and the Civil Government itself. He even had the police at his beck and call, having corrupted it by exploiting its every vice and weakness, and all the villages and small towns were absolutely under his control. In these parts Roure called the tune for many years, and all other politicians, aspiring caciques to a man, were mere puppets he moved at will, so that the Civil Governor was reduced to being his agent and he used the (Civil) Government as though it were his own office. (Maura Archives 1/6/1907)

But the position of the Gerona Governor did not change very significantly as a result of the switch in Madrid from a Liberal to a Conservative Government:

It is said [wrote Moreno Churruca soon after arriving in Gerona] that Joaquín Delclós has made a nice niche for himself under the wing of the Count [of Serra, the Conservative boss of the province] and that he is considered the party's foremost local cacique. The Count introduced him to me when the three of us were alone, telling me that he was his alter ego and that I could trust him as though he were himself, and since then he hasn't left me alone. He visits me daily, bringing me news, letters and warnings of the Count. He constantly writes me cards and notes ... and has set himself up as my guide and mentor when it comes to elections, marshalling even policemen and inspectors to work in the campaign. (Maura Archives 9/3/1907)

The cacique's strength vis-à-vis the Civil Governor, representing the Government at the provincial level (and by implication, vis-à-vis lesser men, civil servants and local employees) sprang directly from the former's position as head of the local party organisation. The cacique whose party was in power had access to the Prime Minister, or to the Minister of the Interior, or to a factional leader who had access to either or both. The Civil Governor, in party terms, could not be seen to be hampering his party's progress or hindering his party's local organisation in the constituencies of the province. In this sense the Civil Governor was not above the local cacique.

Whatever the text and the spirit of the laws governing the behaviour of Governors, they had to be wary of the caciques' complaints. When, in 1905, the Governor of Lerida clashed with Agelet, cacique of the town of Borjas Blancas, who refused to accept the Government's proposed candidate, the Governor felt insecure:

My intervention in this matter by the Government's order ... makes me suspect in his [Agelet's] eyes; therefore, I would ask Your Excellency [Minister of Interior] to pass word to Don Eugenio [Montero Ríos, the Prime Minister] for I fear that he may complain to him of me as weak and irresolute because I have taken pains not to support a patronage system ['Un cacicato'] that is collapsing, but rather to serve the interests of my government and party'. (Ministry of Interior Archives 19/8/1905)

Already in 1903, when Antonio Maura had tried to convince the Governors and the country that he meant what he said when he declared that the next elections were going to be clean, he had both to prompt and reassure his Governors with words such as these:

My instructions were given and must be carried out regardless of any political [i.e., partisan] intentions ... seeking exclusively to fulfill the duties of your office, without regard for [the political affiliation and strength of] persons and without qualms or hesitation. I have not authorised nor shall I authorise anyone's interference in your relationships with myself [then Minister of the Interior] on official matters, this being the basis of [my previous] well-known general instructions [which] I hereby ratify in every detail. (Maura/Almeria 7/1/1903)

Maura's 1903 attempt failed on the whole for even where Governors followed his lead other civil servants did not always do so, and caciques clearly did not. The relationship of caciques and Civil Governors soon reverted everywhere to what it was before, following a pattern schematically described by the Count of Torre-Vélez in a document presented to the King with a collective plea from ex-Governors:

Whether or not a Governor owes his credentials to the cacique, the Government tells him, more or less wrapped in circumlocutions, 'follow So-and-So's instructions'. So-and-so is the cacique. Comes the day when the Governor is loth to follow those instructions and he says so to the cacique, or tells the Government, or both, and within ten or twelve hours at most, he receives a cyphered cable saying: 'Kindly do such and such without delay'. That is to say, whatever it is that So-and-so wanted. And then the Governor either realises that there is no point and forgets his scruples, or he refuses to lie down, causing the Official Bulletin to announce his transfer, at least.

For the 'golden rule' followed in the internal affairs of our political parties has ever been that 'in any conflict between Governors and caciques, it is the Governors who are usually right, but since the caciques cannot move elsewhere, it is the Governors who must go'. [That is] the axis of the whole system. (Torre-Velez, 49-50)

The cacique needed a clientele. In a country where caciques were frequently poor, or very poor, or at any rate no richer than the local middle-classes, and where provincial and local, but also national budgets were relatively meagre, while available resources were not easily divisible, the caciques could not rely for the purpose of building up their clienteles on their control over decisions affecting the distribution of material goods. But centralisation, in the context of the liberal, napoleonic State, had created goods of which there was a cheap and inexhaustible supply, and which were often vital to the citizen: decisions by the administration, constitutive, sanctioning, or whatever. These had to be distributed, and their distribution could be controlled. Authorisation, certificates, court and police sentences, exemptions, and the like, were as important to the cacique, if not more so, than jobs and other resources allocated to clients and non-clients.

Although the State and local administrations, and the Judiciary, were bound by the rule of law, the cacique needed to ensure that decisions would be taken in accordance with instructions when he gave them; and his instructions were bound to be discriminatory. The reason for this is clear: the patron who gives his client what the latter can obtain in the normal way, through the normal channels, is no patron. Caciquismo thus thrived on illicit decisions.

Here, it is worth reminding the non-jurist of the wide scope of illicit action open to the decision-making civil servant, local authority, judge, or magistrate. Failure to act when action is due is of course a very important part of this. Both action and inactivity can, then, be technically illegal on two different grounds – and this technicality is relevant, since it is supposed to rule the behaviour of administrative decision-makers. The distinctions were made long ago by the French *Conseil d'Etat*. They are what it called *excès de pouvoir*, a familiar concept referring to events when the administrator decides *ultra vires*, i.e. rules on matters on which he is not empowered to rule; and the less familiar but equally important breach of the law called *détournement de pouvoir*. This occurs when the administrator, while ruling within his sphere of jurisdiction, does so for reasons and ends which are not those intended by the law. Discretionary powers can thus also be used illegally – and often were – at the prompting of the caciques.

Civil servants and local administrators who were not caciques themselves thus disobeyed the rules they were supposed to abide by, when they obeyed the caciques. The cacique had to be in a position to oblige them, and to protect them. On the other hand, those who governed often resented the power of the caciques which made government inefficient in a thousand ways, and disrupted the chain of command. Why tolerate them, when the strength of the strongest cacique looks infinitely frail compared to the might of the State, or of its delegate, the Civil Governor?

The answer lies in the degree of demobilisation which was obtained in the country. At election time, if the government negotiated with the cacique, an agreed députy would be returned. For many important politically-related matters, including information, the government could rely on the cacique. Whatever the drawbacks of the cacique, in most places there was nothing else in the way of political organisation. The cacique, moreover, knew that the greater his local strength, and the greater his hold over the administrators locally, the greater his power to resist damaging pressure from the top. If the government wanted a deputy of the cacique's party, he was nearly certain to be returned; supposing the government wanted a deputy of the other dynastic party, or of some of the anti-dynastic parties, he would also be returned thanks to the cacique. But locally, the deputy would be nobody, and he would work for the cacique if asked by him to do so. Thus, the strength of its local caciques guaranteed to each party that it would retain a strong minority and considerable influence whenever it was the other party's turn to 'make' the election from the

Government. Of course, it was tempting for the in-coming party or some of its factions to try to destroy the other side's machines. But here the King, who, as we said, could dissolve Parliament, and who chose the Prime Minister, would not allow such a thing to happen: he knew, or thought that it was the case, that such political exclusivisms had brought the Monarchy down in 1868.

Once we look at caciquismo from this angle, what we know about the ways in which political decisions were taken, and through which channels, ceases to puzzle us – at least for those periods and areas within Restoration Spain (1876-1923) for which we have sufficient information.

The system as described was not necessarily based on a traditional mentality. In order to exist, clients did not need to feel as clients are supposed to feel towards their patrons in the face-to-face relationships described in some of the literature. There was often gratitude and respect which did not involve any feeling of subordination in the client – genuine sentiments resulting from favours delivered with grace by the cacique, who publicly called his client *amigo* (friend), even if the latter addressed him as *jefe* (my political chief), a word which in Spanish is very frequently used with no connotation of subordination whatsoever. On the other side, straight bargaining was frequent, with little or no concealment of the clear transactional nature of the relationship. Here, it is perhaps worth taking up a point already made by other contributors, that benefits bestowed individually do not necessarily lead to the formation of a patron-client relationship. There may be social and other conditions favouring the formation of such relationships in the classical sense, but we should remember that, whatever the underlying social positions of giver and beneficiary may be, and whatever the nature of the gift or favour, we cannot start from what we see in them if we want to discover whether or not an obligation is born. That is what Seneca meant when he said that 'a benefit cannot possibly be touched by the hand; its province is the mind' (De Beneficiis). In the context of Restoration Spain, the ideal clientele for the cacique was a very small one, just large enough to keep the machine performing. This was in keeping with the limited scope of demands made by the cacique from his protégés, in a context of massive demobilisation. Once we know this, it is perhaps natural to expect, as appears to have been the case, that clients should very often have viewed their relationships with the caciques as another instance of the sort of negotiations that were going on in their professional and non-professional lives, and not significantly different from those.

Caciques themselves seem to have been more given to feeling what the arch-typical patron is supposed to feel. This is understandable in men who, having performed their role in politics without incurring the obligations of an elected representative, could often feel that they were motivated only by a sense of public responsibility as they saw it. Surely, there were many caciques who shared the sentiments of the

Conde de Serra, writing in 1907 at a time when anti-caciquista feelings in his constituency of Torroella de Montgrí were hemming him in: 'In the service of my country and in particular of Torroella, I have sacrificed the best of my existence, given that my public life has been a continuous Calvary, which I have borne with resignation while I had the strength ... I [now] succumb to fatigue and disappointment' (Maura Archives 12/5/1907).

The way the cacique saw his own role had direct political relevance in that it made him ill-prepared to face the challenge of opponents who chose to take the battle to the field of genuine vote-gathering. His experience of decades of command was of course there to suggest to him that what had been would remain. Thus, after a reverse suffered by the Barcelona Regionalists in 1899, when they had barely started organising as a modern party, the newspaper of Planas y Casals, the mighty Conservative boss, commented confidently:

[This] obviously shows what we have always thought; that is: that however deep the good intentions of public men may be, they will never reach their aims if they live outside the realm of political reality. Ideals are one thing, and practical reality is something quite different. From which we can deduce a strong argument against the ridiculous and vulgar illusion, of late so fashionable, which consists in attributing to people who were not involved in daily politics a regenerationist panacea somehow beyond the reach of men who had spent their whole life in politics. (La Dinastia, 13/10/1899)

But such wisdom was not the only source of the cacique's blindness. In 1899 the caciques of the Vich district equated the local regionalists' method of canvassing for votes to political begging. Soon, they lost Vich to the Regionalists, and Barcelona too, to a combined attack of Regionalists and Republicans. The lesson, though, was lost on them. Having vainly attempted to mobilise the caciques for the Conservative party in the direction of vote-gathering, the Civil Governor of Barcelona complained to the Prime Minister in 1907: 'What does not occur to any of them [the dynastic politicians of the Barcelona province] is to apply to local life that [mobilising] spirit of yours, though they claim to admire you greatly' (Maura Archives 11/2/1908). The Civil Governor of Gerona at the same time pointed out concisely another aspect of the views and the structures set up by the caciques: 'Our friends, though they have acted loyally, lack the organisation required for this kind of combat and especially [they lack] those auxiliaries indispensable for manning the polling stations, for distributing campaign material and other details ...' (González Seara 1966).

However spectacular some of the stories about the misdeeds of caciques, two connected points ought to be made. One is that there was pluralism in Restoration Spain, 'Cacique' pluralism first, with effects similar to those of pluralism in democratic electoral systems. Possibilities of choice were often very great, and the alternatives to choose from were often significantly different in terms of policy at the

local level, although this significance appears to have had little to do
with overall party ideologies. The general constitutional framework of
freedom of the press, of organisation, etc., was not just in the letter of
the law. In varying degrees, but by no means always less than, say, in
neighbouring France, such freedoms were very real. This limited the
freedom of any cacique to abuse the law against too many people in
too many ways. One example, among many: when the Liberal
cacique of San Hilario de Sacalm, in 1906, wanted to get rid of hostile
town-councillors inherited from the previous, Conservative period, he
had to desist, because he could not find anyone in the village prepared
to take the place of the councillors he wanted to suspend; as the
villagers wrote to the Liberal Minister of the Interior:

There is beginning to be an awakening in the district of Santa Coloma [and] all are
making ready to fight with determination against interventions and impositions that
pursue no political ends but only personal advantage ... The struggle against the
cacique ... is not [directed] against the Liberal party but against those who by joining
the party have managed to invest themselves with an unwarranted influence they
exploit without political idealism of any kind. If Your Excellency does not halt the
abuses of the caciques, it is certain that in the district of Santa Coloma de Farnés,
where the only contenders since 1890 have been Liberals and Conservatives, the next
elections will take on a different character, because the existing state of irritability
and tension is bound to entail a coalition of all the villages against the Liberal
cacique. (Romanones Archives)

And in fact this is precisely what happened.

Connected with the relative insecurity of each cacique's hold on his
fief is the fact that the system did deliver. The pressure groups of
different economic and non-economic sectors could usually count on
the caciques to help lobby governments and parliaments effectively.
Even after some pressure groups started operating through modern
parties different from or hostile to the dynastic parties, the system
retained much of its conductivity. It was of course fortunate for the
politicians of the Establishment that the demands made were not
mutually exclusive, and that sectoral interests were asking for
decisions that were mostly complementary; but the ability to deliver
the goods within the range of expectations also shows the flexibility of
the system. Such distributions did not of course generate new clients
for the local patrons, but many of them thought that they kept
potential opponents to the caciques and to the system out of politics,
or at least away from active political behaviour. At any rate, these
distributions allowed the caciques to remain effective with relatively
small clienteles.

As for the poor, the lower strata, the working class, repression does
not explain everything, and was neither constant nor invariably iron-
fisted when it occurred.[2] The statement (much used by critics then
and by historians since) that caciquismo sapped the people's will,
does not tell us very much about the phenomenon and merely
indicates by implication the critic-historian's desiderata. Suffice it to
say that clienteles cut very much across class lines and that many of

the goods and decisions distributed to non-clients as well were of obvious benefit to such social groups. The fact that the law was twisted by the cacique does not entail that it was always infringed to the disadvantage of the poor nor to that of any group in particular. Besides, caciques often feared disturbances far more than the wrath of the local rich, and often bought social peace through imposition upon the latter of decisions favouring the former. The same happened with the government, in certain cases. A typical example was in the use of the army to meet certain demands of the workers in the northern industrial and mining areas. The same happened at times in connection with the local poor and with national institutions, as shown by the widespread and illegal avoidance of the draft thanks to the control of drafting officers by the caciques (R.E. 1898).

The description of caciquismo outlined above is fraught with unresolved difficulties, because the researcher states his case in such a way as to make it understandable, while hoping to avoid further implications as to where and in what way the objects and processes described resemble and/or are identical to other objects and processes evoked in the reader's mind by the words used. The choice of quotations and examples given above was dictated by the hope of preventing such generalising urges as may be suggested by the vagueness of words compounded by unfamiliarity with the context of Restoration Spain. It is – in my view – impossible to escape this trap when we talk of social phenomena (such as caciquismo). To start with we do not have a clear notion of what are the relevant elements, properties, etc., of the factual frame of reference within which we carry out the analysis. I am only warning against a possible, and tempting jump from description to definition. An arbitrary stipulation of definitions would not help at all. The sort of relevance I talk about is that which is established by a satisfactory theory leading to a satisfactory explanation. What is satisfactory in this context is perhaps determined by fashions in the scientific community. The present fashion is both more demanding and more openminded than it used to be in the heyday of strict mechanistic determinism. But I cannot see how to accept as valid explanations/theories the sort of woolly statements that lead to forecasts so imprecise that the range of results taken as corroborative makes almost any results partially corroborative.

What I have described above is coherent in that it divides up what is perceived into facts inter-related in a way which appears familiar and unsurprising while basically unexplained. Since we have no theory worthy of that name, it is pointless to argue about what would have happened had caciquismo not existed, or to ask other questions around which argument is pointless unless deductions can be reached analytically, based on what is usually called a well-established general law. These remarks may be superfluous for most readers, although the way in which some of these matters are discussed suggests that awareness of such difficulties is not always complete. I am reluctant to develop any comparative or definitional arguments on the basis of my and other data in this volume and in the literature. The analogies, differences, and regularities are all rather obvious and vague, as is my guess as to their significance.

NOTES

1. This point is important, in view of the influence of recent works based on electoral results taken at face value; for a more detailed criticism, see my article 'El caciquismo: tentativa de conceptualización', *Revista De Occidente* (Madrid), October 1973, pp. 15-44. The main points of the present contribution are developed at some length in that article, but most of the material now included is new, and the limits and implications of the approach taken appear to me far clearer (and restrictive!) as presented here.
2. See, e.g., notes by A.P. (?), 'Notas sobre la situación del partido liberal en Gerona', n.d.; but, 1906: '[the province] has in the way of policemen 24 men in the coastal border and 13 throughout the [rest of the] province, inclusive of the inspectors', Romanones Archives, Leg. 18, n°20.

REFERENCES

Dinastia, la, (13/10/1899) cited in G. Rubio, *Una inflexión de la Restauración: el Regeneracionismo en Cataluña*, unpub. MA thesis (Barcelona 1963).
González Seara, L. (1966) 'Materiales para una sociología electoral de la Restauración', *Anales de Sociología* 2.
Interior Ministry Archives: Civil Governor to Romanones, Lérida (19/8/1905) A/22, file Lerida
Interior Ministry Archives: Maura to Governor of Almería (7/1/1903) A/21, file Almeria.
Maura Archives: Moreno Churruca to A. Maura, Gerona (9/3/1907) uncatalogued.
Maura Archives: Letter to A. Maura, Gerona (1/6/1907).
Maura Archives: Letter to Moreno Charruca, Barcelona (12/5/1907).
Maura Archives: Ossorio y Gallardo to A. Maura, Barcelona (11/2/1908).
R.E. (?) 'Lo que hay que hacer', in *El Ejercito Espanol* (Madrid) 2/7/1898.
Romanones, Count; Collective Document sent by the inhabitants of the constituencies of Santa Coloma de Farnés and La Bisbal, Romanones Archives, L 72 n.50 (2/6/1906).
Torre-Valez, Conde de (et al.) (1902) *Nuevo régimen local (campaña de los ex-governadores en 1901-1902)*, Madrid.

Alan Zuckerman

Clientelist politics in Italy

Introduction

Clientelism (and the related terms patron-client ties, patronage and dyadic alliances) refers to the social grouping of markedly unequal individuals (termed patrons and clients) in 'personalised reciprocal relationships'. The tie is based on personal loyalty, obligation and the exchange of unequal goods and services (Lemarchand and Legg 1972, p.149; Lande 1973, Scott 1969).

Clientelism was first conceptualised and examples of it described by anthropologists. It is not surprising, therefore, that most examined cases have been in the villages of non-industrial areas. Increasing numbers of studies indicate, however, that patronage is limited neither to a geographic area nor to a 'stage' in the process of modernisation (Lemarchand and Legg 1972, Scott 1969). Rather, it appears that socio-economic change serves to alter the particular bases of clientele relationships though they persist as frequently found modes of social cohesion. Lemarchand and Legg suggest, therefore, a typology in which variations of patron-client relations are associated with different types of political systems. There is also increasing evidence that clientelism is not destroyed with the rise of social class as a basis of social cohesion. Both forms may coexist, and any particular individual may use either or both (Zuckerman 1974). Consequently, the task of theorising is to describe and account for the emergence, persistence and effect of each type: clientelism as well as social class.

With regard to the formation and behaviour of political clienteles (i.e., clienteles seeking to influence or control a social unit's authoritative decision-making positions) two primary types have been distinguished and examples located and described.[1] The first is traditional clienteles which have been transformed into groups engaged in political competition (Lemarchand 1972, Linz 1967, Powell 1970, Heath 1973). The second is political groups with the structural characteristics of clienteles, e.g. political machines (Scott 1969; Weingrod 1968). As with most studies of clienteles, these types have been described with particular regard to the relations between political leaders and their local level sources of support, especially voting support.

It is neither empirically necessary nor theoretically useful to equate clienthood with low social status, precarious economic positions or very limited political power. Rather, local-level patrons frequently serve as clients to patrons 'above' them and so on in the development of the patron-client chain to the national level. The maintenance of these political clienteles is just as dependent on particularistic, material rewards and personal loyalty, though the currency of exchange is not limited to support at the polls.

The literature also contains attempts at theorising about the determinants and consequences of political clienteles. In particular, hypotheses have been suggested in which the presence and characteristics of political clienteles are treated as dependent variables (Lemarchand and Legg 1972, Scott 1969 and 1972, Zuckerman 1974). Here, however, I am concerned with the consequences of the activities of political clienteles for structures of political competition.

Given the crucial importance of personal loyalty and particularistic exchanges for the maintenance of political clienteles I propose that:

1. Political clienteles will act so as to further the political career(s) of the leader(s).
2. Political clienteles will act so as to control governing positions.
3. They will rarely act so as to obtain goals of value to those who are not members of the group, 'collective goods'.
3a. Those 'rare instances' will be occasioned by perceptions of danger to its survival and to the persistence of the competitive system.[2]

Hypotheses relating to their likelihood of success in political competition and to their competitive strategies may be suggested:

4. Given that political clienteles are relatively less bound by packages of policy preferences than are 'trait groups'[3] they are less encumbered in the choice of political allies and, therefore, are more likely to succeed in controlling governing positions.
5. The greater the success of political clienteles in attaining their goals, the more likely that 'trait groups' will adopt similar goals.
6. Given the issue orientation and pronouncements of the 'trait groups', the political clienteles will publicly frame their particularistic demands in issue terms.
7. Competition among political clienteles will result in unstable agreements.

These propositions will be illustrated by examining political clienteles institutionalised (i.e., recognised and persistent) as Italian political party factions. After surveying the place of clientelism in Italian society, the political clienteles' nationwide structures and competitive behaviour in regard to control of Italian national cabinets will be explored. It is hoped that this analysis of clientelism at the national level of a relatively industrial society will help fill a gap in the literature of political clienteles.

Political clienteles in Italy

The locus of most analyses of Italian clientelism has been the villages of the *mezzogiorno*. There, patron-client relations have been frequently found, and their structural features and associated behavioural norms have corresponded with those of highly valued social institutions, the Church, the family and godparenthood.

Increasing industrialisation and the penetration of the society by the government and political parties since World War II have altered the particular characteristics of southern Italian clientelism. These changes have not resulted, however, in the replacement of patron-client ties by social class as the basis of social and political cohesion.

The traditional resources of local patrons which lay in the position of land-owner or mediator to the world beyond the village have been supplanted by control over government and political party positions. While in its earlier form each client had but one patron, this too is diminishing in frequency. Southern clientelism is less multi-dimensional and is now most frequently entered into for specific and limited purposes. At the local level, clients promise their support, particularly votes, to a patron as a means to gain access to government positions. Patrons, in turn, increasingly use their followings in order to advance their careers within the parties and the bureaucracy (Boissevain 1966, Stirling 1968, Weingrod 1968, Tarrow 1967, Graziano 1973, Allum 1973).

While one may argue from recent evidence that the traditional clienteles of local notables have been supplanted by party-associated political clienteles, the behavioural patterns and norms of traditional clientelism have persisted. Stirling's study of social values in the changing society of southern Italy focuses upon the conflict between the 'impartiality' expected in a bureaucratic organisation and the traditional 'personal morality', still found in the *mezzogiorno*. He contends that success is still viewed in personal terms and seen to be achieved only by using *raccomandazioni* so as to obtain efficient protectors (Stirling 1968, pp. 30-51).

Thus, it would seem that at least until the middle of the 1950s clientelism was the predominant, if not the only form of social grouping in the south of Italy. Since then, the alterations that have occurred there have resulted in the change of the bases of clientelism and the scope of particular clientelist groups.

In the analysis of political clienteles in other parts of Italy one must rely on less direct sources: there are fewer field studies; social class and categorical political groups emerged there much earlier than in the south; and perhaps most importantly there existed a scholarly consensus that the North is best seen as another case of an industrialised society, significantly different from the 'traditional' or 'modernising' south (Tarrow 1967, Allum 1973).

There is reason to believe, however, that there exist strong similarities throughout Italy in regard to general norms and behaviour concerning competition and authority as well as toward social cohesion and division. The differences that are present within Italy are not neatly linked to differences in industrial development. This argument is borne out by ecological analyses of voting behaviour (Capecchi 1968), by the survey responses found in the *Civic Culture* study and in more recent analyses by Barnes and Sani (1974).[4] It will be substantiated by describing political clienteles in the Italian north as well as the south, and in national politics as well as at the local level, through the analysis of factions in the Christian Democrat Party (DC).[5]

For the purposes of this essay, I define a political party faction as a structured group within a political party which seeks, at a minimum, to control the authoritative decision-making positions of the party. It is a 'structured group' in that there are established patterns of behaviour and interaction for the faction members over time. Thus, party factions are to be distinguished from groups that coalesce around a specific or temporally limited issue and then dissolve and form collectivities of individuals who, though sharing attitudes and opinions, do not form structured groups. By contrast, in the case of the DC party factions, each is characterised by a decision-making apparatus, a recognised leadership and a nation-wide organisation which extends to the provincial and at times communal levels of government and society. Each has periodic national and local-level meetings and a press agency (Sartori 1966).

Since its inception at the end of the nineteenth century, the history of the Italian Christian Democratic movement has been marked by the presence of competing currents, *tendances*, and groupings. With Christian Democracy's establishment as a nationwide political force during and after World War II, party factions have proliferated to join with and supercede the older divisions (Zariski 1965). Two events, Fanfani's success in the mid-1950s in institutionalising the party as an independent political movement and the decision in 1963 to form a governing coalition with the socialists (i.e. the PSI as well as the PSDI), served to enhance the importance and activities of the party factions.

The factions that competed at the 1969 and 1973 Party Congresses are surveyed in the following table. Their analysis will serve as the descriptive centre of this paper.

In neither Congress did a single faction command a majority of the seats, and hence none controlled the National Council and Secretariat. The governing alliance in 1969, of the *Dorotei*, *Fanfaniani*, and *Tavianei*, mirrored the ruling coalition of factions in the party during the preceding several years. Of the three, the *Dorotei* was the largest and had been so for the previous decade. With the exception of

Table 1 Christian Democrat factions: National Party Congresses, 1969, 1973

Faction (leaders)	1969		1973	
	% votes at Congress	Seats in National Council	% votes at Congress	Seats in National Council
DOROTEI	38.3	46		
Colombo-Andreotti			16.5	20
Rumor-Piccoli				
TAVIANEI	9.5	12	} 34.2	42
(Taviani, Gaspari)				
FANFANIANI	15.9	18	19.8	24
(Fanfani, Forlani)				
MOROTEI	12.7	16	8.7	10
(Moro)				
BASE			10.8	12
(De Mita, Granelli, Galloni)	} 18.2	22		
FORZE NUOVE			10	12
(Donat Catin)				
NUOVA SINISTRA	2.6	2		
(Sullo)				
FORZE LIBERE	2.9	4		
(Scalfaro, Restivo)				
	100.1	120	100.0	120

the two smallest factions, all had existed for at least ten years and some for even longer. The governing coalition was opposed on its left by an alliance of the *Morotei, Base* and *Forze Nuove* and on its right by the *Forze Libere* factions. Coordination among the factions of the left was sufficient to enable the *Base* and *Forze Nuove* to present a united list of candidates to the Party Congress.

In the fall of that year, a split in the *Dorotei* produced two factions: Rumor-Piccoli and Colombo-Andreotti, and a change in the party's governing coalition. Control shifted to a new, more left-looking generation of leaders composed of the left factions, the younger leaders of the *Fanfaniani*, particularly Forlani, Fanfani's lieutenant, and supported by Colombo-Andreotti. This new ruling alliance lasted until the 1973 Party Congress, where, in a demonstration of apparent party unity, all the factions agreed to the return of Fanfani to formal party leadership.

Several factors of major importance emerge from this rapid survey of events. There has been a marked persistence in the particular factions competing for power within the DC. The relative size of the factions has changed very little during the period, and the same party leaders have been present for the past fifteen years. The result of the effort to limit inter-faction competition under Fanfani's direction is quite problematic. It is dependent on the continued willingness of the party leaders to maintain the agreement. This is an unlikely prospect, and an earlier breakdown brought the *Dorotei* into existence.

In describing the kinds of political groups found in the Christian Democrat Party, one of the left faction leaders contended:

As I would say that every political party has a power character, these men are interested above all in the control of the majority and thus in the control of a certain distribution of positions in the party and the government throughout its levels. ...

We see, therefore, that the regroupings of the majority are done in the name of men. That is to say, that there is no 'centre' or 'right' in the party. There are the friends of Fanfani, of Taviani, of Moro, of Piccoli, of Colombo, etc. These are very large clienteles of men who are very powerful. For example, the Minister of the Treasury names men to many powerful positions: heads of banks, commercial houses, directors of credit associations, and thus has many clients and from these forms groups of power. (Personal interview)

This view is echoed by two of the leaders of the other party factions. One said:

Did you think that there were philosophical or ideological bases for these groups? Given the policy differences in the party, there ought to be three groupings: a 'left' (with perhaps two parts), a 'centre' and a 'right'. That there are now nine factions is caused by the importance of personalist groupings and is aided by the presence of proportional representation. (Personal interview)

In a similar vein:

The number of factions has now grown to nine. This is due to personal power games within the party. When a new faction forms, such as the *Tavianei*, or the *Morotei*, it must justify itself in ideological terms, but this is artificial. The factions are power groups. (Personal interview)

The non-left factions are labelled 'groups of power' not only because their primary goal is to control political offices, but also because of the relationship between faction members and leader(s). Of crucial importance is the controlling position of the national leader over his followers, both at the national and local levels. While the factions have recognised structures and periodic meetings, the distribution of power within the factions is highly skewed in favour of the leaders at each level. Faction meetings are not sessions for the equal exchange of information and influence. Rather, they allow the followers to come into contact with the leaders and to learn the leaders' positions and desires. At the centre of the relationship is the exchange of political positions and access to government resources for votes in national and party elections, in particular, and political support in general (Zariski 1965, Sartori 1966, 1971).

A description of the *Dorotei* will highlight the structure of the political clienteles. Before the split in 1969, the *Dorotei* was composed of the alliance of four national political leaders: Rumor, Piccoli, Andreotti and Colombo. Each of them had occupied the highest government and party positions and each of them was supported by long chains of personal followers. The political bases of faction leaders are strongest in their home provinces and regions from which large numbers of the faction members are recruited: Rumor (Vicenza and the entire Veneto), Piccoli (Trento), Andreotti (Lazio), and Colombo (Basilicata). They were all supported by very large preference votes in national and party elections.[6] Indeed, at the 1969 Party Congress, they ranked as the top four party leaders in terms of preference votes. While these personal power bases are crucially important for their positions as party leaders, each was also tied to other somewhat less major party leaders. The secondary leaders had their own electoral and party bases of strength and chose to ally themselves with one or more of the national leaders of the *Dorotei*. Thus, the geographical spread of the faction was tied to the personal sources of power of each of the national leaders and to those second-level leaders aligned with the faction.[7] Each of the factions formed in 1969 was composed of two of the leaders of the *Dorotei* and their personal followers both in their home regions and of the second-level national leaders. The only difference in structure between the *Dorotei* and their successors, the Rumor-Piccoli faction and the Colombo-Andreotti faction, was in geographical spread, and that was conditioned by the personal bases of power of each national leader and the number of second-level leaders aligned with each faction. In addition, the description of each of the four strands in the *Dorotei* serves equally well for the *Tavianei* and *Morotei* factions. Each of these factions is composed of the personal power bases of the national leader from his home district and those secondary leaders aligned with them. This is not at all surprising given that both of them were formed by earlier splits within the *Dorotei*.

In order to develop more fully a picture of the structure of each of the political clienteles, I will describe the political bases of two of the national leaders, Colombo and Rumor. Each has been a DC party leader since the late 1940s and each has served as Prime Minister of the Republic. In addition, Rumor, one of the founders of the *Dorotei* faction, was General Secretary of the DC between 1963 and 1968, and before becoming Prime Minister Colombo served for seven years as Minister of the Treasury.

Colombo's position in his native province of Potenza, and in the region of Basilicata, has been clearly dominant.[8] Not only is there no political leader in the area of equal stature to him but all DC political activists are members of his faction. Several factors serve to indicate further his controlling position. The preference vote for him in both national and party elections has been consistently high. In 1968, 66.7% of those voting for the Christian Democrat Party in his election district cast preference votes for him and thereby set a record for percent of preference votes received by a candidate in Italy (Nobecourt, 1971, p.23). At the National Party Congress of the DC in June, 1969, he received the third largest number of preference votes (*Il Popolo*, July 2, 1969).

Of primary importance to the argument being presented here is the analysis of the DC party factions in Potenza and their links to

Colombo. Though there exist within the province three competing local factions, euphemistically called 'groups', with significant differences between them, they are all *Colombiani*. His control of the party organisation in the region is best summarised by noting that during Moro's tenure as General Secretary of the DC the only region to which he was never invited to speak was Basilicata (Nobecourt 1971, p.58).

Colombo's control of the DC is of major significance because it persists even as new political forces have emerged to control the party in Potenza. The majority faction is composed of a group of young men who proclaim the desire to bring about fundamental change within Potenza and the entire region. This transition has been greatly resented by older party leaders who feel that their rightful position to control the party has been stolen. One such leader, a mayor of a commune, argued: 'It is the third generation which is in the minority and wrongly so. The second generation passed on the power to those of the fourth generation in order to save themselves and in the process cut off those in their forties from their rightful positions' (personal interview).

This new political group of men in their late twenties and early thirties with university degrees is best typified by their leader, Angelo Sanza, the Provincial Secretary between 1968 and 1972 and elected to the Parliament in the 1972 elections. When first elected, he was the youngest Secretary in the DC. Sanza joined the party in 1958 upon returning from a year at school and with relatives in the United States. At the age of eighteen, he became a member of the Youth Movement and was elected the Provincial Delegate and then rapidly came to hold positions of national leadership. After receiving his degree in economics at the University of Rome, he rejected a position at the university in order to return to Potenza. The decision to leave the more developed areas of Italy in which they were educated and to return to Potenza was made by several of the young party leaders and the reasons for the choice colour much of their political activities.

The following summarises both the differences that these new political leaders feel from the others and their perceptions of their tasks:

It must be made precise that we are a group of quite homogeneous persons, young, twenty-five to thirty years of age. Thus we are different from the rest of the party. In the past, in Potenza, they were not homogeneous. They were of all ages and all ideologies and relied on individual actions and leadership much more. They were more restrictive in the making of decisions.

Decisions in a modernising society such as Basilicata cannot be made solely at the top. The people in our region have suffered hundreds of years of misery and have a sense of fear, a lack of confidence in the political leaders. Many political leaders have exploited them in the past.

I believe that it is our task to gain the confidence of the people by this new type of political leadership, and to criticise and condemn that which they feel is wrong. Even

though the DC has received such a large vote the people still have no confidence in
it ... (Personal interview)

Notwithstanding the contrary policy goals of the majority faction,
they too are all members of the Colombo clientele and have very close
relations with him. They have adapted their policy desires to the
pattern of political competition which has been successful in their area
for generations. They have neither joined the class-based political
parties nor the 'trait' based political groups within the DC. Rather,
they have adapted the policy demands of a broad stratum to the
structures of political competition which they perceive to have the
most chances of succeeding. Even in assuming a policy focus, they
have maintained the competitive style of the political group based on
patron-client ties and have joined one such group linked to Colombo.

In sum, Colombo is the dominant political figure in Potenza. All
political activists, no matter how divided they may be from one
another, are his supporters. He has a veto power over all decisions
taken in the party and is consulted on all important issues. To succeed
in political competition within the DC in Potenza necessitates
receiving Colombo's support. The fate of the 'third generation'
indicates this best.

The presentation of the roots of the Colombo clientele in Potenza
parallels the support of other political leaders in the southern areas of
Italy (Zuckerman 1974). It is also found in other areas and serves to
describe the political bases of such leaders as Andreotti (Lazio),
Fanfani (Arezzo), Forlani (Pesaro-Ancona), Taviani (Genoa), Piccoli
(Trento) and Rumor (Vicenza). While none of the northern leaders is
as clearly dominant as is Colombo in his province, strong similarities
exist. One clear example is that of Rumor in Vicenza.

The party factions in Vicenza are not sub-groups of a single
dominant faction as in Potenza but have definite links to competing
national factions.[9] The majority group in the provincial organisation
of the party is composed of adherents to two national factions, the
Rumor-Piccoli (*Dorotei*) and *Fanfaniani* factions. The minority group is
composed of members of a united faction of the two national left
factions and a group with local Vicentine historical roots which has
consistently sought to draw together all the left groups into one
organisation.

Within the controlling *Dorotei* a split has developed over two issues:
the question of what is to be done after Rumor retires from political
life and the desire of some to initiate socially active policies in the
province. At the time of the initial fieldwork, the power of these two
groups was evenly divided, as evidenced by the need to hold five
meetings of the Provincial Committee in order to elect the new
Provincial Secretary. The *Fanfaniani* faction served as a group which
attracted those who for various reasons would not join the *Dorotei* or the
left faction. That there are members of other national party factions in

Vicenza distinguishes Rumor's dominance in his province from that of Colombo in Potenza. However, all members of the *Dorotei* were followers of Rumor and the *Dorotei* controlled the provincial party organisation. All informants agreed that the daily issues of the provincial party were rarely the concern of Rumor. His perceived desires were, however, a focal point for general party decision-making, e.g., even when local leaders had no actual knowledge of Rumor's position on an issue, they claimed that their position was a reflection of his. In addition, and as in Potenza, the resident national leader possesses the right to veto any and all decisions he sees fit and is consulted on all major decisions.

Illustrative of the ties of the Rumor group in Vicenza as well as political clienteles in general are the following comments about the structure of the faction by a Vicentine *Dorotei* leader:

It is impossible to say what will happen when a faction leader dies. Membership in the group is not a matter of having opinions and ideas. It is a matter of having faith in a certain person. ... The only ideas that the members must believe in are those that are publicised by the leaders.

Faction decisions are taken by the leaders. They reason among themselves and decide what is best to do in order to keep power. The leaders decide. The others must follow. (Personal interview)

Though the provincial party leadership possesses wide latitude concerning local policy and activities, they never act so as to embarrass Rumor. In 1963, a majority composed of the united left faction and the *Fanfaniani* succeeded in supplanting the *Dorotei* and gaining provincial power. Their tenure in office lasted six months. The discrepancy between the existence of a left-wing majority in Vicenza and Rumor's position as General Secretary of the party at the head of a *Dorotei*-based national coalition caused the national leadership to unseat the provincial majority.

While the presence of competing factions with national ties characterises the DC in Vicenza, the number of positions controlled by the majority *Dorotei* has been sufficient to give them absolute control of all party decisions. Compromises between the factions of the two groupings have been extremely rare and when they have occurred appear to be favours granted to the minority rather than negotiated agreements. One of the left-wing faction leaders described an example of one such compromise. He noted:

Compromises can happen, and a typical example would be on the selection of the make-up of the electoral lists of the party. At the last national elections [1968], we were given the option of naming either two men for the Chamber of Deputies or one Senator. We said that we would like to discuss this problem in order to have two Deputies and one Senator. They told us either one Senator or two Deputies but not both. We decided to have one Senator and chose the man already backed by CISL. (Personal interview)

The analysis of the provincial bases of Colombo and Rumor applies to the national and secondary leaders of the other non-left factions as well. Each of these leaders is supported by solid and large groups of local leaders linked to him by ties of mutual advantage and personal loyalty. The major distinction between the local bases of Rumor and Colombo is not the internal structure of the factions, but the presence or absence of competing factions. While all in Potenza are *Colombiani*, most of the party activists and the ruling faction in Vicenza are the followers of Rumor.

The *Base* and *Forze Nuove* factions, on the other hand, have been based to a much greater extent on policy and ideological affinities and the desire to represent broad segments of society within the Christian Democrat Party (Galli and Facchi 1962). As with other such groups, they are present where there are political activists in agreement with their issue concerns and who are members of the represented social strata. The *Forze Nuove* faction began as an outgrowth within the DC of the Catholic-linked trade union organisation CISL. As such, it has primarily depended (though somewhat less so over time) on the support of the union, its members, and those DC members sympathetic to the policy demands and issue concerns of labour. It is perceived as the most 'radical' of DC factions. The *Base* faction was formed to represent within the DC the left-wing Catholic tradition and, therefore, was initially strong only in the centres of that movement, Florence and Milan, and particularly weak in much of the south. In recent years, the *Base* has succeeded in spreading to other parts of Italy and is powerful in the area around Naples. Much of this growth has been linked to the success of *Base* leaders such as De Mita in Avellino. De Mita's political victories have been attributed by observers, however, to his formation of a powerful local base much in the manner of the leaders of the non-left factions.

DC party factions and cabinet coalitions

Cabinets in Italy have collapsed with relative frequency (Browne 1971). Between the founding of the Italian Republic in 1946 and 1972, there were twenty-seven cabinet formations and dissolutions, with an average tenure for each of less than one year. Even if one commences counting in 1948, i.e., with the election of the first legislature, the pattern is little different, for between then and 1972 the life-span of each cabinet was approximately one year.[10] In addition, Italian cabinets are not only short-lived, but are difficult to form and are apparently ineffective in making policy (Gurr and McClelland 1971).

Most analyses of Italian cabinet coalitions presume that the political parties are the only parliamentary groups engaged in this competition (Sartori 1966). A number of factors, however, question the utility of this approach. Hypotheses drawn from the literature of formal theories of coalition behaviour which focus on political parties have been of little value in analysing cabinet behaviour. Those derived from Riker's 'size principle' are confounded by the larger than 'minimal' size of Italian coalitions. Browne argues that random predictions of coalition partners prove more useful (Browne 1971, p.403). Even when the ideological distance between potential partners is added to the calculation, the suggested hypotheses fare no better. Predictions about the sub-set of parties composing Italian cabinets have been both larger than the actual and have included the empirically correct sub-sets no more frequently than thirteen of twenty-one times (De Swan 1971, p.427).

In addition, Italian cabinets rest on the support of large, pre-determined and solid party-based parliamentary majorities; the Christian Democrats have controlled the lion's share of the portfolios; personnel turn-over has been relatively low; and cabinets frequently dissolve without the rupture of the inter-party alliances. The specific problem of the Italian case is not that cabinets fall when the supporting inter-party agreements end but that most cabinet collapses have occurred without the demise . of the inter-party agreements.

Cabinet coalition persistence in Italy, therefore, is not to be equated with the maintenance of the alliances between political parties. A very crucial distinction must be drawn between mass political competition and its actors, the political parties, and cabinet competition and its actors, the party factions of the parliamentary coalition. The direct link between the two competitive arenas may be summarised in the following proposition: the persistence of the inter-party parliamentary alliances is a necessary but not a sufficient condition for the survival of a cabinet in office. When a parliamentary alliance dissolves, the cabinet will collapse, but cabinets have frequently dissolved without the break-up of the parliamentary coalition. Table 2 outlines the process by which cabinets form.

Table 2

Stage	Competitive units	Competitive arena	Outcome
I	political parties	parliament	coalition formula: 1. agreement over division of cabinet position
			2. agreement over cabinet policy
	party factions	each party	bargaining strategy and goals of each party
II	party factions	parties of the coali- tion formula	filling of the cabinet positions

A most striking feature of the first stage has been the recurrence of the same outcomes. The consistently similar results of national

elections and the distribution of parliamentary seats to the parties
have granted the pivotal role to the DC and have produced two
possible coalition formulas and three types of cabinets: the Christian
Democrats aligned with one or more of the 'centre' parties (the
Republicans (PRI), the Liberals, (PLI) and the Social Democrats
(PSDI)), the 'centre-left' in which the Socialists (PSI) replace the
PLI, and a single-party DC cabinet.[11] All cabinets are composed of or
are supported by the parties of the coalition formula.

During both stages, party factions are the crucial competitive units.
They compete within the parties to set party policy and strategy and,
thereby, control the formation of the coalition formula. Cabinet
positions are distributed by party and within each party by faction
according to the relative size and policy expertise of each. The factions
are the vehicle for entering into the cabinet, and it is within the second
stage that cabinets have proved so fragile. DC party factions are of
particular importance, because they determine which of the other
political parties (and their factions) will be invited to form a cabinet,
and because their actions have brought down almost all the cabinets
(Grosser 1964).

The persistence of faction coalitions, which exist within and across
the parties of the coalition formula, is the necessary and sufficient
condition for the survival of Italian cabinets. It is the dissolution of the
inter-faction agreements that ends the cabinets. Given the dominant
position of the DC, the behaviour of its factions is the prime
determinant of the pattern of competition for control of cabinet
coalitions in Italy.

As previously argued, five of the seven DC factions are political
clienteles and the remaining two have adopted many of the
competitive goals and strategies of the others. As political clienteles,
they act according to the following behavioural rules:

1. Seek to control cabinet positions. Strive to occupy more and
'better' positions than previously held and to defend those already
controlled.

2. Seek to further the career of the leader. Support him in his effort
to achieve 'better' positions.[12]

3. Seek to obtain goods of value from those who are not faction
members only when the persistence of the faction or the strength of
the Christian Democrat Party is at stake.

The conjunction of these behavioural rules with the factor that
cabinet positions are primarily distributed at the formation of
cabinets has resulted in the following consequences: 1. Party factions
will dissolve a given cabinet when there is a chance to better the
number and quality of positions controlled in the next formation. 2.
Party factions will delay the formation of a cabinet until they obtain
the best bargain possible. Winnings and losings in this political game
are judged by the quality and number of offices controlled, given the

rank-ordering of junior and senior cabinet posts and the relative size of each faction within its party.

The volatility of cabinet coalitions is further increased by their location in time and space. The interlocking nature of the several competitive arenas of party factions – within the political parties' external as well as parliamentary organisations – serves to link faction coalition dissolutions in one arena to the others. The resignation of the Rumor-led coalition cabinet in July 1969 was directly related to the split in the reunited Socialist Party and the reformation of the PSI and PSU (Social Democrats) as well as to internal DC divisions. The latter surfaced in the fall of that year and brought about the split in the *Dorotei* and the formation of a new governing coalition of factions within the DC. Given the shift within the Christian Democrats, the Rumor coalition cabinet which was formed in March 1970 lasted less than four months and was replaced by a Colombo-led cabinet.

Taken together, the behavioural rules by which the party factions compete serve to account for the frequent dissolutions of Italian cabinets and the difficulties exhibited in their formations. Taken individually they may be used to deal with related phenomena. That the party factions act so as to further the political career of the leader underscores the personal bases of the Fanfani-Moro feud. This decade-long conflict between two former Prime Ministers, Political Secretaries of the DC and candidates for the Presidency has not only divided their factions within the DC and constrained the formation of a new governing coalition within the party, but it has had powerful repercussions in cabinet competitions, and in the Presidential election of December 1971.[13]

The third behavioural rule introduces electoral and policy factors into cabinet competitions and thereby ties the latter to the arena of mass politics. The choice of coalition formula partners is linked to electoral appeal and policy affinities. The DC 'left' factions and the dominant factions of the PSI have long proclaimed a common desire to join in a two-party coalition which would eliminate the 'insufficiently progressive' PSDI and PRI from power. The dominant factions of the DC along with the latter two parties have succeeded in blocking the move and in maintaining the four-party coalition formula. When electoral and policy issues serve to split a faction coalition, they will lead to an inter-party alliance dissolution as well as to a cabinet collapse.

The link to electoral and policy factors introduces elements which reduce the fragility of cabinets. Not only do factions work together to assure Christian Democrat success at the polls but their hunger for governing posts is limited by fears of being perceived as unduly selfish. Cabinets are typically provided a period of grace free of sniping. In addition, policy expertise is requisite for the occupation of the most crucial cabinet positions – Prime Minister, Foreign Minister, Ministers of the Treasury, Finance, Interior and Labour.

Other factors serve to support cabinet stability. Each cabinet formation is perceived to be a contest intimately tied to others in the past and future and competitive tactics are modified accordingly (Zincone 1972). The use of proportional representation as the rule by which cabinet positions are distributed first to the parties and then to the factions emerges not as the determinant of the number or volatility of party and faction coalitions, but as a means of conflict limitation.[14] PR provides a standard of fair distribution by holding out to each group within the coalition a portion of the positions roughly equivalent to its membership size in the party and the parliament. Given the position orientation of the factions and the need for the parliamentary support of all the factions to sustain the cabinet, a distribution rule by which only the members of a 'winning coalition' occupied the governing posts would serve to make it impossible for cabinets to form. *Monocolore* DC cabinets, which are examples of winning coalitions controlling all governing positions, are temporary expedients. They hold office only as long as the inter-party faction coalition cannot form.

ACKNOWLEDGMENTS

Earlier versions of this essay received the searching comments of many, and I am especially grateful to Joseph LaPalombara, Eric Nordlinger, Norman Kogan and Harry Eckstein as well as to the seminar participants for their criticisms.

NOTES

1.　I am omitting the rather different conceptualisations and analyses of clientelist systems within bureaucracies examined by LaPalombara (1964) and Schmitter (1971).

2.　Similar hypotheses concerning the competitive goals and strategies of political clienteles are found in Key (1949), Zariski (1960) and Wolfinger (1974).

3.　The terms 'trait group' and 'trait association' are suggested by Lande to refer to associations of individuals based upon perceptions of shared social or economic positions. Examples cited by Lande are interest groups, ideological groups and classes. See Lande 1973.

4.　Regional comparisons of the survey responses found in the data of Almond and Verba (1963) may be found in Zuckerman (1972).

5.　The interviews and observations which are reported here took place during sets of fieldwork experiences in Italy. The first was a year long stay in 1968-69 and the second occurred during the summer of 1972.

6.　The Italian form of proportional representation provides for the selection of 'preferred' candidates from the party list. This, in turn, serves as the primary means of indicating personal political power.

7.　The analysis omits the bases of factions that are tied primarily to specific national bureaucratic sources such as RAI-TV, the radio and television network, whose resources are crucial to *Fanfaniani*.

8.　While the following analysis of provincial level relations within the DC refers specifically to the period 1968-70, it is generally descriptive of the years since then as well.

9.   There were no substantial changes in provincial Vicentine politics and the links between the groups and Rumor between the two periods of fieldwork. I would like to thank David Pusateri for his help during the summer of 1972 in the analysis of Vicenza.

10.   The source for the analysis of cabinet coalition behaviour in Italy is *Italy: Documents and Notes* X, July-October, 1971, Presidency of the Council of Ministers, pp.259-323.

11.   This applies to all cases when the coalition formula has changed i.e., before and immediately after the elections of 1963 and 1972.

12.   When a faction is composed of the alliance of more than one political clientele, each branch will follow its own leader. This is what happened to the *Dorotei*.

13.   See Wollemborg, *Italia al Ralentore* (1966), pp. 483-5. That the party divisions are so closely tied to personal disputes implies equally that professions of unity can be effected by agreement of the leaders as well.

14.   A debate on the importance and role of proportional representation for the existence and behaviour of the party was initiated by Sartori (1971), and responded to by Passigli (1972) and Zincone (1972). The argument here is another response to Sartori and generally supportive of Passigli.

REFERENCES

Allum, P.A. (1973) *Politics and Society in Post-War Naples*. London.

Almond, G. and S. Verba (1963) *The Civic Culture*. Princeton.

Barnes, S. and G. Sani (1974) 'Mediterranean political culture and Italian politics: An interpretation', *British Journal of Political Science*.

Boissevain, J. (1966) 'Patronage in Sicily', *Man*, 1, 18-33.

Browne, E. (1971) 'Testing theories of coalition formation in the European context', *Comparative Political Studies* 3, 393-413.

Capecchi, V. et al. (1968) *Il comportamento elettorale in Italia*. Bologna.

De Swan, (1971) 'An empirical model of coalition formation as an N-person game of policy distance minimization', in S. Groennings, E.W. Kelley and M. Leiserson (eds), *The Study of Coalition Behaviour*. New York.

Galli, G. and P. Facchi (1962) *La Sinistra Democristiana*. Milan.

Graziano, L. (1973) 'Patron-client relationships in Southern Italy', *European Journal of Political Research* 1, 3-34.

Grosser, A. (1964) 'The evolution of European parliaments', *Daedalus* 93, 153-78.

Gurr, T. and M. McClelland (1971) *Political Performance: A Twelve Nation Study*. Beverly Hills.

Heath, D. (1973) 'New patrons for old: Changing patron-client relations in the Bolivian Yunqas', *Ethnology* XII, 75-98.

Key, V.O. (1949) *Southern Politics*. New York.

Lande, C. (1973) 'Networks and groups in Southeast Asia: Some observations on the group theory of politics', *American Political Science Review* LXVII.

LaPalombara, J. (1964) *Interest Groups in Italian Politics*. Princeton.

Lemarchand, R. (1972) 'Political clientelism and ethnicity in Africa', *American Political Science Review* LXVI, 68-90.

Lemarchand, R. and K. Legg (1972) 'Political clientelism and development', *Comparative Politics* 4, 149-78.

Linz, J. (1967) 'The party systems of Spain: Past and future', in S. Lipset and S. Rockan (eds), *Party Systems and Voter Alignments*, New York, 197-282.

Nobecourt, J. (1971) *Italia al Vivo*. Milan.

Passigli, S. (1972) 'Proporzionalismo, frazionismo e crisi dei partiti: Quid prior?', *Rivista Italiana di Scienza Politica* 2 (April), 139-59.

Powell, J.D. (1970) 'Peasant society and clientelist politics', *American Political Science Review* LXVI, 411-26.

Sartori, G. (1966) 'European political parties: Case of polarized pluralism', in J. LaPalombara and M. Weiner (eds), *Political Parties and Political Development*, Princeton, 136-76.

Sartori, G. (1971) 'Proporzionalismo, frazionismo e crisi dei partiti', *Rivista Italiana di Scienza Politica* 1, 629-55.

Schmitter, P. (1971) *Interest Conflict and Political Change in Brazil*. Stanford.

Scott, J.C. (1969) 'Corruption, machine politics and political change in Southeast Asia', *American Political Science Review* LXVI, 91-113.

Stirling, P. (1968) 'Impartiality and personal morality (Italy)', in J.C. Peristiany (ed.), *Contributions to Mediterranean Sociology*. The Hague.

Tarrow, S. (1967) *Peasant Communism in Southern Italy*. New Haven.

Weingrod, A. (1968) 'Patrons, patronage and parties', *Comparative Studies in Society and History* 10, 377-400.

Wolfinger, R. (1974) *The Politics of Progress*. Englewood Cliffs.

Wollemborg, L. (1966) *Italia al Ralentore*. Bologna.

Zariski, R. (1960) 'Party factions and comparative politics: Some preliminary observations', *Mid-West Journal of Political Science*, February, 27-51.

Zariski, R. (1965) 'Intra-party conflict in a dominant party: The experiences of Italian Christian Democracy', *Journal of Politics* XXVII, 3-34.

Zincone, G. (1972) 'Acesso autonomo alle resorse: Le determinanti del frazionismo', *Rivista Italiana di Scienza Politica* 2 (April), 139-59.

Zuckerman, A. (1972) 'Social structure and political competition: The Italian case', *World Politics* XXIV.

Zuckerman, A. (1974) *On the Institutionalization of Political Clienteles: Party Factions and Cabinet Coalitions in Italy*. Beverly Hills.

Jeremy Boissevain

When the saints go marching out: Reflections on the decline of patronage in Malta

Introduction

The growing literature on patronage deals chiefly with its utilitarian aspect. It is conceived of as an asymmetrical, quasi-moral relation between a person (*the patron*) who directly provides protection and assistance (*patronage*), and/or who influences persons who can provide these services (*brokerage*), to persons (*clients*) who depend on him for such assistance. Clients, in turn, provide loyalty and support when called on to do so. A great deal is now known about varieties of patronage, its inner mechanics, its consequences and the way it is modified.

One of the perennial problems remains the question of why patronage emerged in some countries as part of the social, cultural and moral climate. Its emergence is usually related to the partial penetration of the nation-state. Silverman (1965, p.188) noted perceptively that ' ... the mediator represents a general form of community/nation relationship characteristic of an early phase of development of nation states, a form which regularly gives way as the process of interpenetration of the total society advances.' (Cf. Bax 1973, who contests the notion that patronage withers as the state expands.) Others have seen it as an institution linking cultures (Wolf 1956; Bailey 1969).

The world of ideas and concepts in which patronage and brokerage function has all but been ignored. Relatively few anthropologists (Kenny 1960; Campbell 1964; Boissevain 1966; Wolf 1969; and Christian 1972) have noted that there is a particularly interesting relation between religion and patronage. Catholicism in particular, with its range of benevolent patron saints intermediate between God and favour-seeking, dependent humans, provides an ideological world view which closely parallels a conception of society articulated by political and economic patron-client relations. These anthropologists have argued that religious and political patronage reinforce each other.[1] Each provides a model of and a model for the other. The relationship between spiritual and temporal patronage is clearly characterised by the south European custom of referring to both types of patrons as saints. The proverb 'You cannot get to heaven without the help of saints', thus has religious and political significance. Other observers, while noting the congruence of action and values in spiritual and earthly patronage, have criticised the attempts made to relate them to each other (cf. Bax 1973, p.67, and the contributions of Gilsenan and Silverman to this volume). The following discussion seeks to further our understanding of the interplay of religious and secular patronage, of value and action, by exploring social developments, interpersonal relations and political and religious dependency in Malta.

Developments in Malta

The Maltese archipelago is composed of three islands: Malta, Gozo, and Comino. They cover a land area of 120 square miles, and have a population of just over 318,000 people. Malta's history has been greatly influenced by its small size and strategic location in the centre of the Mediterranean. For centuries it was run as an island fortress, first by the Knights of St. John (1532-1798), then by the French (1798-1800), and finally by the British, who gave the country its independence in 1964.

Malta's experience of self-rule was limited by the obvious difficulty of giving full self-government to a fortress. For centuries the islands were ruled by a highly centralised civil/military administration centred in Valletta, Malta's capital. When necessary, representatives were stationed in the villages and areas remote from Valletta to see that the policies of the central government were carried out. Following the First World War a system of modified self-government was introduced. Representatives were elected to the national parliament from multi-member constituencies. This provided institutionalised communication between the grass-roots electorate and the central government. This highly centralised form of government continued following independence. The Maltese parliament now consists of fifty representatives elected from ten districts. The central government employs some 25,000 persons, who, with the exception of police and teachers, all work in the capital.

The official religion in Malta is Roman Catholicism. All but a handful of Maltese are Catholic, and most practice their religion fervently. The centralised hierarchical organisation of the church provides much of the territorial organisation of the islands. Each village forms a parish and some of the larger towns are divided into two parishes. The parishes of Gozo and the island of Comino form one diocese with its own bishop, who falls under the jurisdiction of the metropolitan archbishop of Malta. Until the advent of self-government parish priests provided a traditional but informal channel of communication between village/parish and the central government.

In addition to the increasing autonomy of the central government from outside control following independence, five interlinked trends can be discerned which are relevant for a discussion of developments in patronage: (1) increasing education; (2) industrialisation; (3) tourism; (4) increasing communication and mobility; (5) rising standard of living. These trends have been discernible for many years. Their pace seems to be constantly accelerating, and was boosted by the two World Wars, the sporadic periods of self-government and, finally, by independence.

The push towards public education began just before the turn of the century, at about the same time that the first conflict-ridden experiments in limited self-government took place. Prior to that education had been fairly exclusively controlled by the powerful Church. The development of schools increased steadily, though attendance was partial and to a large extent voluntary. Compulsory education until the age of fourteen was introduced on a part-time basis following the return of self-government after the Second World War. During the next twenty years the school-leaving age was gradually increased to sixteen and school facilities greatly expanded.

During the same period the economy also evolved. The island's economy for centuries was based on furnishing goods and services to the military and naval garrisons of its rulers. In the early days of the Knights of St. John the Maltese provided food and menial services, including physically defending the island against various aggressors. Members of the professional classes were also employed in the central administration. Under the British increasing numbers of Maltese were employed in the garrison, the naval dockyard, ·and the civil service. The numbers of professionals and businessmen expanded as entrepôt commerce flourished following the opening of the Suez Canal. It was a period of considerable economic and social ferment.

The balance of power in the Mediterranean gradually passed from British hands. By the late 1950s this was reflected in the drastic decline of the defence establishment in Malta. Teams of advisors finally began to make serious attempts to find alternative economic possibilities. Foremost among these were plans to convert the giant, over-staffed, naval dockyard to a viable commercial enterprise. Attempts were also made to attract manufacturing industry. In the past the British had systematically kept such industry out of the islands to safeguard the dockyard and military monopoly of employment of local skilled labour. Projects were also undertaken in the early 1960s to encourage tourism.

In spite of these efforts, the economy was stagnant when Malta became independent in 1964. Discouraged by the grim economic prospects, and fearful of independence, more than 9,000 emigrated that year. (The annual average for the previous five years had been around 4,000.)

Since independence Malta's economy has proved to be remarkably robust. Though small, the country has become a diplomatic power to be reckoned with and has been able to increase the rent of its defence facilities from Britain and NATO from £M4 million annually to over £M14 million annually (£M1 = £1.25 Sterling). It has also been able to garner various forms of aid from NATO countries as well as mainland China, which at the moment is building a drydock to accommodate 300,000 ton vessels. The country has also displayed phenomenal economic growth. From 1965 to 1969 there was an economic boom sparked off by new industries and mass tourism. Since 1970 boom conditions have been replaced by a slower but steady growth. Many foreign firms, attracted by various incentives, established themselves in Malta, boosting domestic exports from just over £M4 million to nearly £M32 million per annum in just over ten years. Timely measures taken by the newly independent government enabled the islands to capture an important portion of the wave of tourists which in the 1960s began cascading into the sunny Mediterranean from grey industrial centres in northern Europe. Following currency restrictions imposed in 1965, thousands of British discovered in Malta a Sterling island in the sun. Tourism grew from 23,000 arrivals in 1961 to over 333,000 arrivals by 1975. The expansion of industry and tourism raised the gross domestic product from £M44 million in 1964 to more than £M101 million by 1972.

Increasing education, expanding employment, especially for women, and rising wage rates brought about a considerable rise in prosperity. Between 1964 and 1974 virtually every Maltese household bought a modern gas cooker, a television set and a washing machine. People began to eat more meat. They also began to spend more on leisure activities.

During the past twenty years there has been a veritable explosion in the means of communication in Malta. Not only have contacts with the outside world increased; the means to communicate within the country have improved greatly. Between 1962 and 1972 television became firmly established. There is now one set for every six persons. During the same period the number of telephones increased from 11,000 to 26,000, or from one for every thirty persons to one for every twelve. The growth of television has been particularly significant. It has brought Malta into direct contact with Italy, for the two Italian television channels are received clearly. The amount of local news broadcast has also increased remarkably. In 1954 only an hour and a half of news was broadcast daily. By 1974 news broadcasts from various sources had increased to ten and a half hours a day. A similar growth of the local press took place. In 1954 there were eight daily and weekly newspapers, producing 172 pages a week. By 1974 the number of publications had doubled, and were printing no less than 700 pages a week. The proportion printed in Maltese increased from 40% to 58%. Malta is thus better informed about what goes on abroad and also about what goes on within the country. During the past decade or so public transport increased markedly, as did private transport. Between 1964 and 1972 car ownership increased from 20,000 to 45,000, or from one car for every eighteen persons to one for every seven.

Changing social relations

Interpersonal relations have been affected by the developments touched on above. Relations are becoming less hierarchical and also less many-stranded. These changes can be seen in the family, in the community and in the relations between people in such organisations as the church, unions, and political parties.

Influences are at work which slowly, almost imperceptibly, are reducing differences in relative power in families which have been characterised by strong parental, and especially paternal authority. To begin with, children are now generally better educated than their parents. They know more. Their horizons are wider. They can read documents and sign legal forms for their illiterate parents. This decreases the dependency of parents on outsiders to perform these tasks, but it increases their dependency upon their own children. Increasingly, also, girls are finding jobs, and for much of the day are away from the village and the authority of their mothers. In the early 1960s it was usual for unmarried village girls to remain at home. Now, almost all those who have left school work outside their place of residence, mostly in hotels and, increasingly, in the expanding light manufacturing industries. The money they earn makes them more independent from their parents for clothing, amusements, and even marriage partners. In the past many marriage plans foundered because parents refused to provide their daughter a dowry or layout if they did not approve of her choice. Today a girl pays for these herself. She also contributes handsomely to the wedding reception given by her parents. Sons, who are better educated and have more prestigeful, better-paying jobs than their fathers, are also increasingly less inclined to submit to the traditional patriarchal authority. Moreover, married children are moving out of the neighbourhood of parents as intervillage marriages increase and as distant housing becomes available. These factors are reducing the traditional hierarchical relations in Maltese families.

These developments are also creating new group identifications and activities, thus affecting traditional community interaction patterns. Bonds of loyalty in neighbourhood, parish and club associations are declining in importance. This is partly the result of increased mobility. Improved transportation, work outside parish limits, and housing in distant estates are pulling people out of village and neighbourhood of birth. New reference groups are also being formed. Young people from all over the island congregate between seven and nine in the evening in the main street of Valletta (or the seaside promenade of Sliema, a nearby smart suburb). There they see their friends from all over the island, exchange news, fashions, and companionship. Political party loyalty, especially following the clash in the 1960s between the Malta Labour Party and the church, has also drawn people from different neighbourhoods and parishes together in political interest groups. New reference groups draw people out of traditional groups.

A growing concept of a national Maltese community/nation has followed independence. Before 1964 the primary point of identification beyond the family was the faction, parish, or party. Now, slowly, a national 'we' feeling is also emerging. Moreover, as increasingly more outsiders come to live in the villages, either because they find housing or they marry there, the village becomes less homogeneous. People have less to do with each other. There has been a noticeable decline in the scale and participation in the annual festas celebrating saints important to the villages. Fewer young men are prepared to sacrifice hours of dangerous work to prepare fireworks. They now prefer to spend their free time with (girl) friends at the beach or the cinema. Where just ten years ago young men competed for the honour of carrying the parish saint in its annual procession, today the parish priest is often forced to hire outsiders to do this.

These changes affect the quality of interpersonal relations. In a way, relations between villagers have become less multiplex, more diffuse. Mutual interdependency which existed when the village was more homogeneous, more tightly knit and more closed to outsiders, has decreased. Prestige and honour are no longer attributes which derive exclusively from the judgment of fellow villagers. Most people now also play roles on a much wider stage. They are therefore less dependent upon their neighbours.

There has also been a shift in power relations. Perhaps most notable has been the decrease in the power of the church. At the village level, dependency upon the parish priest has been greatly reduced for a number of reasons. Increasing education has freed people from the need to use their local priest, often the only literate person they knew well, to help them with their paper work. The expansion of government social services has freed poorer parishioners from dependency on church charity controlled by the parish priest. As general well-being increased, people became less dependent upon the parish priest to obtain supernatural help. The bitter conflict between the church and the Malta Labour Party during the late 1950s and the 1960s alienated many from the church forever, thus further reducing the numbers of those tied to the parish priest. Finally, competing politicians, eager to perform services in exchange for votes, have systematically sought to suppress the traditional brokerage activities of parish priests with the central government on behalf of their constituents. These are a few of the many ways that dependency on the church is being gradually eroded at the grass-roots level, thus reducing power differences between priest and parishioner.

Relations in other spheres of social activity are also becoming less asymmetrical. This is partly a result of bureaucratisation and collectivisation. There has been a slow expansion of the degree to which the central government impinges upon people's lives. Government is increasingly asked to provide more education, more housing, more industry, more social services, more traffic control, etc. Government departments thus expand and become more complex. Decision-making in government and private business is becoming more collectivised: decisions are increasingly made by boards instead of single individuals. This reflects the growing ideology of discussion and equality.

Corresponding to the collectivisation of decision-making at higher levels, collectivities at lower levels increasingly represent the interests of their members. In the past twenty years membership in political parties and, especially, trade unions has greatly expanded. Church lay associations have also grown. Associations of farmers, employers, women and students, defend the interests of their members. The power of persons in authority is slowly being fragmented, distributed over committees and boards, which increasingly deal with collectivities instead of individuals.

Increasing prosperity has also been significant in reducing dependency of people upon each other. Education has broadened their horizons and with it their independence, as has the possession of a car, television, and work outside the village, especially for girls. Relative prosperity has increased the margin of safety with which people face the future, thus reducing their vulnerability, and consequently their need to maintain a protective network of patrons and brokers. One retired village dockyard worker, the son of a peasant, put it to me this way.

You cannot imagine the misery, the abject dependence that my father faced when he was my age. Today I have savings, a pension and can get government medical services if I am sick. He had none of these. He had to keep working hard until the end. He also remained servile to the church and to the local big men. I have independence he never knew, never even thought of.

The ability of single persons – whether father, employer, priest, doctor, lawyer, government minister, or department head – to influence the action of others is being affected. Extreme concentration of power potentials in the hands of persons is being reduced, as are relations of dependency which bound people to them.

Transformation of patronage relations

The transformations which have been touched on have affected the interdependency of people. As power is not monopolised by single individuals to the extent it once was, people are no longer as dependent. Old informants described to me how just forty years ago certain persons, including their parish priests, wielded great power in their villages. They disposed of local housing, credit facilities, and labour. They also had access to important government decision-makers who could issue licences, local scholarships and provide employment. They were jealous of their power. They sometimes ruthlessly protected their interests. Such concentration of direct power resources in the hands of magnates has all but disappeared.

But if the power of patrons is declining, the demand for specialised brokers is increasing. The growing demand for influential mediators is not only due to the increasing complexity of government and the collectivisation of decision-making. It is also a consequence of the availability of new prizes, such as overseas scholarships, licences and subsidies for tourist and industrial developments. These prizes are allocated by scholarship committees, licensing authorities, development boards. These often include foreign experts and other unknown people. Most boards attempt valiantly to make decisions according to universalistic criteria. It is difficult, if not impossible, for people, alone, to influence the decision of such collectivities. This is a task for specialised intermediaries who, ideally, have the backing of organisations.

People are thus finding it increasingly efficient to have their interests represented by organisational specialists. An employee asks his union shop steward to argue his pay claim with his employer. A person seeking a scholarship, building permit, government flat or a transfer asks his local member of parliament to help him. A parish priest who has a dispute with his bishop mobilises the secretary of the college of archpriests and parish priests to help argue his case. The Malta Labour Party in particular has sought to strengthen these organisational relations. It has consciously channelled the mass of resources to which it has access as government party through its formal party apparatus. Both clients and brokers have become part of formal organisations, and their relationship is changing. It is a person's *right* to be represented by his union secretary, his professional association manager, or his local member of parliament. He no longer has to grovel, display his dependency, or try to make the relation a moral one to obtain this help. It will be evident that the bureaucratisation of patron/client or broker/client relations is reducing the sense of personal dependency and the moral content which once characterised such relations.

People are now also beginning to sneer at self-confessed clients. Once clients were called the *parrokjan*, parishioners, dependents, of a saint or patron (*il-qaddis*). Today the word *bazuzlu* (teacher's pet, toady) is increasingly used to indicate the abject dependency of personal (political) clients. It is a term of disapproval, of humiliation, of condemnation. The general shift from the use of *parrokjan* to *bazuzlu* to designate personal clients reflects the shift in the content of patronage relations. As opposed to organisational dependency, relations of personal dependency are increasingly being looked down upon. This ethical condemnation of the patron/broker-client tie is also related to another development. The word corruption is on everyone's lips. Patronage relations which once were accepted as normal are now increasingly regarded as corrupt. This is possibly also a reflection of the growing awareness of Maltese that certain private interests must be sacrificed for the new Maltese state. Just ten years ago Malta was a colony. Military and government resources were controlled by Britain. They were fair game. They could be and were plundered on a grand scale without incurring opprobrium. In fact, hoodwinking the British gave prestige. For example, dockyard workers still recount with admiration and awe how a 14 ton ship's screw was pilfered one night from the 'Yard'. With the increasing penetration of a national ideology, a growing separation is taking place between public and private domains. Increasingly the client is condemned as a *bazuzlu* and the patron/broker who personally channels government resources to him is viewed as corrupt.

Three types of dependency relations

It would seem that in the past hundred years relations of dependency in Malta have assumed three dominant forms. These may be termed patronage, patron/brokerage, and organisational brokerage. The first is the classical personal patron/client relation. This is still found occasionally between a wealthy landowner and the family of his farmer tenant or old family retainer. This is a long-term, personal, moral relation. The landowner provides land, advice on investments and influence with important people for his tenant. The latter in turn provides personal loyalty, esteem and small services above and beyond the formal contractual relationship. This relationship was characteristic for people who were bound to the village as agriculturists, as they were more than forty years ago. Farmers and small artisans had very little to do with the remote central government, located far away and scarcely impinging upon their lives.

The second type of dependency relation is that between (industrial) labourer and local big man, often the notary, parish priest or doctor: the patron/broker. It is characteristic of a period in which big government begins to impinge more noticeably upon the lives of villagers. People are concerned with placing their children in school, finding work for them, obtaining building permits. The local patron can provide ever fewer important services personally. But he can use his influence with people he knows well in the increasingly complex government who, in turn, dispense those prizes. There is still a personal relation with some moral overtones between the client and his patron/broker. But the relationship is no longer exclusive. The client has several specialised patrons, and is always on the look-out for new persons who can intervene on his behalf. In return he is prepared to bargain his vote and do other small services. But because the relation is unstable and increasingly pragmatic and transactional, it has little moral content.

The third type of dependency relation is that between a person and his member of parliament, the secretary of his local party club, his shop-steward, or his union secretary. Both organisational broker and client are members of the same group. They thus share a certain group loyalty. Both expect support from each other as members of the same group. Their relationships have become formalised, in the sense that they may be expressed as rights and duties. The party or union secretary represents the interests of his client/constituent/fellow member to civil-service decision makers. He does this not so much as a personal friend but as a representative. If he does not succeed he can mobilise further pressure on the civil servant through political party or union apparatus. He need not maintain relations with such civil servants to the same extent as the patron/broker. It will be obvious, however, that in a country as small as Malta the personal element in social relations will continue to remain strong. Organisational brokerage is becoming the most prominent type of relation with authorities. It is a more egalitarian relation, a relation of incorporation in the same formal group.

The three types of dependency relations are shown in Figure 1.

TRANSFORMATION OF DOMINANT POLITICAL DEPENDENCY RELATIONS IN MALTA

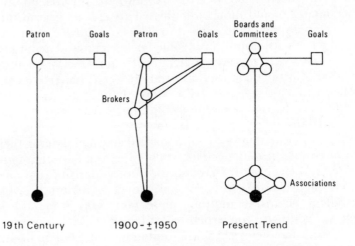

Religious changes

As political saints are slowly eliminated, so too are religious saints. Following the second Vatican Council in the early 1960s there has been a concerted effort to bring about a more Christocentric religious orientation. Increasing stress has been placed by the Church upon the direct link between man and God. In the various parts of the liturgy where scriptures are read, priests are urged to choose passages which lay emphasis on salvation and on the direct link with God. There has also been a conscious, and many Maltese parishioners would say ruthless, effort to reduce the importance of saints. Many have been eliminated on the grounds that they never existed. Others have been downgraded. The cult of Mary is being played down drastically. Linked with this there has been an increasing stress on community participation. People are being urged to approach God directly with their fellow men, as part of a community of equals. The intermediary is being eliminated.

This religious policy was designed to bring the Church in line with developments taking place in the world (cf. Documents 1966: 122). In Malta one of the first steps was to translate much of the liturgy into Maltese. Parishioners now understand the prayers of their priest. He is regarded as one of the community, a specialist who leads them. People now pray together *as a community*. Formerly people contacted God individually. They did this as entrepreneurs in highly personal ways: through their own private intermediaries, their personal patron saints and the Virgin Mary. They planned their own programme of worship and sacrifices. Many in Maltese churches would conduct their own devotions during the mass, reciting the Rosary out loud in a corner. Today people pray together. The importance of God is directly emphasised.

The changes in the rite of baptism clearly indicate the thrust of these reforms. Before the new liturgy was introduced in Malta three years ago, influential persons who could provide prestige and assistance were often chosen as godparents. This meant they often came from outside the parish. The baptism was performed privately by the parish priest at the baptismal font behind the main altar. A small group of intimates attended the ceremony, and the baby was held by its godmother, while its own mother remained at home. Today godparents are supposed to be chosen from the members of the parish community (though this is not yet taking place everywhere). The infant is now held by its mother. The godparents are no longer responsible only to God for the child's moral education. As representatives of the community, they are responsible to the community. More significantly, the baptismal ceremony now takes place collectively. In most parishes it is performed once a month. All babies born that month are baptised together during a public ceremony. Rich and poor stand together. Parish priests have noted that in general this new ceremony has been very successful, although their richer parishioners object to its levelling influence. They still wish to have private ceremonies to which their exclusive friends may be invited. They don't wish to stand together with the poor.

The Church has also consciously tried to bridge the gap between priest and parishioner. For example, the priest now meets a couple to be married at the door of the church and escorts them to the altar. Formerly he waited for them at the altar. This new action symbolises the reduction in the distance between them. They are members of the same community.

These are some of the ways in which the church is consciously stressing its new Christocentric policy. It does this by promoting the sense of equality among the members of a worshipping community, and by downgrading the intermediaries. Communication with God today is less private, less entrepreneurial, more communal. Shifts in the teaching of the church parallel in a striking way the changes taking place in society. Under pressure from bishops from all over the world, the church has consciously tried to modernise itself.

Three types of religious dependency

The conceptualisation of religious dependency relations can also be seen to have assumed three forms. The first is that of the early church, where there was a fairly direct relation between man and God. Salvation was mediated through the intervention of Jesus Christ, who was part of the Trinity. The second form emerged in the Middle Ages and persisted until recently. Intermediaries became progressively more important. The reformed liturgical calendar following the sixteenth-century Council of Trent listed 65 feasts of saints; by 1960 these had increased to 338 (Zarb 1972: 51). A man's path to salvation still led through God, but was mediated by the saints, and, increasingly, the Virgin Mary.[2] She was formally set apart from, and placed well above, all other saints. This special status was confirmed by the doctrine of her immaculate conception in 1854. Finally, the third form reflects the new developments following the Second Vatican Council. Saints and other divine intermediaries have been eliminated or downgraded. The traditional mortal intermediary, the parish priest, has been incorporated into the same community as his parishioners. Salvation is increasingly dependent more upon collective rather than on individual action. That is, while salvation still depends upon the individual's state of grace with the efficacious assistance of the sacrament, attainment of this state is increasingly contingent upon people's collective representations as a congregation. In this the parish priest acts as a first among equals. His monopolistic power to control the access of individuals to the sacraments has been weakened (though certainly not eliminated) by the growing collectivisation of worship. Thus the attainment of a state of grace is less and less the result of dyadic transactions between supplicant and saintly or clercial broker. Increasingly it is the product of collective representations, of relations of incorporation. I suggest this reflects the lengthening interdependency chains of people in the secular world, their collectivisation and the reduction of power differentials between them.

This transformation of religious dependency relations is schematically portrayed in Figure 2. The resemblance to the transformation of political and economic dependency relations is striking.

TRANSFORMATION OF RELIGIOUS DEPENDENCY RELATIONS

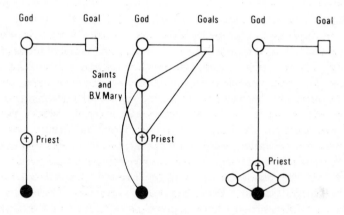

Early Church   Post Mediaeval Church   Post Vatican II Church

Conclusion

In an earlier discussion I drew attention to the similarity between political patronage and the cult of saints and their influence on each other (1966: 30-1). At the time I was unable to establish the nature of the relationship. It now seems quite clear to me that there is a causal relationship between belief and action. The theological conceptualisation of dependency is being changed by the Catholic Church to keep it congruent with economic and political behaviour. In the deliberations of Vatican II this nexus is explicitly formulated. The Christocentric thrust of the new liturgy, the downgrading of the saints and the greater sharing of power within the church are responses to the increasing range of communication and the reduction of power differentials in the wider society. While these secular trends are also present in Malta, they were not sufficiently evolved at the time of Vatican II in the early 1960s to have influenced the changes it advocated. These were set in motion by representatives from societies in which such trends were already well established.

Yet once introduced to Malta, liturgical changes have begun to influence behaviour. Although, as one wise monsignor remarked, 'The theological principles at the basis of the "New Liturgy" have not yet seeped through down to the rank and file. One must wait some time, perhaps years, before this would come about.' In this respect, the teaching of the church is ahead of developments in Malta. It is consequently an agent of change. For example, though the rich now stand alongside their poorer fellow parishioners during the new baptismal service, they don't always enjoy doing so. Some still ask for and receive dispensation to hold the traditional, private ceremonies for guests from their class. Yet most people follow the new teaching.[3] Religion is thus both a model of and a model for social action.

The impetus to change belief systems comes from forces operating at the level at which people interact in family, work place and political arena. These forces eventually modify norms, values and cognitive maps. The relation between social and religious change is evident in the congruence between mortal and immortal patrons and brokers. Both types seem to have thrived in periods when power was concentrated in the hands of a few, when economic and political uncertainty prevailed, when widespread poverty induced dependency. Such conditions existed in the fourteenth and nineteenth centuries following the Black Death and the French Revolution. Conditions have changed in most West European countries. There is a decrease in power differentials, there is political stability and, until the recent (oil) crisis, there was relative prosperity. In Malta, as elsewhere in Europe, the saints are marching out. Are they leaving for good? Only the future will tell. Perhaps, one day, should conditions recur which in the past favoured them, saints will again be called upon to help men reach paradise. Until then, it seems, increasingly impersonal collective brokers will continue to gain influence.

ACKNOWLEDGMENTS

Discussants at a Malta Rotary Club dinner, a Netherlands European Anthropology Association meeting and a seminar at the Department of Social Anthropology of the University of Stockholm constructively criticised earlier versions of this paper, as did participants at the 1974 Rome conference on patronage. Monsignor Professor Carmel Sant, Monsignor Professor Joseph Lupi and Herman Diederiks provided advice on matters religious and historical. The research in 1973 and 1974 upon which the discussion is based was financed by the University of Amsterdam. The Department of Economics of the Royal University of Malta provided important research facilities.

NOTES

1.   While Foster (1963) draws attention to spiritual patronage, he views it merely as a pragmatic extension of earthly relations to include supernatural protectors. He does

not explicitly conclude that the two systems of patronage reinforce each other.

2. Wolf (1969, p.296) citing Christian (1966) noted that the growth of the cult of the Virgin Mary is associated with the representation of private and associational interests as against the growing power of the state. At the 1974 Rome conference Professor John Hale contested this. He argued that the increase of the importance of saints, and particularly of the Virgin Mary, was primarily related to urbanisation and to the plague. Urban growth provided new loci for cults. In the aftermath of the thirteenth-century Black Death, God the Father became a more and more terrifying creature and His Son became associated with judgment and punishment. Saints increasingly provided a means of mediating access to the domain controlled by these stern figures.

But we should also note that the increase in the severity and remoteness of God also paralleled the erosion of local power bases in favour of a more centralised monarchy. The monarch played the rising urban elite off against the regional nobles. This consolidation of powers at the national level gained momentum following the plague. As power was increasingly concentrated at the royal court, a demand developed for personal intermediaries who could represent the interests at court of those remote from it. State power continued to develop. The cult of saints and particularly of the Virgin Mary reached its peak in the nineteenth century, the era of the Immaculate Conception and of Lourdes. Again we must note the relation to political developments, for the last century was characterised by an intensive drive to consolidate the power of the secular state at the national level, in imitation of the Napoleonic state. Thus Wolf, Christian and Hale seem to complement each other rather than disagree.

3. It is probable that the church's great authority in Malta has prevented organised resistence to major Vatican II reforms such as have developed, for example, in the Netherlands. In some places there democratisation of decision-making at the diocesan level has been slowed down, and Latin Masses have been reintroduced. On the other hand, the introduction of the new liturgy to Malta has not always been painless. Some parishioners were highly indignant that their patrons had disappeared from the new calendar. In Gozo the important parish of St. George has not celebrated its annual feast since 1968 out of pique because the bishop, anxious to solemnise the Easter worship in accordance with the new liturgy, prohibited the parish's traditional rowdy Good Friday procession. This boycott has been accompanied by much abuse of the bishop.

REFERENCES

Bailey, F.G. (1969) *Stratagems and Spoils: A social anthropology of politics.* Oxford.

Bax, M. (1973) 'Harpstrings and confessions: An anthropological study of politics in rural Ireland'. PhD Thesis, Faculty of Social Sciences, University of Amsterdam.

Boissevain, J. (1966) 'Patronage in Sicily', *Man* N.S. 1, 18-33.

Campbell, J.K. (1964) *Honour, Family and Patronage: A study of institutions and moral values in a Greek mountain community.* Oxford.

Christian, W.A. Jr. (1966) 'The cult of Mary in Europe: explorations'. MS (Paper written for Anthropology 656: Peasant Society and Culture, University of Michigan.)

Christian, W.A. Jr. (1972) *Person and God in a Spanish Valley.* New York and London.

The Documents of Vatican II, 1966. New Delhi.

Foster, G.M. (1963) 'The dyadic contract in Tzintzuntzan, II; patron-client relationships', *American Anthropologist* 65, 1280-94.

Kenny, M. (1960) 'Patterns of patronage in Spain', *Anthropological Quarterly* 33, 14-23.

Silverman, S.F. (1965) 'Patronage and community-nation relationships in Central Italy', *Ethnology* 4, 172-90.

Wolf, E.R. (1956) 'Aspects of group relations in a complex society', *American Anthropologist* 58, 1065-78.

Ghita Ionescu

Patronage under Communism

The kind of patronage considered here is exclusively modern, i.e., has developed after the First World War. While it would be important to link the traditions of patronage in the history of Russia, China, Poland etc., with the situation prevailing now in these countries, this is not what we are asked. We are asked, I take it, to see whether and how the phenomenon of patronage survived in the specific socio-economic and political regime called either Communist or Marxist-Leninist-Stalinist. As such our comparisons will be made with contemporary non-Communist forms of patronage, and especially with the forms of political patronage still prevailing in the West and which derive from the Jacksonian and pre-Northcote systems of the distribution of public spoils.

It may have been by accident that the original plan of this symposium put only one kind of patronage, *patronage under Communism*, under the conceptual heading of *power*. I must admit that this synoptical arrangement anticipated somehow my attitude. The factor of power so overwhelms the political processes of Communist polities, that the concept of patronage, which where seen from the vantage-point of these polities looks rather like a mitigation of power, can only with great discrimination be used for the study of these polities.

Two of the most relevant aspects of the concept of patronage are, to my mind at least, the nexus of reciprocal interest which forms the relationship patron-clientele, and, on the other hand, the end-product of this relationship: the allocation of posts and dignities. In both respects the concept of patronage does not fit exactly the original political processes of the USSR of before the Second World War. But it becomes more applicable to some of the contemporary Communist states.

If one compares from the above points of view the Western democratic system of patronage, and especially the system of enrolment and of reward on which the Western patronage is based, with *mutatis mutandis* the same functional system in the USSR of before the Second World War, one is bound to find at least the following four differences. (1) The classic Western patronage is ultimately based on an assumption of political stability, and routine, indeed of cyclical constitutional consultations. In the Russian context the background is one of supreme revolutionary tension, and of historical uniqueness. (2) The interest-motivation of the Western clientele is limited, practical and immediate. It does not compare at all with the sacrificial fervour of the Leninist revolutionaries and with their absolute stakes. (3) The very element of bargaining and of alternative choice, which is the trump card of the clientele in the Western democratic relation with the patron ('What do I get if I back you and not the others'?) is replaced in the Stalinist society by the sheer helplessness and fear of the individuals faced only with the monolithic state-employer. (4) Without going so far as to say that patronage in a democracy requires a multi-party system (we know that many no-party or pseudo-democracies of the Third World thrive on patronage), there is no doubt that if the state, or government, or the dictator or the one party (Gramsci's 'New Prince') is so strong that it alone controls all appointments in the society, this situation reduces considerably its duties and worries as patron. Its clientele is a captive clientele.

In the Stalinist society all individuals form a captive clientele for the state organs of employment (*Nomenklatura*) and for the state planning agency (*Gosplan*). The one-party state being the sole employer and the state's one party being the sole political force the individuals have nowhere else to go. Thus the operation of political support becomes an operation of *mobilisation*, and the operation of allocation of jobs an operation of *control*. In Lenin's time the Party captured the key function of controlling all appointments. 'Why have a party,' Lenin exclaimed in January 1921, 'if industrial management is to be appointed by the trade unions, nine-tenths of whose members are non-party workers?' In Stalin's time the Nomenklatura was already the institutionalised procedure whereby all appointments of all *Responsible Positions* (*dolzhnostnoye litso*) in the Beehive State are made exclusively by, initially, joint Party-NKVD teams, but gradually more and more by the latter – so much so that by the time of the purges (1936-1938) the police controlled all jobs in the Party as well. Coming back to the principal question raised in this paragraph I would submit that the more control-by-Nomenklatura expands in a society the less relevant is appointment-by-patronage in that society; and vice-versa, in a proportionate inverse ratio.

There are two exceptions to this monolithic control. The first exception is the rivalry between the Apparats. The passage of the control of appointments from the trade unions to the Party and from the Party to the political police is an example of this rivalry in action. The more important Apparats – the Party, the political police, the army, the trade unions, the administration etc. – are bound, for two reasons, to rival each other and therefore, in principle, should be acting as patrons in quest of their own clientele. The first reason is that each of these corps strives to win supreme political control, dislodging the other (in Stalinist Russia the police took over from the

Party, in China in 1967 the 'Cultural Revolution' and then the army displaced the Party, in 1972 in Yugoslavia Tito warned that if the Party failed in its duties it would be replaced by the army etc.). The second reason is that as professional *corps* they need the best personnel and are on the look-out for candidates of quality for their cadres. Both these reasons lead to a strong *esprit-de-corps*, which in turn leads to the typical patron-clientele relation, even if in an unusual context and in entirely different conditions from those of the Jacksonian patronage. But this kind of patronage is limited on two accounts. On the one hand, it is bound to be implicit. It becomes politically explicit only in the rarefied supreme layers of the respective Apparat. On the other hand, so susceptible to general political control are the communist societies, that the principal Apparat in the USSR, which is now again the Party, has no difficulty in penetrating the other Apparats from within. The CPSU was in this respect particularly successful, until now, in controlling the Red Army from within.

The second exception is the rivalry between factions (or opposition groups) from within the Party itself. The similarity with the struggle between Apparats is evident. Like the Apparats, the factions try to rally around them, but clandestinely, the support of the best and most influential members. Moreover, as we shall see presently, in the industrialised USSR, as well as in all other industrialised communist societies, the factional struggle with a political ideological motivation links up with the Apparat struggle, which is motived by concerns with efficiency of performance. Modern Kremlinologists (Brzezinski, Pethybridge and others) base a lot of their guesswork on this identification of factions with groups of such divergent 'functional' interests from within the industrial Communist society.

We have now indeed come to the point when we can begin to speak of patronage in Communist societies. This is the point when some Communist societies have completed their first industrialisation and become industrial or indeed post-industrial societies. This produces, or allows to re-emerge, functional cleavages from within the formerly monolithic society. The most important cleavage is that, to use here the jargon of some of the Communist societies, between the 'economy' and the 'politicians'. What this means is that once the threshold of industrialisation is passed, and the principle question is no longer 'how to build an industry?' but 'how to run an industry?' *Efficiency* becomes the principal indicator. Unproductive or badly run enterprises must, sooner (in Yugoslavia or Hungary) or later (USSR or Czechoslovakia, with the short exception of 1968), be closed down.

This is very much a matter of management and of cadres. The old *apparatchiki* of the Stalinist age are eased out. New managers with entirely different backgrounds and approaches are brought in. Their technical ability becomes, at least for some Party leaders, of greater relevance than ideological and political solidarity. The results of the individual enterprises of which they are in charge are more important than the duration of their Party membership or their ideological integrity.

Gradually, the Party or 'the politicians' are asked to relinquish the micro-controls of the 'economy' and to withdraw into the rarefied spheres of the macro-economics. Gradually too the 'regulated market' in Yugoslavia and Hungary acts as an objective judge of the economic realities. In these two countries, at least for the time being, the Party accepts the principal conclusions of the change from industrialisation-mobilisation to industrial efficiency: it confines itself, at least on paper, to the responsibilities of *macro-* and *consultative* planning. It also distinguishes political merits from professional qualifications when appointing people in 'responsible positions'.

In such countries too Nomenklatura, our pet 'indicator', hides itself more chastely behind appointment-boards in which it is no longer, or in any case no longer imperatively, the Party and the political police that decide on the appointments. This then leads to much more visible and indeed feasible forms of patronage. The Party, the other apparats, (especially the respective Apparat – army, police, trade unions – in which the appointment is made) the enterprises, the communes, the regions, want to have *their* men appointed, and *their* enterprises or services properly run.

Promises are exchanged between the functional groups and the potential candidates. Mutual preferences and elective affinities come to the fore. Old and new groups, each claiming to have the last word in the appointments, try to rally homogenous rank-and-files behind them. Among the new groups the most influential are the technical and the managerial elite of which more will be said shortly. Among the old 'patrons' there are some very old indeed. In Albania for instance, the clans are still among the most powerful agencies of patronage and cut across the party and the state-administration. Even in modern Yugoslavia the Montenegrin or the Kosmet-Albanian quasi-clans are known to be the main job-dispensers for their kins.

But the most specific cleavage in the industrial communist society is that between the intelligentsias (both the 'creative' and the 'technical' intelligentsias, but the latter is much more important and much more relevant in this particular context), and the previously monolithic Party. Functionally the intelligentsia is bound to take the lead in a society in which, as in all modern industrial societies, scientific knowledge is the principal avenue to success. Ever since 1936, when he knew that he had won the battle of industrialisation, Stalin referred to the new intelligentsia as the 'apple of our country's eye'. What happened since is that, with ups and downs, the intelligentsia acquired, in the wake of their esoteric indispensability, a kind of functional immunity and a status of superiority which break both the monolithic glacis of the egalitarian society and the self-absorbed domination of the Party and of its membership. The word immunity is deliberately introduced here, because professional immunity is one of the antidotes of patronage – this is how the Northcote reform stopped the rot in Britain. In Communist countries where legality has made great progress, even in Yugoslavia which shows inclinations of becoming a Communist *Rechtsstaat* (Fisk, 1969-70), civil service and public appointments are not immune from the strong control of the Party and police. But the combination of larger appointments-boards, more publicity, greatly legality, and, above all, the need for competence and efficiency, which makes the technical intelligentsia's reputation, produced especially in Yugoslavia and now in Hungary more objective conditions. All professional *corps* and all sectors of the economy compete for the services of the new graduates and specialists.

Sociologists like Richard Bendix or Daniel Bell or political scientists like John Armstrong and David E. Apter have drawn the attention to the primacy of the scientific technological and managerial elites as a common characteristic of all highly industrialised or post-industrial societies, capitalist or Communist. In Communist societies this leads not only to distinct manifestations of patronage – but to caste-formation (through inter-marriages only in intelligentsia families) and especially to nepotism (sons of lecturers, of managers and of experts succeed their fathers in the careers). The intelligentsia is a very active patron and actively challenges the Party's monopoly of appointments.

In general, the more pluralist a given Communist society is, the more competitive the appointment system becomes, though with the qualification that in the lingering dictatorial chiaroscuro the competition is not in the open, and the appointments are still made by under-the-counter bargaining between the organised 'corps', each acting as 'patrons' in opposition to the others. In the early sixties Yugoslavia was the prototype of such a functionally pluralised society: the trade unions, the communes, the self-managed enterprises, the republics, the army, the political police, the state-administration (federal and republican) were all engaged in functional competition. In the seventies national pluralism overtook functional pluralism. The total decentralisation·among the republics led to the formation of new administrative bottlenecks at the republican level. From that moment on republican patronage became the most ostentatious. Republican chauvinism within the republics, and republican favouritism in the limited federal appointments became the rule. Whether within the republics themselves the Party was again in the ascendant, taking under its active protection the local interests and acting as the sole patron in the federal rivalry, is a matter which should be studied separately. But, in theory, it comes back to the question of whether an individual Yugoslav republic is less pluralistic in the seventies than the Yugoslav federal state was in the sixties.

In general, the concentration of interests as well as of purposes in and on a smaller territorial area must result in a greater dependence on the leadership. The leadership of an inward-looking republic controls more closely the attitudes and the nationalistic credentials of the supporters. A narrow motivation becomes imperative. Zeal and even fanaticism are seen as marks of distinction, while national and ethnic origins are *sine qua non* conditions of acceptance into the family where spoils are now shared. This is not to say that of necessity a component republic or state in a federation becomes more centralistic minded, and therefore more patronage-prone, if given more autonomy than the federation itself. Generally speaking, decentralisation might be accompanied by a democratisation of the political processes of the decentralised unit, republic or state. But in the special conditions of centralism, even democratic centralism, prevailing in the communist political systems, the fragmentation of power in smaller and more hermetically closed units, with nationalist or ethnic motivations, could increase the two way process of selective dependence which is at the basis of patronage.

Whereas the opening up of political systems dispels patronage, the introduction, or re-introduction of political or ideological barriers, whether with national or with social motivations, re-creates the claustrophobic atmosphere in which patronage flourishes.

NOTES

1.　I must refer to Ionescu (1968) and (1972) for the full explanation of the Apparats and of the Apparat state, as well as for the concept of *Nomenklatura*. For *Nomenklatura* see especially Ionescu (1968), pp. 60-4.

REFERENCES

Fisk, W. (1969-70) 'A communist *Rechtstaat?*' *Government and Opposition* 5, no. 1, pp. 41-53.
Ionescu, G. (1968) *The Politics of the European Communist States*. London.
Ionescu, G. (1972) *Comparative Communist Politics*. London.

Sabri Sayari

Political patronage in Turkey

I

We may define patronage as a mechanism which regulates social relationships between individuals and groups with differential access to economic and political resources. More specifically, political patronage refers to a particular form of reciprocal exchange whereby individual patrons and/or political parties seek to mobilise the support of their followers in return for assistance and various brokerage services. Although a host of factors, ranging from the weakness of centre-periphery linkages to social segmentation, are likely to contribute to the emergence and maintenance of political patronage, its principal cause is socio-economic and political inequality.

Although it is true that higher rates of socio-economic development may change the form and bases of patronage, it is also apparent that varieties of patronage-oriented behaviour exist in societies of different developmental levels. In general, a mixture of both vertical and horizontal types of solidarity networks are to be found in most social systems. But where horizontal group or class affiliations are relatively weak, we would expect to find a greater frequency of clientelist-based social interactions. As Chalmers has pointed out, it is therefore possible to differentiate between systems which are more 'vertical' than others depending on whether or not 'the rate of innovation of new vertical, dependent relationships exceeds the rate of breakdown of the old ones into horizontal patterns' (Chalmers 1974, p.11).

Since there appears to be an inverse relationship between the strength of horizontal solidarities and patronage, a number of social scientists have come to feel that political loyalties in developing countries cannot satisfactorily be analysed through theoretical perspectives derived from the historical evolution of Western Europe and North America (Lande 1973; Scott 1972a, pp. 91-2). In the latter, the modernisation process has been accompanied by the emergence of common class or group affiliations as the bases of political behaviour. The breakdown of most vertical hierarchies and their replacement by horizontal ties has been a critical turning point in the structuring of mass politics in the industrialised Western nations.

However, attempts to analyse politics in developing countries by using the class or pluralist group approaches have been less than successful. Both approaches are based on the premise that individuals pursue their interests in politics primarily through collective action with others who share similar interests, attitudes, and goals. Yet, an impressive array of evidence from studies on the social bases of politics in Asia, Africa, and Latin America indicates that interest representation in these societies is channelled mostly through vertical ties which cut across horizontal solidarities (Weiner 1967; Lemarchand 1972; Sandbrook 1972; Powell 1971).

How are such vertical political loyalties structured and in what direction are they likely to change? According to the emerging model of clientelist politics, vertical networks are commonly built around patron-client ties of personal followings. Patron-client ties are dyadic, they involve face-to-face interaction and rest on a reciprocal exchange relationship. In return for protection and material assistance, the patron receives the personal support of his clients. Individual patron-client relationships are the building blocks for vertical social hierarchies which extend from local to national political arenas.

Traditional clientelist relationships flourish in those settings where, in addition to inequalities of land tenure, the level of societal integration is low, and state authority remains weak. As villages and provincial towns are integrated into the nation-state and the market economy, patron-client relationships are similarly integrated into what Powell calls an 'extended clientele system' (Powell 1971, p.414). The centre-periphery linkages begin to be regulated by brokers or mediators who take over the roles previously performed by traditional notables. In the presence of viable political parties, such brokerage functions increasingly take place through party organisations.

II

We may begin to explore the role of patronage in Turkish electoral politics by noting that manifestations of clientelistic behaviour (e.g., dependency relationships between individuals of differential status and authority, social networks of personal followings, factionalism, favouritism, etc.) can be observed at many different levels of Turkish society, including both formal organisations such as the bureaucracy, trade unions, or civic associations, and informal social groups. The importance of patronage as a means for either strengthening one's status or for achieving particularistic goals is clearly recognised by most citizens. Establishing proper connections with the right people, therefore, assumes priority in all types of social interactions.

This trend is all the more apparent in political life. For example, a visitor to the National Assembly is likely to notice that the busiest sections of the parliament building are the waiting-rooms for the guests. The 'guests' are mostly groups of peasants from the provinces who have come to Ankara in search of assistance from their deputies. The help which they seek usually involves particularistic favours: extension of the deadline for the repayment of the loan borrowed from the State Agricultural Bank, a permit to go to Europe as a worker, or a hospital bed in Ankara for a relative who is critically ill. Deputies spend a good deal of their time trying to secure preferential treatment from various bureaucratic agencies on behalf of their constituents. Although such activity hinders the proper functioning of the legislature (sessions are frequently cancelled for lack of quorum because most deputies are busy taking care of their voters), no deputy can afford to bypass these services since they often determine his chances for re-election.

This type of face-to-face interaction between leaders and followers, which involves the exchange of assistance and favours in return for political support, takes place with much frequency. In rural communities, election campaigns centre around the activities of party-affiliated brokers or notables who increase the size of their personal followings by distributing material or symbolic favours. Similar clientelist transactions, operating through urban political machines, can be observed in the shantytown quarters of large metropolitan centres such as Istanbul, Ankara, and Izmir.

Linkages between local and national political arenas are commonly structured around vertical networks in which sub-leaders, along with their personal supporters, become the followers of high-ranking leaders (cf. Lande 1973, pp.122-6). The maintenance of these vertical networks depends on the downward flow of governmental patronage and on the capability of leaders at each level of the hierarchy to perform brokerage services for their followers. For example, within a typical party organisation, such vertical networks extend from national party elites down to party leaders in the provinces, sub-provinces, or villages. Delivery of goods and services in exchange for political support is essential both for internal party cohesion and for electoral strength.

III

It should be noted here that clientelistic relations between leaders and followers have long been important in Turkey. Studies on Turkish social history often emphasise the relevance of dependency ties between agrarian elites and peasants in traditional Ottoman rural society (Inalcik 1964; Hourani 1968; Mardin 1973). These dependency relationships are usually associated with the rise to prominence of local notables (*ayan*).

Although as early as the fourteenth century the *ayan* were among the influential members of rural communities, they became especially powerful with the disintegration of the traditional land tenure system during the 17th and 18th centuries (Inalcik 1964, pp. 46-7). The *ayan* were able to accumulate considerable wealth by acquiring the right to lease state-owned lands and collect taxes which, prior to that date, had been enjoyed by the fief holders. Control over land was a key factor in the growth of patron-dependent ties between notables and peasants. Equally important was the lack of effective central authority in the provinces. In the absence of governmental protection, the peasants became increasingly dependent on the notables for their personal safety and security of property. This dependency also reflected their need for channels through which they could protect themselves against arbitrary acts of local administrative officials. As Shaw points out (1971), by the eighteenth century, the notables had 'assumed the function of mediating between the people and government officials and, as the latter became more corrupt and tyrannical, of intervening to protect the people from the officials'.

The restoration of the Sultan's authority in the provinces during the course of the nineteenth century, along with the abolition of tax farming, weakened the supremacy of the *ayan*. By the twentieth century, prosperous small-town merchants (*esraf*) and large land-owners in villages (*aga*) had replaced the *ayan* in social influence (Lewis 1961, pp. 441-4). The nature of the dependency relationships also acquired a new dimension with the gradual penetration of the centre into the periphery in the latter part of the nineteenth century, which led to the creation of new brokerage roles for the notables (Mardin 1973, pp. 177-8). The encroachment of the state in the provinces made itself felt in the form of taxes, military conscription, court litigation, and the registration of land titles. To cope with these matters, the peasants sought the aid of notables who could bargain with government officials.

The fact that the notables exercised economic controls over the peasantry *and* acted as their 'protectors' against a powerful state gained additional political significance with the emergence of parties after the turn of the twentieth century. Although the reach of party politics and the scope of mass participation remained limited during both the Young Turk era (1908-18) and the authoritarian one-party period (1923-46), the influence of notables was amply felt in parliamentary politics and in party activities. Between 1908 and 1918, scores of notables entered into the parliament and assumed leadership roles in local branches of the Committee of Union and Progress (CUP). As Rustow (1966, p.117) indicates, the CUP organised its party units in the provinces by recruiting notables into its ranks through 'systematic use of patronage and economic regulation'.

The organisational bases of Mustafa Kemal's nationalist movement similarly rested on provincial notables who were instrumental in the mobilisation of the peasantry against the invading foreign powers. The Republican People's Party (RPP), which Mustafa Kemal founded after the establishment of the Republic in 1923, and which functioned as the ruling party of the authoritarian regime for the next

23 years, maintained the same pattern of alliance between a core group of nation-building elites at the centre and notables in the periphery. Provincial deputies of the RPP in the National Assembly came predominantly from leading local families. Undoubtedly, their access to channels of governmental patronage strengthened their social influence at the local level.

IV

With the beginnings of competitive politics in the late 1940s, dependence and exchange relationships between notables and peasants played a major role in the rapid politicisation of the periphery. A recurrent theme of studies on rural communities covering this period is that hostilities between lineages and intergroup conflicts were the two principal sources of factionalism in the countryside and that factional oppositions were transformed into political competition at the local level with the advent of electoral politics (Stirling 1966, pp. 281-3; Szyliowicz 1966; Eberhard 1967; Meeker 1972).

Undoubtedly, the segmentary nature of the Turkish rural society, with its multitude of ethnic (Turkish vs. Kurdish), sectarian (Sunni vs. Alevi), and intertribal cleavages, provided an ideal setting for the proliferation of factional oppositions. But it is important to note that these factions were essentially segments of extended clientele networks with members of locally influential families assuming their leadership. In general, factions in villages and provincial towns were linked to each other through similar clientelistic ties between leaders and followers. The aggregation of factional followings within vertical hierarchies provided sizable numbers of political supporters for the notables.

Following the transition to competitive politics, party strategies for peasant mobilisation were based largely on the recruitment of notables into party ranks who were then entrusted with the task of providing 'ready vote banks'. Hence, the two major parties (the Republican People's Party and the Democratic Party) competed with each other to win the backing of landlords, merchants, and in the case of Eastern Turkey, sheikhs and tribal leaders. This strategy met a favourable response from the notables since assuming the leadership post of a party's local unit meant that a notable could (a) gain additional status and prestige vis-à-vis rival notables, (b) secure new sources of outside support for members of his faction, and (c) maintain and improve his economic standing through party ties. Quite often, the decision to join one party or another was made according to whether or not the faction led by a rival notable had already established party connections. There were also instances of different party affiliations within the same family to ensure that whatever party won the elections, the family's honour, prestige, and economic interests would not be adversely affected.[1]

Hence, during this initial phase of electoral competition, clientelism of the notables had important political consequences. Since the late 1940s, the politicisation of clientelistic networks between leaders and followers had been a significant factor in the periodic mobilisation of the peasant voters during election campaigns. But the context within which these networks operate, and the degree of reciprocity involved, have undergone considerable changes.

The replacement of notable clientelism with what Weingrod has called 'party-directed patronage' is one prominent aspect of this change. With the exception of Eastern Turkey which I shall discuss later, in most parts of the country a transition has taken place from traditional to more contemporary forms of political patronage. This is not to suggest, however, that the role of the notables in electoral politics has altogether waned. On the contrary, members of notable families have succeeded in getting elected to the National Assembly quite regularly and have continued to hold key positions in provincial party organisations.[2] But as case studies on local-level politics show, the political influence of the notables at present depends more on their roles as party functionaries than on their control of traditional patronage resources (Tachau 1973; Meeker 1972). For example, landlords and prosperous merchants may maintain personal followings through their control of choice land and locally available credit. But these are by themselves rarely sufficient for attaining political power. They are likely to become politically relevant only when supplemented with additional resources that have to do with party patronage as well as possession of skills and knowledge derived from professional or technical occupations (cf. Scott 1972a, pp. 97-8).

The transformation of former notables into party-affiliated brokers and the spread of party patronage may be explained by several factors. First, since the late 1940s, parties have gradually penetrated into most branches of the bureaucracy. This means that a leader who mediates between the government officials and his clients has to have a position within a party organisation – preferably within the ruling party. With the expanding scope of state activities, the peasants' need to find intermediaries to deal with bureaucratic agencies has increased. By virtue of his position, a party functionary stands a better chance of performing this task than a notable without party affiliations. Thus, most of the individual and community demands for assistance are relayed to local party leaders or deputies.

Secondly, the growth of party competition has been accompanied by rising levels of public investments for rural development projects. The allocation of state resources for these projects is controlled by elected party governments. Ruling parties have often used this power to broaden their grass-roots electoral support by rewarding rural communities which vote for them with new roads, electricity, waterways, and various public works. The downward flow of governmental patronage is channelled through vertical networks of brokers within party organisations. Along with notables, increasing numbers of lawyers, doctors, pharmacists, schoolteachers, etc. have assumed important positions in central and provincial party organisations by efficiently regulating this exchange process.

Finally, the replacement of notable clientelism with party patronage is related to the weakening of the deferential political culture of the countryside as a result of socio-economic change. Since the early 1950s, the socio-economic context of political relationships in Turkey has undergone changes with the rapid spread of the social mobilisation process and the growing commercialisation of economic activities. In the rural areas, the net impact of these developments has been the weakening of traditional deferential loyalties and a growing demand for self-improvement through greater reciprocity in the maintenance of exchange relationships (Kelaş and Türkay 1962). Increasingly, these demands have come to involve goods and services which can only be obtained by access to governmental patronage through party affiliations.

The expansion of party patronage and the increase in the number of party-affiliated brokers have introduced an element of choice as well as greater reciprocity to exchange relationships of the clientelist variety. In contrast to their former dependence on one particular local patron, peasants nowadays have greater opportunities of choosing between several competing brokers (Huizer 1965, pp. 142-3). Unlike the notables of earlier times who could easily mobilise their followers for political action, the local party bosses of today can no longer count on such ready support unless they can skilfully manipulate individual and group demands for material self-improvement. As peasants have come to learn the bargaining power of their votes, they have increasingly sought to obtain greater advantages in their dealings with party agents.

Undoubtedly, it is in the shantytown quarters of large cities, with their migrant populations of peasant origins, that the bargaining power acquired through the electoral processes has been most openly used. Election campaigns in these areas involve lengthy negotiations between voters and candidates concerning the benefits which parties promise to deliver in exchange for votes. The mass inflow of migrants into the cities since the late 1950s has vastly expanded the possibilities for urban party patronage. Indeed, party activities among the urban poor have striking resemblances to the way in which political machines functioned in the United States during the late nineteenth and early twentieth centuries (Scott 1972a and b).

The changing form of political patronage outlined in the preceeding paragraphs is much less visible in Turkey's Eastern provinces which, in many ways, display the characteristics of traditional societies. Most of these provinces rank much lower than other sections of the country on indicators of societal development such as urbanisation, industrialisation, literacy, exposure to mass media, etc. This is also true of the relatively limited extent of commercial market processes. Semi-feudal economic relationships still prevail in parts of the region and it is not uncommon that a single notable family privately 'owns' several villages. Inequalities of land tenure are much more pronounced in the Eastern provinces than elsewhere as indicated both by landownership patterns and the high proportion of landless peasants.

The East lags behind other regions in terms of social integration as well. In the periphery of several provinces, state authority is only marginal and some of the functions which should normally be performed by the state (e.g., distribution of justice, maintenance of law and order) are carried out by tribal leaders and sheikhs. Several factors, such as (a) the absence of adequate communication facilities between villages and the outside world, (b) the extreme segmentation of society among numerous tribal groups and religious orders, and (c) the existence of a large Kurdish minority have all exacerbated the problem of integration.[3]

The nature of political patronage in Eastern Turkey reflects the region's low level of development and integration. Unlike other parts of the country, traditional patron-client ties rather than party patronage are of primary importance in the structuring of political loyalties (Kudat 1974). Although party organisations exist, they are not well-established and tend to be personalistic. Influential patrons frequently switch parties which results in the wholesale transfer of the political loyalties of their personal followings. Party switches by notables account for the wide swings in the distribution of votes among parties. The weakness of party patronage and partisan loyalties in the Eastern provinces is also indicated by the rise of independent candidacies, especially since the switch to the proportional representation system in 1961. In recent years, the percentage of votes received by independent candidates in this region has been much higher than elsewhere in Turkey.

V

A discussion of the means by which different parties have sought to utilise patronage to maximise their votes or the role of patronage in internal party cohesion remains outside the scope of this paper. Suffice it to note here, however, that the electoral fortunes of Turkish parties during nearly three decades of political competition have been significantly affected by their adaptability to changing terms of political patronage.

As I have indicated elsewhere, one major reason for the dominance of the Democratic Party (DP) in the Turkish party system in the decade after 1950 lay in its ability to function effectively as a rural political machine (Sayari 1974). One among several factors which contributed to the DP's success in winning the majority of the peasant votes in successive elections following its rise to power in 1950 was its expedient use of governmental patronage to cater for the needs of its clientele. During the course of the 1960s, this strategy was continued with equally successful results by the Justice Party (JP) which replaced the outlawed DP in the party system following the military intervention of 1960. The JP took maximum advantage of its control over governmental sources of patronage to distribute it to its clientele among the peasants and the urban poor.[4]

On the other hand, the RPP's failure to adopt a similar style has adversely affected its electoral strength. The RPP continued to rely on traditional notable clientelism at a time when party patronage had become a critical factor for peasant mobilisation. This may partially account for the fact that while the RPP did relatively well in the Eastern provinces, it regularly lost the majority of the peasant votes in most other regions to the Democrats during the 1950s and later to the Justice Party.

Since the late 1960s, however, the Republican People's Party has begun to experiment with new electoral strategies which reflect the party's attempt to combine ideology with patronage. The increasingly ideological orientation of the RPP indicates its leadership's assumption that horizontal rather than vertical ties will become salient in political competition. But the party leadership has also become much more aware of the political pay-offs of patronage. For example, it has sought to replace the party's longstanding reliance on traditional notables by recruiting politically skilful brokers into the RPP's organisation. It has additionally attempted to form party-affiliated peasant unions and agricultural cooperatives and establish close links with secondary associations such as trade unions. As Tarrow shows in his study on Italy, this strategy facilitates the expansion of party patronage through the creation of 'horizontal clienteles' (Tarrow 1967, p.332). Also, as the RPP's policy of granting substantial price increases for agricultural products during its brief tenure in office in 1974 showed, the party has become much more adept in playing the game of politics in a peasant clientelist society.

The electoral gains of the RPP since 1960 may be interpreted as a sign that horizontal loyalties are gaining in importance in Turkish political life. Indeed, the relevance of ideologies and party programmes in voting behaviour has increased considerably in recent years, especially among the urban voters. However, the emergence of horizontal class or group loyalties should not be taken as an indication that vertical political relationships and/or party patronage are losing their saliency. Rather, as I have argued, vertical hierarchies maintain their significance and a combination of policy-oriented appeals with patronage distribution is likely to remain a characteristic feature of Turkish electoral politics in the near future.

NOTES

1. Eberhard describes one such case of different party affiliations within a prominent. notable family in following terms: 'The Bahadirli, most important in Reyhanli, descendants of former tribal leaders, have as one of their members the mayor of the city and chief of the People's Party; before him, his cousin was mayor, and previously two of his uncles. The candidate for the post is another cousin. One cousin is the founder of the local Democratic Party. ... The family had a clear family policy: professional positions like those of lawyer, judge or doctor are necessary if the family is to keep its prestige in a changing city ... ' (Eberhard 1967, p.320).
2. Examples of notable families who have continued to send deputies to the National Assembly are Karaosmanoglu in Manisa, Bozdoganoglu in Adana, Mursalioglu in Hatay or Ulusoy in Tokat and Amasya.
3. As Yalman has argued, the difference between the official (Turkish) and spoken (Kurdish) languages makes it necessary for the peasants to find intermediaries in their dealings with the buraucracy (see Yalman 1971). In addition, Ayşe Kudat has emphasised the importance of fictive kinship as a source of patron-client relationships in Eastern Turkey (Kudat 1974b).
4. Sherwood underscores this aspect of the JP when he writes: 'A typical villager arriving in Ankara or Istanbul goes immediately to that district populated by people from his own village. The local Justice Party man helps him settle, aids in the problems with authorities, and functions as an employment agency or a marriage bureau as the case may be' (Sherwood 1967).

REFERENCES

Chalmers, D.A. (1974) 'The search for the underlying structure of Latin American politics: Statism, vertical ties, and factionalism', paper presented to the Conference on Authoritarianism and Corporatism in Latin America, University of Pittsburgh (April 4-6, 1974).

Eberhard, W. (1967) 'Changes in leading families in Southern Turkey', in his collected papers, *Settlement and Social Change in Asia*, Hong Kong, 312-26.

Hourani, A. (1968) 'Ottoman reform and the politics of the notables', in W.R. Polk and R.L. Chambers (eds), *Beginnings of Modernization in the Middle East*, Chicago, 41-68.

Huizer, G. (1965) 'Some notes on community development and rural social research', *America Latina* 8 (July-September).

Inalcik, H. (1964) 'The nature of traditional society: Turkey', in R.E. Ward and D. Rustow (eds), *Political Modernization in Japan and Turkey*, Princeton, 42-63.

Kaleş, R. and Türkay, O. (1962) *Köylü Gözüyle Türk Köylerinde Iktisadi ve Toplumsal Degisme*. Ankara.

Kudat, A. (1974a) 'Patron-client relations: The state of the art and research in Eastern Turkey', in E.D. Akarli and G. Ben-Dor (eds), *Political Participation in Turkey*, Istanbul, 61-87.

Kudat, A. (1974b) *Kirvelik*. Ankara.

Lande, C.H. (1973) 'Networks and groups in Southeast Asia: Some observations on the group theory of politics', *American Political Science Review* LXVII (March), 103-27.

Lemarchand, R. (1972) 'Political clientelism and ethnicity in tropical Africa: Competing solidarities in nation-building', *American Political Science Review* LXVI (March), 68-90.

Lerner, D. (1958) *The Passing of Traditional Society*. New York.

Lewis, B. (1961) *The Emergence of Modern Turkey*. London.

Mardin, S. (1973) 'Center-periphery relations: A key to Turkish politics?', *Daedalus* 102 (Winter), 169-90.

Meeker, M.E. (1972) 'The great family Aghas of Turkey: A study of changing political culture', in R. Antoun and I. Harik (eds), *Rural Politics and Social Change in the Middle East*, Bloomington, Indiana, 237-66.

Powell, J.D. (1970) 'Peasant society and clientelist politics', *American Political Science Review*, LXIV (June), 411-25.

Powell, J.D. (1971) *Political Mobilization of the Venezuelan Peasant*. Cambridge, Mass.

Rustow, D. (1966) 'The development of parties in Turkey', in J. LaPalombara and M. Weiner (eds), *Political Parties and Political Development*. Princeton.

Sandbrook, R. (1972) 'Patrons, clients and factions: New dimensions of conflict analysis in Africa', *Canadian Journal of Political Science* V (March), 104-19.

Sayari, S. (1974) 'Some notes on the beginnings of mass political participation in Turkey', in E.D. Akarli and G. Ben-Dor (eds), *Political Participation in Turkey*, Istanbul, 121-33.

Scott, J.C. (1972a) 'Patron-client politics and political change in Southeast Asia', *American Political Science Review* LXIV (March), 91-113.

Scott, J.C. (1972b) *Comparative Political Corruption*. Englewood Cliffs, N.J.

Shaw, S. (1971) *Between Old and New: The Ottoman Empire under Selim III; 1789-1807*. Cambridge, Mass.

Sherwood, W.B. (1967) 'The rise of the Justice Party in Turkey', *World Politics* XX (October), 57.

Stirling, P. (1966) *Turkish Village*. New York.

Szyliowicz, J. (1966) *Political Change in Rural Turkey: Erdemli*. The Hague.

Tachau, F. (1973) 'Turkish provincial party politics', in K. Karpat (ed.), *Social Change and Politics in Turkey*, Leiden, 282-316.

Tarrow, S. (1967) *Peasant Communism in Southern Italy*. New Haven.

Weiner, M. (1967) *Party-Building in a New Nation: The Indian National Congress*. Chicago.

Yalman, Nur (1971) 'On land disputes in Eastern Turkey', in G. Tikku (ed.), *Islam and its Cultural Diversions: Studies in Honor of G.E. von Grunebaum*. Urbana, Illinois.

Peter Loizos

Politics and patronage in a Cypriot village, 1920-1970[1]

Four areas of social relations each connected with politics and patronage are important in understanding a Cypriot village as it was in 1970. These are changes in the organisation of credit; changes in education and the role of teachers in electoral politics; changes in the office of *mukhtar*, village headman; and changes in the operation of party politics at the village level.

Approaches to patronage and derived notions have been diverse. They range from a precise but restricted use employed by Peters (1968) to deal with a Libyan case, the broader, more flexible interpretation of Campbell (1964) in his monograph, and more recently the shot-gun tactics of Powell (1970, p.411) a political scientist who makes rather wide claims for the usefulness of the term 'clientelism'. Weingrod (1967-8, pp. 377-81) argued that anthropologists and political scientists have attached different emphases to terms like patronage, patron, client and their derivatives. Here, *patron-client relations* will be used in a restricted sense to identify rather rare, long-term contracted relations in which the client's support is exchanged for the patron's protection; there is an ideology which is morally charged and appears to rule out strict, open accounting, but both parties keep some tacit rough account; the goods and services exchanged are not similar, and there is no implication of fair exchange or a balance of satisfactions, since the client is markedly weaker in power and needs the patron more than he is needed by him. Most men in the particular village studied were not, in this sense, anyone's clients. By *patronage* is meant the capacity for particularistic distribution of benefits, inherent in an office or agency. Both these terms need to be kept distinct from other instances of dependency and exchange relations, particularly from exchanges such as bribes, gifts, extortion, blackmail, and favours between friends who are equals, which tend to have different structural implications.[2]

The recent arguments (Asad 1972) involve problems about choice and contract. Choice need not imply 'free choice', that is, broad freedom of action, for people meaningfully choose between the lesser of several evils, for example, to live without protection or to pay a high price for it. Nor is a contracted relationship always 'freely' contracted if this implies that both parties enter it with equal satisfaction about its terms. The notion of contract is needed to help distinguish the condition of a press-ganged mariner or a junior age-set from that of a wage-labourer, who cannot meaningfully choose not to work, but can choose which of several jobs he does, and bargain over terms.

Later in the paper issue is taken with the suggestion from Italian studies that villagers now enjoy more ways of getting what they need than in the days when a single patron class guarded the junctures between state and local community. For in Cyprus, at least, men now need both *more*, and *very different* things from what their grandfathers needed, so this extension of dependency on non-local decisions means that increase in choice, a plurality of links, or competition between patronage systems may be more apparent than real.

Debt

Many writers agree that in the nineteenth and early twentieth centuries, Cypriot peasants were debt-ridden, and frequently dependent on moneylenders, both land-rich fellow-villagers, and members of the urban bourgoisie. Jenness (1962, p. 126) cites evidence that in 1879 one in twenty-five of the population of Limassol district was sued for debt; in these first few years of their administration, the British reduced the frequency of imprisonment for debt but they did not make any substantial attack on rural credit and moneylenders for another fifty years, in spite of the many other administrative reforms they introduced. This may have been because of the financial burden to the Colony of the Tribute, since rural credit was one thing which could not be introduced without surplus funds.

Obviously, the power of moneylenders over peasant debtors does not have to lead to patron-client relations, narrowly defined: the debtor either goes on paying interest, or he loses what he has pledged.

The relationship may remain single-stranded and purely economic, if the moneylender is satisfied with his material return and sees no need to convert the relationship to political power. However, in 1882 the British set up in Cyprus an experiment in representation, a Legislative Council. The franchise included all males over 21 who had paid *verghi*, an income tax paid by people of most classes (Hill 1952, p.245). Election to the Legislative Council became an important means of consolidating power and prestige for a few Cypriot notables. Governor Storrs, in office from 1926 to 1932, described the Council's composition. There were 15 elected members, 3 Muslim and 12 Christian; having told us that a major source of income for advocates was actions for recovery of debts, and that 70% of the peasants were indebted to 'usurers and merchants', he adds (Storrs 1939, p.491):

I found on the Council eight advocates, three of whom were moneylenders; one landowner who was also a moneylender; one bishop of the Greek Church; one merchant and one farmer. Thus though the real interests of the Colony were those of the peasant producer, the interests represented in the Legislature were exclusively those of the numerically insignificant class of parasites who made a living out of him.

But the picture was not without shading, for he remarks (p.505) that his government was not able to control the ravages of goats, and re-cover the island with forests, because

the goat is for Cyprus what the pig is for Ireland or the camel for Arabia, the irreplaceable means of subsistence for the very poor. Moreover, in the democratic days of the Legislative Council, goatherds had to be placated, and goats meant votes.

Much more research is needed on the workings of the Legislative Council, and the way it articulated with village-level relations, so my remarks here are speculative. But it seems most probable that the economic leverage available to some of the elected members would have been used to secure votes, and where there were 'goatherds to be placated' who were also indebted to their representatives, the potential was available for *enduring* patron-client relationships to emerge.

These need to be distinguished conceptually from either simple use of debt control to insure compliance, or vote-buying as such. A member must have got votes in a number of different ways, and would have had one or two committed clients, to mix metaphors, in any particular village. He would probably have had rather more simple debtors, whose votes he might have sought to influence more crudely.

The British started to make more serious attacks on the problem of rural indebtedness by the 1914 Cooperative Credit Societies Law, which allowed villages to set up their own credit societies which they managed themselves.[3] By 1925 there were only 29 in the island, but this year saw the foundation of an Agricultural Bank, and the next four years saw a further 175 local societies formed. At the very least, these societies provided the peasant with an *alternative* source of credit to the individual moneylender, but Storrs (1939, p.509) makes larger claims for them, claiming that governmental initiatives were 'diminishing the prestige of the Honourable Member *qua* Member, no less than the rapid growth of Cooperative Credit Societies were loosening his grip *qua* Usurer'. How far this tendency might have gone remains obscure, since in 1931, following the uprising (an unexpected outburst of nationalist agitation which resulted in the burning of the Governor's residence and a military repression of unrest), the Legislative Council was suspended, and with it, its potential for patronage.

The Credit Societies did not wipe out all moneylenders overnight; during my fieldwork in 1968-70 there were still a few villagers who used to lend their surplus cash at interest to other villagers. But the societies by providing a supply of agricultural credit at a low, controlled interest rate, reduced the short-term economic insecurity of the peasant, and loss of tenure by foreclosure declined dramatically in the later 1930s and early 1940s. Nowadays, a farmer who has invested in a long term crop such as citrus fruit may have debts at the Credit Society, other debts to local banks secured by portions of his land, and yet further debts to private individuals. Prior to 1930 most villagers would have been in debt to private moneylenders only, and the more likely to propitiate them by becoming their clients if called upon.

In meetings of the five-man village committee which administers the Kalo village Credit Society, the members take pains to make an assessment of a man's ability to undertake debt without damage to his overall economic interests. The main decisions about who may receive loans of a particular size are assessed by men elected from the village, who have reputations for administrative ability and honesty. The ceiling on the loans made is set by the Commissioner of Cooperatives, and he allows this to vary from village to village, according to the productivity of the land. But he is not involved with the day to day decisions. To this extent, the credit societies have given villagers more power of decision in their own lives.

Mention of the Commissioner's Department brings the issue of patron-client relations back into the foreground. So far we may note a shift from the inferred political use of debt, to a situation where much rural debt is controlled by a two-tier administrative agency. No instances where Members of Parliament between 1960-70 were elected through the manipulation of credit ties are known to me. But there are senses in which the Cooperative Development Department has a patronage role in rural society, that is a role which permits the distribution of some rewards to be made on partisan lines. The Commissioner's Office fixes the salary of the officials who work in village units, both Credit Societies, and retail stores. It is believed that the salaries of committed left-wingers may be kept lower than the volume of business they handle justifies, a kind of 'negative patronage', which is explained by the fact that the Commissioner was formerly the Secretary of PEK, the right-wing and nationalist farmers' association founded in the 1940s to combat leftist influence. It is also widely believed that in spite of his civil service post, the Commissioner remains active in right-wing politics. He is considered personally loyal to President Makarios, and hence he could be in a position to reward similar loyalty (or punish disloyalty) in the Cooperative movement.

So much for the patronage potential of the Cooperative Department. There was in the village studied one clear case of patron-client ties, narrowly defined, between one villager and the Commissioner, and described in detail elsewhere are some consequences of that relationship.[4] To summarise briefly, one young villager, a secondary-school graduate of proven administrative ability, on his own admission moved between 1966 and 1969 from the open political support of a socialist political leader to a more right-wing position, for a complex of reasons which can be simply expressed in the assertion that his civil service boss became his patron: a single-stranded tie, became a more complex, enduring one. The villager took a long time to reach his decision, and it was much more emotionally-charged than a simple decision to switch from one commercial supplier to another – it had for the villager implications of betrayal both of a person and an ideological position.

This villager was able to help certain close relatives and affines through his relationship with the Commissioner, but there was no-one else in the village who could have been called a client of the Commissioner. This point needs to be made, for it seems to me that the Commissioner only needs one good client per village, or even in a cluster of villages. It would be a waste of his resources to have several, and for him the critical question must have been the early identification of the right man for the role. Suppose a man is needed to do something as sensitive as make sure that at one of the Cooperative movement's small factories, no left-wingers are employed? This assignment takes knowledge, tact, the ability to work quietly and so forth. One does not entrust such a task lightly. This is why real patrons and clients, as opposed to assorted dependency relationships, are few and far between – the commitments on both sides are of *major* resources such as jobs and whole political positions. It is unsatisfactory to pin down patrons and clients by a shopping-list of what they do, but it is worth saying that, qualitatively, these are different orders of dependency.

Education

The Legislative Council was provided with other resources for the creation of patron-client relations. The British decided to support the expansion of primary education in the island, and by the Education Law of 1895 and its Amendment in 1897 set up a system in which villages annually elected committees to appoint (or dismiss) teachers and to fix their salaries. The six Districts of the island had District Education Committees, also mainly elected, to which appeal could be made by village or teacher, and at the top of this was the Board of Education. Since revenues were considered insufficient at first for a separate Board, and since the British had decided to deal separately with Christians and Muslims, the Christian Schools Board was composed of the Chief Secretary to the Government, the Archbishop, three Christian Members of the Legislative Council, and six other Greeks elected by the six District Committees. This Committee had the power to recommend to the High Commissioner which villages should receive grants-in-aid for schools. In 1905 the Rev. F.D. Newham was asked to report on the state of education in the island. He states that the examination for the appointment of new teachers is of a very low standard, and does not necessarily require any teaching experience, but that the low salaries do not so far ensure a steady supply of even poorly qualified men. He goes on (Newham 1905, p.417):

Teachers are appointed by Village Committees for one year only; and, since the Village Committees are themselves elected annually, and the elections turn on questions of politics foreign to education, constant changes of masters are the natural result.

One of the many *lacunae* in our knowledge of Cypriot rural politics is the extent to which the 'politics' of these committees were those of purely village-level factions, based on personalities; and how far if at all such factions articulated with alignments at District or Legislative Council levels. In short, were there stable village factions with the same personnel and ideologies as the followings of Members of the Legislative Council? Only further research can answer this, but meanwhile there are hints of how the situation was working at a later period. Surridge (1930, p.20) comments:

The old type of Greek-Christian schoolmaster is gradually being eliminated. He was the advisor of the villagers. He wrote their petitions and on the visit of higher Government officials or of the Greek Orthodox Bishops he delivered an oration ... He was the party 'boss' in politics and was forced to bow the knee to the local Member of the Legislative Council to whom, not infrequently, he owed his appointment.

A little later he describes how some teachers have become helpful to villagers, by taking up the role of Secretary of the Cooperative Credit Societies (a role which by 1968 they were no longer willing to perform in the area I studied). But he adds: 'Occasionally they are to be found meddling in village politics and supporting one leading man as against another, but this habit is dying out as their appointment no longer depends on popularity with one or another of the village factions.'

Here we have the suggestion of two discrete levels of political activity by village teachers – as local agent for the Member of the Legislative Council and as the placeman of a village faction. But the question of articulation remains open.

Storrs, who was responsible for changing the system of appointment with the Elementary Education Law of 1929, explains why he did so and sheds further light on the potential for patron-client relations in the link between the Legislative Council and teachers (1939, p.522):

The method of appointing, transferring and dismissing teachers, male and female, by the Greek Members of Council was open to grave objections. The politicians too often exercised their power for political or petty personal aims. The teacher was usually the only educated man in the village; as a political agent he was therefore almost indispensable to the politicians who were exclusively town-dwellers. Being dependent upon the politicians for advancement in his profession he had to serve the political purposes of his masters ... In order that a Member of the Board might promote a friend, or vex an enemy, some unfortunate schoolmaster of Paphos would find himself transferred more than a hundred miles to the Karpass peninsula.

Nor can one suppose that Storrs was mainly animated by the

possibility of nationalist agitation by teachers, since he insists (p.521) he was against anglicisation of the curriculum, or diminishing the study of the Greek language and classical traditions. His reform, which transferred all responsibilities for appointment, promotion, transfer and salary to the Government, was greeted with 'a howl of discerning rage' by the politicians.

As with the issue of rural debt, we can see hints that the structure of legal powers linking the Legislative Council and village education allowed a fruitful situation for some form of patron-client relations to flourish, and that as with rural debt, this situation was modified by British administrative action. It is worth noting that after independence, in 1960, control of the Ministry of Education passed into Cypriot hands. I have heard a number of allegations involving the punitive transfer of teachers for their political beliefs, and again, it is widely believed that known leftists are unlikely to be employed as teachers in Greek schools. The Ministry was regarded as a nationalist stronghold during the tenure of Spyridakis in the 1960s, and this reflects the inevitable link between Hellenistic curricula and political nationalism discussed elsewhere.[5] But during the height of the attempts by Grivas and his supporters to undermine President Makarios, 1969-74, the President's supporters gained the upper hand in the Ministry. This could be seen when large numbers of civil servants signed statements of support – later published – for the President, a definite confusion of administration with politics, and it was also maintained that the supporters of Grivas in the Ministry were known and inevitably handicapped in their careers. Once again, as with the Cooperative movement, since independence branches of the civil service hold potential both for the formation of a few enduring patron-client relations, and more generally and diffusely, for the 'private' political alignments of individuals to affect their careers in public roles. In both cases, the small scale of the island must play an important part, since it is relatively easy for key individuals to gather information about the alleged alignments of individuals.[6] In a larger-scale society, this would probably require the relatively costly use of either state security services, or of private investigators.

Mukhtars

The office of *mukhtar* was yet another role in the administrative system which provided opportunities for skilful men to become patrons to their fellow villagers. The election of *mukhtars* annually was in operation when the British arrived on the scene (Dixon 1879). Their duties included the registration of births, deaths, and land transfers, the execution of various public health enactments, the lodging of visiting officials, and the reporting of crimes to the police. *Mukhtars* are, then (for they still exist in much the same roles) the arm of the government at the village level. Like African headmen, they face two ways, since while responsible in law for a number of activities, they are also locally-born members of the village community (*not* outsiders foisted on the village) and hence have social relations and obligations to their public, and are in certain ways subject to its social control.

Two qualities desirable in *mukhtars* were wealth and literacy. Wealth because they needed to be men of substance in order to offer hospitality to visiting government officials, and this the more so in days before good roads and motor cars made overnight stays in villages unnecessary; and also because poor men would not have had the time to spare from daily wage-labouring, to handle the *mukhtar*'s duties. Literacy was obviously desirable, to be able to read government circulars, fill in forms and so on.

From my own fieldwork and other sources it is clear that factions formed in villages over the office, and that it was undoubtedly a valued prize. In the same way that the British Government in the 1920s appears to have been trying to tighten administrative control over rural debt and education, so there appear to have been attempts to introduce an element of control in the choice of *mukhtars*. Orr (1918) described the system as one of simple election by villagers. But law 18 of 1923 set up a system in which villagers selected or elected a list of persons to represent them, and these were forwarded to the Mejlis Idaré (District Council) who would then select two names from this list; the elected Members of the Legislative Council would select another three. Finally, the Governor would pick one man from these five to be *mukhtar* and the other four would be his *azades*, advisors. This odd blend of local election, intermediate and executive selection was again modified after the 1931 uprising, since the Government decided that many *mukhtars* had been in effect subversive of colonial rule, and sought to change the system to one of direct appointment, which it remains at time of writing.[7]

During 1931 disturbances in fact occurred in some 209 of the 598 Greek or mixed villages in the island. In Kalo village, the man who was *mukhtar* at the time told me that he knew the names of those villagers who had cut the telegraph wire linking the capital to the local market town, but had refused to give them to the police. A village man who was prepared to give their names to the police was later made *mukhtar* by the Government, but villagers took reprisals against him by stealing his sheeps and harming his crops.

During fieldwork in Kalo there were many references to the previous Kalo *mukhtar*. It was said that he was a 'fine' man who 'helped many people'. He had 'friends all over Cyprus', he 'knew all the government officials, and went into their offices', and he 'brought' the electric light and other improvements to the village. He was also supposed to have found minor government jobs for a number of villagers. The extravagant way people spoke about him, and his known wealth make it likely that he was a local patron of some importance. From a few villagers could also be heard stories which showed him in a harsher light. His successor was never spoken about in strong terms, one way or another, was in no way distinguished, and was given little weight in village life. It is likely that only a 'big man' can turn the *mukhtar's* office into an important patronage position – it is not the case that the office itself inevitably brings much power. In several adjoining villages there were really powerful *mukhtars,* and they always turned out to have had key positions in EOKA, the nationalist guerilla organisation which in 1955-59 fought the British to obtain *Enosis* (Union with Greece). The appointment of *mukhtars* after 1960 was in the hands of the Minister of the Interior, the EOKA militant Yorgadjis, and he probably rewarded those former militants he trusted, and who in 1959-60 showed themselves loyal to Makarios rather than to Grivas in their attitude to the Treaty of Zurich and other issues. The advantage to the Interior Ministry of having loyal agents in every village who would report on activities of both right and left wings of the political spectrum need hardly be stressed. The issue of returning the office of *mukhtar* to village election is periodically aired in the Greek press, and the government usually states that it intends to do this when the intercommunal problems with the Turkish minority are settled, but that to do so before then would be to weaken 'national solidarity' among Greeks. While it is unlikely that all *mukhtars* are active on behalf of the government of the day, their role is an ambiguous one which in the current political climate in Cyprus inevitably lends itself to politicisation, and to the alleged exercise of state patronage. If a *mukhtar* refuses to assist a villager in documenting his claims to various benefits such as old age pensions and cheap medical care, or is punitive in assessing him for local taxes, or forwards his name to the Ministry as a politically unreliable person, then he brings this public office into the political arena.

The following case is cited to give something of the flavour of a powerful *mukhtar* in village politics. In Kalo village, the post of secretary of the Cooperative Credit Association became vacant because the elected village committee decided that the incumbent, Old Fanos, could no longer carry out his duties properly.[8] This made his children very angry; one of them was the client of the Commissioner of Cooperatives, who seemed unwilling to intervene on his behalf. One Kalotis however was godchild of Old Fanos, and when he heard of the family's difficulty he visited their house. His name was Katchios; he had for many years been regarded as a leftist. However he had a few years previously started to work regularly driving a heavy machine for Paschis, the *mukhtar* of a neighbouring village. This man had been an EOKA militant and had become very wealthy in the years since Independence. He had invited Yorgadjis to baptise one of his grandchildren, and the Interior Minister had accepted. At the very large celebrations Katchios was to be seen working as a helper in cooking and serving the food that his patron Paschis was providing.

Katchios now told Old Fanos that he would get his 'friend' Paschis to intervene in the case. They were drinking companions, and Katchios insisted that the *mukhtar* looked on him like a brother. I gently pointed out that the decision was in the domain of the Commissioner, Azinas. Katchios said 'Paschis will *eat* Azinas. He does what he likes. I'll bring him here tomorrow night, and then you'll see what sort of man he is' and much more in this vein, designed to show this *mukhtar* 'friend' as infinitely powerful, and Azinas as negligible beside him. In the event, the dispute was settled by other means. At its crudest the language of patronage is a language for talking about relative power.

Some illustrations

The Career of Pavlos.[9] Pavlos, son of a shepherd, is a truckdriver with a useful landholding in Kalo village. He was among a small number of young men in Kalo village who were EOKA militants; one of his closest comrades-in-arms, Levendis, was shot to death in obscure circumstances, in 1963, and it was widely believed in Kalo that his killer had been protected by the powerful Minister of the Interior, Yorgadjis. Pavlos had sought from this Minister a license to import a vehicle, but this had not been given him, and he felt that the Minister should have recognised the prior moral claim of a former fighter for Independence.

Another powerful EOKA militant, Nikos Sampson, had been hidden in Kalo village during the 1955-59 Emergency, and he now took up the cause of his dead friend (and client) Levendis, whose village friends and kin accordingly started to support Sampson in national politics. This was a complicated matter in some ways since during the first decade of Independence, Sampson's newspapers were so erratic in their political policies that they earned their owner the nickname of The Political Windmill. However, he managed to get Pavlos a vehicle import license, and the services of some EOKA militants who felt that the Makarios government had not repaid adequately their nationalist self-sacrifices. These men were disgruntled, but not to the extent of burning their bridges and joining the supporters of Grivas, the really intransigent critic of the Makarios group.

In 1969 there was a wave of minor attacks on police stations and government officials around the island, in the name of *Enosis* (Union with Greece); the literature of this underground attacked a number of Makarios' key supporters for alleged corruption or betrayal of the *Enosis* ideal. In a village near Kalo, a pro-government *mukhtar*, himself an ex-EOKA man, was given a public and rather close haircut by six masked and armed men. Later six men from Kalo were arrested and held for a few days for this attack, among them Pavlos. They were released without trial. By the cultural standards of Cyprus, this armed haircut was a relatively *mild* form of protest, for no-one was maimed, beaten or killed.

Pavlos was the key Sampson man in Kalo in the late 1960s and he became an active organiser for Sampson's party in the campaign which preceded the 1970 election. Sampson's party was successful in his own district, but not in the district where Kalotes voted.

In 1972 Pavlos received a minor government post, in his own village. It offered a secure salary, easy hours, light work, and some social status, since it was a white-collar job. Pavlos became strong in his praise of the man who headed his department, Andreas Azinas, who had been one target of pamphlet criticisms in the 1969 disturbances, and is widely held to be completely loyal to Makarios.

Pavlos represents the pure type of strictly defined or old-fashioned, *genuine* client. It could be said by cynics that his public ideology and his private pursuit of advantage remain in close harmony. But in his favour it needs stressing that he does not chop and change overnight, and he does get himself involved in the politics of militancy and crisis; if he is something of an opportunist, he also sticks his neck out. He is not simply a small-time petitioner for favours, but a public political man. He did start out by serving in EOKA, when he certainly didn't have to. He did support the champion of his dead comrade for more than seven years. If he has changed political masters more than once, then it must also be said that at the national level, these political masters have also played musical chairs with their coalitions and alliances; if this is the lesson they teach so well, then Pavlos hardly deserves special opprobrium for having learned it from them.

There are perhaps twenty men in the village with comparable histories, involving durable political links with powerful outsiders. What distinguishes them from other villagers is that their commitments are more long-term, they involve them in greater risks, and mark them out from their fellows as men with serious commitments to outsiders. They may be mistrusted and feared by their fellow villagers, who also may seek to take advantage of their connections.

One indicator that a Cypriot is a real client of a powerful patron is the way others speak of him. If they describe him as *anthropos tou Yorgadji* (Yorgadjis' man), or simply say *en tou Yorgadji* (he is 'of Yorgadjis', 'with Yorgadjis') this suggests a *total* commitment, almost as if the patron *possesses* the client, or the party *owns* the loyalty of the supporter; and patrons often speak of someone being *dhikos mou anthropos*, 'my man', although the same phrase in another context would mean 'my kinsman' *or* 'my friend'. Men do not use these phrases lightly although as with many other markers of patron-client relations, they can imperceptibly shade off into weaker forms of dependency relations, and the social or linguistic context must remain decisive. This is unsatisfactory if we seek a formula which will always distinguish stronger from weaker forms of institutionalised dependency, yet it is in the nature of social relations that they are prone to shadings, or spectrum effects (Finley 1973, p.67), and if this can be the case with legal statuses, themselves a matter of legitimate, public definition, how much more likely it is with less formal, interpersonal relations, and those of dubious propriety.

Here, in contrast to the case of Pavlos is a quite different kind of situation, but it connects with other themes in this paper. Gligoris is a farmer and tractor-driver married into Kalo twenty five years ago. He is politically a stable leftist, of long standing. His small daughter suffered serious spinal injury in an accident and he sought medical help. He went first to the General Hospital in Nicosia, because there he had a *koummara* (female co-godparent); she told him she had heard the doctors speaking English and that they would not be able to help the child, so he would have to take her abroad. He went to a leading Nicosia surgeon, who did some minor work, but said, yes, the child would have to go abroad. He then went with his friend Sklyros, a left-wing committee man in Kalo village, to see the General Secretary of the Communist trade union PEO, because he had heard that there was a scheme whereby there was free medical treatment to be had in East Germany. They were told that 150 people had just gone on this scheme, and while it was possible that more would be accepted, it depended on further negotiations between the Cyprus Government and the East Germans. It might take weeks, or months. Gligoris could not wait – the child needed urgent attention. He went to Athens where he contacted a woman who was a friend of a Kalo EOKA militant, and whose son made trips to stay in Kalo. She took him to the Ministry of Health in Athens, and helped him with the arrangements. He commented at this point 'How would I have known how to approach the Ministry of Health in Athens?'. The child stayed in the best hospital in Athens for months, and was cured, at no charge. This was partly because Gligoris had managed to get the appropriate form filled in by the Cypriot Archbishopric. He was legally entitled to this benefit, but, he pointed out, there might have been delays, or he might in any case have been refused his rights. He happened to know a man there, a monk who was related to a Kalo woman, the wife of a boyhood friend of Gligoris.

When the child was cured he took her to the shrine of the Virgin on a certain island, because his wife had promised the Virgin this pilgrimage if the child recovered.

In this case, we can see the use made of social relations between kin, co-villagers, friends, and other contacts of various kinds. We see an attempt to use the patronage of a left-wing organisation, which could have worked, and illustrates the network of advantages which a small country like Cyprus can create through keeping all its political options open (a concrete benefit of non-alignment). But Gligoris did not stop being a left-winger, simply because he could not get what he needed in a crisis. Nor did the help he received from his various other contacts turn him into their client, though it does put him under a general obligation to help them if need be. This kind of case is very common, but it is neither in any obvious sense 'corruption' nor 'patronage'. It simply shows that in situations where obtaining rights is uncertain, or the possibility of material help obscure and undefined, people will use personal contacts to give themselves a fighting chance. Of course, only by sitting inside the agencies which control valued assets would it be possible to relate precisely the written rules to actual outcomes, and this falls under the heading of 'utopian research'.

Space does not permit discussion of the many ramifications of patron-client relations in Cypriot life – the special role of an elected President who is also the elected Archbishop, who is *also* the traditional political representative (*ethnarch*) of all Greek Cypriots; nor enlargement on the uses to which *koumparía* (wedding and baptismal sponsorship, similar to *compadrazgo*) are put by Cypriot politicians, although it is suggestive enough to point out that several national politicians had taken the trouble to baptise children in Kalo village, and the fathers of these children tended to be their ardent supporters. When Independence started EOKA became briefly an informal duplicate government, and enabled patron-client relations, as well as weaker exchanges, to take place. But there is space to conclude with one other brief case-history.

Kammari village, next door to Kalo, had for some years been in dispute with the Water Department over its right to deepen a bore-hole in a particular place. One problem appeared to be that this act was illegal without a permit; another seemed to be that two wealthy men had land nearby and feared that they would lose *their* water supply. Also, a relative of the President had recently obtained a bore-hole permit nearby. The villagers continually discussed the partiality of Government in this matter. However, one of their number was a minor official at the Archbishopric, and seeing the potential for presidential unpopularity in the issue arranged for the Irrigation Committee of this village to visit the President. Several village notables not on this committee also went. The Irrigation Committee stated their case to the President – the bore-hole was traditionally on their land, they were farmers and completely dependent on this water, and they had heard that outsiders with powerful interests were opposing them. They named these men stressing that they were not farmers. The President listened sympathetically, but said, what am I to tell these outsiders? The villagers hoped the President would help them. He said he would do what he could. Later a Water Department official told me the villagers had no legal case, and that their position was 'a put-up job'.

Later, they decided to go and see the Minister of the Interior, Yorgadjis. This initiative seems to have come from Sostis a former EOKA militant from a mountain village who had (it was said) saved the life of the Minister when he was on the run in the mountains. He was now a teacher in Kammari village, and married to a local girl. His very posting to the village may well have been due to an administrative favour. He was in any case concerned to be of help. The committee was granted an audience with the Minister, and I attended. Once again there was a close personal link to the Minister, in that one villager on the Irrigation Committee had a son who was a policeman in the Minister's body-guard. Technically, the Minister is the man with authority in the case, and the visit to the President ten days previously was going over his head.

The committee spokesman in an indirect way mentioned the outsiders and their interests in the case. Yorgadjis seemed not to be well informed, and called the District Commissioner on the 'phone. He first spoke about several other bits of business, then said, 'I'm interested, by the way, in the Kammari case; what's it all about?' He listened to the ensuing explanation, but of course the Committee could not hear it.

Later in the meeting Yorgadjis asked the Committee 'Why didn't you come to me directly?' and he seemed quite piqued. At this point, the teacher Sostis, the EOKA militant who was his client, declared with some emotion:

I simply must say this: You know me and my opinion of you. In Kammari village everyone was getting angry. They were speaking loudly against you. Now I am an outsider in that village so you can see that I say this without any question of the need to support my own village, but I have to tell you that they had some right on their side. Now you are my *mastros* (boss/leader), mine and everyone else's. [Here Yorgadjis broke in to say that he was not his or their *mastros*, but the teacher continued] And so I said to them that we must take the matter to you. They were ready to have a demonstration with placards. I told them, no, we must go to you and you would set it right.

After this meeting, another member of the Committee, an educated secondary school teacher, Vourros, complained to me that the primary teacher Sostis had spoken 'like a simple villager' and that this was not the way citizens should speak to a civil servant; they should not praise him personally, but get into a frame of mind to seek their rights. However, the same man had stayed behind after the meeting to press the Minister to provide compensation to an employee whose son had died in an accident during national service. And although he could speak the language of 'modernity' and citizenship, his outward behaviour often contradicted or modified these principles. Like everyone else, he knew the Minister was very powerful and dangerous, and feared him.

It is worth noting that the client Sostis presented himself as a complete outsider to Kammari village, even though he has close affinal connections there and is virtually a permanent resident. Also his speech is a mixture of two messages. Partly, it 'warns' the Minister of serious grass-roots discontent in Kammari village and shows the speaker as loyal to the Minister; partly it presents the speaker to the villagers as a man determined to help them to avoid a dangerous confrontation with state power by using mediation, and supplication to the Minister, portrayed in this speech as a man who would find the just solution (i.e., one helpful to the village). The statement 'you know me and what I think of you' in this context simply meant 'you know how much I admire you and how loyal I am to you'; it was also a way of stressing to the Committee men his *intimacy* with the powerful Minister, and thus obviously his own importance. For Ministers do not normally *know* ordinary villagers. This visit to the Minister did not bring success, and in the relevant election two years later this village had a very high vote which did not go to the Minister's party.

Politics and anti-politics

There were political ideas in the world before the French Revolution, but once that event had given expression to ideas of popular sovereignty, with an accompanying franchise, then peasant politics were destined to become 'politics in a new key', a politics of ideas as well as interests (Kedourie 1960, p. 18; Hobsbawm 1974, p. 5). By 1925, to set an arbitrary date, European communism had joined Greek nationalism in Cypriot villages, as ideas which encouraged men to oppose and reject each other, whole classes and ethnic groups in a more total and intransigent way than anything had done in the Ottoman period.

Recent history in Cyprus has been one of continual political ferment. 1920-30: national parties contested elections; 1931-43: nationalist rebellion, parties suspended, colonial rule by decree; 1943-54: municipal elections, violent left/right antagonism, constitutional bargaining; 1955-9: nationalist armed struggle against British rule, leftists and Turks not participating, major Greek/Turkish violence; 1960-3: Independence, intercommunal deadlock, then fighting; 1964-7: sporadic intercommunal fighting; five years' negotiations; fascist coup by mainland Greek officers against Makarios, Turkish invasion. Throughout this period the political interests of the USA, USSR, UK, Greece, Turkey and NATO have directly affected Cyprus. At various times in the last fifty years, the left, the right and the centre, the British, the Greeks and the Turks have been on top, only to be brought down by events. The point is clear – political alignments lead to denial of benefits, imprisonment, torture, invasions, refugee camps, death.

During the same period the villagers experienced in economic matters a fairly impressive improvement of their material conditions. (until 1974). This can be appreciated by a brief sketch of how social structure changed. The villagers were always a class in relation to the government and urban bourgoisie, in that their surplus produce was exchanged on terms they could rarely control. But the internal structure of the village was complex. In 1931 only 21 out of 169 families – roughly 12% – were landless, while a handful of families were moneylenders and regular employers of labour.[10] At the extremes then, a class structure existed. But between these extremes something akin to a ranking system operated, since virtually everyone owned land and worked with his hands. There was no landlord or latifundist class, no leisured aristocrats, no literate elite. The land-rich peasant was prepared to take a man with little land as son-in-law, and the notion of social honour as the key to a family's local prestige is important. Although the villagers were affected by the politics and economics of the island, and beyond, their dominant concerns and interests were local – local land, local honour and local marriage partners.

The last fifty years altered the structure of the village in a way which involves more men in relations with outsiders, and sharpens the distinctions of wealth, political power and status which exist,[11] so that a class structure is emerging. But the village continues to be the main arena for prestige competition, so that there is a tension between the continuation of the village as a moral community, and the increased dependence on outside decisions, and non-local economic forces. One expression of this tension (some would call it a contradiction) is in the village ideology of anti-politics. This does not refer to the fact that perhaps between 25 and 50 of the 750 voters were politically active and committed in 1970, or that many men described themselves as 'neutral' or 'independent' in politics, or ready to vote 'wherever my self-interest lies'.

It means rather that in many small ways they sought to restrict the scope of modern politics in village social relations, and their lives generally: for example, they defined the functions of village administrative committees as 'out of politics'; they expressed normative rules enjoining men of opposed political beliefs to remain calm and civil with each other; they insisted that kinship was too important for kin to let politics ever divide them; and they frequently exhorted each other 'not to get mixed up with the parties'. Finally, they tended to describe political activists as 'fanatics', while suggesting a degree of irrationality in their conduct. The growth of party politics coincided (until 1974) with economic development, but the villagers rarely connect this with the political system, the vote, or mass parties.

In this volume Sydel Silverman explains aspects of a 'myth of patronage'. In a very general way the Kalo villagers' anti-political ideas are understandable in light of the recent political history of the island just mentioned. But how do the particular institutional changes of the last fifteen years articulate with this history, in the context of the village?

Before answering this question it is worth mentioning studies from Italy. In their earlier writings, Sydel Silverman (1965, p.187) and Weingrod (1967-8) suggested that changes in the growth of the Italian state's agencies, party politics, and certain social structural changes have given the rural citizen what boils down to greater choice, or more freedom of action. 'The junctures can no longer be guarded by any group' wrote Silverman, and mentions 'direct participation' by individuals in the national system, 'alternate links' and the like. In a similar vein, Weingrod adds that no single figure has recently dominated the politics of Surughu. 'Rather than a single line of authority, there now exist multiple links and competing systems' (p.397). Previously, he points out, a local boss and a grand patron were the key figures. Davis (1970, p. 77) has certain suggestions which make similar points for a South Italian town.[12]

It would be idle to deny that peasants in Italy and Cyprus have often become materially better off – they live longer, eat better, and so forth. The problem is that in Cyprus the notion of more links, alternative systems, and the functional specificity of bureaucracy leave something essential out of the picture. It is right to stress the demise of a specific patron class where this occurs. It is the nature of the new dependency which is the problem. The writers on Italy all show that the modern state requires more and different transactions compared with those it required of the nineteenth century citizen. The villager now needs and has grown used to certain new goods; but he is also required to enter into new relations, as will be clear in a moment. It would only be helpful to say that he now had more choice if what he once needed and now needs were the same, but now he had extra ways to get what he wanted. He now in fact needs a host of *new* things, has other *new* things demanded of him, so his area of dependency on external decisions has increased, in some senses. If there are more ways of doing things, then there are more things that have to be done. The suggested increase in rural autonomy is at best debatable; it will take further research to settle the issue. To give a hint of the argument, here is a brief list of goods and services which suggest the qualitative extension of rural dependency:

Heavy machines: second-hand trucks, cars, tractors, bulldozers require special import licences, and major cash outlays, often through bank loans. Bus and taxi operators require special passenger franchise licences. Loans and licences can be obtained through connections.

Military service lasts two years, but some students can get one year's exemption. If the boy is posted to a distant camp and rarely gets leave, his labour is lost to his family. Sons of leftists may be punished by the mainland Greek Army officers by heavy duties or remote postings; sons of 'friends' or right-wingers can be helped.

Legal proceedings: in a number of cases of the illegal use of firearms, vehicle offences, beatings, and indecent assault, police were persuaded to lighten or drop specific charges.

Scholarships to Greece were given to children of good 'nationalist' families, either in the centre faction or more right-wing factions; these were not available to leftist families, who sometimes however got scholarships to Eastern European Communist countries. Scholarships to the USA would probably have been vetted from political information obtained from the Ministry of the Interior, since police reported regularly on leftists.

Civil Service promotion was sometimes helped or hindered by relations with relevant superiors. Some civil servants have been sent for special training to the USA, probably as a reward for anti-left activities and for political training. Some extreme rightists have been blocked for promotion or sent to remote parts of the island, which hurts them socially and economically.

Permits to sink boreholes, to plant certain crops (citrus), to transfer land (particularly for building plots), could depend on political alignments to powerful persons.

There is no space to discuss the implications of compulsory education, and the great increase in regulatory laws which control the villager's behaviour and bring him into contact with civil service officials.

The situation is not of one (or several) top-to-bottom integrated patronage systems, or party machines; and all sorts of things can be obtained for personal rather than political reasons. But different sections of Cypriot society tend to be dominated by different political groups. Education and the police tend to be held by right-wing nationalists; the government information services by moderates and progressives; the unions and cooperatives by leftists (but with rightist counterparts); the National Guard was officered by pro-Junta fascist officers from mainland Greece, and so on. There are various *foci* of power in Cypriot society, and in some senses this means competition for followers; but very often it simply means that in some sectors patrons of a particular political standing are powerless. A leftist politician cannot usually challenge a decision inside the Ministry of Education, or the National Guard; and a known rightist will not get much help from socialist patronage channels.

True, patrons sometimes hope to win over the discontented clients of opposed patrons; but this is probably rare and costly, and for the client in the nature of an irrevocable choice, rather than a continuous option. A decision to go to university in a Communist country will either make or break a man for life, in all probability, because with the wrong men in power, his degree may be seriously devalued. This reduces the meaning of choices between alternatives – for many people the choice is once-and-for-all.

It is now possible to understand better the philosophy of anti-politics in Kalo village. To obtain concrete benefits from a political party or patron involves setting outsiders (and their values) higher than local social relations. If mediation is a local virtue, then intransigence in national politics is an obvious vice. Political commitment – whatever the motives of the villager – is a high-risk activity which is most uncertain in its delivery of tangible benefits. Is it worth the risk? Does it matter if others label one an 'ideologist' (the Greek word also means 'idealist') or a 'fanatic'?

The danger is that political leaders outside the village may ask an activist to do certain things which are locally defined as reprehensible, and will lose a man his good name; things like passing information on the movements and loyalties of co-villagers, starting up political clubs in the village, propagandising and much else.

One problem about an analysis in terms of patron-client relations is that it is so easy to slip unwittingly into a cynical posture, to treat most exchanges as based on a tit-for-tat instrumentality, to ignore the man who is committed to a party or a creed, or to conclude that if a man who sticks to his party through thick and thin (in Cyprus there has been a great deal of 'thin') finally receives a reward for loyalty, then this casts suspicious light on his original motives. Yet logically, there is no contradiction between being loyal, and being rewarded for loyalty. Simply, most analytic schemes are so far inadequate to handle such issues.

The value in keeping patron-client relations analytically distinct from other weaker exchange relations is that the former are of major structural importance. They are one reason why some men participate in extraordinary political acts like conducting coups or revolutions (of course there are many other reasons). Prior to modern politics, villagers were exploited by the state, but in many respects left alone by it, to survive as best they could, in a kind of subsistence political economy, and many of the things they wanted were within local control, though far from freely available. More recently, the growth of state and party have been accompanied by new external dependencies. Strangers in Nicosia, Athens, Ankara, Washington or Moscow make decisions which directly impinge on village relations, and if these decisions are based on the political alignments of individual villagers, they can prove very costly. In July 1975 the villagers of Kalo were refugees; what they had acquired from personal hard work had been lost when politics, in the shape of the Turkish invasion force, drove them from their village.

NOTES

1.   The fieldwork which led to this paper was generously financed by the UK SSRC and the Nuffield Foundation. In July 1975 the people of Kalo (a pseudonym) were refugees, so this paper is written in the ethnographic present with a vengeance. For more details, see Loizos (1976).
2.   The approach taken here to patron-client relations closely follows some notes written by Gellner, and circulated to participants in the Rome conference. It owes a good deal to Campbell (1964), Silverman (1965) and Weingrod (1967-8), but where the first two writers speak of 'patronage' I follow Weingrod and use this term to mean something different from patron-client relations.
3.   In this volume Michael Attalides writes on similar themes, for a quite different region of Cyprus. In my fieldwork nothing was discovered as specific and concrete as his two brokerage factions, although other sorts of factions existed. But the Kalo area at this period was probably more subsistence-oriented, less involved in market production. Attalides' remarks on the colonial government and its alliance with the

peasantry have been particularly helpful to me, and I have greatly benefited from discussions with him and from reading his material.
4. Loizos (1975), pp. 150-75, 210-34.
5. Loizos (1974).
6. Benedict (1967) has a valuable discussion of small scale and its political implications.
7. Shenis (1962).
8. Loizos (1975), pp. 166-75, has other information on this incident.
9. Other information on Pavlos in village politics is in Loizos (1975), pp. 235-88.
10. But the figures in Loizos (1975), p.307, contain two errors: in 1931 there were 37 (not 27) households with obviously inadequate land holdings, i.e. reported as under 5 *donums*; that is roughly 22% (not 15%) of 169. See Cyprus 1931.
11. Loizos (1975).
12. A similar sort of hint appears in Paine (1971), p.105.

REFERENCES

Asad, T. (1972) 'Market model, class structure and consent: a reconsideration of Swat political organisation', *Man* 7, no. 1, 74-94.
Benedict, B. (ed.) (1967) *Problems of smaller territories*. London.
Boissevain, J. (1965) *Saints and Fireworks: Religion and Politics in Rural Malta*. London.
Campbell, J.K. (1964) *Honour, Family and Patronage*. Oxford.
Cyprus (1931) *Report and General Abstracts of the Census*, Nicosia: Government Printing Office.
Davis, J. (1970) 'Honour and politics in Pisticci', *Proceedings of the Royal Anthropological Institute* 1969, 69-81.
Dixon, W.H. (1879) *British Cyprus*. London.
Finley, M.I. (1973) *The Ancient Economy*. London.
Hill, G. (1952) *A History of Cyprus*, vol.IV. London.
Hobsbawm, E.J. (1973) 'Peasants and politics', *Journal of Peasant Studies* 1, no. 1, October, 3-22.
Jenness, D. (1962) *The Economics of Cyprus: a survey to 1914*. Montreal.
Kedourie, E. (1960) *Nationalism*. London.
Loizos, P. (1974) 'The progress of Greek nationalism in Cyprus, 1878-1970', in Davis, J. (ed.), *Choice and Change: essays in Honour of Lucy Mair* (London School of Economics Monographs on Social Anthropology, no.50), London.
Loizos, P. (1976) 'Notes on future anthropological research in Cyprus', *Transactions of the New York Academy of Sciences*.
Loizos, P. (1975) *The Greek Gift: Politics in a Cypriot Village*. Oxford.
Newham, F.D. (1905) *The System of Education in Cyprus* (Board of Education Special Reports, no.12).
Orr, C.W.J. (1918) *Cyprus under British rule*. London.
Paine, R. (ed.) (1971) *Patrons and Brokers in the East Arctic* (Newfoundland Social and Economic Papers no.2; Institute of Social and Economic Research) Memorial University of Newfoundland.
Peters, E. (1968) 'The tied and the free: an account of a type of patron-client relation among the Bedouin Pastoralists of Cyrenaica', in J.G. Peristiany (ed.), *Contributions to Mediterranean Sociology*, Paris, The Hague.
Powell, J.D. (1970) 'Peasant society and clientelist politics', *American Political Science Review* vol. 64, pp. 411-25.
Shenis, J. (1962) *Provincial and local administration in Cyprus in comparative and historical perspective* [PhD thesis, New York University].

Silverman, S.F. (1965) 'Patronage and community-nation relationships in Central Italy', *Ethnology* 4, no. 2, 172-89.

Storrs, R. (1939) *Orientations*. London.

Surridge, B.J. (1930) *A Survey of Rural Life in Cyprus*. Nicosia.

Weingrod, A. (1967-8) 'Patrons, patronage and political parties', *Comparative Studies in Society and History* 10 (July), 376-400.

Michael Attalides

Forms of peasant incorporation in Cyprus during the last century[1]

Social scientists who have studied Mediterranean societies have generally emphasised the predominance of patronage, brokerage, non-corporate groups, and generally free-floating particularisms. The idea that this is the dominant fact about such societies has been reinforced by intensive study of face to face relations in village communities. There is a tendency in what has been called the 'village outward' view (Fox, n.d.) of peasant communities to see them in terms of relations linking individual villagers to urban centres through patron-client ties.

It seems theoretically possible that individual linkages are a historically specific type of interrelation between peasant communities and urban centres, or at least may predominate at a certain phase of development. It is argued here that peasants may be seen in a wider perspective: as well as being part of the village, a vertical segment of a region or a state society, peasants are also members of horizontal segments, such as classes (see Steward et al. 1956). Class linkage is not a conceptual alternative to 'non-corporate' linkages (Schneider et al. 1972), but rather the two are interacting principles of social organisation.

Wolf (1966) has broken down into logical components the possibilities for different kinds of peasant coalitions, but here the chief concern is with the broad distinction between two kinds of coalition which are termed horizontal and vertical. Horizontal coalition may be on the basis of class interests, as for example the producers of a certain crop as against the merchants. By contrast, vertical coalitions have to do with the defence of individual or family interests through relationships across class lines. Vertical coalitions such as patron-client ties are not just characterised by being particularistic or informal, but also by linking people individually across class lines, and providing at certain times a means of control of rural populations by urban merchant and professional elites. Competition between such elites may result in village-based factions of their clients (Powell 1970). To the extent that such factionalisation takes place, organisation of peasants on a class basis is impeded (Mouzelis and Attalides 1971).

This paper attempts to outline the conditions which favoured the relative degree of predominance of vertical as against horizontal coalitions during three phases of social development in the Karpasia region of Cyprus. These conditions have to do with credit supplies, forms of marketing and idioms of political appeal to village populations. Field work was conducted during some months of 1973 and 1974, mainly in the administrative centre of the region, Yialousa, and is here supplemented by historical sources. During the first phase, the development of a well articulated brokerage network is described, in which the supply of credit, marketing outlets and political control coincided. This network linked peasant producers in vertical coalitions to urban political factions composed of merchants and professionals. The idiom for the relationship was one of 'friendship'. The second phase involved a challenge to this form of social organisation both by the British colonial government (with whom the merchant and professional group was in conflict) and by peasants on a class basis. This resulted in the increasing separation of credit and marketing relationships from the political control of the brokerage network, and opened the way for increasingly ideological appeals. In the last phase the situation was complicated not only by the coexistence of both vertical and horizontal forms of coalition, but also of nationalist appeals deriving from conflicts over the island's international orientation. Patron-client ties reminiscent of the period of unchallenged brokerage co-existed with ideological appeals from right-wing nationalist and left-wing parties, each claiming to represent the interests of the producers. The resulting structure allowed the peasants to be manipulated easily, since they could never be certain about the results of supporting one national grouping rather than another.

1. The development of vertical coalition

Even before the British occupation of Cyprus in 1878, villagers were tied to competing groups of merchant intermediaries through the loan of money both for subsistence needs in bad years, and also for the necessity of paying various taxes.

The base line of 'undisturbed' or 'corporate'[2] villages recedes into the depths of history for Cyprus. The preconditions for the type of incorporation that existed in the late Ottoman Empire are an insecure and corrupt state authority; great scarcity of credit, combined with high demand for agricultural products; and attempts to extract the maximum taxation. The Ottoman governor of Cyprus vied with the Greek Orthodox Church as the predominant authority on the island and in representation of the island to the Sultan. The very extension of representative powers to the Church was motivated by the desire of the government in Constantinople to have a check on a potentially disloyal or even rebellious governor in a relatively distant province

(Luke 1921). Part of the power granted to the Church consisted in the allocation and collection of taxes. Until 1821, the Archbishop, aided by the Bishops assessed each village's share of the tax and sent out clerks to collect the money. Clerks sometimes diverted this money to their own purses and with this capital entered the grain and wine trade (Jenness 1962).

At the same time European merchant ships competed for a share of the island's agricultural produce and to further their chances in competition, European governments set up consulates in Larnaca, the chief port of Cyprus at that time. These helped channel Cyprus products towards their own shores and protected their nationals (Jenness 1962, pp. 59-60). The consulates were privileged with extraterritorial rights which they could also extend to their employees. Agents, interpreters and middle-men attached themselves to each consulate, aiding the consuls in their manner of trade. This consisted of lending money to peasants at high interest rates and being repaid in silk, wine, cotton or wheat, estimated at the buyer's own price (ibid., p.61). The position of the traders was unchallengeable due to the fact that until 1864 there were no banking facilities in Cyprus at all. For credit facilities one had to have access to Smyrna, Constantinople or Beirut.

After 1821, when under the impact of the Greek War of Independence the scales in Cyprus weighed definitely in favour of the Ottoman governor, the privilege of taxation was removed from the Church and the autonomy of villages was further broken down, as from this time taxation was extracted through tax farmers. Essentially, the tax farmer came to an agreement with the government to pay a certain amount, and in return was empowered to collect all he could from the population in his jurisdiction (Jenness 1962, pp. 102-3).

In a way that has been described, partly through corruption and partly through trade, a small merchant class had developed by 1878, the time of the British occupation. Naturally these were the first people the new administration made contact with, to the exclusion of the Orthodox Church which, presumably for reasons of Western secularism, the new regime did not accept as a representative of the Christian population (Hill 1952). The merchants, mainly centred in Nicosia, the capital, had previously influenced the Archbishopric and with their new British contacts became even more important. They were soon used in the administration and one of the most prominent was made mayor of the capital. In an advisory capacity they came to control the appointments of teachers, native civil servants and *mukhtars* (Katalanos 1914). They clearly derived some benefits from the British presence.

Before twenty years had passed however, the British authorities had created preconditions for a challenge to this group through the indirect consequences of their reforms, particularly of transport. By

1881 a carriage road was built into Karpasia, previously only accessible by camel. A Legislative Council was established and new judicial institutions which created novel career opportunities. Sons of wealthy peasants and merchants and individuals sponsored by the Church studied law and medicine in Greece and other European countries. By the beginning of the twentieth century a group of young professionals was ready to challenge the power of the 'old clique' (Katalanos 1914). The ideology of the challenge was nationalism. Not unnaturally the 'clique' adopted a compromising attitude on opposition to the colonial government. They argued that raising the issue of union with Greece (*Enosis*) would disrupt the chances of deriving further advantages from the British administration. The conflict was fought out over the next decade through the election of a new Archbishop, and in the process both groups attempted to establish a popular base over the whole island, so that after 1900 island-wise parties came into existence for the first time (*ibid.*).

In Karpasia these parties were coterminous with two chains of merchant brokerage. Almost until the Second World War, and long after the original issues were eclipsed, factions were named after the two candidate Bishops for the Archbishop's seat: The *Kiriniaki* and the *Kitiaki*. There were two competing merchant houses in the region. One, based in a village in the west of the area, Tricomo, supported the *Kiriniaki* or establishment party. The other merchant house, with its headquarters in Komi Kebir, supported the *Kitiaki*, the uncompromising nationalists. In each village of the region there were representatives of each house and the two networks were firmly established. Political relations were hardly distinguished from economic ones, although over time the issue of nationalist commitment no longer separated the two factions, uncompromising nationalism being common to virtually the whole merchant and professional class.

A clear hierarchical relationship of dependence existed, with brokers (*mesites*) in each village. Literacy was important in becoming a broker; many of them were or had been teachers. It also helped to have a larger landholding than ordinary peasants. The two merchant houses advanced credit to their respective brokers, who advanced it in turn to farmers and thus put them in their debt. On occasions when a broker bought on his own account rather than on account of his usual merchant, he was unable to dispose of the merchandise since both merchant houses refused to buy from him.

Brokers actively sought out new suppliers, attempting to put them in their debt in order to increase the amount of merchandise which they collected. In fact brokers went to fairs and 'cried' the availability of loans. Often these loans were given without any written agreement. If a borrower was unknown to the broker, it was frequently sufficient for a fellow villager who was known to the broker to vouch for him. Products that were sold through the brokerage network were carobs, silk, cotton and tobacco, all in demand for export. Other products which had a local demand, such as wheat, olives, olive oil and animals were sold at fairs or by the brokers on their own account. Each part of the broker's business reinforced every other part, so once established they tended increasingly to accumulate wealth and many were shop keepers or innkeepers as well as being merchants and money-lenders on their own account. Eventually they would become large landowners.

The generalised power which such people acquired over ordinary villagers is related to the nature of the transactions which they entered into. It has already been pointed out that money was frequently lent on the basis of 'word of honour'. In general the idiom of the relationship had to be one of friendship, as the frequently illiterate peasant was virtually at the mercy of the broker. Not only did he depend on him for his annual credit and sales, but also for keeping an account of these transactions. If, for example, at a certain time of the year the client needed some cash in order to pay taxes which had become due, he would go to the broker who would give him that sum. The same might happen in the case of an extraordinary expense or emergency. When his product was collected the peasant would take it to the broker who would credit him for it. It was only through exhibitions of friendship and if possible with bonds of fictive kinship that the client could hope to limit the broker's rapacity. The addition of an extra nought to the amount lent and entered into the broker's accounts, omitting to note a repayment, and the underweighing of produce,[3] were regarded as fairly normal business practices. The condition of indebtedness even resulted on occasion in sexual exploitation of the debtor's womenfolk.

It is not implied that all such relationships were fraudulent. In fact the bonds they resulted in might often be true exceptions to self-seeking relationships. But this was all the more reason why friendship towards powerful individuals (from whom benefits or merely the withholding of exploitation might be expected in return) should become a psychologically powerful part of the culture.

In this context, political alignment was part of the relationship of friendship and dependence. Generally people simply voted for whomever the broker they dealt with told them to vote for. Brokers related that they wrote on a piece of paper the people their clients should vote for so that they would not forget on the way to the polls. So the issues of the elections were likely to be of little significance, and any 'floating voters' were more likely to be attracted by the rival feasts which the candidates organised before elections than by their promises to bring wheat to the area, which was in chronic shortage, to have a bridge built, or to bring about *Enosis*.

The merchant and broker network was reinforced by its overlap with the government administrative system. This was partly because the necessary qualifications were similar, that is literacy and a chain of contacts which would secure appointment. One of the prominent brokers of the pre-war period started his career as a tithe collector, and was at the same time a government road-building foreman. He was able to get these jobs for the same kinds of reasons as those which enabled him subsequently to become a broker. His father had himself been an overseer in government road-building, had been financially able to send his son to school, and had made contacts which helped in his son's appointment. The produce of the tithe was collected at two points on the coast, and there auctioned to the same two merchant houses of Komi Kebir and Tricomo. The system was not necessarily corrupt.[4] However, small favours cannot have been unknown, to judge from the number of officials checking on each other.[5]

The *mukhtars*, the lowest level of administrative officials, also had to be literate, and sometimes were themselves teachers or brokers. At the beginning of the century they were, according to a contemporary description, virtually absolute rulers of a village. They were given extensive powers by a law to limit the carrying of arms, which it is plausibly claimed they used not only in genuine cases, but also against innocents ' ... whenever they disapproved of the conduct of their *mukhtar* or the powerful of the day, from whom the position of *mukhtar* depended' (Katalanos 1914, p.125). A simple statement from the *mukhtar* to a policeman was sufficient for a court order to be made prohibiting someone from carrying arms. He was then known as a *kakourgos* (criminal) and was subject to close supervision by the *mukhtar* (ibid., p.126). Even in later years the *mukhtar* was held in awe. The *mukhtar* of Yialousa between 1941 and 1955 was described as being dominating and was reputed to have such influence in government circles that 'he could save a man from the gallows'. He had been a teacher, was one of the largest landowners of the village and one of the brokers of the Komi Kebir merchant house.

Through a series of individual vertical coalitions, the pre-war brokerage system provided the urban and rural merchant class with an extremely tight control over the peasant producer. The market system was regional in the sense that the relationships between the national merchant/professional factions and the colonial government, on the one hand, and individual villages and peasants on the other, was mediated by two regionally oriented merchant houses. But these houses were not interested in engaging in a 'struggle for domain' (Schneider et al. 1972) for the region, since they were in turn dependent on nationally operating merchants for credit and outlets for regional merchandise. The national factional conflict cut across class lines, since it aligned producers and merchants of one faction against producers and merchants of another, and peasants pursued their economic interests through individual relations with brokers and through them to national factions. The merchants and brokers had more interest in maintaining this structure than the peasants since the competition between the factions in no way improved the bargaining power of the peasant,[6] who was stably tied to one or another faction, and where there were sanctions against brokers raising the price in order to go into trade on their own account. The stability of the system was largely maintained because two national factions monopolised credit and channelled it down to the peasant in a system that also ensured political control.

Competition for peasant allegiance and horizontal coalition

The form of peasant incorporation that is described by the brokerage networks was increasingly weakened by the social changes involved in two conflicts on the national level. One was a conflict between the merchant and professional group and the colonial government. The other was the conflict between this group and the Communist Party of Cyprus, known after 1945 as AKEL. These two conflicts had lasting effects on the form of peasant incorporation. On the one hand they resulted in the elimination of the brokerage network's credit monopoly which thus weakened the patronage relationship between broker and peasant. In the long run they also resulted in the elimination of the merchants' monopoly of marketing agricultural products. The breakdown of these personally mediated links opened the way for increasingly ideological appeals to the peasant population.

The merchants and professionals who sat in the colonial Legislative Council came into conflict with the government over the financial relationship between the colony and the metropolis, and over demands for the expansion of their constitutional powers. Increasingly they rejected the legitimacy of British colonial government and advocated the union of Cyprus with Greece. Since the Legislative Council was severely limited in its powers, the Orthodox Church became an important agency for the pursuit of the nationalist conflict with the British administration.

The British colonial government, faced with these agitators in the Legislative Council, turned to the peasants whom they thought to be more interested in bread-and-butter issues and less interested in 'politics'.[7] On his arrival as Governor of Cyprus in 1926, Storrs notes that the Greek members of the Legislative Council were eight advocates, of whom three were money-lenders, one a landowner who was also a money-lender, one a Bishop, one a merchant and one a farmer. By 1929 the opposition he was experiencing in the Council, partly due to the fiscal changes of 1926 (see p.144), was such that he suggested to the Colonial Office in London several changes in the constitution of the colony: that three quarters of the Legislative Council should by law be engaged in agriculture; that money-lenders should be ineligible; and that the elected members should be in a minority, with a majority of elected members (Storrs 1943). These proposals were not adopted but they do emphasise local colonial preference for peasant interests against those of the Cypriot elite.

Credit for the indebted peasants had become an issue as early as

1904, when the Government approved the efforts of the Commissioner of Paphos district to promote village credit cooperative societies. In 1914 the government legislated the possibility that villages or groups of villages could organise such societies. There was little actual progress until a government-financed agricultural bank was established in 1925 to provide credit for them. Their eventual success must be linked to the government's eagerness to break the power of the brokerage networks. Between 1925 and 1929 the number of village societies increased from twenty-nine to four hundred and twenty-two (Surridge 1930). Government officials ensured that they actually worked.

In Yialousa a credit society was established in 1923 by a landowner, broker and *dikolavos* (a broker in the transaction of legal or government business). He was one of the brokers who had been boycotted by the merchant houses when he attempted to go into the carob trade on his own account, and according to his son's report had resorted to setting up the cooperative in order to find himself a source of credit independent of the merchant houses. Four or five years later he was ousted as secretary of the society by another of the prominent brokers. The very people whom the cooperative societies were designed to displace could initially gain control of them since both the secretary and committee of each one were elected by village members of the society who were often indebted to local brokers. But before the 1939-45 war the colonial government acted to provide more central control, so that appointees to the secretaryships of credit societies would then have to be confirmed by a government-appointed Commissioner of Cooperative Development. The first Commissioner appointed was Surridge, the government official who had surveyed the extent and consequences of peasant indebtedness in 1928.[8] What the change meant is indicated by the letter which he wrote to the broker who was secretary of the Yialousa society in which he pointed out that 'no man may serve two masters'. The successor, confirmed in office by the Commissioner, was a leftist schoolteacher who had had experience in cooperative management in one of the towns. Up to this time the cooperative had been 'in a latent state' according to village accounts.

In addition to credit cooperatives, in 1940 the colonial government initiated rural debtors' courts which discounted farmers' debts by up to thirty per cent. Brokers and money-lenders lost substantial sums of money and some went out of business. The two merchant houses were not substantially hit since their creditors were mainly brokers and not farmers, and they were thus eligible for full repayment of loans.

In 1926, the colonial government had largely shifted the burden of taxation from peasants paying through tithes, to merchants, in the form of import and export duties (Jenness 1962, p. 32). In 1931 the depression hit government revenues, but the Legislative Council refused to approve a further increase in customs duties, and the raising of duties was achieved by the government by an extra-legislative process. This was the immediate cause for widespread disturbances on the island, which involved the burning down of the Governor's residence, and rioting in about a third of all villages in Cyprus (Storrs 1943, p.505). Even though the peasants had been the major beneficiaries from the change in taxation, they followed the leadership of the National Organisation, formed by the Church, merchants and professionals, in assaulting police stations and government tithe and salt stores in one hundred and nine villages. In Karpasia farmers and fishermen were instigated by school-teachers, doctors and brokers under the slogan of *Enosis* to burn down police stations in several villages, and they also took the opportunity to loot the government salt stores. In spite of the substantial changes the government had set in train, the riots of 1931 were an indication that it had been unsuccessful in detaching the allegiance of the peasants from the leadership of merchants and professionals and the Church. Until 1923, and in many respects until 1937, education had been left in the hands of the Church and the village authorities, who had used it to convert the peasants to following an ideological nationalist opposition to the colonial government. When this became increasingly evident, the government attempted to anglicise the educational system. The belated attempt was self-defeating and increased rather than effectively curbed nationalist opposition (Gavriilidi 1972, in Greek).

Though the colonial government weakened the credit hold of the brokerage network on the peasants, the extension of the nationalist movement meant that peasants remained faithful to the Church leadership. This alternative means of control to the credit relationship was mainly ideological.

The second important conflict which influenced the pattern of peasant relationships to brokerage networks was connected with the development of a Communist movement in the island, AKEL, and the partly spontaneous and partly Communist-led group selling schemes for agricultural products which developed. The immediate pre-war years were a period of rapid population increase in Cyprus. The war marked a period of rapid urbanisation, increased military and civilian construction and the development of an urban working class. Membership of the Communist-organised trade unions increased from 2,544 in 1939 to 12,961 in 1945 (Republic of Cyprus 1969). After 1941, when party organisations were legalised, there was a rapid increase in leftist influence in villages. Leftists organised farmers' associations and supplied militant leaders for various kinds of cooperative activities. It is not clear how far leftist influence in the cooperatives disturbed the colonial government, which had the administrative powers to limit them but did not use them. The church used its financial resources and political influence in an attempt to counterbalance left-wing strength by organising its own farmers' associations, but the leftists were the most important organised force in the villages of Karpasia until the beginning of the armed anti-British campaign in 1955.

Both the cooperatives led by leftists and the right-wing farmers' associations took initiatives in organising collective sales of the region's most important commercial products, tobacco and carobs, to merchants in the post-war years. Merchants retaliated. On one occasion at least they refused to buy at all from the Yialousa tobacco cooperative so it had to process and export the crop itself, assisted by an AKEL-owned trading organisation. There was competition between the cooperative credit societies and the right-wing farmers' association as to who should lead the group-selling moves. The cooperatives had an advantage since they had the credit resources with which to pay farmers, at least in part, on delivery. The cooperative group-selling schemes also gained in popularity after a failure of the right-wing farmers' association in the early fifties. After taking delivery of the tobacco crop it was unable to dispose of it and many producers remained unpaid. By 1957 a 'Central Committee of Karpasia Tobacco Producers' was distributing printed pamphlets calling on the government to subsidise tobacco prices, help in finding new markets abroad, give incentives to Cypriot industries to use more locally-produced tobacco, and to help in financing and organising a marketing cooperative for the disposal of the tobacco.

The colonial government's peasant credit policies had been designed to weaken merchants' control over peasants, since this elite group were leaders of the anti-colonial movement, and the brokerage system weakened as a result. Social changes during the war made possible horizontal peasant coalitions. The struggle between group-selling schemes and merchants indicates an attempt by peasant producers to alter their articulation with the market. In this they were helped by the fact that AKEL existed as a national party with a strong base in the urban areas. They were also helped by the fact that as a counter to Communist influence the church also promoted the creation of peasant associations.

These conflicts resulted in the increasing separation of individual economic linkage and political control. The weakening of the brokerage system did not mean that there were no more merchants. On the contrary, it opened up the market for agricultural products to all who wished to trade. The crops of Karpasia were bought by merchants from all over the island. Some of the Karpasia brokers became merchants on their own account. But the competition for purchasing products combined with the fact that the peasant was not bound to seek credit from the man he sold his products to, meant that there was a rupturing of the political link between peasant and merchant. The merchant who lived in a town belonging to a different electoral district, and bought carobs directly from a peasant in Karpasia, had less interest in the politics of the producer who sold to him, and much less effective means of compulsion. The cultural patterns created by the brokerage system survived to complicate contemporary politics, but the coercive basis behind patronage links weakened. Finally the horizontal coalitions, whether promoted by the Communist Party or by the Church, had the irreversible consequence of promoting the idea of common producers' interests as against individual vertical coalition.

3. Nationalism and Communism in the historical context of brokerage

In the 1950s the opposition between the church-led nationalist movement and the colonial government culminated in a violent anti-colonial campaign. An explanation has been offered of the eruption of violence at this time in terms of the strength of the Communist challenge to the church after the war (Markides, forthcoming). It is true that the underground anti-colonial organisation, EOKA, also turned against the AKEL organisation.[9] Since the Communist leadership had in many respects been the organisers of horizontal peasant coalitions, its suppression had a tendency to re-establish a system of vertical ties, based now not on a regional marketing system, but on the organisation of the underground anti-colonial fight. However, after independence the EOKA organisation factionalised, and one faction allied itself with horizontal peasant coalitions, since unlike the pre-war brokerage networks, members did not have stable interests in common. In any event, the changed structure of rural society made it impossible for a system involving the same degree of control of the rural population to re-impose itself.

During the anti-colonial campaign, a policy of economic boycott and intimidation was followed by EOKA against leftists in the Karpasia region, as in other parts of Cyprus. As a result numbers of people wanted to leave AKEL and some of them were channelled into the religious and farmers associations, and right-wing trade unions, collectively known as the 'Nationalist Bodies', which had been relatively unsuccessfully organised by the church as a counter to leftist influence in the early forties. In the late fifties they were revived so that people leaving the left-wing organisations 'would have somewhere to join' as an ex-EOKA leader said. It is not possible to estimate numerically the extent of the shift, but there is no doubt that the aggressive leadership of the left which had developed in the post-war period was curbed.

By similar means to those used against AKEL, control was also gained over institutions which had been in the hands of merchants and brokers. This was partly because, as power-holders, they were associated with the colonial government, and partly because they could not be expected to lead the independence fight with the self-sacrifice of the young, propertyless and unmarried EOKA men. In Yialousa, the *mukhtar* who could 'save a man from the gallows' was forced to resign together with all other *mukhtars* in Cyprus. The secretaryship of the Development Council[10] of the village was taken over by an EOKA militant. There were cases when merchants and their families were humiliated by young EOKA members whose families had previously been in their debt.

The young men who had joined EOKA acquired the power to assert themselves over all the forces which were locally competing for power before their appearance. But at the opening stage of the anti-colonial campaign it was free-floating power and not attached to social institutions other than the organisation of violence and the legitimation of the nationalist ideology. But since EOKA was not a unitary social force, after independence in 1959 its constituents divided and adapted to the various structural conflicts which crystallised around two issues: cooperation with AKEL, and continuation of the struggle for *Enosis*.

The EOKA members in Yialousa divided into three factions. The first, about ten in all, remained faithful to the man who was their area commander during the struggle, and through him to Grivas, the uncompromising military leader of EOKA who advocated both anti-Communism and a continuation of the struggle for *Enosis*. The second group, about twenty men, were led by the Minister of the Interior who was anti-Communist, but who supported Independence. He was to be a co-founder of the United Party ten years later. This group were known as the hard-liners and were uncompromising both in relation to the Communists and in relation to the Grivas group. The third group, also about twenty men, were known as the moderates and were prepared not only to go along with the post-independence government's decision to accept AKEL support, but were prepared to accept AKEL support themselves. This group was linked directly to the Archbishopric, and presumably therefore to the president. These young men in spite of their nationalist pedigree saw no reason for refusing to cooperate with the region's leftists, for example in establishing the Tobacco Marketing Cooperative in opposition to merchants and some of the cigarette manufacturers. Their parents had been, or they themselves were by now tobacco producers, and they knew, either from their parents' experiences or their own, of the problems of the relations between producers and merchants. Their opposition to AKEL was only ideological, based on the latter's wavering on following the nationalist line of EOKA.

On the other hand, it was equally easy for the hard-liners to argue that uncompromising opposition to the leftists was a continuation of the EOKA tradition, particularly if it coincided with the possibility of a government or police job, or merely if they had friendly ties with an influential man who followed this position.

The various factions did not form overnight and always retained some degree of fluidity, partly at least based on the rewards that became available. Leftists were ousted from the cooperatives and some of the jobs taken by former EOKA fighters. Scholarships were awarded and government jobs. If in 1974 one cross-tabulated the names of the five most prominent fighters who had remained in the village with five of the most important committees of the village, each man was a member of at least three of the committees. Those who became the elite of the region were those who took over the Tobacco Cooperative, and the process of its formation illustrates the process of fission of EOKA, whereby the moderate faction ousted the leftist leadership and then took over some of its functions in terms of peasant representation.

The break-down of the brokerage system meant only that its regional organisation disappeared, and with it the close links between merchant office and political faction. In purely economic terms, it opened up the field for merchant enterprise. There was a great increase in the number of merchants dealing in tobacco for example, many coming from outside the region. The number varied greatly from year to year depending on success in locating purchasers abroad. The producer had to bear the insecurity of the international market, because in years of low international demand the merchants withdrew from the market and left the tobacco in his hands. Efforts at group selling continued therefore after independence and culminated in the formation of the Cooperative Organisation of Tobacco Producers in 1961, with some governmental financial assistance.

By 1974, the Tobacco Producers' Cooperative was one of the largest cooperative organisations of the island, and its management positions were held by individuals who were known to be EOKA moderates. After displacing the leftist leaders of the group-selling schemes, they had used the continuing solid support of the leftist producers to build the cooperative up, not only into a selling organisation, but also into a processing and exporting one. The EOKA hard-liners refused to have anything to do with cooperating with Communists, and many of the right-wing producers were, in the initial steps, finding it difficult to free themselves from personal relations and obligations to merchants. The leaders of the Cooperative used organised pressure on the government, including demonstrations and, at one stage, threats to move away politically. At the same time they pressed (and on some occasions intimidated) producers to stop selling to merchants and sell to the Cooperative. By 1974 merchants were operating only in the interstices left to them by the cooperative, that is with special varieties of tobacco or with specialised processing. The moderate leaders of the Cooperative had not necessarily been moderates from the beginning. In some cases they moved to this faction politically as they became involved in the activities of the Cooperative, or were given a job in its administration. On the national level these people supported the Progressive Party which was willing to cooperate with AKEL and supported the government's policy of independence for Cyprus.

Though national parties (other than AKEL) were only given formal shape in 1968-69, the factions on which they were based pre-existed them, as is indicated by this account of political processes in Karpasia. The factions into which EOKA and its political successor, EDMA, splintered had by 1970 received names and official leaders as follows:

The only complete opposition to the President's policy of cooperation with AKEL and the pursuit of independence came from the *Enotiki*, who received guidance from Grivas, the military leader of EOKA, and while there was dictatorship in Greece from the Greek Government and the Greek army officers in Cyprus.

By 1970 there was a division among the President's supporters, reflected by the Progressive Party on the one hand, and the United Party on the other. The United Party joined together the rural-based hard-line EOKA factions, and middle-class urbanites. As well as opposition to Communism and pro-Western orientation, elements of this party came to advocate curbing the cooperative movement,[11] which after independence had grown to be a threat to some fields of private enterprise trade. The Progressive Party grew from a section of EOKA/EDMA which had acquired the leadership of the cooperative movement and the right-wing farmers' associations (Georgiadi-Kyproleonta 1970; Hajidemetriou 1974). They were prepared to suspend anti-Communism and strongly supported the entrenchment of cooperative power.

None of the parties lacked the possibility of bestowing patronage[12] in the new development-oriented organisation of the independent state. Members of the United Party had influence in the state machinery, the police and local administrative appointments. Members of the Progressive Party controlled the cooperative organisations, and members of the *Enotiki* movement a system of violence based on the army and the ideological legitimation of being the only true nationalists (Loizos 1974). The century-old pattern of allegiances between peasants and elite remained: it involved the coincidence of economic expediency and political alignment described as 'friendship', in a hierarchical relationship. There was also the confusion provided by public office being used for private favour. These transactions however had consequences beyond the individual aims of those who were immediately involved in the relative power of forces shaping the development of the whole society, because the national parties to a much greater degree than the pre-war merchant factions represented real differences in class interests and different international orientations.

The linkage of people at grass-roots to factions of EOKA notables was achieved in various ways. They have in common a tradition of village politics which established the necessity of relationships in idioms of friendship with representatives of national factions which can reward or penalise. Whether true or not there was a tendency to believe that the cooperatives might refuse to give loans or to take tobacco from those who opposed their leaders' political alignments; that others had the powers to give jobs; and that it is wise to vote for people one is economically dependent on. The relevance of the secrecy of balloting is weakened by the fact that people frequently want to vote for their benefactors, and because many of the older people cannot bring themselves to believe that powerful individuals cannot find ways of circumventing the secrecy.

The character of these processes is indicated by the great differences in voting patterns from village to village within the region.[13] Due to the importance of the Tobacco Cooperative in Karpasia, a higher proportion than the national average voted for the Progressive Party in the 1970 elections for the House of Representatives. However in many villages the United Party retained considerable support for reasons which varied from village to village. In one, a native of the village was a candidate on behalf of the United Party for the whole electoral district, which was wider than Karpasia. In another village, which grew a variety of tobacco not handled by the cooperative and where the local merchant supported the United Party, most electors voted for that party. Two of the merchants who had been largely displaced by the competition of the cooperative gave some support to the *Enotiki* party. This party, with their help, produced a pamphlet for Karpasia arguing that the management of the Tobacco Marketing Cooperative was corrupt and extravagant and would lead to the bankruptcy of the village credit societies which had largely financed it.

The similarities with the pre-war brokerage system should not however obscure basic differences. The first group of differences are structural and the second ideological. There are numerous structural reasons making the people of the area much less dependent on any one national faction. The cooperative movement has radically altered the economics of being a peasant farmer, both in terms of access to credit and in terms of marketing. Since credit and marketing are freely and relatively impersonally available, they do not necessarily lead to individual political ties. The Communist Party continues to exist as an option, both in terms of individual choice and in terms of national politics. As a personal option it has similarities to the other parties as an avenue for individual benefits. But as a national party it involves a great difference. Its presence contains the threat of a possible resurgence of trade union and peasant militancy, which has to be borne in mind by other parties; these include the cooperative movement and the Progressive Party which, though based on a horizontal peasant coalition, is vertically controlled by people whose class alignments would not normally be with peasants. Thirdly, the impact of modernising changes means that Karpasia is no longer an area of farmers and craftsmen exclusively dependent on local patronage connections. The occupational structure is much more diversified and includes many more opportunities for employment, particularly in retailing and construction. Also the possibility of employment through migration to a town is high. Finally access to the state machinery is not solely channelled through a powerful local agent, the *mukhtar* and one or two other influentials. The office of *mukhtar* continues, but with a shadow of its former powers. There are many more means of mediation than the purely political ones for access to the administrative bureaucracy of the district town or capital. With migration, educational mobility and a great expansion of the urban middle class, kinship is one of the most important. National factions needing peasant votes face the fact that vertical links are weakened in significance for villagers and have to be supplemented by ideological appeals. The idiom of the appeal is a dual one reflecting the two most important vehicles of political change that have been examined: the Communist movement on the one hand and nationalist anti-colonialism on the other.

The activities of AKEL before the EOKA period, and its current existence, though in a quiescent state, made a significant difference. The pre-war factions competed with each other, but merchants could also agree on matters of common interest. The group-selling schemes however had created the concept of common producers' interests. No matter whether they served the producers' interests well or badly, there were certain limits placed by the fact that this conception now existed. No group aiming at peasant votes could now attack the actual existence of the cooperatives. An attack had to be phrased in terms of a demand for reform against mismanagement.

Secondly, no group, including AKEL, could denounce the ideology of nationalism and anti-colonialism, *Enosis*,[14] even if in practice supporting policies which maintained independence. The autonomous power which the ideology had acquired was such that all parties had possibilities of acquiring followers, independently of economic issues or personal relations, by competitive demonstration of close adherence to it. In fact, some of the appeal of the violent *Enotiki* movement which developed after 1969 was probably due to the directness and simplicity of its programme, in contrast to the complexity of class politics conducted competitively in idioms of patronage and nationalist appeals by clientelist parties.

The relationship of the region to the state society after independence is complicated by several factors. Vertical coalition continued to operate as shown by the pattern of interrelation of villagers to the new EOKA-derived elite and through them to the national factions and later parties. But they are rendered confused and unstable by the coexistence of principles and institutions of horizontal coalition, initiated by the colonial government and AKEL, and also adopted by the church. Though recruitment to the various factions remained to some extent patronage-based, on the national level they represent genuinely different class interests and international orientations.

The three phases may, in conclusion, be summarised as follows: the first phase is one of pure vertical coalitions; peasants are incorporated into merchant and professional factions in a competition which has nothing to do with the interests of peasants as a class. At the second stage, with the help, or at least connivance of the colonial government, peasants organise horizontal coalitions aimed at eliminating the previous form of incorporation based on the credit and marketing outlets of brokerage networks. In this they were assisted by the emergence of the Communist Party as a national political organisation which opposed the political and economic pursuits of the merchant and professional class. At the third phase, the conflict of the church-led groups and the Communist Party and the victory of the first, tends towards the re-establishment of vertical incorporation, assisted by the continuation of a tradition of patronage. However the presence of the ideology of producers' interests, the fact that the EOKA fighters lacked a unitary class interest in favour of reimposing a system of vertical coalition, and the differentiation of village society, means that what in fact results is a mixture of principles of vertical and horizontal coalition. Though on the national level differences of class interest and international orientation are real, the mixture of the forms of coalition makes it difficult for a villager to know what tendency he is supporting by allying himself to one rather than another party. Unlike the unchallenged brokerage phase, appeals are made to him on ideological grounds and he responds to this idiom as well as the older clientelist one, but it remains true on the whole that villagers 'live out the conflicts and contradictions of the social structure and in the ideology it imposes on them,' which means that they 'politick without controlling the political process' (Rosenfeld 1972).

NOTES

1.   An earlier version of this paper was read at the New York Academy of Sciences Conference on Regional Variation in Modern Greece and Cyprus, February, 1975. I would like to thank Peter Loizos for making extensive and valuable suggestions for revision in this version.

2.   'Corporate' is used here as opposed to 'open' as these terms are defined by Wolf (1955). A similar view is implied in the use of the concept of incorporation in Pearse (1971). However the term 'incorporation' as used by Pearse implies an 'open' village community, and this is the sense in which 'incorporation' is used in this paper.

3.   The practice had a long tradition. At the beginning of the nineteenth century, the Ottoman Government had established a state monopsony for carobs. The government bought from the peasants at eight piasters for 220 okes, but it was well known that the scales which the government agents used weighed only 180 (Jenness 1962, p.77).

4.   During the early years of the British occupation an attempt had been made to collect the tithe in cash, but this attempt had to be abandoned after the uncovering of the involvement of government officials in corruption, and also due to the fact that it drove the peasants to closer dependence on usurers, a matter to which British colonial

administrators were very sensitive, presumably because of the 'disloyalty' of the merchant class.

5. The *Memouris* had to give his permission for winnowing to take place and afterwards was responsible for measuring the tithe. The actual measurement with wooden boxes was done by his assistant, the *Kkiretzis*. A *Kortzis* supervised the threshing floor until the actual tithing was done. He had a wooden seal with which he patterned the pile of wheat at different places so that no amount could be removed without disturbing the impressions of the seal. A *Neziris* was responsible for supervising a group of villages. If he came across a *Memouris* in the process of tithing, he made him remeasure the tithe in his presence. A further official, an *Epoptis*, supervised the *Nezirides*.

6. Powell (1970) points this out as a generalised fact of clientelism.

7. They also turned to the Turkish Cypriot representatives in the Legislative Council. Though this had far-reaching consequences, they are beyond the scope of this paper.

8. In 1927-8 when he conducted the survey, 73% of all farm-holders were in debt, the average amount of debt being a quarter of the value of their holding (Surridge 1930).

9. This is evident from the EOKA documents reproduced in Papageorgiou (1961 in Greek). It is also made clear in the account of the campaign by its military leader (Grivas-Dhigenis 1961, in Greek).

10. Development Councils were established in 1950 in the larger villages. They were composed partly of elected members and were part of a programme of self-government and economic development designed to curb pro-*Enosis* feelings.

11. A pamphlet issued by the Tobacco Cooperative in 1966 contains the following statements: 'When we ... were creating the tobacco cooperative, the government was subsidising the manufacturers ... they moved about the drawing rooms of Nicosia smiling ironically at our expense.' 'We must all be prepared for any struggle so that the cooperative movement may preserve its freedom and independence, as a genuine defender of our interests.' The Chamber of Commerce and industry, on the other hand, in a message to the President of the Republic, which was also released to the press, referred to its views which were well-known as far as the government was concerned, on the subject of the cooperative movement's 'continuously expanding activities' with 'unacceptable advantages granted to it and with favourable treatment in comparison with private enterprise'. *Eleftheria* newspaper, 9 Feb., 1971, Nicosia.

12. There are many points of correspondence between what has been described here and the transition from patron-client ties to party directed patronage described by Weingrod. However there the interest is in analysing changing bases of patronage, while here it is in patronage as against other bases of coalition. From the latter point of view, it is more important that the parties here described gained part of their support through patronage than that this patronage is ultimately derived from the state rather than the resources of the patron himself. This is on the assumption that there are variations in party organisations, and patronage-based or 'clientelist' parties have specific implications.

13. Kitromilides (1972) discusses the election results of 1970 in terms of a pattern of 'personalised politics'.

14. Loizos (1974) discusses the social bases for the appeal of the *Enosis* idea.

REFERENCES

Fox, R. (n.d.) Realm and Region in the Anthropology of Complex Societies.

Gavriilidi, A. (1972) *Ethnarchic Rights and the Enosis Plebiscite of 1950.* Nicosia (in Greek).

Georgiadi-Kyproleonta, A.A. (1970) 'Deductions and conclusions from the elections', *Eleftheria* newspaper, 17 July.

Grivas-Dhigenis, G. (1961) *Memoirs of the EOKA Struggle, 1955-59*. Athens (in Greek).

Hajidemetriou, T. (1974) 'Anatomy of the right', *Ta Nea* newspaper, March. Nicosia.

Hill, G. (1952) *A History of Cyprus*. Vol. IV. London.

Jenness, D. (1962) *The Economy of Cyprus: A Survey to 1914*. Montreal.

Katalanos, N. (1914) *Cyprus Diary*. Nicosia (in Greek).

Kitromilides, P.M. (1972) 'Patterns of politics in Cyprus'. Unpublished dissertation, Wesleyan University.

Loizos, P. (1974) 'The progress of Greek nationalism in Cyprus, 1878-1970', in J. Davis (ed.), *Choice and Change: Essays in Honour of Lucy Mair*. London.

Luke, G.H. (1921) *Cyprus Under the Turks 1571-1878*. London.

Markides, K. (forthcoming) 'Social change and the rise and decline of social movements: The case of Cyprus', *American Ethnologist*.

Mouzelis, N. and M. Attalides (1971) 'Greece', in M. Scotford-Archer and S. Finer (eds), *Europe: Class, Status and Power*. London.

Papageorgiou, S. (1961) *Archive of Illegal Documents of the Cyprus Struggle, 1955-59*. Athens (in Greek).

Pearse, A. (1971) 'Metropolis and peasant: The expansion of the urban industrial complex and the changing rural structure', in T. Shanin (ed.), *Peasants and Peasant Societies*. Harmondsworth.

Powell, J.D. (1970) 'Peasant society and clientelist politics', *American Political Science Review* 64, 411-25.

Republic of Cyprus, Ministry of Labour and Social Insurance (1969) *Annual Report*. Government Printing Office, Nicosia.

Rosenfeld, H. (1972) 'An overview and critique of the literature on rural politics and social change', in R. Antoun and I. Harik (eds), *Rural Politics and Social Change in the Middle East*. Bloomington, Indiana.

Schneider, P., J. Schneider and E. Hansen (1972) 'Modernisation and development: The role of regional elites and non-corporate groups in the European Mediterranean', *Comparative Studies in Society and History* 14 (3), 328-50.

Steward, J.H. et al. (1956) *The People of Puerto Rico: A Study in Social Anthropology*. Urbana, Illinois.

Storrs, R. (1943) *Orientations*. London.

Surridge, B.J. (1930) *A Survey of Rural Life in Cyprus*. Government Printing Office, Nicosia.

Weingrod, A. (1968) 'Patrons, patronage and political parties', *Comparative Studies in Society and History* 10, 377-400.

Wolf, E.R. (1955) 'Types of Latin American peasantry: A preliminary discussion', *American Anthropologist* 57.

Wolf, E.R. (1966) 'Kinship, friendship and patron-client relations in complex societies', in M. Banton (ed.), *The Social Anthropology of Complex Societies*. London.

Amal Rassam

Al-taba'iyya:
Power, patronage and marginal groups in northern Iraq

In the summer of 1974 I went to visit Jamal Beg, scion of the Muftis, one of the most prominent and wealthy *sada* (holy) families* of Mosul. As I drove into the large, Ottoman-style compound where he lived, I saw that the courtyard was full of men, women and children dressed in the distinctive clothing of the Shabak, a rural, extremist *shi'a* group who live in several villages to the north-east of the city. The Shabak were formerly sharecroppers on land belonging to urban *sada* families, but since the land reform efforts of the present regime, the majority had become landowners themselves. When I enquired about his rural guests, Jamal Beg replied 'No, these are not my sharecroppers anymore – they are now independent – but since they are still my *ra'iyya* (flock, people, clients), they stay here when they come to the city. There are usually ten to fifteen of them around, and of course, they eat and sleep here. My father used to host them like this and I continue to do so. We have a special bond between us; they are still "counted on us" '.

The expression 'counted on us' or 'mahsubin 'alayna' implies that it is the duty of the *sada* to guide and protect the helpless peasant, and underscores the patron-client relationship that prevails between the two groups. This clientelistic pattern is one of the various ways in which marginal, semi-autonomous groups in northern Iraq adapt themselves to their socio-political environment.[1] The concept of patronage, despite its vagueness, nevertheless provides a useful framework for the isolation and analysis of these networks of dependencies that seem to exist in segmented, plural societies like that of Iraq.[2] For it is not sufficient to define the different groups and locate them in time and space (the 'ethnic mosaic syndrome'); equally important is to discover the basis of their differential access to resources, religious, social or economic, and the patterns of their articulation. These groups do not (and did not) exist in a political

---

* The term *sada* is used in Iraq to refer to those families who claim descent from the Prophet Mohammed through his daughter Fatima.

vacuum, but were themselves often adaptations to the nature and form of the power superstructure, the State. Thus, an historical analysis becomes crucial for the proper assessment of the factors involved in the formation of these groups, their encystment, and their patterns of relatedness to each other and to the State. Within such a context patronage networks create important links between the State and the local groups as well as serving to diffuse the tension inherent between them (Pitt-Rivers 1961, p.156).

My argument assumes that patron-client relations represent a special kind of personal exchange, one where two individuals of different socio-economic status enter into a relationship in which the individual of higher status uses his influence and resources to provide protection and benefits for the person of lower status, the latter reciprocating by offering his personal services, loyalty and general support. Among the distinguishing features of patron-client relationships are 'their basis in inequality, their face to face character and their diffuse flexibility. All of these features are most apparent in the ties between a high-status landlord and his tenants or sharecroppers in a traditional agrarian economy – a relationship that serves in a sense, as the prototype of patron-client ties' (Scott 1973, p.93).

By presenting two different case studies, I hope to point out some of the variations in these ties as they exist in Iraq. My concern is with the enduring, institutionalised, clientelistic patterns and not with the analysis of the shifting and open-ended individual choices and strategies within a given socio-political field. By incorporating such differentiating factors as ethnicity, occupational status, lineage and rural-urban distinctions, the concept of clientelism makes it possible to determine in functional terms the operation and boundaries of the political system. It allows us to bridge the gap between the study of politics as an urban, elitist phenomenon and the political behaviour of the rural and urban masses in the historical societies of the Middle East.

It is interesting and perhaps significant that there really does not exist a special word in Iraq which approximates in meaning the term 'patron' or 'patronage'. Informants would give me several words that referred to clientage, but had difficulty in finding a term for 'patronage'. The only word on which there was some general agreement was *wajaha* for patronage and *wajh* for the individual patron. The Arabic word *wajh* means face, or outward appearance; it also means pre-eminence, nobility and pride. The traditional upper class or notables of the city were referred to collectively as *wujaha'*, or those who have 'social visibility', and it is thus that the patron is the *wajh* of his client, in other words, it is the patron who confers social recognition and visibility on the faceless and socially insignificant client. For the complementary concept of clientage, informants gave the following terms: *taba'iyya, mahsoubiyya, ra'iyya, jama'a,* and *da'ira.*

These invariably were used with reference to a specific patron or 'taba'iyyat flan', 'the clients of so and so'. In their usage of the two terms, informants gave the impression that the function of patronage was a self-evident corollary of being a notable – all of the traditional elite could and did function as patrons by virtue of their high status and power, whereas among the masses, one had to distinguish the different constellations of followers by means of their individual patrons. Informants would classify the residents of Mosul in terms of 'whom they were counted on', i.e. the circle of clients of which they were a part. Furthermore, informants agreed that the two major functions of the patron were protection and mediation, *himaya* and *wisata* respectively. In the first case, the patron acts as a buffer between the agents of the State, or any other potential exploiter, and the client. In the second case, the patron provides the link, in his capacity as an intermediary, between his client and a second party (usually of higher status) to whom the client has no direct access.

Both the roles of the Protector and the Mediator are basic to Iraqi society, having their historical roots in Arab culture. The notion of mediation is an integral one in the religious sphere where the doctrine of intercession (*'aqidat al-shafa'a*) forms a key concept in Islam, finding its highest development among the *shi'a*, who believe that one of the major functions of their *Imams* is to intercede with the Godhead on their behalf. The counterpart of *shafa'a* in the secular sphere is the *wisata*. Both rest on a shared belief in the inscrutability and remoteness of Power and the inherent helplessness and unworthiness of the average person. The system of patronage is thus sustained by a peculiar combination of deference to a hierarchical ordering of society and simultaneous fear of the power which this hierarchy implies. Kenny wrote that the reason for the success of patronage in Spain is that there exists 'a general acceptance of the idea of hierarchy on earth and the inequalities – sometimes crippling – that go with it ... But a singular respect for authority arising out of this is accompanied by a fear of power misused. Patronage is one method of levelling out some of these inequalities and avoiding the abuses of powerful superiors' (Kenny 1966, pp. 135-6). This is equally true for Iraq.

The concept of protection between different status groups found its expression in early Islam in the institution of *mawali* and the notion of *wala'*. When a member of a conquered tribe or nation converted to Islam, he usually sought the patronage (*wala'*) of a powerful Bedouin tribe. The convert then acquired the status of a *mawali* or client which allowed him to assume the tribal name and guaranteed him the protection and support of his surrogate clan. In return, he pledged his full allegiance. This institution survived in Iraq under the Ottomans and was known as the *kutba*, a ritualised procedure by which an individual or group (Arab or otherwise) would enter into a client status with a powerful Arab tribe.

Beginning with the Ottoman times and persisting into the thirties,

Mosul was organised into a number of named quarters, each with its own leader who was also its representative vis-à-vis the government. This leader, who was known as 'sheikh al-mahalla', was usually a member of the most prominent and powerful family in that quarter. These families could be grouped into three categories, the first being the *sada* or 'holy' families, representing those who claimed descent from the Prophet. In Mosul, there were five of these families, all of whom had originally been brought over by the Ottomans from Najaf and Hijaz to lend prestige to the Ottoman *wali* (governor) and help keep the generally restless population quiescent. The second category comprised a number of 'secular' notables, chief among these being two families that claimed descent from the second Caliph, 'Umar. In keeping with their policy of discouraging the development of a unified political front, the Ottomans had welcomed these families in order to balance the *sada*. Not only were the *sada* and 'Umaris political rivals competing in the same power arena, but they also had a long history of mutual suspicion and hostility. These two groups of families comprised the *wujaha'* or notables of the city. The third group was made up of what the Ottomans collectively referred to as *aghawat,* or tribal chiefs. These were Arab or Kurdish chiefs of nomadic and semi-nomadic tribes who lived in Mosul for most of the year. For example, the paramount chief of the Shammar, a large Bedouin tribe, maintained one of the largest houses in the city.

Each of these families formed the nucleus of a group of diverse clients, or *ra'iyya*, who lived nearby and who directly or indirectly depended on the patron family for a living and/or protection. This system was not exclusive to the Moslems, but included Christians and Jews as well. Although the majority of the Christians and Jews lived segregated in 'ghettos' grouped around their churches and synagogues,* a number of them chose to live scattered in the city, each placing himself under the protection of one of the aforementioned patrons. Since the Jews and Christians were primarily craftsmen, they paid for their 'protection' by serving the patron families as jewellers, weavers, and tailors. In addition, their women and children worked in the house as domestics.[3] In theory, these client families could choose between the different available patrons. In practice, it was rare for a family to move house and go to another quarter; dependency relationships tended to be passed from one generation to the next.

Each of the notables held a weekly 'open house' or *majlis* at his home. His visitors included other notables, merchants, friends, and kin. They came to exchange information, discuss a common problem, gossip and just chat. The weekly *majlis* served as the public arena where the patron-client clusters manifested themselves. As informants put it: 'When you walked into the *majlis* of so and so (the scion of

---

* The segregated Christian and Jewish quarters were under the direct protection of the Ottoman governor of the City.

notable family), you knew who his *taba'iyya* were. Everybody attended, even the *d'eef* (weak, unimportant) who normally sat near the door (in winter) or on the edge of the garden (in summer). Some of these would be serving coffee or helping in the kitchen.' In other words, all the clients had the right (and the duty) to be present at their patron's *majlis*; the notables took turns visiting each others' *majlis* accompanied by a number of their important clients. I should add that the last occasion on which the notables of Mosul acted as a self-conscious group was in 1920. As the British army approached the outskirts of the city, the Ottoman governor fled Mosul, and the notables met in council and elected two among them to 'receive the British and hand over the city to them'.[4]

The patronage network of these notables often extended far beyond the confines of the neighbourhood and the city to include some of the nearby rural groups. The Mufti family was one such wealthy *sada* family. The area where they lived was known as the Sada Quarter (*mahallat al-sada*). It was dominated by a large mosque and school, both built and financed by the family. To compensate them for various services, an Ottoman Sultan had given them large tracts of State land (*miri*) in an area that lay approximately 30-40 kilometres outside the city. They proceeded to register the land in title (*tapu*) as private property of the family. The area included three villages inhabited by the *Shabak*, a Kurdish-speaking, extremist *shi'a* marginal group. Landless, the vast majority of the Shabak became sharecroppers, cultivating land which now belonged to the Muftis. In return for a share that varied between 1/5 and 2/5 of the crop, they planted wheat, barley and lentils. In addition, they tended large flocks of sheep which belonged to their landlords, getting to keep part of the wool and butter.

The traditional Mufti-Shabak relationship was an all-pervasive patron-client one. The patrons in this case were urban landlords, of high status and prestige, endowed with religious charisma and political power. As the *sada* (and in this case, the term *sada* itself regains its original meaning of Lord, overlord or master) the Muftis provided the links between the rural, illiterate Shabak and the representatives of the State, as well as serving as the protectors of the Shabak from other groups in the area. If one of the Shabak villages was harrassed by a nomadic Arab or a Kurdish tribe, the Shabak turned to their *sada* for help and protection. The *sada* would try to use their religious prestige to settle the dispute; should they fail in that, they would turn to the State for military aid. A police force, or even an army unit would then be sent out to 'restore order in the area' and to protect the property and clients of the urban notables.

When a Shabak peasant came to the city to sell his grain, see a doctor or buy provisions, he stayed at the house of his landlord who saw to it that his client was not cheated by the shopkeeper nor ignored by the doctor. In addition, each Mufti household included a number of resident Shabak (many of whom were widows and orphans) who served as retainers and domestics.

It should be clear from the above brief description that the Mufti-Shebak patron-client relationship combined elements of the 'patrimonial', 'feudalistic' and 'saintly' types of clientelism (Lemarchand 1972). It is noteworthy that within the traditional, pre-revolutionary context the emphasis was on the 'saintly' dimension. As I interviewed the older *sada* and Shabak, I was struck by the compatibility of their world views and the similarity of their idiom; both 'legitimising' their unequal socio-economic status in terms of their unequal religious prestige. As descendents of 'Ali, the *sada* saw themselves as having inherent rights to wealth and authority; as extremist *shi'a*, the Shabak believed that all prestige and obedience must be accorded to the descendants of 'Ali who possess Blessing (*baraka*) and can intercede on their behalf with the Hidden *Imam*. In more functional terms, one may argue that this emphasis by the Shabak on the sanctity of their landlords checked the inherent explosive potential of the lopsided relationship, since it obliged the *sada* to live up to the full standards of noblesse oblige and charity expected from true descendants of the Prophet.

The land reform laws of 1958 and 1963, promulgated by the revolutionary government of Iraq, put an abrupt end to the landlord-tenant relationship between the Muftis and the Shabak. Expropriated land was offered to the landless peasants at low rates and long-range terms. Encouraged by the newly-formed agricultural cooperatives in the area, a number of Shabak bought small pieces of land and became independent farmers. However, for a variety of reasons, the Shabak continued to maintain their cautious and distant attitude towards the agents of the government and to rely on their former landlords for credit, guidance and general help. Despite their relative political impotency under the Ba'athi regime, the *sada* continued to enjoy a large measure of social and political credit among their former sharecroppers, who still assume that their former landlords possess influence with the government. Rendered bewildered and insecure by the rapid transformation of their environment and the arbitrary and shifting policies of the regime, the peasant's dependency on his former *sayyid* intensified, particularly in view of the latter's role as a mediator or broker. It is the educated members of the Mufti family, the lawyers, teachers and clerks who are now helping the Shabak to cope with the new bureaucratic demands such as that of getting a son into high school or registering a piece of land.

Perhaps the single most significant trend in the former relationship, signalling the transformation of the old patron-client relationship from an all-comprehensive, religiously sanctified dependency system to a more specialised and instrumental one, is the newly formed sheep-raising partnerships. Under this kind of arrangement, a former landlord extends cash to his former peasant who then proceeds to move out of his nucleated village and buys land near the major highway. He builds himself a house and a large enclosure for animals. With his partner, he buys a number of sheep which are raised and fattened in stalls, the labour being provided by the peasant's family. Mature sheep are taken to the urban market and sold, the money divided between the two partners according to the terms of the original agreement.

It is premature at this stage to estimate the durability and success of this emerging contractual pattern between a former landlord and his former sharecropper, but it certainly indicates the erosion of the old ties and their replacement by open-ended ones since the Shabak can seek this kind of relationship with any interested party, be it a Kurd, a Christian villager, a city merchant or even another Shabak. The *sada* seem to be aware of this, and it is no accident that a few years back one of them hired a religious teacher, an *akhundi* from Najaf, and sent him out to the Shabak villages 'to teach the people the principles of *shi'a* Islam and to remind them of their heritage and responsibilities in order to combat the heresy of Communism'. It was a last effort by a *sayyid* to regenerate the beliefs and ideas that had hitherto provided moral legitimacy for generations of his family in their role as grand patrons and overlords of the Shabak peasants.

No shared moral ethos existed to cement the ties between the peasants of Tel Yaqo, a Christian Chaldean village, and the wealthy Moslem family of Hadi. One afternoon in 1959, a young man drove out of Mosul to Tel Yaqo. The next morning his body was found in the village square; it had been riddled with bullets and driven over by a tractor. The incident became an immediate *cause célèbre* in a year full of political troubles in Iraq. It signalled the dramatic end to an ordered social universe built on the principle of ascribed inequality and inter-group dependency, and ushered in an era of political and social experimentation. The young man had belonged to the Hadi family, a family of grand landowners, and the traditional patrons of the peasants of Tel Yaqo. His trip was a routine one. He had intended to collect meat and eggs from 'his village' since there was a shortage of foodstuffs in the city. Instead of the usual welcome by the peasants, he was ambushed and killed. Four years later, five villagers were apprehended, put on trial and hanged for the murder. In their joint statement at the trial, they said they had 'done our duty and put an end to an exploiter of our people'.

The case of the Hadi family and Tel Yaqo illustrates the equivocal nature of patronage as well as its inherent instability in a plural society when the patrons and the clients belong to two different ethnic groups. It seems to be true that 'where cultural cleavages not only are prominent, but tend to coincide with patrons and clients, these cleavages may help break up the patron-client nexus. Thus, the greater the cultural differences between them, the greater the likelihood of violent ethnic strife in conditions of rapid social mobilization' (Lemarchand 1972, p.84).

Tel Yaqo lies about thirty kilometres to the north of Mosul. Its Christian inhabitants are known as hardworking peasants and superb weavers. The villagers bought the wool from the nearby nomads, spun and wove it and then exported it to nearby villages and tribes. Although the majority of the peasants owned their land, a number were sharecroppers on land belonging to the Hadis, a powerful family that lived in Mosul, but of nomadic origins. The Hadis had acquired their land in and around Tel Yaqo through a combination of legal and not-so-legal means. One way was through the consolidation of small parcels of land that reverted to the family after the failure of villagers to repay loans. The Hadis also would apply direct pressure to force peasants to part with all or part of their land – the threat of inviting nomads to settle on village land (already owned by the Hadis) was sufficient. Fearful lest the nomads would molest their wives and children while their animals destroyed their fields, the peasants usually agreed to sell the desired plot. In time, the Hadis emerged as the grand landlords of the area and began to assume the role of the patrons of the village.

Christian peasants generally tend to rely on their priests for leadership. Through their ties with the urban-based bishop, priests provided the necessary links with the city. But the local priest was no match for the Hadis who came to assume an important place in local level village politics. By employing village elders as their local agents to look after crops and supervise the sharecroppers, the urban-based family came to be in a position to manipulate village factions and influence decisions. Simultaneously, through their connections in the city, they were in a position to interfere in the high level decisions that affected the lives of the villagers. As a consequence of this key role, the villagers came to depend on the Hadis for the traditional functions of patronage, that is to say, mediation and protection. In return, and in addition to the general support and allegiance offered the patrons, the villagers supplied the landlords with free domestics, and seasonal 'gifts' of honey, fruit and woven blankets. During the forties and early fifties, the village used to 'deliver its vote' to the member of the Hadi family who ran for the Parliament.

Underneath the seemingly traditional patron-client relationship with its attendant ritual of deference and solidarity, a tide of frustration and resentment built up. This was to find its focus in Communist ideology which was seriously introduced into the village around 1945.

Fifteen years earlier, a Dominican father from the Mosul mission went up to Tal Yaqo to recruit a number of boys for the mission school. Some of these went on to obtain a teaching certificate and become teachers in the primary schools of Mosul and Baghdad. Soon after, relatives followed them into the cities; those that did not go to school became cooks and waiters in the newly-established hotels and restaurants. It was among this urban immigrant group of school teachers and unskilled workers that Communism took root and spread. Since the immigrants maintained their ties with the village, by 1958 an active, clandestine Communist network was operating in Tel Yaqo. The spread of Communist, egalitarian principles helped to undermine the 'premise of inequality', with the result that many came to see the 'protection' offered them by landlords as exploitation. This shift in view was articulated beautifully by an informant who said 'Alra'iya saret shuyu'iya, wal atawa saret shaqawa' ('As the clients became Communists, protection became oppression').

The peasants of Tel Yaqo had particularly resented the habit of the Hadi family of holding large-scale banquets in the village for which the peasants had to provide food, service and even the locally-distilled liquor. This form of indirect taxation of the peasants continued until 1959, a year after the revolution.

Taking advantage of the political crises and upheaval that year in nearby Mosul, the youth of Tel Yaqo put a dramatic end to their dependency by murdering one of the Hadi family. For the moment, the revolutionary atmosphere and their Communist beliefs had provided them with the necessary ideological justification and self-confidence to challenge the traditional 'premise of inequality' and inter-group dependency. It matters little for our purpose that their dream was short-lived.

The two examples discussed illustrate some aspects of power as manifested in the phenomena of clientelism or *taba'iyya* in northern Iraq. In an early article (1956) Wolf pointed out that the task of pulling town and village, state and peasant society, together is the specific mediating function performed by different groups at different points in the development of the society. One may add that some groups may play different roles at different times, depending on the demands and obligations of clientage. In the case of the Shabak, recent bureaucratic centralisation, land reform and the expanding market economy have all contributed to the transformation of the *sada*. Whereas formerly their role was that of protectors, acting as buffers between the Shabak and the larger society, today they are mainly brokers, who serve as links between the individual peasants and the expanding market. In this manner, the patrons of the Shabak have survived by bridging the traditional-modern transition through changing their roles. In contrast, the patrons of Tel Yaqo were simply removed, and their functions were taken over by local priests and members of the Communist Party. Although the traditional patronage system of Tel Yaqo might have been considered perverted, it nonetheless helps to illustrate the fragility of patronage as a means of maintaining order and protection in an ethnically fragmented, low-resource environment, such as that of Northern Iraq.

Anthropologists have traditionally stressed lineages and other kin organisations as the key groupings in the Middle East. An analysis of the patron-client linkages reveals the important part that non-kin based groups play, their modes of competition and conflict, and the resulting accommodation. This provides a more balanced view of the complex social organisation in the Middle East mosaic.

NOTES

1.   In an earlier paper (Vinogradov 1974) I have examined the special adaptation of one of these groups in terms of their different sets of patrons.
2.   For a definition and discussion of pluralism and plural society see, among others Desperes (1968), Morris (1967), and the various essays by L. Kuper and M.G. Smith in *Pluralism in Africa*, 1969.
3.   The domestic service of the Christians and Jews was limited to the households of the secular notables and tribal chiefs. The *sada*, who abided by a strict code of ritual purity and pollution, refused food prepared by non-moslems.
4.   I cannot go into the effects of British rule on the traditional patronage system of Mosul. Suffice it to say that notables who became clients of the British, soon attained national prominence – one of them becoming a perennial prime minister. The *sada*, in general, did not collaborate with the British.

REFERENCES

Desperes, L. (1968) 'Anthropological theory, cultural pluralism and the study of complex societies', *Current Anthropology* 9, 3-26.

Kenny, M. (1966) 'Patterns of patronage in Spain,' *Anthropological Quarterly* 33, 1, 14-23.

Lemarchand, R. (1972) 'Political clientelism and ethnicity in tropical Africa: Competing solidarities in nation-building', *American Political Science Review* LXVI, 1, 68-90.

Morris, H.S. (1967) 'Some aspects of the concept "plural society" ', *Man* 2, 169-84.

Pitt-Rivers, J. (1961) *The People of the Sierra*. Chicago.

Scott, J. (1972) 'Patron-client politics and political change in Southeast Asia', *American Political Science Review* LXVI, 1, 92-113.

Vinogradov, A. (1974) 'Ethnicity, cultural discontinuity and power brokers in Northern Iraq: The case of the Shabak', *American Ethnologist* 1, 1, 207-18.

Wolf, E. (1956) 'Aspects of group relations in a complex society', *American Anthropologist* 58, 1065-78.

Wolf, E. (1966) 'Kinship, friendship and patron-client relations in complex societies', in M. Banton (ed.), *The Social Anthropology of Complex Societies*, London.

Michael Gilsenan

Against patron-client relations

There is a fair measure of agreement over what is meant in sociological usage by 'patron-client relations' (the inverted commas hereafter to be understood as always present). Let us take it that the phrase is commonly held to characterise relations between two persons or groups one of whom is in some way in a superior or more favourable position than the other. From the first flow favours, rewards and protection; from the latter perhaps specific goods and services but also more diffuse returns of loyalty, support or allegiance. One usually understands a multi-stranded pattern that is continuous over time, often cast in the idiom of ritual or other forms of kinship (godparenthood for example), honour and respect, friendship, attachment, and so forth. The range and scale of patronage is presented as depending on many factors: the nature of the State and the degree of effective centralisation of political power; the modes of violence and control in a society; the nature of the significant social units and their interrelations.

Typologies have been developed of all 'dependency relations in traditional Africa' in which the 'type of clientelism' is seen as characterising the overall system of domination (Lemarchand 1972). On the other hand writers have used the term in settings as disparate as Mediterranean politics *in toto*, New York City bossism, not to mention Spanish and Portuguese maintenance of a subservient labour force in their Latin-American colonies (Hall 1974). Patronage is even discussed as 'anxiety-reduction behaviours by which the peasant attempts to build some security in the face of his perceived environmental threats', a phrase that not only probably applies better to academics than peasants, but that also reduces the relations under discussion to a psycho-cultural level of subjective perception and nullifies attempts at a more structural analysis (Powell 1970, p.411). De Coulanges, of course, used it in a strict and limited jural sense for a legal-ritual status of inferiority in *The Ancient City*. In short, it has become a concept for all seasons, applied quasi-universally to a multiplicity of relationships in a wide diversity of social and economic formations.

It follows from this confusion that stipulative definitions ('when I say patron-client ties I mean ... '), based as they are on a cobbling together of 'traits' based to an uncertain degree on specific empirical situations, are inevitably inadequate. They have no real theoretical base and lead merely to endless additions to or subtractions from various lists of 'characteristics'. Where, moreover, patron-client terminology is employed as a framework for a discussion of whole systems I would argue that it is part of a functionalist-consensus view of society that obstructs a deeper analysis of social structures in quite fundamental ways.

A second complementary but distinct point should be made. Clearly patron and client are terms that are sometimes used in particular societies to classify and constitute certain relationships (as are also 'friends' or 'kinsman' for example). These categories are often very much part of local thought and behaviour, and in that regard require analysis as do any other social elements. But it is precisely because they are so often an integral part of local ideology that they must be abandoned for heuristic purposes. The local ideological-normative model cannot be used to analyse itself. Only by such a critical rejection can one begin to show how the ideology and social practices of which patron-client relations are a part are connected, and the complex linkages of ideology and practices to the factors that generate and structure them. For conscious models, to use Lévi-Strauss' term, have important objective factors behind them. Indeed without such factors this way of constituting and thinking of relationships in the everyday world could not be maintained and legitimated.

The area in which I worked, Akkar in North Lebanon, is one of the last regions to be incorporated into the political and economic hinterland of Beirut. It is one of the characteristically undeveloped peripheral provinces that until recently formed effectively a political and quasi-autonomous enclave, in which only the ruling class of Beys (or lords) had outside connections with the governing stratum. Put simply, the lords' modern dilemma has been to maintain strictly personal-factional politics, localism and village bounded loyalties, and a supply of cheap labour by preserving traditional relations of exploitation. For there have developed considerable pressures to invest, diversify and generate far larger surpluses in order to participate in a rapidly widening political arena on a national scale (in which of course other lords were their rivals on the electoral lists). A rise in land prices and the relatively late cultivation of cash crops in the 1960s has compensated to some extent for the sale of land into which many were forced. The old extensive agriculture, mostly cereals with primitive technology, and semi-servile villages in which often all means of production were owned by the Beys, has gradually, but not entirely, given way to wage labour and capitalist agriculture as a side investment (orange groves, etc.) by the Beirut commercial elite and by those lords who early on in the French period had seen what was happening. (This at a time when agriculture as a whole was in decline in terms of share of the GNP and numbers employed.)

Under this form of rent capitalism many of the landowners (and there was hardly any peasant smallholding) either lacked the resources or the political understanding to transform their own positions. They had only limited interest in the process of production but merely skimmed off the proceeds without any corresponding reinvestment. As a fundamentally sterile and parasitical ruling class, they kept going a system of underdevelopment. As Lebanese political and economic relations slowly changed many of such Beys' families were forced to sell land. Expenditure on cars and prestige goods, the exigencies of elections where they themselves had direct political ambitions, or where that was the only avenue to keeping the flow of rewards going out and propping up social prestige in a highly competitive situation, undercut their positions.

Some therefore went for isolation (of which more later). Others went for development, tractors, the use of fertilisers, rationalisation of production methods, while trying to preserve old 'feudal' patterns of dominion over labour and recruitment. These, in the main, became the current big men, owners of villages across the plain into Syria, hand-in-glove with the French between the two world wars, controlling elections, and marrying into the old Syrian ruling class and into other wealthy, aristocratic Lebanese families.

Another part of the attempt to perpetuate this system lies in the use of staffs of retainers drawn from given villages and used mostly in their home villages or, up to 1958, as bailiffs-managers on the plain or in Syria. In the village in which I carried out research one descent group was and is incorporated into the hegemony of status honour, though not all of them were in the service of the lords. They are men of the sword and horse (old Ottoman marks of prestige and nobility and restricted to certain strata) and now of the car and gun (though only as driver and paid gunman). Strong men, sitting and walking a certain way, swaggering, moustache stroking, with a profound contempt for the despised *fellahin* ('peasants'). In short, men of honour. Work and honour are opposed, one *is* a *gabadi*, or a hunter etc., but one does not *work*. One *is*, and one demonstrates it in a certain style of honour which includes an ethic of careless, spendthrift display and throwing away of money in reckless gestures. There is a radical devaluation of productive processes and of labour (and associated ideas of planning, the 'rational' pursuit of profit, attitudes to the future and time, etc.). This is very important because it has played a vital part in undermining their position, as indeed it has that of some of the less successful of the lords who are also imprisoned in an ideology of honour and the traditional 'feudal' relations on which honour is based. What had been the expression of an on-going domination in one structural setting became 'false' consciousness as that setting changed; it worked to the self-undermining of those members of the once ruling groups whose ideology of status, honour remained unchanged, not taking account of altered circumstance. (Interestingly enough, the 1970-1 peasant movements on the Akkar plain were concentrated in those settlements in which Beys, in a kind of 'feudal reaction', were attempting to preserve traditional relations of production, and *not* on the new estates worked by wage labour nor in the mountain villages.) Honour became more and more a ritualised model of expression that less and less reflected the emerging realities, even though men still hold it up as a mirror of the truth.

An identification in a status honour hierarchy of landowners and staffs was made concrete in privileges, rewards, and a monopoly of the means of coercion and violence exercised by the staffs. These remain local, not connected to those of other villages. Objectively they were opposed to the interests of the exploited labourer class, though their relationship to the lords was marked by deep ambivalence. But it is crucial to note that the Beys have in fact over the years gradually undercut the independent position of members of the staff, buying them out of land, hiring individuals as retainers on a purely personal basis and making them completely dependent for livelihood and status on the lord. Honour legitimised them, marked them out as different and superior while the material basis of that honour was being whittled away. The contradictions in their position have become all the stronger as they objectively share more and more in the life chances, economic and occupational level of the *fellahin* and become at best mere henchmen. There is now an extreme emphasis on honour, at the same time as there is equally heavy emphasis on actual social practices which are dedicated to avoiding the application of the code so assertively proclaimed. The unity of the descent group is precarious and its internal politics are marked by endless, shifting, day-to-day factionalism which makes any leadership uncertain. Yet the group's position depends on at least a fictional sense of unity sustained by an increasingly fictional shared status honour.

Where do the sheikhs, of which there are several varieties, fit into all this? Descent groups of sheikhs are found in different kinds of location, geographical and structural, which can be roughly identified as follows:

(a) On the mountain tops. One group is a major lineage in a large village on the heights of the mountain, the last of the major Sunni Muslim villages set in a line at right angles to the sea from the plain to the summit. A second well-known sheikhly group lives at the north end of the mountain range in an isolated area once the centre of an independent local ruling family, the Beni Saifa, long since faded into history. In both situations they are of considerable importance in village affairs and of relatively high prestige even in regional terms. But I would hesitate to call them the dominant lineages of their villages either in numbers or resources.

(b) In the foothills and on the plain. Here the picture is slightly different. In the two villages inhabited by such groups, defined by the criteria of sacred genealogy and wearing the green turban as a mark of status, they are politically and economically dominant. In both they are the single largest descent group and the major landowners or lessees.

(c)   Finally, there are several other villages, two of which are centres of Beys' 'houses', in which there are men called 'sheikhs'. They wear no distinctive dress, claim no corporate genealogical character, and their activities are limited to writing talismen, operating oracles in domestic disputes (e.g., over thefts, though one does not have to be a 'sheikh' to do this), and living lives of a kind of diffuse quietist piety with no great pretensions.

The important thing to note is that, with the exception of the last marginal category, sheikhs and lords are *not* found in the same villages. This separation of domains is instructive and reminds us of Barth's studies (1959) on the Pakhtuns and Saints who also live in separate settlements. There are other parallels too. The Pakhtuns are conquest-based in origin, have a genealogical charter that presents them all as being of one descent, are defined by an effective local monopoly over land and the means of coercion (a monopoly which in the case of the Beys of Lebanon has only recently begun both to break down and to be less significant in political and economic terms). In both cases the only group ideal-typically presented (by non-lords particularly) as equivalent in prestige and standing in the stratification system are the sheikhs. In both the sheikhs are locally linked and defined and have a limited, parochial range in authority, genealogy and geographical jurisdiction, in contrast to the regionally dominant lords. In both they maintain apparently separate domains with spatial and ideological boundaries.

The ideological separation is quite clear. The lord's power (*sulta*) is founded in popular account on force, oppression (*zulm*) and domination (*masaitra*). Opposed to, indeed a contradiction of this set of characterisations, are the authority, Quranic learning and ritual specialisation, sacred genealogy ultimately derived from the Prophet himself, and rights to the emblems and images of religion that mark out the sheikhs. In the many stories of miracles of several prominant religious men who died in the thirties and forties the common theme was one of the discomfiture of the Bey by the sheikh, power overcome by authority. A lord insulted the holy man only to find that his favourite horse had fallen and broken a leg, or his car overturned, or he suffered an illness, and so forth. The miracles are seemingly very political and speak of a specific confrontation of both individuals and of principles, of men and of concepts, of the order of the world and of the order of God.

For ultimately the sheikhs, as men and ideology have it, are links with the Divinity. Not the only or essential links, but links none the less. And one way of judging the strength of those links in a particular case seems to have been measured by encounters with the Beys and the notion that the latter were *compelled* to respect the sheikh in question. He mediates with God and dispenses food, hospitality, and blessing to those who come to the ever-open reception room (the *manzul*).[1] He protects those who respect him by making successful requests on their behalf to the Bey, with whom he is, as it were, on equal and opposite terms. His role is ideal-typically presented by many as that of mediation between strata, 'filling the gap', dispensing blessing and protection, and receiving respect and marks of honour in offerings and gifts.

A sheikh might be said then (both locally and sociologically if one adopted the patron-client approach) to serve as an important semi-independant element in the political system by extending his patronage to others, a patronage that is legitimated and made an economic possibility on the one hand by his link with God and on the other hand by the lords' 'respect' for him (*biyihtirimu* – 'they honour him'). I had initially thought in these terms and taken my analysis in the field precisely to this point. But doubts arose occasioned by an unexpected response to an enquiry. I questioned a local sheikh about his very celebrated maternal uncle, dead some twenty years. Had he not been at odds with the great, not to say notorious, lord of our area? 'Oh, not at all. They got on famously'. But, I persisted, were there not all these stories of antagonism and opposition? 'Well, of course, we had to teach him a lesson first' (literally, 'beat him'), said my interlocutor with a smile, 'but after that they were very close'.

That remark said more perhaps than he knew, certainly more than I at first realised. In the notion of 'teaching a lesson' and enforced respect lies the core of the ideology of the sheikh's worldly role. From our perspective, the strength of the link with the Divinity is very much a function of the supposedly oppositional relation with the principle and reality of lordly power. The popular account *reverses* this reasoning, of course, and respect becomes a function and further proof of the connection with the Divine. Either way both persons and principles are inextricably combined. Indeed the connection is even closer than this and of a rather different nature from that which ideology proclaims. For the Sheikhs are, in fact, the dependents of the Beys, their dependence masked by miracles and the supposed triumph of authority over power.

One clue to the true nature of the relationship lies in a remark which I heard several times when discussions turned to the subject of the political system. Someone would say, perhaps indicating a member of one of the sheikhly houses: 'These are our Beys.' I interpreted this initially simply as deference and a statement about the normative order – that these are the men whom we really respect and regard as our superiors. Yet particularly in the case of our second category (b) above, the sheikhs of the plains and foothills villages, the remark will bear a different interpretation. Namely, that these are the men who are in the same position vis-à-vis ourselves as the lords are in their areas. They rule local affairs and are economically the leading stratum. In this sense sheikh and landless labourer/peasant are as opposed in practice as sheikh and Bey are in theory. In one small village in which the sheikhs are very much the dominant group there has been blood feud for several years between them and the peasant families and the holy men carry guns that their sacred status theoretically makes redundant. Here it is the sheikhs as a group who dominate, rather than any specific individual. Where any sheikh in one of the villages has an independent reputation as a holy man it is quite likely to be outside his own locale. For on his home ground he is the member of a 'ruling class' who share the characteristics of the Bekawat.

Moreover it is still true that the leading members of the sheikhly lineages are maintained in significant part by direct support from the Beys. The famous saint who 'beat' the equally famous Bey received the wherewithal in food, wheat and money supplies to maintain an ever-open sanctuary and *manzul* from that same lord, over whom he had gained the miraculous victories that are quoted as proof of his powers. Insofar as he supported men who regularly came to the *manzul* he did so in material terms by grace of his alleged adversary, with whom he was, as his relative said, 'very close'. The lord 'respected', even 'feared' him and kissed his hand and no other's. He 'honoured' him, and as in the honour code of dominance and challenge, this honour derived ideologically in men's accounts from the sheikh's triumphs, his successful ripostes to the challenges of the lord. The idiom, in other words, is exactly that of the honour code that prevails in the wider society as a model of value and interaction.

This pattern extends to other groups. The leading figures among the sheikhs of the mountain have close ties with the major lords who are politically significant in the national and regional arenas. They act as prestigious supporters and mobilisers of voters and opinions. Their men's houses, which is functionally what the *manzul* amounts to just as among the Pathans, have an important part in the day-to-day and election politics of the mountain villages. On the plains it is more a matter of a class composed of those who have limited land holdings and are part of local dominant descent groups supporting the big power-holders on whom their own place in the system fundamentally depends.

This support takes many forms. The lords often provide cash or food, gifts of fruit, olive oil in season, a welcome in the *manzul* in their village places or in their Tripoli homes. Weddings and funerals are dignified by the sheikhs' presence and the sheikhs dignified by invitations to weddings and funerals. Indeed at major funerals of the Beys, many sheikhs attend, and the larger the numbers and the more well known they are, the greater the status of the event and the religious weight and prestige of the occasion. It is not unusual to see the sheikhs competing with each other as to who will eat fire or chew glass, or who will be 'taken by the exalted state' (*akhadhahu al hal*) in the ritual of chanting the names of God (the *zikr*). At such functions they hold places of high honour and are made much of, particularly by the older lords. The sons of the latter may be impatient of a ritual specialism with which they have little or no contact, but they nevertheless know local society well enough to sit silent and respectful as the sheikhs whirl around and cry out ecstatically. Those lords who still live on the plain in their fortress houses amidst the 'peasantry' observe these vital forms when in the village. A young doctor trained in Beirut, the son of a leading Bey, married a wealthy girl from Iraq with all the trappings of upper-class Lebanese society. The whole entourage travelled in Mercedes convoy to the utterly impoverished settlements on his father's lands and the wedding feast could not begin until the sheikhs had held a *mulid* (a ritual of recitation of *Quran* and the chanting of religious texts and hymns) in which the lord himself participated.

More specifically the Bekawat lease out land to some of the sheikhs at low cost and in this way play an important role in the land holding basis of the sheikhs. It is said that in the past outright gifts of land were made to specific individuals. Whatever the truth of this assertion it is worth noting that such land tends to be of poor quality, heavy soils on the plain that give low yields according to local information and are not irrigated (again this is parallel to the saints' grants of land from the Pakhtuns). Resources may be granted at virtually no cost to the lord himself, but the level of exploitability seems to be fairly low and the sheikhs of course must bear all the costs of seed, machinery time, labour and so on. None of them becomes wealthy as a result of such an arrangement. The man who cultivates 30 acres may be of course a good deal less well off than the mere number might indicate and people have a very practical knowledge of exactly what kind of income a given holding will generate.

They do not, therefore, grow rich as the result of such assistance and none occupy independent positions of regional significance as large land owners or lessees. Yet in local and parochial terms this cheaper letting of land by the lords stabilises and maintains the particular members of the religious descent groups. It enables them also to act as hosts for specifically ritual occasions at which men must also be fed and given proper courtesy and hospitality in the *manzul*. Land, in short, is the most significant factor that cements both a sheikh's position and the 'dependency-alliance' of subordinate and superordinate social strata. In the mountain villages, where the sheikhs form only one descent group among several others commanding equal resources of men, arms and rights to pasture and water, support comes in money and produce in return for political mobilisation and mutual displays of 'respect'.

Since personal relations are so important in national politics and as part of the regional base in elections, such links on plain and mountain, different though they are in specific elements, are of considerable significance to the positions of both sides. Moreover, the relations of exchange diffusely imaged in the idiom of respect are part of the armature of the wider political economy. The real conflict of interests and class position on the plain is *not* between sheikhs and lords, despite all the ideology of authority versus power, but between landholders and labourers. The relations here between sheikhs and peasants are marked by ambivalence and often outright hostility or tension in their home villages. I have myself seen a leading religious figure urging men to drive down to the coast with their automatic rifles to confront labourers who were ploughing up the land of a lord with whom the holy man was connected. The labourers were doing so, it should be added, on another lord's orders and not on their own account. This is a common enough situation of encroachment and sounding a rival's determination to defend his boundaries, a tactic by which the workers are sent out to 'test the water' before a decision is made on a more permanent claim or trespass. Similarly in the 'troubles' on the plain of Akkar in 1970-2 in which the labourers were led by a Tripoli-based agricultural union, the sheikhs of the area, amongst others, rallied men to the defence of the traditional order and the rights of property and land possession.

There are thus very practical purposes to the alliance of landholders. The sheikhs served as defenders of that shared interest far more than as mediators. In very concrete ways, they legitimate the structure of domination in apparent contradiction to the principles on which their own claims to status and uniqueness are founded. The particular links between themselves and the lords are links of dependency, masked as opposition, autonomy and enforced respect and honour. (I would, incidentally expect this to be true of the Saint-Pakhtun relation, both in local idiom and reality.)

It would be quite wrong, however, to say that their position is based purely on dependency on the lords. Even though their 'generosity' is derived ultimately from the lord's material support, it is still 'by their hand'. In the quasi-ritual setting of the *manzul* men eat commensally together, the fire is always alight and endless jugs of coffee are kept hot, hubble-bubble pipes are set before prominant men, and people constantly move in and out. In one *manzul* I attended, packets of cigarettes and tobacco were literally hurled at everyone as if to emphasise the free scattering of things that should not be dignified as 'gifts' or as part of reciprocal relations with some kind of expected return. This paradigmatic situation of hospitality, the almost profligate distribution of food and bounty, the ritualised and communalistic association of friends, strangers, clansmen, kin, leaders and followers, are what go to make the reception room such a complex, open-ended and crucial social institution of village life. Men who keep such a *manzul* take on a heavy burden in running this kind of mobilising and clearing centre for goods, loyalties, information and alliances. And a great deal depends on their own resources of character and kinship and other networks and political associations. This is their organising centre, as it is for any man who wishes to have local influence. That the paradigm has a more specifically religious dimension should not be forgotten. Especially so because of the importance religion has traditionally had in local-level, regional, and national Lebanese politics in the definition of groups and their political and social rights (an importance that goes back to the Ottoman system of state government). The sheikhs are, as it were, 'markers' and symbols of the Sunni identity in North Lebanon. That identity is in certain situations of conflict with other groups, for example, Christian or Shi'a, seen to be quite dominant and indeed primordial. (The history of the area is closely linked with struggle with the Shi'a families now over the mountain for control of the plain and pasture.) The claim to religious competence, associated with holy descent, is quite independent in principle of the patrimonial structure. Both conceptually and theologically 'sheikhness' *is* in some senses opposed to 'power', and were there not factors supporting this opposition the ideology could never have persisted.

In this regard it is noteworthy that those who are spoken of individually as saints and miracle workers lived and were active in the inter-war decades of 1919 to 1940. This was a period characterised by French occupation and the rule of the great local lords who acted in concert with them and ran very large landholdings comprising in some cases many settlements. It seems that at least one or two of the sheikhs were seen as symbols of indigenous and Islamic traditions of identity and authority as distinguished from the Kurdish-descended lords and Christian French. No doubt, too, they may have intervened on many occasions with a lord on behalf of an individual and played the classical role of mediator. No serious movements under sheikhly leadership took place however (cf. North Africa and Cyrenaica), though there are stories of French officers being 'compelled' by miraculous deeds to treat them with 'respect' – a familiar enough theme now. Such revolts as there were took place in the traditionally insurgent area of the Shi'ite Alawite mountain that forms the northern boundary of the plain and *were* led in that region by the sheikhs. On the Akkar plain quietism and control were maintained.

Today there are *no* figures at all who are regarded as miracle workers. When asked why they always speak of saints and saintliness in the past and deny anyone's right to that title and those powers on the contemporary scene, men say: 'Well, there are no Beys anymore, so there are no real sheikhs'. This phrase highlights the notion of opposition of which I have spoken. But it also hints at fundamental changes in Akkari politics.

I observed that even the notion of *baraka* (loosely translated as 'blessing'), so fluid and omnipresent in Egypt and North Africa, was almost totally absent; to the point, indeed, where no sheikh was ever spoken of as 'possessing' *baraka* though one of the saints was described as *mabruk* or blessed. Power here is structured, hierarchy and domination are institutionalised in what is, at least conceptually, a rigid model of social stratification in which free-floating 'blessing' has no part. Nor have the sheikhs monopolistic control over the religious sphere. For, unlike priests, they are not essential to the performance of the prescribed rituals of Islam and they are not organised into any collective body such as a Muslim religious brotherhood (*tariqa*). It was not, then, so much that a given holy man had access to uniquely held resources and meanings as that he represented in concentrated form certain fundamental truths about the nature of things, in part based on the polarity of authority and power.

This polarity concealed a relation that derived its real sustenance from a close link between sheikhs and lords. But again, it was a relation that the sheikhs shared with others. They had no monopoly over entry to the Bekawat. The staffs and retainers were collectively and in personal terms more significant in this respect when it came to favours and interventions. Moreover, the sheikhs were not established as a class of ritual specialists without whom certain vital processes of peace-keeping could not be fulfilled. The pollution of blood and vengeance is not dealt with by ritual but by manoeuvre, factional alignments, the mobilisation of support and much to-ing and fro-ing by big and lesser men or their agents. It is a crucial setting for gaining or demonstrating influence and men who will 'owe' you something for your good offices, but it is not one in which the sheikhs play a major part. It is the lords and their subordinates who try to exploit such critical arenas, and the sheikh's moment comes when the real business is over and he can appear perhaps at a public reconciliation if there is to be one.

The most important Beys have moved to Beirut and Tripoli and they are seen in person much less in the villages and on their holdings. The agents and bailiffs and chauffeurs are the important linking figures for most people. This is the sense in which 'there are no Beys now'. They have been merged in a wider national ruling class operating in the urban centres and broadly speaking dealing through key men in the region. As they have moved out and come to exercise less direct personal control, the sheikhs have been left a little out on a limb. For they are not, particularly on the plain, the men who seem to have either independant standing or privileged access. Some of them are not unimportant at this level, for example on the mountain, but most are rather peripheral to the links of spoils and favours. Even ideologically there are restrictions, for a sheikh's position accords ill with travelling around lining up votes and dependents and fixing jobs and permits as the local first lieutenants to the lords do. As the personal ties have ramified particularly in electoral politics, and as the range of spoils has increased, so the emphasis on a cult of saints and the position of saintly men has declined.

This contrasts with the idea that 'patron-client configurations are structurally related to a specific orientation towards the supernatural world in which the cult of Saints stands out as a dominant element', an idea developed from material on Catholic societies of southern Europe (Blok 1974, pp. 214-15). There is certainly in our case *no* obvious parallel of saintly and political formations, for while personal connections have increased in range and complexity through the social hierarchy, the importance of the holy men has diminished. Since the 'state', in so far as it exists, *is* the ruling elite, access to benefits and resources hangs on personal connections of man to man in a chain of dependence. As Guenther Roth has observed (1971, p.58): 'Some of these new states may not be states at all but private governments of those powerful enough to rule.' This seems to me true in large measure of Lebanon. Furthermore, such personal power is already sanctified in the code of honour, manliness and individualism. Particular religious figures are important of course, and in a very different way from that of the sheikhs; the Maronite church for example, has played a major role in Lebanese politics. But in Akkar the religious specialists have too narrow a base to attempt to operate beyond the *manzul* and their limited spheres of influence. Some of the sheikhs play a local village part in patronage, as do many others. But they do so as dependents themselves, and none plays an independent role on a level with the Bekawat, nor do they mediate between one lord and another. It is not that the state is in some Weberian sense 'rationalised', far from it. But men do have access to 'it'; and, to reverse the usual emphasis, '*it*' *has access to them*. Patron saints are thin on the ground, not a kind of parallel government.

In one dimension it could be said that the ruling group helps to maintain the holy men by links of dependency in order to ensure underdevelopment. The lords have a vested interest in blocking political development even as they themselves, or the successful ones among them, have moved into new economic fields of diversification and investment. Such 'blockage' takes many forms at the level of everyday politics – controls on school building, the provision of clinics and post offices, poor infrastructure of roads and transport, an extremely low level of services and amenities, and so forth. All these things have been either prohibited in areas where the lords are paramount, or they have been used as part of the spoils and rewards for distribution as government and law broadened the patronage possibilities – a road 'at his hand', a clinic because of electoral support. These are ways of preserving personal politics through underdevelopment, and vice versa, limiting the life chances of what amounts to an impoverished and subject population; an attempt to keep up the level of exploitability through control of resources and avenues to income, jobs, and any degree of social mobility. Here what is *withheld* is more important than what is granted. In the maintenance of parochial loyalties, confessionalism, and the traditional symbolism of power, the sheikhs are 'in the interest of the lords', part of a distributive system for the domination of certain social classes by other social classes in a social and economic system of a specific character. But to analyse such a system, incorporating the features of blockage and exploitation, in terms of a 'patron-client system' stands the problem on its head and itself blocks analysis of ideology and structure. It is to mistake symptom for cause.

Clearly the nature of the Lebanese state and the level or stage of state formation is of major significance in determining the character of the distributive system and the control that certain sectors exercise over it. It is generally suggested in the literature on patronage, for example, that the more centralised the state apparatus and the greater the degree of control over a 'rationalised' system of law and sanction, the less likely it is that 'patronage networks' will be politically significant. Further, if people have access to government-controlled resources and benefits through formal bureaucratic agencies, the 'informal' links of patronage will become far more limited in scope, except perhaps at the top of the bureaucratic structures themselves. At the same time the political parties may become the directors of pork barrel patronage and build up local support groups on that basis if the scope of state activity expands. So in this argument patronage reappears in another guise, depending in part of course on the nature of the 'client' constituency. It was of New York that Boss Tweed remarked: 'This population is too hopelessly split up into races and factions to govern it under universal suffrage, except by the bribery of patronage, or corruption.' One gathers that he made virtue of this sad necessity. Or, as we might see it, bribery reinforced ethnicity, in a way helped to create and stabilise it as an element in politics associated with certain kinds of loyalties supposedly in conflict with the 'rationalised', 'modern' system of democracy. It could only work that way, says Boss Tweed, because in that social situation democracy and the formal organisation of the suffrage are impossible without the informal modes of bribery. Or was it because certain groups and classes had a vested interest in only that kind of political order?

The Boss Tweed argument is often put forward for Lebanon by local politicans and by social scientists alike. Confessions and factions, as in New York politics, *are* highly important in the mobilising of followings and the handing out of rewards. Both government office and the legal system *are* part of the political system of distribution and exchange directed from the top by ruling strata. The apparent continuity of this pattern over time and in personnel should be stressed, because it means that from the point of view of the composition of the elite and ruling families there *appears* on the surface to be no radical break in the overall form of political domination, *even though the economic basis for that structure has in fact changed profoundly*. By an emphasis on families is very often implied a *structural* continuity and this gives a completely false picture of the nature of Lebanese society. Study of the transformations of the economy, social stratification and class formations are put to one side while we focus on the surfaces of day-to-day political behaviour, which in very important ways *does* run on personal connections and on individual chieftains' militia, bodyguards of 'client' followings, and so forth. The overall pattern of social change is in this dimension concealed (both for locals and sociologists) by a kind of false concreteness of individualism, a notion that politics and 'the system' are just an aggregation of person-to-person relations. For law and the use of force are the monopoly of no one, and of no central institution. Chieftain, village, region, confession, all are part of the mosaic of power. Unless you have the links, unless you have the services and connections, unless you know someone's local 'key' man, you cannot gain access to these necessities and benefits only the ruling groups can bestow.

So there are very powerful objective factors *at this level of behaviour* which can be ideologically described in the sociological and the native-conscious model as 'patron-client relations'. Yet to assert that 'patron-client links' form a *system*, or are the *framework for analysis* of the political economy, or are the *basis* of the social order, will clearly have a very different effect on our view of a society and how it should be understood than to focus on the organisation of production, the market and labour supply, and the cash nexus. On the one hand is a picture of patrons linked to clients across class lines; on the other, a conflict between owners and labourers.[2]

The mosaic and dyadic ties view tends to see a 'fragmented' system characterised by separate atomised cells or elements between which there are 'gaps' unplugged except by mediators and clientage. The major point about such ties of patronage so-called then becomes that they 'cut across' other dimensions of social stratum and class. Weingrod, for example, sees 'gaps' between locations as generating power and mediators. 'It is this gap between levels (i.e. of the political system, MG) or locales (i.e. between village and village, town and country, etc., MG) which leads 'clients' to search for 'patrons' and which places such power in the hands of mediators' (Weingrod 1967, p.383). In this view, as the social and economic role of the state expands, patronage increases (e.g. through the political parties) and the profound switch from 'traditional' to 'mass' society occurs. As Shils (quoted by Weingrod) puts it, 'the mass of the population has become incorporated into society'. The gaps, presumably, are finally plugged as the state and 'society' reach their final destination, though that society may still run on the fuel of patronage, man to man, link to link, all down the line. The links are seen as running vertically from top to bottom, cross-cutting 'horizontal' ties.

Now it is tempting to say that all this is completely true. In one dimension this *is* precisely what happens in everyday political life and it is certainly how men conceptualise it for visiting anthropologists and for themselves. Peters and others have shown (Peters 1967) how the Bedu conceptualise relations and practice by genealogies, genealogies which can obviously in some sense be said to be 'true', but which cannot be taken as having explanatory power or as serving as the basis of any sociological model of feud in that society. You *have* got to make a connection, know someone, juggle kinship, 'friendship', 'respect', 'dependance' and so forth to get anywhere. And indeed in doing so you may get quite far. Violence itself is not a bad avenue to social ascent (à la Sicily). But in another way this view seems to me also completely false.

In the first place this view of what constitutes social relations is tied to and limited by the notion of face-to-face contact. A villager may say to me 'we have no relations with them over there' and in face-to-face terms this may be perfectly accurate. But that does not mean that it furnishes an adequate characterisation of the social structure as a whole, or a framework for analysis and explanation, or a ground for characterising the society as 'fragmented'. Unless the village exists in some vacuum of total autonomy and self-sustenance, which no village does, it is part of a wider and sociologically more crucial set of relations and structures.

It is extremely difficult to point to a 'gap', except where it has already been 'filled' (teleological functionalism rides again). Mediators are generated by reified 'gaps'. But it seems quite clear in fact that mediators are *not* generated by gaps but by transformations of the economic and political systems such that, for example, a new class or stratum arises out of specific conditions and structures because of specific factors (e.g. the emergence of the estate managers and guards of Sicily who were so important in the mafia in Blok's excellent description). It is banal to say that because, in a stratification model (either local or sociological), stratum B comes 'between' A and C, it 'mediates' between them or fills a 'gap'.

Moreover, the whole notion of mediation, so closely related to the general gap thesis, can be very misleading, as I hope to have shown in my discussion of the role of the holy men. I suppose one could say also that the peasant-lord relation was mediated by rent or taxation or dues, but it hardly advances the argument to say that rent fills a gap or is part of a patron-client tie. This simply misrepresents the nature of the relationship altogether. Indeed it is interesting that the *locus classicus* that is always cited for this view of landlord-peasant relations, Marc Bloch's *Feudal Society*, does not actually support it. Patron-client relationships get three references, church patronage two and patron saints two. The most positive thing he has to say (1961, p.188) is that: 'In the Byzantine provinces, oligarchies of landowners, warriors, and often merchants also, dominated the mass of the humble folk who were sometimes bound to them by a sort of patron-client relationship.' In what I think is a very significant passage he goes on:

But however great the contrasts may have been the transplantation of feudal and vassal relationships was made easy by the fact that they were class institutions. Above the peasant class, and in some cases the burgher class, both of hereditary type, the ruling groups, composed essentially of invaders ... formed so many colonial societies governed by usages which like the rulers themselves, came from abroad.

Obviously Bloch did *not* see 'patron-client' links as either descriptively or analytically primary for an understanding of feudal society.

Having suggested a reversal of perspective which would focus on the access of the state and ruling groups to subject populations, rather than of 'clients' access to the state, let me stand finally another proposition on its head. Instead of placing the emphasis on dyadic links and cross-cutting connections, let us say rather that it is precisely the horizontal dimension that is structurally most significant. All writers in fact agree that the 'patrons' attempt by every means, including force, to maintain monopolistic control over access to resources, information and so on. Let us look at this on the micro-level in Weingrod's discussion (1967, pp.391-2) of a Sardinian village:

At Surughu the influential men included several of the larger land owners, two families of lawyers, the village priest, and preeminently, the village *sindaco* ... The economically advantageous position held by the larger landowners was frequently translated into political influence ... they formed close ties of mutual benefit with village political leaders. ... The *sindaco* was the major political force in the village. ... In alliance with several of the landowners, in league with the local *segretario*, with the tacit and sometimes active assistance of the priest, Serra emerged as the local 'boss' of the village.

What seems to be happening here is alliance and consolidation *at the top*. The most important element, I would argue, is the cementing of ties between the favour givers who have a common interest (and structural position) in excluding favour seekers and keeping them dependent, and incidentally *making sure that everyone thinks in terms of 'gaps' which these big men so providentially fill*. In other words, we are dealing with the crystallisation and consolidation by the dominant group of shared class position at either end of the stratification scale. There is a *reinforcement* of the horizontal dimension rather than a cross-cutting. The cross-cutting comes in the realm of the local model and ideology which does indeed speak of the face-to-face, individual relations, and which is significant in the class and status consciousness of both rulers and dependents. It also comes into the sociologists' model of consensus to which the notion of a patronage glue is fundamental. The sociologist, operating in part with his own functionalist model and in part with the conscious model of sections of the society he is studying, celebrates the integrative power of clientage. But in doing so he makes it impossible to study objectively both his own and others' ideologies and the structures of domination from which they were generated.

ACKNOWLEDGMENTS

I should like to thank all the members of the seminar for their comments and criticisms, and the American Universities Field Staff offices in Rome for their kind hospitality. I owe particular thanks to friends and colleagues who gave time to reading the paper and raised major and minor issues with me: Talal Asad, Ken Brown, Ernest Gellner, Joel Kahn, Julian Lait and Sami Zubaida. They are not responsible for the views expressed.

NOTES

1. A lord wishing to build up and maintain a position for himself, especially at election time, must also keep a *manzul* open for meeting, largesse, exchange of information, the trading and granting of favours, very much on Pakhtun lines. It is an item of major expense and frequently leaves a loser with unpleasantly large debts, even leading to the selling of land.
2. I am referring here to Martinez-Alier's trenchant critique (1971) of Pitt-Rivers' work on a Spanish village.

REFERENCES

Barth, F. (1959) *Political Leadership Among the Swat Pathans*. London.
Bloch, M. (1961) *Feudal Society*. London.
Blok, A. (1974) *The Mafia of a Sicilian Village, 1860-1960*. Oxford.
Boissevain, J. (1966) 'Patronage in Sicily', *Man* 1, 18-33.
Fustel de Coulanges, N. (1870) *La Cité antique*. Paris.
Hall, A. (1974) 'Patronage', *Journal of Peasant Studies*, 1, no.4.
Lemarchand, R. (1972) 'Political clientelism and ethnicity in tropical Africa: Competing solidarities in nation-building', *American Political Science Review* LXVI (March), 68-90.
Martinez-Alier, J. (1971) *Labourers and Landowners in Southern Spain*. London.
Peters, E.L. (1967) 'Some structural aspects of the feud among the camel-herding Bedouin of Cyrenaica', *Africa* XXVII, no.3, 261-82.
Powell, J.D. (1970) 'Peasant societies and clientelist politics', *American Political Science Review* LXIV, no. 2, 411-25.
Roth, G. (1971) 'Personal rulership, patrimonialism and empire-building: The new states', in R. Bendix and G. Roth (eds), *Scholarship and Partisanship: Essays on Max Weber*. Berkeley.
Weingrod, A. (1968) 'Patrons, patronage, and political parties', *Comparative Studies in Society and History* 10, 377-400.

Samir Khalaf

Changing forms of political patronage in Lebanon

> All human societies and their institutions are, at the root, a barrier
> against naked terror.
> (Peter Berger, *The Sacred Canopy*)

A cursory review of any daily Lebanese newspaper is bound to reveal
a preoccuption with stories such as the following:

1. Sabri Hamadeh, the traditional political *za'im* of the Shi'ite
community of Baalbeck, declared his intention to seek his 25th
nomination as Speaker of the Chamber of Deputies – the second
ranking position in the formal hierarchy of power in Lebanon. Like
most other veteran politicans (*aqtab* as they are popularly labelled by
the press), Hamadeh is an absentee landlord, a descendent of a feudal
family that can trace its genealogical descent to the 15th century and
the undisputed head of an extensive clan. Typical of the traditional
zua'ma, he has been a prominent figure in the political life of Lebanon
for close to half a century, and has succeeded in representing his
constituency in every parliamentary election held thus far. He served
as minister a score of times and has had a virtual monopoly over the
speakership of the Chamber of Deputies. Of all forty-two regular
parliamentary sessions since independence, Hamadeh was elected
twenty-four times. During the remaining sessions the speakership
rotated between two other prominent Shi-ite feudal families of the
south: Assad (nine times) and Usayran (eight times). In declaring his
intention to seek the speakership yet another round, Hamadeh
identified no program or platform other than his purely personal whim
to cap his political career by celebrating a golden jubilee.

2. Camille Chamoun, though not a scion of a feudal family, has
also been one of the most ubiquitous and entrenched political figures
of contemporary Lebanon. He was first elected to the National
Assembly of 1934-37, and like the spirited politicians of the day, he
participated in the national struggle for independence, served as
minister in successive cabinets, and became President of the Republic
(1952-8). Rather than retiring after his eventful term as President, he
established his own 'National Liberals' political party, regained his
parliamentary seat, and has since been instrumental in the formation

of several coalitions – often with some of his earlier and most bitter adversaries – to assert his continued influence on the political life of the country. Like other *aqtab*, he has formed his own militia group – a paramilitary organisation of trained and disciplined retainers – for the professed purpose of assisting in maintaining law and order and safeguarding Lebanon's sovereignty. In recent months the whole question of the presence of private militias within a nation state, because of their growing visibility in public places and the concomitant display of arms and explosives, has become a hotly contested issue with charges and counter charges of arms smuggling, espionage and the demise or erosion of state power.

Practically every day, the papers carry sensational headlines of a new 'scandal' involving deals, kickbacks, *quid-pro-quos* and other evidence of corruption, nepotism, graft and squandering of public funds. Some of the most recent are the 'Régie scandal' (the state tobacco monopoly) involving the sale of defective tobacco, mismanagement and bribery; the sale and resale of municipal real estate property; technical incompetence of government officials; ministers taking advantage of their short term in office to appoint some of their own clients in excess of positions available; the disproportionate allocation of public funds for projects in politically 'desirable' regions to the exclusion of others currently out of favour; the personal and often arbitrary intervention of the President of the Republic in expediting certain public projects while obstructing or suspending others.

Papers also carry repeated stories of long-standing family and tribal feuds being liquidated without retributive justice; of mutinous *qabadayat* (henchmen) of known political leaders taking the law in their own hands in defiance of government authority; of offenders wanted for honour crimes seeking the protection of their local *za'im*; of marginal and interest groups (Shi'ites, Palestinian Resistance, banana growers, fishermen etc.) demonstrating their grievances against government abuse and indifference by imposing road blocks and cordoning off urban districts and neighbourhoods; of dismissed university students seeking the patronage of politicians and religious leaders.

Monday morning papers, at least during the three months of summer, almost always carry engaging accounts of a day in the life of President Frangieh while on his family homestead in Ihden. Every Sunday, and often on other days, the President literally holds an open house. All protocol is lifted and any person, regardless of station or background, can seek his audience without previous appointment. He personally enquires about each of his visitors' relatives, recalling nostalgically past moments they might have shared together, listens to their grievances and promises prompt attention. Much like the fief holder of old, presiding over the private concerns of his estate, he is more the affable, benign and personable 'Bey' displaying genuine empathy and compassion in the lives of his subjects than a President carrying on with the affairs of state. He is no longer President Frangieh but 'Abou Toni' or 'Suleiman Bey', the tribal *za'im* (boss, chief) of a tightly knit community.

Though seemingly unconnected, all these instances – the resilience of traditional leaders, veteran politicians seeking to extend their political clientage, corruption, tribal feuds and the grievances of dispossessed groups and marginal communities, and the personal and affective style of political leadership – are manifestations of essentially the same phenomenon: the ubiquity and survival of patronage in Lebanon. This is far from unusual in a pluralistic society marked by persistent disparities in status and opportunity and sustained by highly personalised networks of reciprocal obligations and primordial loyalties. To a large measure, much of the socio-political history of Lebanon may be viewed as the history of various groups and communities seeking to secure patronage: client groups in search of protection, security and vital benefits, and patrons seeking to extend the scope of their clientage.

Within such a context, the middleman, the *wasit* and the broker, who provides greater access to opportunity, needed services and protection, emerges as the most prized and viable political actor. Likewise, patron-client ties become one of the most fundamental of all social bonds. In their most rudimentary form, all such ties involve the 'reciprocal exchange of extrinsic benefits'. Both the patron and the client (Blau 1964, p.314; Lemarchand 1972, pp. 75-6) have a vested interest in maintaining this kind of mutually beneficial transaction. Despite their asymmetrical nature – and all patron-client ties bring together people with marked disparities in wealth, status and power – they remain essentially an exchange partnership. As will be shown, clients in Lebanon have no more accessible avenue to secure some of their personal services, favoured treatment and protection, than through their allegiance to a patron, and patrons can only maintain their power by extending the size of their clientage support. Herein lies the ubiquity and survival of patronage in Lebanon.

1. Feudalism and patronage

In its broad features, the socio-economic and political organisation of Mount Lebanon during the latter part of the eighteenth and early nineteenth centuries may be easily characterised as 'feudal'. In both its origin and evolution, the *iqta'* system of Mount Lebanon had much in common with other feudal societies. Yet as several writers have suggested (Chevallier 1971; Harik 1965, 1968; Poliak 1939; Polk 1963) it had also unique features of its own which distinguished it clearly from the *iltizam* system of tax-farming prevalent in other provinces of the Ottoman Empire. It is not too difficult to trace the origin and some of the persisting peculiarities of patronage to that special variety of Lebanese feudalism.

As the term itself suggests, *iqta'* denotes a socio-economic and political system composed of districts (*muqata'as*) in which political authority was distributed among autonomous feudal families (*muqata'jis*). The *muqata'ji* was subservient to the *Amir* or *Hakim* who, as supreme ruler, occupied an office vested in a family – in this case the Shihabi Imarah or principality. Within the context of the Ottoman system of government, the Sultan was formally the highest authority over the rulers of Mount Lebanon and their subjects. The *Amir* received his yearly investiture through one of the Sultan's representatives, the pashas of Saida, Tripoli or Damascus, under whose administration Lebanon and its dependencies were divided. Through the pashas, the *amir* also forwarded his annual tribute (*al-miri*) which he owed the Ottoman Treasury. In effect, however, neither the Sultan nor the pashas – with the noted exception of al-Jazzar's governorship of Saida (1776-1804) – meddled very much in the internal affairs of Mount Lebanon. Most historians seem in agreement that the *amirs* enjoyed considerable autonomy in exercising their authority. One, in particular, goes so far as to assert that the Ottoman government in Mount Lebanon 'was virtually a fiction – the Sultan was recognized as the supreme lord, yet he was so far removed in distance and power that the Amir al-Hakim was the actual supreme ruler in the land' (Harik 1965, p. 409).

As supreme ruler, the *amir* had the double task of dealing with the demands of the Ottoman pashas and acting as arbitrator among the *muqata'jis* in case of internal conflict. The specific duties of collecting taxes, maintaining peace and order, raising a limited annual amount of unpaid labour from the peasantry, exercising judicial authority of first instance over all local, civil and criminal cases involving penalties short of death, were all part of the traditional authority of the *muqata'ji* (Kerr 1959, p.3).

One of the unusual political features of the *iqta'* system of Mount Lebanon, one which had implications for patron-client networks, was its non-military character. It was clearly not organised as a military fief. Unlike the fief holders in Syria, Egypt and Palestine, those of Mount Lebanon had no fixed military duties and were not required to maintain a specific contingent of troops. The Shihabi *amirs* did keep a small number of retainers mostly for administrative purposes, but they had no army or police force to speak of.

This non-military feature reveals a subtle but basic characteristic of the nature of political legitimacy and allegiance in the *iqta'* system. Legitimacy is based more on personal loyalty than on coercive obedience to an impersonal authority. In other words, the *amir* need not resort to coercion to generate and sustain conformity to his authority. Instead he relied on the good will of his *muqata'jis* and the personal allegiance of their followers (*atba'* or *'uhdah*). Furthermore, this form of political allegiance was not sectarian or confessional but predominantly personal. The mutual moral obligations and feelings of inter-dependence inherent in such personal ties are aptly described and documented by Harik (1965, p.411):

> To be of the *'uhdah* of a *muqati'ji* placed moral obligations not only on the followers but also on the *muqati'ji*, who would come to the aid of his men and protect them. This duty was usually expressed as *haq al-riayah wa al-himayah* (to tend and protect). To maintain his integrity and position in the political life of the Imarah, a *muqati'ji* was well aware that he had to have a strong following and a loyal one. Sometimes *muqati'jis* went so far in protecting their followers as to place political considerations above accepted rules of good conduct.

This is clearly a form of a patron-client tie, involving the exchange of support for protection. This form of patronage, with all its moral undertones of mutual benefit and avowed loyalty between protector and protegé, could be easily sustained under the special variety of Lebanese feudalism. Unlike the system of *iltizam* prevalent in other Ottoman provinces, where the *multazim* was essentially a government official with no special ties to the village or tax farm under his control, the *muqata'ji* usually lived in his own village among his own *atba'*. Much like the bureaucrat of a centralised administration, the *multazim's* sole concern was to remit the yearly tribute and maintain law and order in his district. Since his tenure in office was usually at the mercy of a pasha's capricious whim, he developed little interest in the welfare of his subjects and tried instead to enrich himself at their expense.

In contrast, the *muqata'ji*'s power and economic well-being depended on the continuous support and loyalty of his *atba'*. Accordingly, he was less likely to be oppressive and rapacious toward them. The beneficial effects of such a system of patronage, particularly since it involves propinquity between feudal lord and peasant, should not be overlooked. More important, the *iqta'* system permitted more responsibility to be exercised at the local level than was the case under *iltizam*. The *multazim* was essentially a representative of the government in the village. As an autonomous feudal chief, the *muqata'ji* enjoyed a much larger measure of independence in his jurisdiction. Indeed, both the *amir* and the *muqata'ji* did all they could to ward off Ottoman encroachment on their own traditional rights. The Shihabi *Hakim* himself had no direct relations with the subjects; and if he had any particular wish or grievance with regard to any particular subject, it had to be mediated through the *muqata'ji*. In such a differentiated hierarchy of authority, the *muqata'ji* emerged with almost undisputed sovereignty over his own district. This sovereignty was further reinforced and perpetuated by the hereditary character of the *iqta'* system. 'Power and transference was subject to blood relationship. ... Both title of nobility and government rights were passed from father to son and thus authority was kept within the patrilineal kinship group' (Harik 1965, p.420). The *muqata'ji* lived on his fief, attended personally to the affairs of his subjects, and was clearly not part of a court aristocracy. Nor was he a tribal leader, although political authority and succession were kept within the same family. The feudal districts he presided over were composed of heterogeneous kinship and religious groups (Harik 1968, pp. 64-73).

2.   *Varieties of political patronage*

Throughout the nineteenth century, most of the conditions associated with the survival and vitality of patron-client networks – marked disparities in the distribution of wealth, status and power; isolated and closely knit communities; factional and partisan rivalries and highly personalised and diffuse social obligations and loyalties – continued to display themselves under varied forms. They also generated different forms of patronage. A brief word about each is in order.

1.   A recognised hierarchy of ranks among the feudal elites had evolved as a rather formalised system of social prestige sustained by elaborate forms of social protocol and rules of conduct (Shadiaq 1954; Shihab 1933; Harik 1965; Salibi 1965, pp. 8-12). The distribution of prestige among the different families was far from arbitrary. It reflected a continuity of traditional considerations, of which the following seem the most prominent: the actual power each of the families held (such as the hierarchy of noble titles differentiating that of an *amir, muqaddam* and *sheikh*), the vintage of their kinship genealogy, and the esteem the families happened to enjoy in the eyes of the ruling Shihabs. For example, only three houses held the title of *amir* (Shihab, Abillama and Arslan), one *muqaddam* (Muzhir), and several (Jumblat, Imad, Abu Nakad, Talhuq, Abd al-Malik among the Druzes, and Khazin, Hubaysh and Dahdah among the Maronites) were entitled to the rank of *sheikh*. Together these eight families formed a special class of 'great sheikhs' (*al-mashayikh al-kibar*), differentiated from other feudal families (such as Azar, Dahir and Hamada) in terms of titular prestige and the extent of their feudal tenure and control over their respective *muqata'as*.

2.   The social structure of Mount Lebanon was also differentiated horizontally into isolated and closely knit village communities. The mountainous terrain and the division of the country into distinct geographic regions, each with its own particular customs, dialect, folklore and social mannerism rendered the village community a fundamental unit in the society. Strong endogamous ties, continuities in the patterns of residence and landownership, attachment to feudal families who also resided in the village, along with geographic isolation from other communities all tended to reinforce village loyalties and make the villager conscious of communal interests. So strong were these loyalties, that village identity often superseded kinship, religious or class attachments (Polk 1963, p. 70).

This is all the more remarkable since the village communities, like the feudal districts, were generally of mixed confessional composition. Neither the predominantly Christian communities of the north nor the pre-dominantly Druze communities of the south were homogeneous in their sectarian structure. In fact, of all the feudal districts only three in the North (Bcharri, Zawiya and Futuh) were Maronite, and one in the South (Jabal al-Rihan) was Shi'ite (Chevallier 1971, pp. 61-3).

The implications of such communal and regional isolation for patron-client networks are self-evident. Villagers, among other things, required protection from the oppressive tyranny and rapacious controls of distant pashas and *amirs*. They also needed protection from the excessive demands of the central administration, particularly the ruinous impositions of *corvée*, taxation and arbitrary conscription. Warding off the encroachment of competing factions or other village communities was also a persistent need. Any person or group that could offer the needed security and protection and that was in a position to alleviate the heavy exactions levied on the peasants was bound to inspire allegiance among clients. Initially, the *muqata'jis*, by virtue of the authority and autonomy they enjoyed, were the most likely group to offer such patronage. No other group, at least until 1820, could have challenged their supremacy or offered alternative avenues for protection and security.

3. The feudal society of Mount Lebanon, all other integrative evidences of harmony and balance notwithstanding, was far from factionless. There were deep splits and rivalries between feudal families competing for power positions or seeking to win the favours of a governing *amir* or an Ottoman pasha. In fact, the Ottoman pashas so encouraged such rivalry that it became a policy of theirs to play off one *amir* against another as a means of containing the growing influence of powerful vassals. All such factional splits, at least initially, were predominantly of a partisan or kinship nature. They rarely took the form of a class or confessional conflict. They were also fairly fluid and loose in that the factions could easily reorganise themselves into new alignments.

The factional and kinship rivalries soon developed into broader class and confessional conflict. The peasant uprisings of 1820, 1840 and 1856 and the outbreak of confessional hostility in 1841 and 1860 generated new forms of patron-client relationships. The peasant seditions ushered in the church as an alternate source of patronage and political leadership. For the first time in the history of modern Lebanon, commoners and clerics took the initiative in organising a revolt against some of the abuses of the *iqta'* system. Though the sedition was limited in scope to a protest against the imposition of additional taxes by the Ottoman Pasha of Saida, it generated some unanticipated consequences which influenced the nature of political legitimacy. Clerics helped organise the peasants into village communes and asked each village to choose a *wakil* (representative) as a spokesman who could act on their behalf with other *wakils* and government authorities (Shidiaq 1954, p.45; Shihab 1933, p.685). Simple as it may seem, this innovative institution had revolutionary implications for transforming the political perspectives of peasants and challenging feudal authority and the nature of political allegiance to it. Insurgents from the Maronite districts of the north (Christians of the Druze-dominated districts of south Lebanon did not participate) drew up a convenant in which they pledged their solidarity as *'ammiyyah* (commoners), their unswerving loyalty to their *wakils*, their determination to oppose additional taxes and to struggle collectively in safeguarding their communal public interests (Harik 1968, pp. 213-14).

By choosing a *wakil* from among the *'ammiyyah* and entrusting him with the task of being their spokesman on all matters of common interest, such covenants were, in effect, articulating a new concept of authority; one which necessitated a shift from the ascriptive ties of status and kinship to those based on communal and public interest. In much the same way, this also involved a change in the peasant's political perspectives: he no longer perceived himself as being bound by personal allegiances to his feudal lord. Instead, and perhaps for the first time, he was made conscious of his communal loyalties and the notion of public welfare – *al salih al 'umumi* (Harik 1968, p. 221).

Despite such new perspectives and the new enthusiasm touched off by the initial stages of the rebellion, the *'ammiyyah* revolt remained essentially a Maronite phenomenon and was predominantly confined to the Christian *muqata'as* of the north. Only one Druze feudal family – the Imads of the Yazbaki faction – expressed willingness to support the *'ammiyyah* cause. Efforts to seek the assistance of others in the south proved futile. The uprising clearly failed to spark the same spirit of revolt among the *'ammiyyah* of the Druze. In this sense, one might argue, the ideological nationalism generated and encouraged by the Maronite clergy was parochial not civic. Even when perceived as a class rivalry, the commoners of the south remained overwhelmingly loyal to their feudal sheikhs and refused to heed the call of 'class' or 'public' consciousness articulated in the north.

All other efforts in the nineteenth century to undermine the authority and local autonomy of the feudal sheikhs proved equally futile. For example, the decade of centralised and direct Egyptian rule (1831-41), in which sweeping reforms were introduced by Ibrahim Pasha from above, had little visible effect on subordinating the powerful feudal chiefs. True, the power of some of the prominent Druze feudal families of the south was temporarily destroyed by Amir Bashir in 1825. Much of their property was confiscated and they were forced into exile. Most of these families, however, had little difficulty in restoring their usurped rights and privileges. After 1840, they began to reclaim their former estates and regain their feudal prerogatives.

The same is true of the efforts of the Ottomans, following the outbreak of sectarian hostilities of 1841 and 1845, in reorganising the administrative divisions of Mount Lebanon. Both the double *qu'immaqamiyyah* (the partition scheme advanced by the European powers in 1843 to divide Lebanon into separate Christian and Druze districts each with its own sub-governor) and the so-called Règlement Shakib Efendi of 1845 (which attempted to rectify some of the jurisdictional inadequacies inherent in the scheme) did not undermine the power of the feudal chiefs (Jouplain 1908, pp. 297-353). Indeed, as some observers have argued, the traditional authority and privileges of the feudal families remained virtually untouched (Churchill, pp. 109-10).

The same outcome accompanied other Ottoman efforts to organise local councils (*majlis* or *diwan*). Both Christian and Druze feudal sheikhs again perceived such arrangements as an attempt to undermine their local autonomy and refused to participate. In the coastal cities, the system of local councils reinforced rather than undermined the power of notables and *'ayan*. The general population was barely represented on the councils, and consequently local notables and Muslim religious leaders were able to consolidate and extend their patronage by playing their traditional role as intermediaries between the general population and the central government. In fact, throughout the *Tanzimat* period (1839-1856), a form of cooperation between the urban elite and Turkish officials was gradually evolving into a consistent feature. The power of urban notables also extended to rural areas, and they were able to form alliances with feudal families. This was particularly true after the demise of the Shihabi dynasty when the sphere of power and influence gradually shifted toward Beirut. Different families or factions in the mountain began to seek new contacts among the bourgeoning urban elite. It was in this period, for example, that the alliances between Druze feudal sheikhs of the Shuf and Muslim notables of Beirut began to be established (Hourani 1968, pp. 62-3).

The *Mutasarrifiyah* (governorate) of Mount Lebanon (1860-1920) generated new forces which reinforced rather than undermined the power of the traditional feudal families. The Règlement Organique of 1861 called for another geographic rearrangement of the country. Lebanon was now stripped of its three major coastal cities (Beirut, Tripoli and Sidon) and its fertile regions of al-Biqa' and Wadi al-Taym, and divided into seven districts (*qada'*) each under a sub-governor (*qaymakam*) with further divisions into smaller counties (*mudiriyahs*). The Règlement also called for a central Administrative Council composed of twelve members presided over by a Christian governor who is designated by the signatory powers. The distribution of seats within the council was purely on a confessional basis, i.e., each of the major six sects (Maronite, Greek Orthodox, Catholic, Druze, Shi'ite and Sunni Muslim) claiming two seats.

These and other provisions of the Règlement no doubt undermined the security and social standing of the feudal families and threatened to make a disgruntled class out of them. So did the growing agricultural and commercial class, mostly urban moneylenders, who were already vying for a greater share of the influence and exclusive privileges the feudal famililes had been enjoying. Accordingly, the *mutesarrif* 'undertook to keep them content by arranging for their gradual absorption into the new administration. During the seven years of (Dawud Pasha's) *mutesarrifate* no less than sixteen feudal emirs or sheikhs were appointed to the leading government positions, the later *mutesarrifs* followed Dawud Pasha's policy in this respect' (Salibi 1965, pp. 111-12).

The gradual absorption of prominent families into the new government bureaucracy generated some of the conditions conducive to the emergence of a new breed of political leadership or patronage; a patronage more bureaucratic than feudal in nature, and one which came to play a prominent role in the political life of Lebanon in subsequent decades. Individuals with legal and bureaucratic skills began to develop their political careers under the tutelage of the Ottomans and the French. The political power and social prestige which this new 'administrative aristocracy' came to enjoy was a reflection of their participation in the movements of reform, independence and Arabism which consumed the intellectual resources of the emerging elite at the time. Consequently their status was relatively more achieved than ascribed.

The leadership which emerged during this period, along with their second and third generation descendants, constitutes today the bulk of the political elite of Lebanon. If the country can boast of any political heroes, ideologists, reactionaries or popular urban activists, they all received their political socialisation – in one form or another – during this eventful period. The Khuris of the Shuf, the Solhs of Saida, the Khalils of Sour, the Salams, Beyhums, Daouks, Taqlas and Chihas of Beirut, the Karamis of Tripoli, the Eddes of Batroun: these and a score of other prominent names were drawn – partly by accident and partly by design – into the political and national struggle of their communities. Little wonder that they began to offer new sources of patronage.

The composition of the parliament continues to reflect the intimate association between this form of legal and administrative patronage and political leadership. With the declining influence of feudal families, lawyers, magistrates and government officials became the closest groups to the loci of power and consequently were in a better position to offer the needed benefits to their clients. This may partly account for the continuing popularity of the legal profession in Lebanon. It is still considered, by many political aspirants, as the natural and most effective means for extending their political clientage. The Chamber continues to draw 35 to 40 percent of its deputies from legal and auxiliary professions (Zuwiyya 1968, pp. 96-7).

The socio-economic and political transformations after the Second World War in the form of rural exodus, expanding economic opportunities, rapid urbanisation and the growth of political parties and pseudo-ideological groups, led to the emergence of a new form of political patronage. Self-made entrepreneurs and popular political activists, more receptive to the secular and ideological interests of urban masses, began to offer novel sources of patronage. The new patrons derived much of their support from the relatively amorphous and heterogeneous urban masses, and were more politically oriented and prone to resort to catchy and popular slogans to incite mass appeal. Leaders like Saeb Salam of Beirut, Rashid Karami of Tripoli, Ma'ruf Saad of Saida, the late Emile Bustani of Shuf, and, more recently, younger upstarts like Abdel Majid al-Rafi'i of Tripoli, Ali Khalil of Sour and Najah Wakim of Beirut, to mention a few, have all invoked ideological and pseudo-ideological slogans to capture a transient political mood or to capitalise on concern over some overriding public issue. When not courting Ba'athist, Pan Arabist, Nasserist, Nationalist and, more recently, Palestinian resistance rhetoric, some of the leaders within this group have formed their own parties and parliamentary blocs. Others sponsored or patronised labour organisations and established benevolent voluntary associations to extend the scope of their clientage.

More than the other forms of patronage this pseudo-ideological variety, no doubt, subsumes within it a mixed and heterogeneous group of political leaders. They all display, however, one underlying feature in common. The basis of their patronage remains largely personal and tightly circumscribed. In supporting a Salam or a Karami, the followers pledge their support more for the person than his programme. In this sense, this form of patronage shares some of the attributes of the other more traditional types.

This sketchy overview of the three forms of patronage (to a large measure they represent three different stages in the political history of Lebanon) should have made it clear that what sustains the *za'im* as a political figure – whether feudal, administrative or pseudo-ideological – are the personal and communal ties of fealty. His political assets remain reciprocal loyalties and obligations. Thus the seemingly more liberal and emancipated political leaders have much in common with the *aqtab* they frequently admonish and deride. Younger aspirants for public leadership, with rare exceptions, all seek to establish their political base not by articulating a programme or identifying critical issues or specific problems requiring reform but by building up a personal entourage of clients and followers. Much like the *aqtab*, the bulk of their time and effort is devoted to interceding with public officials on behalf of their clients. Both the private interests of clients and the political careers of patrons are served by patronage.

Politicians in Lebanon rise or fall more on the size of their clientage and competence at dispensing personal favours than on their merit in articulating the coping with public issues and problems. To refuse favours is to risk losing votes, and ultimately diminish one's base of support. Instances of this kind of failure are legion in Lebanon. Resourceful and spirited young intellectuals, sparked by a genuine concern for public service and civic reform, have consistently failed in national elections. The few that have succeeded are invariably ones who have been adopted or sponsored by a traditional *za'im*.

3.   Survival and consequences of patronage

What perpetuates political patronage in Lebanon and how do patrons – whether 'feudal', 'administrative' or 'pseudo-ideological' – retain and extend the scope of their clientage? The discussion thus far has underscored some of the socio-historical circumstances associated with the survival of patronage. We turn now to a consideration of two further, and perhaps more vivid, conditions which account for the ubiquity of patronage in the contemporary political life of Lebanon; namely kinship loyalty and the peculiarities of the electoral system.

Familism

The whole political history of Lebanon may be viewed as the history of a handful of leading families competing to affirm their name, power and prestige in their respective communities (Khalaf). Over the entire span of 50 years of parliamentary life, only 359 deputies, representing 210 families, have won parliamentary seats. This amounts to not more than 8 percent of the total number of families in Lebanon.[1] The extent of such exclusiveness is strikingly different among the various religious groups. While 65 families have represented the Maronites, the proportion declines to 50 among the Sunni Muslims, 34 among the Greek Orthodox, 26 among the Shi'ites, 13 among the Greek Catholics and only 9 among the Druze. Furthermore, of the 359 deputies, slightly more than 300 may be considered to have 'inherited' their parliamentary seat from a family descendent (al-Nahar 1972).

This is particularly true of the so-called *aqtab* of today. With rare exceptions, they are heirs of a long political tradition and continue to exercise much of their political influence by virtue of kinship ties. Like their fathers and grandfathers before them, they too are initiating their own sons – at least those who have politically inclined offspring – into the political life of the country. What needs to be underscored here is that when patronage is supplemented by ties of kinship it is bound to acquire added intensity and survival. The son, himself his father's client, attains more credibility as a patron if the source of his patronage is reinforced by family loyalty. Even if he were to disavow such primordial heritage, as Kemal Jumblat has attempted to do, it is questionable whether his traditional clientele will accept such disavowal. To them he is a Jumblatti, a member of a Druze community before he is a progressive socialist.

Electoral system

The electoral system, which was promulgated by the constitution of 1926 and has since undergone no fundamental modifications, is based on a combination of a single electoral college and proportional representation of the various communities or confessions. Conceptually, the system was conceived to enable each community to be represented in the parliament in proportion to its size,[2] but without becoming a sort of state within the state.

To accomplish this, the electoral system, to a certain degree, compels each candidate to depend on votes outside his own religious community. For example, in the district of Aley two Druzes, two Maronites and one Greek Orthodox are to be elected. Two or three contesting lists or ballots are formed bearing the same confessional composition. Electors are free to vote for any candidate from among the lists as long as they observe the confessional proportion established for that district. In this case, the second Greek Orthodox who might have received more popular votes than the other successful Maronite and Druze candidates will not be elected. What this single college system has meant is that each elected candidate, though competing with a confessional rival, is, to a large measure, a representative of communities other than his own. In fact, in mixed electoral districts (and of all 26 districts only 9 are homogeneous confessional communities) a candidate cannot be elected unless he is reasonably well-accepted by other confessional groups of his constituency. Indeed, in some instances it is the religious communities other than that of the candidate which guarantee his success or failure. In the last national elections of 1972, Najah Wakim, a virtually unknown candidate – supported by the so-called Progressive Nasserist coalition popular among the urban Sunni Muslims – won one of the Greek Orthodox seats in Beirut while in fact receiving little of the votes of his own religious sect.

These safeguards or constitutional peculiarities of the Lebanese electoral system, reinforced by the National Pact of 1943, may have done much to promote harmony, justice and balance among the various communities but they accomplished little in curtailing the power of the *zu'ama*. If anything the division of the country into small electoral units gives the *zu'ama* a freer hand to assert their influence and perpetuate their power over local communities.[3] Each of the *aqtab* reigns supreme in his own district and runs virtually unchallenged electoral contests. They exercise complete authority in selecting the candidates on their lists, set the going or market price for each candidate (i.e., the sum they owe the *za'im*) and dictate whatever strategy or policy the list as a collectivity is to follow. The candidates are usually more than happy to oblige. In addition to paying the set tribute, they defray the full financial burdens of the campaign, act on behalf of their *za'im* in dispensing favours and services and, in some instances, declare their total obedience to him. In short, they are no longer partners in a joint venture but 'clients' in a reciprocal though asymmetrical exchange. A poignant manifestation of this extreme form of patronage appears in a pledge signed by those on the list headed by Suleiman al-Ali in the elections of 1953.[4] The text reads as follows:

We swear by God Almighty, by our honour, and by all that is dear to us, that – having agreed to participate in the battle of legislative elections on the same list – we pledge ourselves, in the case of victory by the grace of God, to follow in the Lebanese Parliament the directives and the policy that will be dictated to us by His Excellency our companion in the struggle, Suleiman Bey al-Ali el Mara-aby, and to act in a manner to carry out all that he wills. We pledge ourselves to back him in all that he desires, in the Ministry or outside of it, and not to swerve one bit from the attitude he intends to adopt with regard to the authorities as a partisan or as an opponent. If we do not keep our promise and fail to fulfill this oath we recognize ourselves to be unworthy of the human species, and deprived of honour and gratitude.

The relationship between the *za'im* and his clients nonetheless remains fundamentally one of reciprocity. The *za'im* throws in his political weight, influence and social prestige, and his clients reciprocate by providing other resources he (the *za'im*) may lack: money, youthfulness, advanced education, a progressive, forward-looking outlook, and most significantly a kinship, regional or communal affiliation that might weaken the strength of an opposing list. Kamal Jumblat, for example, has persistently and skilfully relied on the latter – i.e., incorporating some of the Maronite notable families in the Shuf – to erode the electoral strength of his arch rival in the area, Camille Chamoun. Alternatively two or three of the *aqtab* may resort to coalitions, mostly in the form of temporary *ad hoc* alliances to extend the scope of their patronage and to ward off possible defeat at the polls. The Triple Alliance (*al-Hilf al-Thulathi*) betweeb Chamoun, Edde and Gemayyel in the wake of the 1967 Arab-Israeli War was one such effective though short-lived coalition.[5]

Certainly not all the coalitions between the *aqtab* are prompted by ideological or national interests. In more cases than not purely Hobbesian motives of self-interest and political survival underlie such coalitions. During the last national elections of 1972, Kamal Jumblat and Majid Arslan, traditionally rivals in the feud for Druze supremacy which had lasted over two centuries, found it politically expedient in the face of emergent political threats to ignore their traditional enmity and assist each other in their respective districts. The alliance guaranteed the return of both leaders with their clients and safeguarded Druze hegemony against new challenges.

The survival of primordial allegiances (particularly in the form of kinship, fealty and confessional sentiments), the peculiarities of the electoral law along with the adaptability of the traditional politician have enabled some of the *aqtab* and lesser *zu'ama* to enjoy a measure of power that is not commensurate with their own personal electoral strength. The consequences of such allegiances for political change are many and grievous.

First, it has doubtlessly meant the persistent failure of any truly secular and ideological parties or candidates in making a significant dent in the power of the *aqtab*. The only notable exceptions have been the election of Ba'thists Ali al-Khalil in Sour and Abdul Majid al-Rafi'i in Tripoli and the Nasserite Najah Wakim in Beirut during the last elections.

Second, and more important, the survival and extension of this form of political clientelism, as several writers (Yamak 1966; Kerr 1966) have observed, has crippled the role of the legislature as a forum for national debate and eroded the powers of the state. The cabinet has been fairly independent of the collective will of the deputies. Indeed, no government since Lebanon's independence in 1943, has had to resign because of a vote of no confidence. The so-called 'parliamentary game' – often invoked during the frequent cabinet crises in Lebanon – is no more than a game of musical chairs among its *aqtab* jockeying to extend their share of clients in the government. In this sense, 'politics exists only in Laswell's limited sense of "who gets what, when, and how", as a competition for the honours and spoils of office' (Kerr 1966, p.190). The abiding concern of ministers, once in power – particularly since their tenure in office rarely exceeds a year – is to enlarge the scope of their patronage. Accordingly, cabinet politics becomes a delicate art of distributing and managing patronage. Squabbles over civil service appointments, jurisdictional competition, allocation of public funds – all essentially patronage squabbles – assume more importance than controversies involving substantive issues of national and public policy (Kerr 1966, pp. 193-6).

Finally, the erosion of legislative and executive powers and the reduction of the entire political process to one of squabbles over patronage rights and boundaries relegates to the chief executive exceptional powers. Since ultimate executive authority is vested in his office, it is with his consent that the government submits all legislative and budgetary proposals to parliament and conducts foreign policy. He reserves, in some instances, the powers of veto over the passage of legislative acts and constitutional amendments. He may, with cabinet approval, dissolve parliament before the termination of its regular term; or he may summon it to a special session. Unlike the cabinet, the president is not accountable to parliament except, of course, in instances of constitutional or criminal violations.

More formidable is the amount of unofficial powers and prerogatives he can easily muster and mobilise. With or without his consent, an unofficial retinue of opportunists, troubleshooters, middlemen, self-appointed experts, political entrepreneurs, brokers and retainers emerge to claim their share of privilege. Once again, the distribution of material benefits and opportunity begin to be the prominent concern of the highest office in the land. In this sense the president as patron and his unofficial entourage of clients fulfill one of the distinguishing features of all patron-client ties: he becomes, as James Scott would argue, in a position of monopolist or oligopolist over vital services (protection, security, employment and access to other critical needs etc.) the demand for which is highly inelastic (Scott, p.93).

Both President Khoury (1943-52) and Chamoun (1952-8) thrived on political manipulation and used their unofficial powers to the fullest. Both conducted, if not blatantly fraudulent, then scarcely impartial national elections in which many of their prominent rivals were excluded from office. Accusations of corruption, nepotism, and excessive personal influence were rife; the views were slightly more favourable in the case of Chamoun (at least in the eyes of the public) because they were associated with visible economic prosperity and development in the country. President Shihab (1958-64) carried a clear distaste for political manipulation and waged an almost self-righteous crusade against professional politicians whom he derisively dubbed as 'fromagists'. His Deuxième Bureau (internal intelligence), however, assumed exceptional powers and developed its own tightly controlled and subtle system of patron-client networks. The Bureau became notorious for employing state machinery in dispensing favours for its clients and undercutting its critics and opponents. President Helou (1964-70), despite his initial efforts at civil service reform, never really managed to disassociate himself from the Shihabist mold. Nearly the same networks of forces continued to operate almost unabetted throughout his tenure. While President Frangieh (1970-) has succeeded in eradicating virtually all signs of 'dualism' the Helou regime suffered from (i.e., the coexistence of military and civil powers), he has clearly resorted to the more traditional pattern of patronage without even the subtleties of some of his predecessors.

Prime minister, often victims of such unofficial powers, have persistently complained of their excessive use by presidents. Sami Solh who served as premier under Khoury and Chamoun wrote bitterly in 1960 about presidents who relied more on the advice of their unofficial 'sultans' than their own prime ministers. 'Every sultan' he wrote then in his *Memoirs*, 'had an entourage and a group of followers, relatives, in-laws, in-laws of in-laws, associates, middle-men, and hangers-on from every faction and class and every village and street. Whichever of us should come to power, to the crematorium of cabinet office, found himself obliged to pay homage to those sultans and their followers and the followers of their followers. It is they who govern and direct, plan, and execute policies, while we are only the instruments which they set up before the eyes of the public to bear responsibility for their errors and misdeeds' (Solh 1960, p.380).

4. Concluding remarks

At the expense of some oversimplification I have suggested that the political history of Lebanon may be seen as the history of three forms of political patronage. Though not mutually exclusive, each of the three forms made its appearance at different epochs and was generated by particular socio-political and economic circumstances. They have, nonetheless, much in common. Whether 'feudal', 'administrative' or 'pseudo-ideological' they continue to be sustained by highly personalised, tightly circumscribed and reciprocal obligations typical of all patron-client networks.

The survival of such patronage, it was suggested, is not too unusual in a society which continues to be characterised by a large residue of primordial allegiances. The ascriptive ties of family solidarity and communal loyalties have for a long time provided the only reliable and meaningful basis for integrating the social order. Any other form of collaboration, particularly if it is sustained by the rational instruments of a nation state – i.e., anonymous large-scale organisations such as political parties, civil bureaucracies or class loyalties – has not had an enthusiastic reception in Lebanon.

All efforts to bring about any significant transformations in the basic structure of society throughout the nineteenth century were neither lasting nor substantive. The peasant uprising, a decade of centralised Egyptian rule, the Ottoman reforms and the *mutasarrifiyah* no doubt generated some far-reaching institutional and infra-structural changes. Other dimensions of the social structure, however, especially those that have traditionally held the society together, remained almost untouched. Kinship loyalty, village solidarity, ties of patronage, and to a considerable extent the power and autonomy of feudal chiefs survived tenaciously.

Recent efforts have scarcely been more successful. The two attempts of the Syrian National Party (Parti Populaire Syrien, P.P.S.) in 1949 and 1962 – the only organised revolutionary attempts to bring about political change in Lebanon – have both been abortive. The impact of other progressive parties has certainly not been more decisive. In fact, the distinction between a political party and a client group is not always very clear in Lebanon. The fact that a party has an internal structure, formal bylaws, elected officers and specific aims does not mean, as Arnold Hottinger has suggested, that it no longer serves as a locus for patron-client networks (Hottinger 1966). A sizeable number of the *aqtab* and lesser *zu'ama* have formed their own blocs and parties. The basis of support in most such collectivities remains essentially confessional or personal, and to a much lesser degree ideological.

Even the more gradualist effort directed at undermining the traditional *zu'ama* has accomplished very little in eroding the extensive patronage such leaders continue to enjoy among their clients. The so-called 'Shihabist' doctrine associated with President Shihab and his followers was, if anything, an effort to discredit or bypass the traditional *zu'ama* as the exclusive intermediaries or spokesmen for underprivileged groups and communities. Measures were taken to modernize the state bureaucracy to gain more effective and direct access for individuals in remote communities. State planning was encouraged to curtail or moderate the adverse effects of free enterprise. Specific administrative reforms – geared mainly toward rescuing the bureaucracy from the direct pressure of *zu'ama* – were also undertaken. Finally, national social security and other state agencies emerged to provide citizens with much of their needed welfare and services. None of these measures, however, as Shihab himself painfully admitted after his retirement from politics, accomplished their intended objectives. Like confessionalism, patronage has become institutionalised into Lebanon's body politic.

Continuities of this kind prompt us to argue that patronage is not, as some writers have suggested, a transient phenomenon, one which is bound to disappear as other more secular agencies and institutions emerge to offer alternate avenues for gaining access to privilege and opportunity. In assessing the nature of political change in Lebanon, Leonard Binder, to cite one such instance, has suggested that the extension of roads, health, electrification and other amenities to remoter parts of Lebanon, the emergence of a modern middle class capable of exerting its influence among rural communities, and the recruitment of younger political aspirants are bound to ' ... open a gulf between traditional political leaders and the increasingly educated and politically alert population' (Binder 1966, p. 302). It is doubtful, in the light of evidence supplied earlier, whether this 'gulf' has developed. Even if it has, it certainly has not weakened the traditional patron-client ties; nor has it eroded much of the political legitimacy of patrons.

More important perhaps, patrons have been able, by skilful manoeuvring and abaptability, to forestall and circumvent their possible obsolescence. All the *aqtab*, at one point or another in their political careers, sought to extend the scope of their patronage by incorporating secular and ideological elements. By forming political coalitions, parties and blocs, sponsoring labour organisations and other voluntary and benevolent associations, and by invoking liberal and progressive rhetoric, they have been able to return and extend their clientage support which could have, under other circumstances, sought alternate sources of patronage. Expressed differently, the persisting influence of patrons stems from their ability to provide services, goods and values that no other group has so far been able to match.

Indeed, the power veteran politicans continue to enjoy in Lebanon is partly due to their monopoly over such vital benefits. Two simple but effective strategies are often pursued to retain this form of monopoly. First, access to alternative suppliers of these or substitute services is blocked. Much like the patrimonial manager who uses every ploy to discourage his workers from joining labour unions, often the *za'ama* resort to similar measures to retain the allegiance of their clients. In instances where more than one *za'ama* happens to be vying for supporters within one electoral district or region, direct efforts are sought to withhold a service from individuals unless they turn to a particular patron for support (Gubser 1973, pp. 181-2). Second, the traditional scope of patronage is extended to meet or incorporate a variety of new demands and services. By establishing benevolent or welfare societies, political parties, militia groups, or by sponsoring labour unions and other voluntary associations many political leaders have been able to extend or secularise the scope of their patronage without eroding their traditional basis of political support.

The shortcomings and abuses of patronage are many and grievous and have been variously underscored by several observers: endemic corruption, nepotism, favouritism, the erosion of legislative and executive power; the reduction of the entire political process to one of squabbles over patronage rights and boundaries; the absence of any serious concern for formulating broad policy issues of national and civic significance; and the consequent 'sacrifice of long-range planning for short-run expediency' (Lemarchand 1972, p.71).

We should not, however, overlook some of the inherent advantages of patronage. Beginning with its feudal variety, patronage has been able to generate and absorb new forms of reciprocal and universalistic loyalties, provide some measure of political integration and the means for maintaining a modicum of stability and harmony in an otherwise differentiated and pluralistic social structure. More important, it has offered a relatively viable form of political action – among others which have thus far been less effective – which allows individuals and groups a greater measure of leverage in securing benefits, services and a more equitable distribution of resources. In this sense, patronage in Lebanon is one of the most accessible and effective strategies for coping with vulnerability and relative deprivation. That it has survived when access to resources was made possible through other means – such as the spread of the market economy, centralised bureaucracy, class-consciousness, party-based and ideological loyalties – attests to its tenacity and continued viability.

In this sense political patronage is at one with other adaptive instruments of modernisation. Much like the family firm, kinship associations, confessional and communal voluntary associations, patronage has been effective in meeting some of the secular and rational demands of modernisation (i.e., openness, receptivity to change, the ability to cope with tensions and imbalances) without diluting primordial loyalties or dehumanising the fabric of society (Khalaf 1972). If the central task of modernisation is the reconciliation of continuity and change, cultural reconstruction and institutional transformation, rediscovery and borrowing, coherence and dynamism, then the convergence of tradition and modernisation becomes the only viable and feasible course for Lebanon. Patronage has survived because it has been a device for achieving such a synthesis.

NOTES

1.   The term 'family' here is naturally employed in its broader and extended sense to include several independent family units or households bearing the same name.
2.   The often-invoked Article 95 of the constitution states that 'in order to promote harmony and justice, the communities will be equitably represented in government employment and in the composition of the Ministry without jeopardising the good of the State'. Translated into quantitative and operational terms this system of apportionment has meant that the chamber must always include a number of deputies divisible by 11 (i.e., 33, 44, 77 or 99) so that for every 6 Christian deputies there would be 5 non-Christians (Sunnis, Shi'ites and Druzes).
3.   For example in 1951 there were a small number of relatively large districts, 9 altogether for 77 deputies; in 1953, 33 districts for 44 deputies; 1957, 28 districts for 88 deputies; and since 1960 the number has stabilised at 26 districts for 99 deputies.
4.   The text quoted in Bahige B. Tabbarah, *Les Forces politiques actuelles au Liban,* Thèse pour le Doctorat en Droit, Université de Grenoble, April 1954, p. 167, was reproduced from *al-Jaryda*, Beirut, September 7, 1953.
5.   Initially conceived as a loosely organised alliance to defend the national integrity of Lebanon against the emergent socialist-revolutionary trend sweeping Arab countries at the time, the *Hilf* evolved into a cohesive political coalition with a unifying ideological base and concern for national priorities. It struck a receptive note among the electorate and managed to secure 23 seats in the 1968 elections: nearly one-fourth of the entire Chamber. For further details see Entelis (1974), pp. 161-72.

REFERENCES

Aouad, I. (1953) *Le Droit privé des Maronites au temps des Emirs Chihab (1607-1841)*. Paris.
Binder, L. (1966) 'Political change in Lebanon', In L. Binder (ed.), *Politics in Lebanon*. New York.
Blau, P.M. (1964) *Exchange and Power in Social Life*. New York.
Chevallier, D. (1971) *La Société du Mont Liban à l'époque de la révolution industrielle en Europe*. Paris.
Churchill, C. *The Druzes and the Maronites*.
Entelis, J.P. (1974) *Pluralism and Party Transformation in Lebanon, al-Kata'ib, 1936-1970*. Leiden.
Gubser, P. (1973) 'The Zu'ama of Zahlah: The current situation in a Lebanese town', *Middle East Journal* 27, no.2 (Spring).
Harik, I. (1965) 'The Iqta' system in Lebanon: A comparative political view', *Middle East Journal* 19, no.4 (Autumn), 405-12.
Harik, I. (1968) *Politics and Change in a Traditional Society: Lebanon 1711-1845*. Princeton.
Hottinger, A. (1966) 'Zu'ama in historical perspective', in L. Binder (ed.), *Politics in Lebanon*, New York, 85-105.
Hourani, A. (1968) 'Ottoman reforms and the politics of notables', in W. Polk and R. Chambers (eds), *The Beginnings of Modernization in the Middle East*. Chicago.
Jouplain, M. (pseudonym of Bulus Nujaim) (1908) *La Question du Liban: étude d'histoire diplomatique et de droit international*. Paris.

Kerr, M. (1959) *Lebanon in the Last Years of Feudalism, 1840-1868.* Beirut.

Kerr, M. 'Political decision-making in a confessional democracy', in L. Binder (ed.), *Politics in Lebanon.* New York.

Khalaf, S. 'Primordial ties and politics', *Middle Eastern Studies* 4, no.3 (April), 243-69.

Khalaf, S. (1972) 'Adaptive modernization: The case for Lebanon', in C. Cooper and S. Alexander (eds), *Economic Development and Population Growth in the Middle East,* New York, 567-98.

Lemarchand, R. (1972) 'Political clientelism and ethnicity in tropical Africa: competing solidarities in nation-building', *American Political Science Review* LXVI, no.1 (March), 68-90.

Nahar, al- (1972) 'Elections: Fifty years', special issue, Beirut (January), pp. 39-60.

Poliak, A.N. (1939) *Feudalism: Egypt, Syria, Palestine and the Lebanon, 1250-1900.* London.

Polk, W. (1963) *The Opening of South Lebanon.* Cambridge, Mass.

Salibi, K. (1965) *The Modern History of Lebanon.* London.

Scott, J. (1972), 'Patron-client politics and political change in southeast Asia', *American Political Science Review* LXVI, no. 1, 91-113.

Shidiaq, Tannus ibn Yusuf al- (1954) *Akhbar al-'Ayan fi Jabal Lubnan* (ed. Munir al-Khazin). Beirut.

Shihab, A.H. (1933) *Lubnan fi 'Ahd al-Umara al-Shihabiyyin* (ed. A.J. Rustum and F.E. Bustani). Beirut.

Solh, Sami al- (1960) *Mudhakkirat* (Memoirs). Beirut.

Yamak, L.Z. (1966) 'Party politics in the Lebanese political system', in L. Binder (ed.), *Politics in Lebanon.* New York.

Zuwiyya, J. (1968) *The Parliamentary Election of Lebanon.* Leiden.

Michael Johnson

Political bosses and their gangs: Zu'ama and qabadayat in the Sunni Muslim quarters of Beirut

Among the vast amount of literature on patron-client relations in the political systems of developing countries, there is the notion of a fundamental difference between western and developing democracies, where western democracy is generally considered to be organised according to a class or pluralist model, while developing democracies are usually characterised by a hierarchy of patron-client transactions or dyads (Lande 1973). This does not mean that class and pluralist politics are absent in new nations, nor that clientelist politics are unheard of in 'developed' countries, but it does imply a continuum of dominant modes of political organisation between pre-industrial and industrial societies. Recently, attention has been turned to the specific relationship between clientelist systems and a particular stage of economic development. In 1971, for example, the *British Journal of Political Science* carried an article about Kenya that argued (Leys 1971, p.344):

The continuing vitality of clientelism in politics can be seen as a reflection of the failure of capitalistic development to transform social relationships by transforming the mode of production of an underdeveloped country.

The assumption seems to be that political clientelism will give way to self-conscious class politics when the commercialisation of agriculture transforms the peasant economy into capitalist farming, and the growth of investment in industry transforms mercantile capitalism into an industrial mode of production. Because of the constraints on such economic change occurring in developing countries (Baran 1973; Sutcliffe 1972) the characteristic pre-capitalist social relationships persist in their political systems, irrespective of whether the 'cultural diffusion' of western values takes place (Gunder-Frank 1967; Ocampo and Johnson 1972). Broadly speaking, I accept this argument. But in this paper, although I explain the 'vitality of clientelism' in Beirut in terms of the structure of the Lebanese economy, I am more concerned to show the strength and flexibility of the urban political machine as an agent of social control, and to indicate its potential ability to resist the social changes that are likely to occur with industrialisation. A change in the economic structure might eventually lead to the dying out of clientelism in Lebanon. However, it will not be an easy death, because politicians have built machines that not only exploit individualism, but also encourage its persistence.

Lebanon is at a peculiarly interesting stage of economic development. In terms of the National Product, the agricultural sector is of minor importance, and the dominant mode of production is mercantile capitalism, where production (perhaps a misnomer in this context) is largely confined to banking and trade services. As yet, the commercial-financial bourgeoisie has not invested any substantial proportion of its capital in the industrial sector (largely because the latter is not as profitable as the service sector), and in Beirut, the banking centre for the Arab Middle East, the overwhelming majority of the labour force is employed in the service sector. Just as there is peasant individualism in Lebanese villages, so Beirut's society is characterised by what can be called 'petty bourgeois individualism'.[1] There is little or no class consciousness, and political parties (with one Christian exception, the Phalanges) are weak to the point of insignificance, as are trade unions and other interest groups. Religion divides Beirut, as it does the rest of Lebanon, into two roughly equal confessional groups, the Christians and the Muslims, which are further sub-divided into a plethora of sects.

Partly as a result of the fragmented and individualistic electorate, Lebanon's democratic political system is dominated by locally powerful leaders, called *zu'ama* (plural of *za'im*), who in the cities have developed sophisticated machines to recruit a clientele. In this paper, I am particularly concerned with what seem to me to be the most important elements of the urban machine, the neighbourhood strong-arm men (*qabadayat*) who recruit and police the *za'im's* clientele. My fieldwork was carried out in the Sunni Muslim quarters of Beirut, but there is every reason to expect that a similar *qabaday* system prevails in other Lebanese cities, in Christian as well as Muslim quarters.

Za'im

At the end of the First World War, to the delight of Lebanese Christians, the League of Nations awarded the Mandate for Syria to France. At first, the Sunni notables of Beirut, accustomed to being the agents of Ottoman rule, refused to have anything to do with what they regarded as a foreign and Christian imposition on a Muslim majority. But Sunni *zu'ama* gradually began to participate in the new democratic institutions, and they eventually co-operated with the Christians in founding the independent state of Lebanon in 1943. Parliamentary democracy provided access to governmental patronage, and, in order to maintain a large clientele, it became essential for *zu'ama* to be regularly elected as deputies and appointed as ministers. As part of the elaborate system of confessional checks and balances in Lebanon, the office of president was reserved for a Maronite Christian. But the Sunnis were given the premiership, and present-day conflict between Sunni *zu'ama* in Beirut is mainly concerned with competition for this powerful office.

Today, most of these Sunni *zu'ama* are descended from the notable families of the early twentieth-century Ottoman period. They inherited both the wealth and clientele of their fathers, forming the basis of their electoral support in independent Lebanon. The clientele is bound to the *za'im* by a network of transactional ties, where economic and other services are distributed to the clients in exchange for consistent political loyalty. This political support usually takes the form of voting for the *za'im* and his allies in parliamentary elections, but the clientele may be required to support the *za'im* in other political conflicts, and may even be expected to take up arms in disputes with other *zu'ama*. A considerable amount of ritual support is involved in the patron-client relationship, and clients must publicly demonstrate their loyalty in a variety of ways: on feast days, clients visit their *za'im* to wish him the compliments of the season; and when a *za'im* returns from a journey, his supporters usually turn out to welcome him home. Recently, when the Prime Minister returned from a pilgrimage to Mecca, his Beiruti supporters honoured him by slaughtering many sheep and holding a great reception, during which a number of enthusiastic *qabadayat* terrified the peace-loving inhabitants of Beirut by firing machine-guns into the air – a popular method of expressing loyalty, political strength and jubilation.

The *za'im* maintains his support in two important ways: first, by being regularly returned to office, so that he can influence the administration and continuously provide his clients with governmental services; and secondly, by being a successful businessman, so that he can use his commercial and financial contacts to give his clients employment, contracts and capital. Depending on the wealth and influence of his clients, the *za'im* provides public works contracts, governmental concessions, employment in the government and private sectors, promotion within the professions and civil service, free or cheap education and medical treatment in government or charitable institutions, and even protection from the law. In order to survive electoral defeats and periods in opposition, the *za'im* must himself be rich, or have access to other people's wealth, so as to buy the support of the electorate as well as the acquiescence of ministers and officials responsible for particular governmental services. Although election to the Assembly is of considerable advantage, it is not always essential, and a *za'im* can survive temporary periods of opposition and political weakness by using the credit he has built up in the past. Thus, for example, a judge, who owes his original appointment to a particular *za'im*, would probably continue to be lenient to the *za'im*'s criminal clients even if the *za'im* were no longer in office; and a businessman, who has been enriched by the *za'im* granting him a contract or concession, could be expected to donate some money to the campaign fund when the *za'im* is in opposition. In both cases, the grateful clients might eventually be bought off by rival *zu'ama*, with offers of promotion for the judge and another contract for the businessman. Such changing allegiances are not uncommon, and lower down the social hierarchy, large-scale defections from the clientele take place when a *za'im* fails to deliver the goods.

Zu'ama are not elected on the basis of a programme, but on their ability to provide their clientele with services. In this sense, the clients' support is a transactional obligation, rather than a form of moral, ideological loyalty. But although national and programmatic appeals are not made by *zu'ama*,[2] they do make some moral appeals, and seek to woo their electors by posing as local champions and confessional representatives. Thus a Beiruiti Sunni *za'im* appeals to Beirutis *qua* Beirutis, and to Muslims *qua* Muslims. It has been pointed out elsewhere that *zu'ama* do win the support of constituents who are not of their religion (Gubser 1973; Khalaf, this volume). Indeed, the electoral system compels them to do this.[3] But the major part of their support usually comes from their own sect. During the 1950s, for example, Sunni *zu'ama* in Beirut put forward demands for increased Muslim representation in the administration, and increased influence in what they described as a Christian-dominated state. Similarly, by providing governmental services like electricity, water and roads for his constituency, the *za'im* is able to demonstrate that he is an active local representative. Such services have, of course, long been in existence in Beirut, and a *za'im* cannot use their provision as a political resource. But during the period 1960 to 1968, when President Shihab and, to a lesser extent, President Hilu diverted governmental resources to the poorer, outlying regions of the country, Beirutis complained that governmental contracts and jobs were going to non-Beirutis at their expense. Sa'ib Salam,[4] consistently excluded from the premiership under both presidents, was thus able to capitalise on this feeling, portray his Shihabist competitors as traitors to their city, and maintain the support of a large part of his clientele even though he was politically weak for such a long period of time.

Qabaday, pl. qabadayat

A defining characteristic of the *za'im* is his close coercive control of the clientele. All Lebanese politicians enter into transactional relationships with their constituents, but what distinguishes the *za'im* is his sophisticated machine and his willingness to use force, not only in attaining political objectives, but also in maintaining the loyalty of his clientele. A *za'im* may not set out to bully his clients into accepting his leadership. But in building his apparatus to recruit and control the machine, he makes alliances with strong-arm neighbourhood leaders whose support is based, in part at least, on coercion. Such a neighbourhood boss is called an *qabaday*, and all consistently successful politicians make use of his local organising ability.

The word *qabaday* is generally supposed to be derived from the Arabic verb 'to grasp or hold' (*qabada*). But the same word is found in Turkish (*kabadayi*), where it means 'swashbuckler, bully; tough; having guts.' in Lebanon *qabaday* is an ambiguous word which can have positive or negative connotations, although it is usually a sign of approval and is used to describe someone who is quick-witted, physically strong, heroic, or possessed of some other supposedly masculine attribute. Negative connotations include bullying, throwing one's weight around, and other forms of unruly and obstreperous behaviour. In its most specific sense, *qabaday* is a title given to a street or quarter boss who combines both positive and negative attributes into a leadership role. Here the *qabaday* recruits a following on the basis of his reputation as a man of the people, as a helper of the weak and the poor, as a protector of the quarter and its inhabitants, and, most important, as a man who is prepared to defend his claims to leadership by the use of force. All these characteristics might apply to the *za'im* as well as the *qabaday*, but where the two leaders differ is in their social origins and their levels of leadership. Whereas the *za'im* is born of a rich notable family and is recognised as the leader of a large following, the *qabaday*'s parentage is of low socio-economic status and his political influence is limited to his immediate neighbourhood. Typically, the *qabaday* is a criminal involved in protection rackets, gun running, hashish smuggling, or other similar activities. The *za'im* provides him with protection from the police and the courts, in return for his political loyalty and services. These services include recruiting and controlling the *za'im*'s clientele, organising mass demonstrations of support, and, if necessary, fighting for the *za'im* in battles with other *zu'ama*.

The *qabaday* is particularly well suited for ensuring the loyalty of the *za'im*'s clients, because although he can use his relative wealth and his underworld connections to help the inhabitants of his quarter, he can also use the physical force of 'gangland' to control the clientele. One informant described in the following way how an *qabaday* establishes himself:

An *qabaday* starts by throwing his weight around, picking quarrels and beating up those who don't treat him respectfully. For example, if he is sitting on the street corner playing *tawilah* (a type of backgammon), and someone from the quarter walks by without wishing him a good day and enquiring after his health, he might beat him. Later he'll probably shoot someone. Perhaps he'll kill another criminal, perhaps someone in a quarrel. The important thing is not so much who he kills, but the way he does it. Anyone can shoot someone. An *qabaday* has to do it openly and be willing to accept responsibility, and possibly go to prison for about four years.

In other words, the importance of the killing is the symbolic nature of the act. An *qabaday* is someone who is prepared to promote his leadership claims by an open murder in complete disregard for the law. He accepts the risk of imprisonment and a protracted vendetta, but in committing the act openly he wins the respect of his fellows. Because physical strength and notions of honour are highly prized values, the *qabaday* attracts a local following, and can therefore expect the protection of a *za'im* and a reduced prison sentence for his crimes. He acts outside the law, but is governed by another code of norms accepted by the society in which he lives. Some Beirutis, particularly the highly educated, do not accept this code, and for them the *qabaday* is *az'ar*, a criminal, thug or murderer. But in the poorer quarters, where the *qabadayat* are particularly powerful, *az'ar* is a term reserved for a man who kills dishonourably, for a robber of the poor, and, most significantly, for an *qabaday* who works for an opposing *za'im*. One man's *qabaday* is thus another's *az'ar*, but most people have ambiguous feelings about their local strong-arm men. They support them partly out of respect for their honourable *qabaday* qualities, and partly out of fear of their willingness to use force.

One way Muslim Beirutis express and attempt to resolve this ambiguity is to indulge in myth-making. The *qabadayat* are not a new phenomenon (Lapidus 1967, pp. 163-65 and 170-7), and there are countless myths, particularly about those who operated in the early part of this century. In these stories the *qabaday* aided the weak and the poor, fought against Christian attacks on Muslims, and protected the Sunni quarters against the excesses of the Turkish and French governments. Although the myths admit the criminal activities of many of these leaders, they always emphasise the *qabaday*'s basically honourable character and the services he performed for his neighbours. Of course, the stories change according to who is the narrator and who the listener, and it is interesting to note that, as a 'Christian foreigner', I was often told the *qabaday* was a repository of all Arab virtues, that he was hospitable to strangers, and that Muslim and Christian *qabadayat* were friends who regularly visited one another's houses. So according to the myth, the paradigmatic *qabaday* is the strong, honourable, quarter leader of the Ottoman period. A coffee shop that I visited on occasions was owned by just such a leader. As an old man of some ninety years, he was able to lay claim to the 'true *qabaday* status'. He never smoked cigarettes, nor drank alcohol; he wore traditional dress, and much regretted the decline of traditional moral standards. His predominantly youthful customers accorded him great respect, greeting him with elaborate courtesy and ritual, including kissing his hand. Although they broke most of the old man's rules of morality, they always favourably compared him with what they called the 'new *qabadayat*':

The real *qabaday* has disappeared. Nowadays the new *qabadayat* drink in night clubs, smoke hashish and deal in cocaine and heroin. In comparison with the *Hajj* (the coffee shop owner had made the pilgrimage to Mecca) they are all weaklings. Look at

him; even at his age he is still physically strong. These new men are only strong
because they carry a pistol.

Nevertheless, despite their opinion, which they shared with many
other people, most of the young men respected the new *qabadayat*,
valued their friendship, and even had *qabaday* aspirations themselves.
These contradictions required an extension of the *qabaday* myth,
which in its completed (and rather oversimplified) form runs as
follows: today's *qabadayat* are different from and inferior to their
Ottoman predecessors, but occasionally, because of their exceptional
qualities of daring, honour and generosity, one or two stand out as
close approximations to the traditional model.

It should be noted that many quarter bosses, who are called
qabaday, are in fact employed in legal occupations. At the lowest level
they are bodyguards and port workers, shopkeepers and taxi-drivers;
and at the head of the *qabaday* hierarchy, they are the rich businessmen
who owe their wealth to the commercial and financial assistance of
their *za'im*. These businessmen are sometimes known by other titles,
such as *ra'is* (chief), which indicate their higher status, but their
leadership style is that of *qabaday*, and they are referred to as such by
their followers. All these middle-level leaders in legal occupations are
classed as *qabadayat*, whatever their status, because of their strong-arm
reputation: they will turn out to fight for their *za'im* in factional conflicts
and wars, and will defend their quarters against incursions.

Part of the *qabaday*'s strength rests on his proven ability to defend
his local community in the communal fights and skirmishes that occur
with unfortunate regularity. In 1903, 1936 and 1958, there were
serious battles between the Muslim and Christian quarters. In 1958,
for example, the civil war, between rival *za'ama* throughout Lebanon,
degenerated in Beirut into bloody fighting between Christian loyalists
and Muslim insurrectionists. In 1973 and 1975, during the street
fighting in Beirut between the Lebanese army and the Palestinian
commandos, armed *qabadayat* erected road blocks around the Sunni
Muslim quarters of Tariq al-Jadidah and Burj Abi Haydar, while in
the Christian quarters the loyalist, right-wing Christian parties
mobilised their militias. These confrontations between the Muslim
and Christian halves of the city encourage the local population to see
the *qabaday* as their communal protector. Most of today's more
powerful *qabadayat* established themselves during the civil war of 1958
when, as young men, they demonstrated their ability to mobilise
armed bands of *shabab* (young bloods) to fight for the insurrectionist
za'im, Sa'ib Salam, against the government of President Chamoun.
Their bravery in battle, and their ultimate victory over the Chamoun
regime, turned them into heroes. Often uneducated men from
relatively humble backgrounds, they emerged as popular leaders of
their quarters, and, as such, were extremely useful to the *zu'ama*. The
za'im, born of a rich notable family, has great social and economic

status, and he wins support partly because of this. But by working through the *qabaday*, he is able to show his willingness to come down closer to his low-status clientele. While he gains increased moral support through his alliance with a popular leader, the *za'im* also derives considerable pragmatic advantage, because the *qabaday*, as local boy and local hero, is in an ideal position to recruit and maintain a loyal clientele.

The qabaday as part of the za'im's apparatus

The most important part of the *za'im*'s apparatus is the core of *qabadayat*. During elections, they act as 'election keys' (*mafatih al-intikhabat*) and ensure that the *za'im*'s clientele vote for him and his allies. Between elections they recruit supporters, channel requests for services, and organise mass demonstrations of support. This core is what characterises the *za'im*'s machine. All politicians use intermediaries to recruit and maintain support, but the *za'im*'s strength lies in his ability to give protection and assistance to the popular leaders of the street. Other politicians are either unable to offer this protection, because they are new to the game, or unwilling because of their commitment to some form of social change.

Successful *zu'ama* recognise the necessity of keeping their organisation as simple as possible. Even if the *za'im* could find the time to see each of his clients when they asked for services, he would find it impossible to ensure their loyalty. In the predominantly Sunni constituency of Beirut III, Sunni *zu'ama* can expect between twelve and sixteen, or even eighteen, thousand votes. A proportion of these voters would be clients of other politicians on the electoral list, but the majority would in some way be beholden to the *za'im*. In constructing his machine, the *za'im* seeks to organise these voters into manageable groups, where he can leave the responsibility of controlling the clientele to his lieutenants.

The *za'im* keeps the number of lieutenants to a minimum, and usually has something in the region of fifteen to twenty *qabadayat* in his core group. Typically, a member of the core is an established political boss who controls a network or gang of lesser *qabadayat*. But as he is likely to have begun his political career as a minor *qabaday*, and still has a strong-arm style of leadership, Beirutis usually use the term *qabaday* to describe such a leader. Three major types of core *qabadayat* can be distinguished: quarter bosses, who look after the *za'im*'s interests in particular localities; family *qabadayat*,[5] who are often also organised by quarters; and, in addition, there may be 'immigrant' *qabadayat* who lead clienteles of new voters recently settled in Beirut. Immigrants from rural areas tend to settle in quarters where families from their village or region are already living. In Muslim quarters, most of them are Shi'ite rather than Sunni, which means that they have confessional as well as regional identifications to distinguish them from their Beiruti neighbours. Often they continue to vote in their villages of origin, and form clubs and associations that perpetuate their communal ties. Because they have been brought up in an exclusive environment, those second generation immigrants, who are registered to vote in Beirut, do not readily accept the leadership of established quarter bosses. However, they do have their own *qabadayat*, and *zu'ama* adopt some of these and use them in their apparatus to recruit and control the immigrant clientele.

Perhaps the most important type of *qabaday* is the boss of a quarter. The boundaries of Beirut's administrative districts are virtually the same as those of the nineteenth-century quarters, which were established as Beirut developed beyond the walls of the old city. The confessional war of 1860 prompted thousands of Christians to settle in the relative safety of Beirut, and the expansion of trade attracted members of all confessions to seek their fortune in the service sector of the economy. The different confessions tended to settle in particular districts, and the quarters took on confessional characteristics. The Christians settled in the east, the Muslims in the west, and these two confessional regions were sub-divided into quarters dominated by particular sects. Native Beirutis, generally Sunnis, also moved to a pleasanter environment outside the walls, and while immigrant Muslims (usually Shi'ites) tended to settle in the inner and outer rings of the western city, the native Sunnis were predominant in the quarters of the middle ring. The Sunni merchantile families were the first to move, but the large residences of rich merchants were soon surrounded by the homes of poor and middle class Sunnis. Although this meant that the Sunni quarters were not inhabited by homogeneous occupational groups or classes, they did acquire some socio-economic characteristics. Bastah, with its port workers and stevedores, had a more popular character than Musaytibah where established mercantile and sheikhly families tended to settle; and the quarters of the inner and outer rings (respectively, Bashurah and Tariq al-Jadidah) were considerably poorer than the generally middle class quarters of Mazra'ah. In recent years, the process of urbanisation has changed the character of these quarters. The quarters of the middle ring, in particular, are much more heterogeneous than before, and the boundaries between quarters are less precise. Nevertheless, there is a sense of inhabitants 'belonging' to a quarter. There are still differences between quarter dialects; particular families or clans continue to be associated with particular quarters; and it is still advisable for Sunni politicians to live in the centre of Muslim Beirut, in the quarters of Musaytibah and Burj Abi Haydar.

Thus the *za'im* can conveniently organise his clientele by quarters, and he establishes local bosses to control the quarter clientele. Sometimes these bosses are associated with the traditional occupation of the quarter. In Bastah, for example, one *qabaday* has inherited a family business in the port where there is an *qabaday* tradition of gang fights, between competing families and factions, over such prizes as government concessions to manage the barges and to transport cargo from the ships. Some quarter bosses are protection racketeers, others are alleged to be political assassins or agents in the pay of foreign embassies, but most are outwardly respectable businessmen. The important thing is that they are powerful *local* leaders who know their quarter and its inhabitants, are always ready to see and help the *za'im*'s clients, and can mobilise lesser *qabadayat* to fight for the *za'im*.

   The other important type of core lieutenant is the family or clan *qabaday*. In a sense, every *qabaday* represents both his family and his neighbours in the quarter, but some *qabadayat* come from such large clans that they are particularly important for ensuring the loyalty of their kin. In Sunni Beirut, the 'Itanis form perhaps the largest family. In their Family Association there are claimed to be over 6,000 subscription-paying members, including women and children, but the family is probably larger than this. In terms of their political importance, there are some 4,000 'Itani voters. Traditionally, they have supported the Salams, both Sa'ib and his father Salim. But because the family is so large, and nowadays spreads all over the Sunni quarters of Beirut, it needs a certain amount of organisation if it is to form an efficient unit in Sa'ib Salam's clientele. Other *zu'ama* recognise the value of the family's votes, and various attempts have been made to woo the 'Itanis away from their traditional *za'im*.

   So as to maintain his hold on the family, Salam has established a number of 'Itani *qabadayat* to control their kin. This is not a novel nor a unique tactic. What usually happens is that the *za'im* chooses particular individuals who have a certain amount of support in the family, and then builds them up to a position of monopoly leadership. Thus according to some informants, Salam let it be known that any 'Itani living in Musaytibah, who wanted a service from him, should first see Hashim 'Itani, his chosen representative and the 'official' 'Itani *qabaday* of the quarter. In 1958, Hashim had been a minor *qabaday* fighting under Salam's leadership. Over the years, he increased his local influence, and it is said that when Salam recognised Hashim's strength, he gave the *qabaday* considerable economic assistance. It is certainly the case that from being the owner of a small coffee shop, Hashim 'Itani extended his business interests such that he became part-owner of two of Beirut's biggest cinemas, and one of the directors of a company that owns restaurants, bars and cafés in the fashionable quarter of Ras Bayrut. Although the amount of governmental patronage that Salam could dispense was limited in the 1960s, he was able to capitalise on his close relations with right-wing Christian politicians, including his old enemy, ex-President Chamoun, and give help to his clients in the fields of business and commerce. Thus a number of informants told me that Salam helped to find Hashim 'Itani Christian capital and expertise, and that in doing so he created an indebted ally. These same informants claimed that by refusing services to those 'Itanis not vetted by Hashim, Salam could control his 'Itani clientele in Musaytibah through one loyal and grateful lieutenant.

The example of Hashim 'Itani emphasises the moral, as opposed to transactional, relationship between the *za'im* and his *qabadayat*.[6] All *zu'ama* have a moral core of lieutenants, who over time have received so many transactional benefits from their patron that the relationship has acquired a degree of permanency. Members of the core remain loyal to the *za'im* not simply because of the expectation of future services. They also have a debt of gratitude for past services. This debt has changed the character of the *za'im* – *qabaday* dyad from a patron-client exchange to a leader-follower relationship, which is often further transformed into a condition of friendship. Perhaps Sa'ib Salam's greatest strength was his ability to make such a transformation with a few key people. Reference has already been made to his exclusion from high office during the so-called Shihabist regimes of Presidents Shihab and Hilu. During that period, the agents of the Shihabist *Deuxième Bureau* (intelligence apparatus) skillfully operated the *za'im-qabaday* system against Salam and other *zu'ama* opposed to Shihab (cf. Khalaf, this volume). They suborned criminal *qabadayat* who needed government protection, and they established their own powerful *qabaday* network to organise the clientele of Shihabist *zu'ama*. But although Salam lost a large part of his clientele to the Shihabist *qabadayat* and their masters, he was able to maintain his apparatus by giving commercial and financial assistance to his lieutenants, and by forming close moral relationships with them. Thus a man like Hashim 'Itani, who did not rely on criminal activities for his economic well-being, was not subverted by the *Deuxième Bureau*.

The core *qabaday*'s role should be contrasted with that of the notable (*wajih*). Notables are accorded high status because of their wealth, philanthropy and reputation for religious piety. But they are not usually significant as election keys, as they are not prepared to spend time dealing with the individual problems of the poor, and are not able to coerce the clientele during elections. If a notable does use his contacts in government to build up a large client following of his own, he is likely to become a politician in his own right, and ultimately pose a threat to the *za'im*'s dominance. For this reason, the notable cannot be trusted. The *qabaday*, on the other hand, 'comes from the masses', is protected or enriched by the *za'im*, and is much more easily controlled. In addition, because he usually lacks education and the statesmanlike qualities required of a politician, he is not likely to stand as a candidate in parliamentary elections.

The qabaday's functions in the machine

In using the *qabaday* as an intermediary, the *za'im* cuts down the risk of performing services for his rivals' supporters, leaves the policing of the machine to a few individuals over whom he has close control, fragments the electorate into politically artificial entities of quarter and family groups, and further binds his individual clients into the patron-client debt relationship.

The *za'im*'s patronage resources are not infinite, and he must carefully supervise the recruitment as well as the loyalty of his clientele. Thus he and his secretaries operate a selective procedure when a potential client requests a service. Most attention, and a personal audience with the *za'im*, are granted to rich clients, clients from large families and other voters who can provide the *za'im* with significant monetary and electoral resources in return for patronage. A second category of clients are those poorer and politically less important voters who make up the majority of the *za'im*'s support base, but individually can only pledge their own votes, the votes of their nuclear family and possibly the votes of a few friends. Usually, such people have relatively simple requests and are dealt with by the *za'im*'s secretarial assistants. On behalf of the *za'im*, secretaries write a note or make a telephone call to the relevant government department or whatever institution or individual is concerned with the client's case. A third category of clients includes those who vote in another constituency and those who are not enfranchised. An example of the latter group is the Kurdish community which migrated to Beirut from Iraq. Many Kurds have not been granted full civil rights in Lebanon, do not have the vote and, as a result, have nothing to offer the *za'im*. Such people are refused services, while Lebanese citizens from other constituencies are told to approach their own *zu'ama*.

The *qabaday* is particularly important with regard to the second category. As scores of people come daily to the *za'im*'s house or office to ask for services, the *za'im* and his secretaries cannot easily distinguish which potential clients are voters in the constituency, and which of those are consistent supporters. Elaborate records are kept, but the best way of establishing a client's credentials is to insist on his first seeing a quarter, family or immigrant *qabaday*. The *qabaday* has extensive knowledge of his local domain, and is well placed to vet the client's loyalty and political reliability. He can see which clients regularly present themselves on feast days, and other similar occasions, to demonstrate their ritual support and continuing allegiance to the *za'im*. He can also ensure that clients vote in the way they are instructed, for although the ballot is secret, there are ways of checking on how electors actually vote. It should be noted here, though, that a client who regularly pays his ritual respects to a particular *za'im* soon develops a reputation for being that *za'im*'s supporter and is usually denied services by rival *zu'ama*. If the client is so identified, he has an interest in his patron being elected, and he is not likely to vote for other *zu'ama*. The *qabaday*'s role during elections is nowadays more concerned with seeing that the client remembers to vote, rather than with checking on individual ballot papers. But as an indication of the *qabaday*'s continuing importance as an election key, it is significant that the government often arrests opposition *qabadayat* a few days before an election.

The use of the *qabaday* also serves to fragment the electorate and prevent the emergence of self-conscious, horizontally-linked social categories such as interest groups or classes. By forcing clients to approach him through their quarter or family *qabaday*, the *za'im* encourages the individual client to see himself as a member of a particular quarter or family grouping, and discourages the formation of other social categories that might pose a real threat to the *status quo*. Although urbanisation has tended to lead to the break-up of the quarter as a homogeneous unit, and the extended family has given way to the nuclear family, the *za'im* capitalises on his clients' mythological conceptions of social organisation, and in some cases actually creates artificial quarter and family identification. As a political scientist has already noted (Yamak 1966, p.153): 'The clan ... exists not so much for its own sake as for the sake of the notable. Politically, it exists not in its own right, but in order to be manipulated by the *za'im*.'

The same point can be made about the quarter. But although the *za'im* uses family and quarter as units of organisation, he does not deal with them as corporate groups with their own elected spokesman. He does not, for example, make a contract with the President of the 'Itani Family Association to provide the family with a sum of money, or a certain fixed number of services, in return for the whole family's support. Nor is a contract made between the *za'im* and the *mukhtar* of a quarter, where the elected quarter leader[7] pledges the votes of the local inhabitants in return for an increased water supply or cleaner streets. The electorate is further fragmented because the contracts are made between the *za'im* and individual members of the family or quarter. This is a crucial distinction between the *za'im* machine and the machine of a politician in a place like rural India, where a contract might be made with a broker representing the interests of a whole village. There the villagers' votes may be exchanged *en bloc* for the politician's promise of governmental provision of tube wells or service roads, and in such a society the political system is characterised by a hierarchy of patron-client dyads, with transactional links between villager and village broker, broker and politician's agent, politician's agent and politician. By comparison, there is no significant patron-client hierarchy in Muslim Beirut, for here the contract is usually made directly between the *za'im* and his client. The *qabaday* might recruit the client for the *za'im* and police the transactional relationship, but he does not usually act like the Indian broker with his own independent clientele. The Indian broker, as an ideal type,[8] uses his contacts in the administration to perform services for his own personal clientele, and during elections he delivers his vote bloc to a candidate, where the clients may not even know the politician, let alone feel beholden to him. On the other hand, although the *qabaday* might independently perform some services, such as mediation of disputes, protection of the quarter, and charitable distributions of small sums of money, his access to governmental patronage is limited. He therefore tends to act as a broker who does not speculate in his own right, but effects and facilitates the formation of contracts between the individual clients and the *za'im*. Claims that election keys in Beirut deliver vote blocs must be treated with some scepticism. When informants told me that an *qabaday* was worth at least two thousand votes to a particular *za'im*, this did not mean that if the *qabaday* defected the *za'im* would lose all two thousand votes. He would inevitably lose some, but he would only lose a large number if he failed to find another *qabaday* to take over the defector's role. Even if a client goes first to his street *qabaday*, then to the quarter boss and only after this goes to the *za'im*'s house, where he perhaps sees a secretary rather than the *za'im* himself, the contract is made between the client and the *za'im*, not between the client and the street or quarter *qabaday*. The important function of the *qabaday* is to reinforce this *za'im*-client relationship. When a client receives a service from the *za'im* or his secretary, he is making an agreement with a notable who is socially distant and only occasionally seen in a face-to-face situation. But the transaction is channeled through the *qabaday* whom the client sees in the quarter possibly every day, and this regular face-to-face contact between the client and the *qabaday* serves as a continual reminder of the client's debt to the *za'im*.

The urban machine and social control

The distinctive and peculiar quality of the Lebanese economic system is its domination by the service sector, which in 1970 provided 68 percent of the Gross National Product. The agricultural sector, by comparison, accounted for a mere 10 percent, and the industrial sector for 22 percent (République Libanaise, 1971, p.426). The most profitable sub-sectors of the economy are banking and trade. Lebanon is often referred to as the Switzerland of the Middle East, and its bank deposits help to finance the country's trade, where Western and Japanese manufactured commodities are imported, some to be consumed locally and others to be re-exported to neighbouring Middle Eastern markets. The centre for this financial and commercial activity is Beirut, and according to the 1970 sample population survey, 77 percent of the active population was employed in the service sector, including bankers, merchants, professionals, clerks and shopkeepers. Unfortunately, the categories used by the survey do not permit an accurate quantitative description of Beirut's class structure, but it can be said that only 22 percent of the active population worked in the industrial sector, including employers and employees in the electricity, water, construction and manufacturing industries (République Libanaise, pp. 114 and 124). On the basis of these figures and my own observations, some tentative conclusions can be made about the class structure of Beirut. First, there is virtually no industrial working class, and manual workers are usually either self-employed or employed by small businessmen and artisans. The vast majority of the labour force is employed in the service sector in a range of occupations, including hotel and domestic service, small shopkeeping, teaching, the civil service, and clerical work in commercial and financial establishments.

In Beirut, white collar employees in the service sector, as well as small businessmen and artisans, see their continued relative prosperity and their future upward mobility as closely tied to the increasing profits of the commercial and financial sectors. At present, there is not a large group of educated unemployed as there is in other developing countries, and there is little indication of an impending slump in the service sector. As a result, the petty bourgeoisie continues to believe that its interests are allied with those of the mercantile or commercial-financial bourgeoisie. Even if conditions changed, and this class, or sections of it, developed a class-consciousness in opposition to the bourgeoisie and the *zu'ama*, the strength of the *za'im's qabaday* apparatus would still present a substantial obstacle to concerted action. In the meantime, the precarious existence of the poor, the small size of the working class, and the individualistic ethic of the petty bourgeoisie, all contribute to intra-class relationships being competitive rather than co-operative. The poor compete with each other for welfare services; worker competes with worker for free education for his children; and clerk competes with clerk for promotion in the office hierarchy. By comparison, some sense of co-operation, albeit limited, *is* found in the vertical structure of transactional links headed by the *za'im*. At the very least, there is a degree of temporary solidarity in the relationships between the clientele, the *qabadayat* and the patron. The links are constantly reinforced by ritual visiting and by face-to-face contact between the *qabaday* and the client, and the individual client is encouraged to see himself as part of a quarter or family that fits into a grand alliance of the *za'im's* men.

There have been some attempts by sections of the petty bourgeoisie and proletariat to organise in horizontally linked groups, but as might be expected, manual workers and employees in the service sector have very weak trade unions. There are at least 130 unions in Lebanon, including, for example, ten in the commercial sector and fourteen in the petroleum industry (Commerce du Levant 1973, p.55). Such effective industrial action as does occur is usually put down by the government with considerable severity. At the end of 1972, security forces opened fire on picket lines outside a biscuit factory, killing at least two people, one of whom was a passer-by. A week or so later, the same security forces brutally attacked demonstrators and bystanders alike when pupils and students demonstrated in support of striking teachers. Both strikes, of biscuit workers and teachers, failed to win significant concessions from the employers, and served only to emphasise the repressive power of the *zu'ama*. The Prime Minister at that time was Sa'ib Salam, and a number of informants complained that he and the President, Sulayman Franjiyyah, 'were little more than *qabadayat*'. In other words, they were disciplinarians who could not tolerate organised opposition to a *za'im* system that required individual contracts between the patron and his clients.[9]

The insistence on individual contracts is an important feature of the clientelist system in Beirut. Among the *zu'ama* that I interviewed, a number told me they could not countenance dealing with the demands of organised groups. If one of their supporters wanted a better salary, they would be pleased to help him win promotion. But they would not tolerate disruptive industrial action. A salary increase is a gift of the *za'im*, not something that can be negotiated between employees and employer. Similarly, the marked reluctance, on the part of governments, to introduce a comprehensive social welfare scheme should be explained not only as the result of a lack of resources (if tax laws were enforced, the exchequer would be substantially richer), but also as a result of the resistance by *zu'ama* to any policy that reduces their control of patronage. There are some government-financed and charitable institutions that provide a minimum of social welfare services. These are usually controlled by *zu'ama*, who are able to distribute such services as patronage. By deciding who is admitted to the few free hospital beds, or whose children are to receive free or subsidised education, the *zu'ama* are able to maintain the loyalty of their clients. They can also serve the general interests of their class, because the client is encouraged to see such services as charity for which he must compete, rather than as something to which he and others like him are entitled.

Thus as well as responding to an individualistic electorate, the machine also encourages individualism. Even the limited solidarity of the quarter or family is essentially mythological, because the inhabitants of a quarter and the members of a family or clan are recruited as individuals, not as groups. The *qabadayat* cannot represent the demands of their quarter or family, nor of any other social group. They are merely the retainers of the *zu'ama*, and are the prisoners of their role as much as the clients are. Because they rely on *zu'ama* for protection from the police and the army, the criminal *qabadayat* dare not use their influence as local leaders to rebel against the patrons. They may be able to change their allegiance from one *za'im* to another, but they cannot reject the *zu'ama* altogether. Those *qabadayat* who are 'respectable businessmen' do have some independence from their *za'im*. However, rebellion is still unlikely as they have a debt of gratitude to the patron who has enriched them, and have an economic stake in the system as it presently operates.

Potential alternatives to the *zu'ama* and *qabadayat* do exist. But party politicians and union leaders have an extremely difficult task if they are to build new political structures to compete with the *zu'ama*'s apparatus. Any attempt to defeat the *zu'ama* will involve a long term strategy to persuade individuals to revalue their interests. If industrialisation develops, this revaluation will be more likely to occur. But it is by no means certain that it will be easily accomplished. Not only is the machine particularly well designed to recruit support in a fragmented electorate, it is also sufficiently sophisticated and adaptive to fight a sustained rearguard action against the social repercussions of changed economic circumstances.

ACKNOWLEDGMENTS

The research for this article was carried out in Beirut (1972-3) when I was a Research Fellow on a Manchester University Project set up to investigate Lebanese politics and society. The Project was funded by the British Social Science Research Council, and I should like to take this opportunity to thank that body for all the assistance that it gave me.

NOTES

1. A former Foreign Minister of Lebanon, in his contribution to Leonard Binder (ed.), *Politics in Lebanon* (New York 1966), approvingly describes Lebanese society as 'individualistic and petty bourgeois'. However, he erroneously concludes from this that the petty bourgeoisie is somehow the Lebanese ruling class. See Georges Hakim, 'The Economic Basis of Lebanese Polity', in Binder (1966), esp. pp. 60-1.

2. One notable exception was Riyad as-Sulh, the first Prime Minister after Independence, who had a strong national following among Christians as well as Muslims.

3. The seats in the Assembly are allocated to the various sects according to the supposed size of the sects in the population. In the constituency of Beirut III, for example, four of the five seats are reserved for Sunni Muslims, and one for a Greek Orthodox Christian. In order to win, a Sunni candidate has to recruit the support of Christians as well as Muslims.

4. Since 1958, Sa'ib Salam has been the most powerful Sunni *za'im* in Beirut. During the 1960s, other *zu'ama* (Sami as-Sulh and 'Abdallah al-Yafi) declined in importance, and their place was taken by younger men ('Uthman ad-Dana and Rashid as-Sulh). After his appointment as Prime Minister in 1973, an older leader (Taqi ad-Din as-Sulh) also achieved *za'im* status. All other Sunni politicians in Beirut cannot be considered as *zu'ama*.

5. By family I mean a clan of people bearing the same surname and having the same confession, who trace their genealogy to common ancestors. Often such clans have family benevolent associations, open to all members of the clan, and these give some organisational solidity to the group.

6. Much of my 'clientelist vocabulary' (concepts such as 'moral' and 'transactional politics', 'core group', 'broker', etc.) is influenced by F.G. Bailey (1970), esp. pp. 36-49.

7. For some time now, *makhatir* (pl. of *mukhtar*) in Beirut have been appointed, but it is planned to revert to the earlier practice of electing these officers.

8.   It should be emphasised that I am using the 'Indian broker' as an analytic ideal type to illustrate a particular quality of the *qabaday* role.

9.   It was also pointed out that the members of the Ghandur family, who owned the biscuit factory, were close allies of Salam and contributed to his electoral campaign fund.

REFERENCES

Bailey, F.G. (1970) *Stratagems and Spoils*. London.

Baran, P.A. (1973) *The Political Economy of Growth*. Harmondsworth.

Commerce du Levant, le, March/April 1973, n. 4448/151.

Gubser, P. (1973) 'The Zu'ama of Zahlah: The current situation in a Lebanese town', *Middle East Journal* 27, no.2 (Spring).

Gunder-Frank, A. (1967) 'Sociology of development and underdevelopment of sociology', *Catalyst* (Summer).

Khalaf, S. 'Changing forms of political patronage in Lebanon', in this volume.

Lande, C.H. (1973) 'Networks and groups in Southeast Asia: Some observations on the group theory of politics', *American Political Science Review* LXVII (March), 103-27.

Lapidus, I.M. (1967) *Muslim Cities in the Later Middle Ages*. Cambridge, Mass.

Leys, C. (1971) 'Politics in Kenya', *British Journal of Political Science* 1.

Ocampo, J.F. and D.L. Johnson (1972) 'The concept of political development', in J.D. Cockcroft, A. Gunder-Frank and D. Johnson (eds), *Dependence and Under-Development: Latin America's Political Economy*. New York.

République Libanaise, Ministère du Plan, Direction Centrale de la Statistique (1971), *Receuil de Statistiques Libanaises*, n.7, Beirut.

République Libanaise, Ministère du Plan, Direction de la Statistique (1972), *L'Enquête par sondage sur la population active au Liban: Novembre 1970*, Vol. I, Beirut.

Sutcliffe, R.B. (1972) 'Imperialism and industrialization in the third world', in R. Owen and R.B. Sutcliffe (eds), *Studies in the Theory of Imperialism*. London.

Yamak, L.Z. (1966) 'Party politics in the Lebanese political system', in L. Binder (ed.), *Politics in Lebanon*. New York.

Amina Farrag

The wastah among Jordanian villagers

While Jordan has been an independent sovereign state only since 1946, its army dates back in one form or another to 1921. The army, that is, preceded the emergence of a sovereign independent state in Jordan. In fact one could argue in this case that the army created the state. ... The army was a vehicle and an instrument for the pacification and integration of a predominantly tribal society into a state to whose central authority the tribes became responsive and to whose administrative control they became subjected. (Vatikiotis 1967, p.5)

The army in present-day Jordan is still one of the main props of the monarch, who, even under the present constitution, has extensive powers over the executive, legislative and judicial branches of the government. However, the younger generation has recently shown increasing resistance to the idea of an army career. In order to control and manipulate the growing potential threat, the regime is using other mechanisms, besides the army, to ensure conformity. These include: the perpetuation of customary tribal law, the intelligence service, and the *wastah* (go-between).

The purpose of this paper is to examine, through analysis of a Jordanian village, how the *wastah* is both a mechanism for ensuring conformity, and at the same time a threat to the existence of the very status quo which it is supposed to protect. It is a threat insofar as it intensifies conflicts of interest between those opposed to the perpetuation of traditional systems on the one hand, and the state and those who conform to its mechanisms on the other.

Village background

The village that is the focal point of this study lies about 30 miles north of Amman. It is surrounded by hills which are about 2,000-3,500 ft. above sea level. The houses are tightly clustered up and around the steep sides of the valley. The reason for this is economic – the best land lies in the bottom of the valley, where the villagers are reluctant to build; so the village spreads first upwards and then outwards along the hillsides.

Under Ottoman rule, which ended in 1918, the village economy depended mainly on farming and a limited domestic 'industry'. The main crops then were grapes, olives, grain and onions. The 'industry', which was mainly in the hands of the women, was concentrated on goat's cheese, mats, and raisins.

With the establishment of the Emirate (1921-3), the villagers began to enter the army. To begin with, those who enlisted were the poorer peasants, that is, those who owned little or no land; by the 1940s, more of the villagers enlisted in the army. Today, those who work in the service of the regime, i.e. army, police, intelligence service, are about 50-55% of the village labour force.

The villagers who farm the land today are: the older people who cannot enlist, or who cannot find other jobs; those who have retired from the army and own either very little land or none at all, and who cannot obtain other jobs; those who have one disability or another, who could not enter the army, and had not the means to continue their education; and the Palestinian refugees who had to leave the West Bank in the Arab-Israeli war of 1967, and who now live in a refugee camp on the outskirts of the village.

Most of the cultivation, which today is largely grapes and olives, some vegetables, and other fruits, depends on rain. Rainfall usually begins at the end of November and goes on till about March – January and February being the height of the rainy season. The average rainfall is 20 inches and sometimes approaches 30 inches. Some plots of land are situated near the wells and are irrigated by traditional means, as the villagers are unable to afford the pumping equipment which would be necessary for a major irrigation project.

Briefly there are three crucial categories in the village:
1.   villagers who remained farming peasants
2.   villagers who enlisted in the army
3.   villagers who deliberately opted out of the army, i.e. who refused to have army careers.

Within this context, while the villager who enlisted in the army has thereby helped to reinforce and support the power and interests of the regime, the interests of the villager-opted-out stand in opposition to those of the state and the enlisted. On the other hand, the farming peasant seems to fall in between the two.

In order to understand the process of development of the *wastah*, it is necessary to give a brief historical survey of the tribal, political and administrative system of the village. As there are no written historical accounts of that particular village, most of the information is based on informants' statements.

Tribal, political, and administrative system

There are nine *ashiras* in the village, the largest numbering 3,000 of the total village population of 5,000. The *ashira* does not seem to be more than the largest descent group, and according to statements from the older generation, this was also the case in the past. The *ashira* divides into *hamulas,* which divide into *fakhds,* which in turn divide into *lazam,* and finally into the extended patrilocal family.

The largest political unit in the village was the *hamula*. It seems that its effectiveness as a unit in relation to other units did not depend so much on its kin links to other units as on its numerical strength.

While each *hamula* had an elder as a mediator and go-between, the most prominent *hamula* was headed by a Pasha who was chosen by the Turkish authorities to mediate on their behalf. It is said that he was chosen as their spokesman, not only because he was head of the largest *hamula*, but also because he was willing to play the game, as it were, according to their rules. He saw to it that taxes were collected, and at the same time exploited the peasants (it is said, excluding members of his own *hamula*), by exacting higher taxes than was necessary, giving the right amount to the authorities, and taking the rest for himself. He was also given contributions in kind by members of his *hamula*, which he was then supposed to redistribute back in the form of meals at social gatherings in the *madafa* (guest house). However, it is claimed that on the whole he used the contributions mainly to entertain Turkish authorities who visited the village. According to the villagers, the Pasha was mistrusted because he identified with the interests of the wider authority and was not in opposition to it, as were the rest of the peasantry. His power concerning village matters (other than taxes) was however checked by the elders of the other *hamulas*. He could not, for example, ask the authorities to intervene if bedouin raids became too frequent, without consulting the elders first, and having their consent and approval.

Members of each *hamula* chose their elder on the basis of wisdom, age, generosity, etc. Each elder was responsible for the welfare of his *hamula*. For example, when there was a dispute within the *hamula* which kinsmen could not resolve, then the elder intervened. If a dispute or homicide took place between members of different *hamulas* or *ashiras*, then a *jaha* was formed. This was a deputation consisting of the elders of different *hamulas*, other than the ones involved in the homicide, which mediated between the victim's kin and that of the offender. The *jaha* made sure that the *utwa* (truce money), and the *diya* (final reconciliation money), were paid as quickly as possible by the offender's family to the victim's family. When this was done, the victim's family resumed its relationships with the offender's family.[1]

Apart from the income the elders earned from their land, they were also given contributions in kind by the members of their *hamulas*. However, unlike the Pasha, it is said that they used their income mainly to entertain members of their *hamulas* and other elders, and only when it was advisable or necessary, did they entertain Turkish authorities. According to the villagers, the elders were more trusted than the Pasha because they did not identify with the wider authorities. They tried for, example, to persuade the authorities, either directly or through the mediation of the Pasha, to decrease taxes as they were beyond the peasants' means. Although the complaints voiced by the elders were not successful, this did not detract from their power or influence within the village. They were successful mediators within the context of the village, and their failure with the wider authorities and the Pasha was not attributed to the elders themselves, but to oppression and exploitation by the authorities and the Pasha. The elders were looked upon as the upholders of village norms and values. This was considered to be of great importance by the peasants because they regarded their village as threatened by relations with the external groups. In a sense, while the Pasha's role as a mediator and go-between tilted the balance on behalf of the authorities, and the elders tilted it back on behalf of the peasants, or at least tried to, the *mukhtars* had a foot on each side of the balance.

There were two *mukhtars*, who were chosen by the elders. The *mukhtars* had to be fairly literate, and they were supposed to be reliable and neutral. That is, they were not to favour their own *hamula* at the expense of the other *hamulas* they were representing. If a *mukhtar* did favour his *hamula*, he was summoned by the elders and admonished.

The main duties that they had to carry out were to collect taxes and hand them over to the Pasha who then handed them to the authorities. They also had to see that deaths, births and marriages were recorded. Again apart from what they earned from their land, they lived mostly off the fees paid to them in kind by the peasants, either for services rendered, such as drawing up a marriage or birth certificate, or in the form of bribes from those who tried to escape conscription,[2] and whom the *mukhtars* were supposed to report to the Pasha, who then reported the offenders to the authorities. Although the *mukhtars* could have used this as a form of blackmail and increased their hold and power over the villagers, it is said that it did not generally happen because they would not only have been dismissed by the elders, but they would have lost the support of the villagers. However, occasionally, the authorities threatened to increase taxes because they were not satisfied with the number of conscripts, or they threatened to imprison some of the villagers who avoided conscription. In this case, the *mukhtars* were allowed by the elders to sacrifice a few villagers for the good of the majority.

The *mukhtars* stood in an ambivalent position. They were the ones who had to do the 'dirty work', as one villager expressed it. On the one hand, they represented Turkish interests by virtue of the fact that they had to collect taxes, and at times had to enforce conscription. On the other hand, unlike the Pasha, their position did not depend so much on support from the Turkish authorities, but more on that of the villagers.

On a more personal basis, there were two levels of mediation: the head of the extended patrilocal household, and the *lazam*. The latter was a patrilineal unit which traced its descent to the fifth paternal grandfather, i.e. to the fifth agnatic generation. Among other things, the *lazam* was responsible for paying the *utwa* and *diya*. Those who had to pay, as well as leave the village until the final reconciliation took place, were the first three generations. The fourth and fifth generations had to pay a certain amount of money, but in return they were allowed to stay in the village and were guaranteed protection.

Within the family, sons were not only economically dependent on their father but they were also socially and politically fully aligned with him, and they could not make decisions without his consent. If a son wanted to carry out a trade he could not do so without the consent and/or mediation of his father. If he wanted to get married, it was his father who had to discuss it with the members of the *lazam*, and the latter was then responsible for arranging the marriage with the girl's family; and if the son was involved in a dispute, he could not go to the elder of the *hamula*, the *mukhtar*, or even to members of his *lazam*, without his father's mediation.

It is said that a villager could not have gone very far in terms of acquiring land, getting married, settling disputes, etc., without some form of mediation. What level of mediation was used depended upon the type of problem that required mediation. What was important was that a villager could not by-pass mediators of his own *hamula* and go to mediators of other *humulas* or to non-villagers.

Under the Amir Abdullah (1923-1951), the village became integrated into a wider centralised system. What seemed to be a significant factor of change was the peasants' acceptance of the new ruling power (unlike the bedouin tribes, who to begin with were opposed to it). As part of his policy of appeasement, as well as his attempts to incorporate the rural areas within a centralised system, Abdullah perpetuated and manipulated various traditional factors. For example, he recognised the customary tribal law as a means of settling disputes. One way of centralising it was by having the offender imprisoned (instead of just having him leave the village) until the final reconciliation took place, after which he was released. Another factor was appointing some of the tribal and village leaders into his government and administration. Thus the former Pasha's son, who took over the leadership from his father and whose *hamula* was still dominant, was given a job in Abdullah's government. He and his family left the village and settled in Amman. According to the villagers, they continued to mistrust him, but no longer because he identified with the wider system, rather because, as the villagers became incorporated into the wider system, they had expected him to improve their conditions: providing supplies of electricity, water, improving roads, etc., none of which he did. His failure to do so was apparently not attributed to the government, but to his having 'inherited his father's tyranny and ability to deceive', said some of the villagers. However, he did help some of his near relatives to settle and work in Amman. As his contact with the village became less and less frequent, members of his *hamula* chose another elder. However, this did not mean that the Pasha's son was altogether rejected. When for example, a dispute broke out between members of his *hamula* and members of another *hamula,* then the former used his position in the government as a threat to bring pressure upon the latter.

With the integration of the village into the wider political and administrative system, the elders retained their importance in settling disputes within the village, but they were no longer looked upon as upholders of village interests and values. According to the villagers, this was no longer necessary as they were not in opposition to the wider system, but regarded themselves as part of it. The elders continued to be paid contributions in kind, but only for acting as a *jaha,* and no longer because they were elders who had additional expenses of feeding large social gatherings at the *madafa.* Consequently there were fewer social gatherings and eventually the *madafas* were turned into houses and shops (with the exception of the Pasha's *madafa,* which still stands empty and derelict).

The ones who actually gained more power were the *mukhtars.* While their nomination under Turkish rule was only approved by the elders, now their nomination had to be approved by the administrative officer residing in the nearest town. They became officially responsible to a centralised administration and they were given additional duties such as handing over an offender to the police until the final reconciliation between the families involved took place; the responsibility for seeing that schools were built, drawing up official papers, etc. They were paid a monthly salary, as well as contributions in kind by the villagers for services they may have rendered.

As their administrative powers within the village increased, so did their actual or potential power as intermediaries. Some of the villagers, who because of old age or other reasons, did not go into the army, but wanted to work in Amman, appealed to the *mukhtar* in charge of their *hamula.* They believed that with the increase of his administrative powers and his wider range of administrative connections, he would be able to find them work in the towns. A *mukhtar* did at times succeed in finding work for a villager, such as shop assistant, or porter, and where he failed to satisfy the demands and expectations, failure was attributed to somebody along the line of contacts. If a man thought that his own *mukhtar* was not efficient, he could not seek the help of another *mukhtar.* If he did, not only would he have incurred the disapproval of his own *mukhtar,* but also that of his kinsmen, as the *mukhtar* could refuse to render any more services not only to the offender but also to his near kinsmen. A *mukhtar,* therefore, could not increase his power before or during his office by rallying supporters from *hamulas* other than the ones he was in charge of.

On the level of the extended family, sons who previously had little chance of escaping their father's economic domination now began to enter the army. This decreased the father's economic control as sons earned their independent salaries, and the father was no longer in charge of the purse, nor of his sons' labour. Within the context of the village, a son still could not get married without his father's and *lazam*'s mediation; nor could he, for example, go to the *mukhtar* and ask him to mediate on his or someone else's behalf without his father's mediation. On the other hand, through their army career and contacts with the towns, sons could in their own right act as go-betweens for kinsmen or friends who wanted jobs done in town and did not know who to go to.

Thus within the wider context of the village, integration diversified the range of intermediaries. Within the village boundaries, it changed the emphasis on the power of some of the intermediaries: it limited that of the elders and increased that of the *mukhtars*. But the individual within the village was still unable to by-pass certain traditional channels of representation: the representatives of his *hamula*, and *lazam* and the head of the household.

The present period

Under King Hussein (1952 to the present), the *mukhtars* retained their importance until about 1965, when the village became a *baladia* (small municipality), with a *majlis baladia* (council), and a *ra'is baladia* (mayor). The *majlis* consists of seven members including the mayor, all of whom are elected by the villagers, the length of office being four years. Elders no longer have the authority to nominate or approve candidates. Candidates now have to be approved not only by the administrative officer in the nearest town, but also by the Ministry of Interior, and more important, by the security force.

According to the mayor and a pamphlet published by the Ministry of Interior, to qualify for nomination candidates must: (1) be Jordanian and not under the age of 24, (2) be politically reliable, (3) have been in the area for at least 12 months before election, (4) have no police record, (5) have paid taxes, and (6) be literate.

Some of the functions carried out by the *majlis* and enforced by the mayor are: to promote road construction, to see that the village has electricity and water, to control food prices, to inspect merchandise, to see that taxes are paid, etc.

The *mukhtars* still perform certain functions such as identifying couples who are to be married, or preparing papers for passports. However, on the whole, they have become powerless, and according to the villagers nobody goes to them for mediation. It is also said that in a year or two their offices will be abolished and their duties performed by the *baladia*.

The elders on the other hand still act in the capacity of a *jaha*. However, they seem to have lost completely their role as upholders of village values. Young men show disrespect by openly making fun of them: 'their place is in the museum,' commented one young villager.

Thus the village is now firmly under the control of the state machinery. Under Turkish occupation, one could perhaps say that the elders ordered social, economic, and political relations within the village boundaries, independent of the wider system (apart from taxes); but the present day relations can only be ordered within the framework of the wider system. To obtain office now, a candidate no longer needs wealth, or headship of a *hamula*, but rather the ability to operate within the rules set by the state, such as customary tribal law, *wastah*, etc.

The *wastah* in Jordan applies to both village and towns, and on all levels of employment except for people who want to become ordinary soldiers. Previously doctors, engineers, etc., were badly needed in the army and therefore they were encouraged to enter it. Now however, as the ratio of applicants to vacancies has increased, a doctor or engineer must have a *wastah* if he wants to work in the army.

S. Farsoun, in his article 'Family structure and society in modern Lebanon', defines *wastah* as follows (1970, p.270):

The *wastah* system is generalised in the society and performs important functions within the family and clan as well as outside it. One needs a *wastah* in order not to be cheated in the market place, in locating and acquiring a job, in resolving conflict and legal litigation, in winning a court decision, in speeding governmental action and in establishing and maintaining political influence, bureaucratic procedures, in finding a bride. ... The *wastah* procedure is complex, its rules varied depending on the sphere and nature of activity whether it is legal, familial, economic, etc. ... the higher the degree of training and education the lesser the use of the *wastah* procedure, except in the form of recommending and sponsoring.

This definition applies to a large extent to the way the *wastah* is used in Jordan. However, unlike Lebanon, the use of *wastah* in Jordan does not necessarily diminish with the higher degree of training and education. In fact in many cases it is quite the contrary.

Unlike the past, an individual now does not have to comply to the traditional channels of representation. Theoretically he can, for example, go straight to the mayor or elder of his *hamula* without having his father act as go-between. He can also go to a different member of a *hamula* if he finds him more useful as a go-between than somebody from his own *hamula*. In practice however, the responses vary according to which category the *wastah*-seeker belongs to. If he is a peasant farmer and he tries to go straight to the mayor for a favour, he may not have his request fulfilled by the mayor unless he brings him a *wastah*. An officer and soldier would have their demands fulfilled by the mayor without approaching him through a *wastah*. On the other hand, opters-out, especially the educated ones, do not usually ask the mayor, or any other member of the village, to act as *wastah*. The opters-out do not live in the village for long periods and they have contacts in the towns who are more useful to them than members of their village. However, if it so happened that an opter-out did ask the mayor for a favour, then he too would need a *wastah* to approach him.

The interaction between the *wastah* and *wastah*-seeker varies. The relationship between them need not be stable or lasting. Nor does the use of *wastah* necessarily create a relationship of friendship. For example, a university graduate in economics (village or townsman) hears of a job which is related to his field, either in a ministry or in a company. He may have a friend who has enough influence to act as a *wastah* and get him the job. The friendship so far has been symmetrical. After the friend has acted as a *wastah* the relationship, as far as both men are concerned, is still symmetrical, but in actual fact it has become asymmetrical, implicitly at any rate, by virtue of the fact that one has more effective power or say within the system than the other. In this case, unlike for example Campbell's Zagori villagers, friendship does not 'begin where one man accepts a favour from another' (1964, p.230). The friendship in this case was already in existence before the favour. The graduate is expected to return the favour one day, although this is never explicitly voiced. Again, like the Zagori villagers, 'the person who gives the favour will assert that he expects no return; it would be insulting to suggest his act of friendship had a motivation. It is, however, the very altruism of the act, whether this is simulated or not, which demands a counter favour' (ibid).

On the other hand if the graduate's friend has no direct influence to get him the job, then the friend acts as a *wastah* on behalf of the graduate, to another man who has enough influence to secure the job for the graduate. The graduate is then sent to the second *wastah* to discuss the problem, and once he gets the job, the relationship between them is terminated, unless later the graduate is in a position to return the favour to his *wastah*. Alternatively, the graduate may never see the second *wastah*. The graduate's friend simply deals with the second *wastah* directly and then relates the progress to the graduate.

In the sense above, the *wastah* does not seem to fall in either the patronage or the brokerage categories as defined by Mayer, Boissevain, and others. However, it can perhaps be used in the sense of broker when applied to the mayor's position in the village.

During the elections for the *baladia* (1970), there were candidates for the mayorship from two dominant (in the numerical sense) *hamulas*. The candidate from *hamula* A called for a 'united' village where relationships were not to be dominated by the system of *ashiras, hamulas*, customary tribal law, and *wastah*. On the other hand, the candidate from *hamula* B called for a 'working' village. He promised the villagers that he would act in the capacity of a *jaha* any time he was called upon, and that he would solve their disputes as quickly as possible. He also claimed that he had enough influence with the government officials to persuade them to approve the extension of electricity and water in the homes, and to have the new road project approved. He also promised to act as a *wastah* for the villagers to help them find work and solve their problems.

Each candidate catered to the different interests of the various groups. The man from *hamula* A catered to the younger villagers who had opted out of the army, and who wanted to see some changes in the traditional tribal, political and economic system. On the other hand, the candidate from *hamula* B seems to have catered to the villagers who enlisted in the army and for some who remained farming peasants and who believed that he would act as *wastah* for them, especially as they have a more limited range of contacts than the enlisted or opters-out. Since the majority of the villagers still work in the service of the state, which means that conformity to the rules set by the wider system still rates high, victory went to the candidate from *hamula* B.

The mayor is forty-six years old. He left school when he was in the fourth primary, after which he helped his father on the land (his father has since sold the land). The mayor then entered the army at the age of 20 and served for 21 years. He himself owns no land, and is in a difficult financial situation.

After being elected, he did bring electricity and water to the houses and initiated road construction. He also willingly agreed to act in the capacity of a *wastah* for some people, but others found it much more difficult to get him to act for them.

Case 1: One retired soldier had a son (also in the army), who had been sentenced to jail for having been absent from barracks without leave. The father then asked the mayor to act as a *wastah* in order to have the sentence reduced. The mayor went to Amman where he knew people in the right circles, and the sentence was eventually reduced.

Case 2: A peasant farmer had asked the mayor to persuade the foreman on the road construction site to employ his son as a labourer. The son had very little schooling, and had gone into the army as an ordinary soldier, but then decided to leave it. The mayor agreed, but did nothing about it. Another peasant farmer was sent to act as a *wastah* to the mayor on behalf of the boy, but that did not work either. The mayor then claimed that he could not act as *wastah* for anybody and everybody. He further claimed that he did not really approve of the *wastah* system, but he did it because it was part of the rules of society. Eventually after yet another *wastah*, this time an officer friend of the boy's father, the mayor agreed to speak to the foreman, and the boy was employed on the site. The father then gave the mayor a basketful of fruits and vegetables, for which the mayor thanked him and then pointed out that he would much rather they showed their gratitude by voting for him in the next elections.

Case 3: A family consisting of the father, a retired soldier, mother, two married sons, both soldiers, two sons in school, and one son who has left school after finishing first year of secondary school, and then joined the army. He then decided to opt out and returned to the village. A quarrel broke out between him and his brothers and his father. He told them that he would rather work as a labourer and that the army was not for him. His father and brothers accused him of shaming them (a soldier's social status is higher than that of the labourer both in terms of the state and of the village). The boy then went to the foreman on the road construction site and asked him for work. The foreman refused and told him that he should get a *wastah*. The boy went to the mayor, but the latter scolded him and said that he had shamed his family by leaving the army and wanting to work as a labourer. Furthermore, he was not going to act as *wastah* for him as he would be going against the father's wishes. The boy tried to persuade his father once more, but it only led to more quarrels and accusations of disloyalty. The boy eventually left for Amman, where he stayed with his mother's brother, who found him a job in a private company as a messenger boy.

The mayor is least popular with those who have opted out of the army, and who want to seek opportunities better than those in the army, and changes in the existing structure. They say that while it is all very well for the mayor to provide electricity and water, he still behaves like the old traditional leaders, accepting customary law and the *wastah*, which, they claim, he does not even use constructively or beneficially. Some of the young village teachers had asked him to build more classrooms, and he said that it was not up to him but up to the authorities in Amman. Furthermore, there was no more money as it was all going for the construction of the road.

The mayor's role and position reinforce the mechanisms used by the state to ensure conformity. His relation to the opters-out seems to reflect the fundamental conflicts of interest between them and the state. This has manifested itself within the context of the village by creating a division of allegiance within and between *hamulas*. While in the past, people sided with their own *hamula* in opposition to other *hamulas*, during the elections for the *baladia*, of 140 men from *hamula* B, 35 voted for the candidate of *hamula* A, and of 90 men for *hamula* A, 12 voted for the opposition. Although at the outset this is a small number, its significance lies in the fact that in the past it would have been inconceivable for an individual not to support the elder or *mukhtar* of his *hamula*.

On the other hand, the opposition has little impact upon the overall tribal, political and administrative system. That is, while the villager can choose to opt out of the army, it is more difficult for him to opt out of or ignore, for example, customary law, or the *wastah*. If he is involved in a dispute, or homicide, he cannot go very far without recourse to his *lazam* and *hamula* (except for political offences against the state), and if he wants to obtain a job he must have a *wastah*, regardless of qualifications.

Case 4: A, who has a degree in electrical engineering, has four brothers and three sisters. Three elder brothers are in the army, and the youngest is in secondary school. When A had finished secondary school, two of his elder brothers tried to persuade him to go into the army, but A said that he wanted to continue his education as there was more future in it. The brothers resented his comments, accused him of disloyalty and swore that they would not give him a penny to help him through his education. The third enlisted brother sided with A. Their father, who had been a gardener in an administrative building in one of the towns, and who was now retired, owned 10 dunums of land. He decided to sell some of it to see his son through his education. The two brothers tried to dissuade him, claiming that A had a better prospect in the army, but the father disagreed. Quarrels broke out and the two brothers stopped talking to their father and to A, as well as to the third enlisted brother. When A finished university, one of his brothers, who was an officer, tried once more to persuade him to enter the army saying that he could easily find him an effective *wastah*. A refused. He said that first, he did not want to go into the army, and second, he did not approve of the *wastah* and was not going to use it, and so further quarrels broke out. There was a vacancy in one of the companies in Amman, to which A applied. There were three other applicants besides A: one had only finished secondary school, one had done two years of commerce at the university and then left, and the third was an engineer. They were all interviewed, and the final question that was asked was whether they had a *wastah*. A said that all he had was a letter of recommendation from the university. The interviewer asked him if he could not get a *wastah* and A said no. He was then told that they would let him know. Ten days went by and A heard nothing, and so he went to see them. He found that the job had been given to the student who had dropped out of university. A was then told by one of the employees' that had he had a *wastah* – and a good one at that – he would have probably obtained the job as he had made a good impression. A then pointed out that what he could not understand was how they could employ somebody who had no engineering training at all. The employee replied that this was no problem as they would train him and if worst came to worst, they would create a job for him and readvertise for the original job. What was crucial was that of the four applicants, one had no *wastah* at all, three had *wastahs*, but two were ineffective in the face of the commerce student's *wastah* – his *wastah* having been a high ranking officer. When A's brothers heard of his fate, they lost no time in pointing out that had he listened to them he would not have been in this predicament and that they could still help him obtain a good *wastah* to go into the army. But A did not give in, and his decision was backed by his father and his third brother. He then successfully applied for a job in one of the Gulf states. He sends his father money every month to repay his debts, and he has promised to see his youngest brother through university.

Case 5: D has three older brothers in the army. Before he entered university he had asked one of his brothers, an officer, to help him with his fees until he found a job and then would repay him. His brother refused and told him that if he could not afford to go to university, he must go into the army and help support their mother. D accused his brother of living in the Middle Ages, believing in the tribal system and the *wastah*, which he considered to be the ruin of the country. Social relations were disrupted between the brothers. The mother then borrowed some money and helped her son go to university. He then tried to find a job without a *wastah* to help pay for his keep while he was studying, but he was unsuccessful. Finally after some persuasion from one of his friends, C, he accepted a *wastah*. The *wastah* was a friend of C's maternal uncle. D had met the latter but not the uncle's friend, F. The latter wrote a note to yet another friend E, which he gave to the uncle, who then passed it on to D. D had never met E, but when he gave him the note, E employed him as a part-time cashier. D was therefore, implicitly, under obligation to his friend, his friend's uncle, to F and to E. C was under obligation to his uncle, and the latter owed a favour to F. E, who employed D, was repaying a favour which F had done him sometime ago.

Summary and conclusion

The functions of go-betweens under Turkish rule were defined by the relation between the rulers and the villagers. Relations with the wider system were characterised by contradictions between the services and allegiances demanded by the rulers, and the extent to which the latter met the economic, social and political demands and expectations of the majority of the peasants. That is, Turkish rule imposed high taxes which were beyond the means of the peasantry, and they imposed conscription. In return, they neither offered a wider range of opportunities to the peasants, nor were they interested in the economic, social, and political development of the area, nor in bridging the gap between the centre and the periphery. The authorities gave contributions in kind or in cash, only to those who were willing to manifest their political allegiance – in the case of the Pasha who implemented their demands, and to some villagers who willingly entered the army. On the other hand, most of the peasantry showed its opposition by trying to avoid conscription: sometimes successfully, and at other times not. However, they could neither evade taxes, nor dispense altogether with the Turkish authorities, as every now and again, they needed their intervention against some of the raiding tribes.

Each level of representation within the village, thus, stood for the interests of diverse groups and constituted the basis upon which the community operated internally as well as externally. Each elder represented the interests of his *hamula* in opposition to other *hamulas*, and all elders united to represent the opposition of the peasantry against the wider system. The Pasha represented the interests of the Turkish authority, while the *mukhtars* cut across both, representing both opposition to the wider authority, as well as the inability to escape it. Representation enhanced kinship, family and local ties and loyalties; it did not bring about complementary values and expectations between the villagers and the wider system.

It can be said that representation under King Abdullah was one factor, among others, which helped bring about political integration. And while goods, services, economic, political and social alternatives, were also limited, nonetheless the system gave a slightly wider range of opportunities to individuals than had been offered previously.

The state today has introduced some reforms in education, property, agriculture, housing, and has created limited industry. However, it continues to perpetuate certain traditional systems, such as the *wastah* and customary tribal law, which in turn continue to limit opportunities and alternatives.

In a sense, the position of the opters-out is reminiscent of the position of the villagers under Turkish rule, but naturally under different conditions. While in the past, opposition to the wider system involved more or less the majority of the villagers, for example by the avoidance of conscription, today opposition is manifested by refusing an army career. However, unlike the past, opposition involves only some of the villagers and not the majority. And while in the past group representation was an important condition of their existence, and while under Abdullah it was one of the factors that furthered political integration, today it is no longer a satisfactory means of articulation; it is considered more of a handicap to their demands and expectations. As Lemarchand and Legg suggested, once patronage becomes 'a mere exchange of favours among individuals enjoying differential social status', then it becomes 'too fragmented, personalized and status quo oriented' to lead to 'innovative and integrative transformations' (1972, p.174).

The necessity to conform to traditional norms of behaviour seems to have two effects: first, it perpetuates the status quo. Second, the inconsistencies between the necessity to conform to traditional systems amongst limited opportunities on the one hand, and the growing demands and expectations on the other, intensify conflicts of interest between the opters-out and the state, and between the former and some of the enlisted.

It can be said that at present conflicts of interest between the opters-out and the state are submerged. Perhaps they would only surface in a context where these same conflicts of interest also dominate relations between the enlisted and the state.

NOTES

I would like to stress the fact that this is only one chapter of a doctoral thesis. When the thesis is completed, I may well have modified some of the views expressed in this working paper.

1.   Homicides between the different *hamulas* and *ashiras* did not lead to a state of feud in Peters's sense where 'the feud knows no beginning and it has no end'. (Peters 1967, p.268.)
2.   According to the villagers, it was a lucrative business for the *mukhtars* as many of the peasants tried to avoid going into the Turkish army.

REFERENCES

Boissevain, J. (1966) 'Patronage in Sicily', *Man* 1, no.1 (March).

Campbell, J.K. (1964) *Honour, Family and Patronage*. Oxford.

Farsoun, S. (1970) 'Family structure and society in modern Lebanon', in L. Sweet, (ed.), *Peoples and Cultures of the Middle East*. New York.

Lemarchand, R. and K. Legg. (1972) 'Political clientelism and development: A preliminary analysis', *Comparative Politics* 4.

Mayer, A. (1967) 'Patrons and brokers: Rural leadership in four overseas Indian communities', in M. Freedman (ed.), *Social Organisation*. London.

Patai, R. (1958) *The Kingdom of Jordan*. Princeton.

Peters, E. (1967) 'Some structural aspects of the feud among the camel-herding Bedouin of Cyrenaica', *Africa* 37, no.3.

Vatikiotis, P. (1967) *Politics and the Military in Jordan*. London.

Sawsan El-Messiri

The changing role of the futuwwa in the social structure of Cairo

Introduction

The purpose of this paper is twofold. First, it seeks to further our understanding of the role of the *futuwwa* (pl. *futuwwat*) in Egyptian society, a role that is associated with urban violence and, in particular, protest movements. Second, it attempts to ascertain the power resources inherent in the role.

The term *futuwwa* is used to denote a strong, bold man, but beyond that, the epithet may refer to groups with a basically religious orientation as well as to groups with a criminal or outlaw orientation. Generally, it has been applied to the masses but occasionally to members of the elite as well. In all cases the element of protection has been seminal to the role.

In Cairo, until the twentieth century, each locality in the popular quarters was identified with one or several strong young men who excelled in using cudgels, clubs, knives, swords, and guns. The quarters of old Cairo, the core area of the medieval city, came to be identified by and with their *futuwwat* and, correspondingly, the *futuwwat* by their quarters. Some names mentioned even now in these quarters are Muhammadan of Tulun, Hassan Kina of Birket al-Fil, 'Urabi of al-Hussiniyya, Mahmud Subhi of al-Darb al-Ahmar, Filfil of Darb al-Gamamiss and 'Aziza al-Fahla of al-Migharbilin. By definition the *futuwwat* are young men, yet among them were several *futuwwa* women, such as the above-mentioned 'Aziza al-Fahla. These young men and occasional women were and to some extent still are responsible for the protection of the locality against outsiders. As a protector and informal leader, an essential question to be asked is, whom does the *futuwwa* protect and what are his power resources?

The major attributes of the *futuwwa* are best defined in terms of the local culture itself rather than in reference to western typologies of patronage. Accordingly, we may classify the *futuwwa* broadly within the terms of two ideal types commonly referred to by Cairenes in their everyday life. The first is the *ibn al-balad*, 'son of the country', but a term that contains far more than its literal meaning. It is a very positive term, denoting 'real', salt-of-the-earth, indigenous Egyptians or, in the case of Cairo, the true Cairene with those traits that the bulk of the working classes have in the past attributed to themselves (El-Messiri 1970). The second type, with strongly negative connotations, is the *baltagi*, the thug or tough. He shares with the *ibn al-balad* a reputation for physical strength, manliness, and courage, but he puts these assets to work in his own selfish interests, and, rather than protecting the people, he oppresses them. In general the salience of the *futuwwa*, regardless of type, has dwindled in the twentieth century, a process accompanied by a sequential change in role attributes. In the eighteenth and nineteenth centuries, there is evidence that the *ibn al-balad* type predominated. By the early twentieth century, however, both models were represented, while in the last twenty-five years, there has been a clear tendency for the *baltagi* type to prevail.

Pre-twentieth century

In pre- and early Islamic times the term *futuwwa* was not applied to a category of individuals. *Fata* (pl. *fityan*), meaning 'young man', was the noun used metaphorically to indicate manliness, valour, and generosity. The *fityan* epitomised male vigour, courage in warfare, nobility, chivalry and keeping one's oath even with one's enemy. Generosity was expected from the *fata* to the extent of self-denial and self-effacement. Protecting the weak was the truest expression of manliness and chivalry. These values were carried over into the Islamic tradition and are mentioned in several verses of the Qur'an and the sayings of the Prophet Muhammed (*ahadith*).

In the complex society of the Islamic empire a variety of groups bearing different names identified themselves with these values of *fityan* and developed structured organisations to affirm this identity. These involved elaborate rituals, initiation ceremonies, rules for membership and correct conduct (*adab*), and for settling disputes. Members, at the time of the induction of a new devotee, would communally drink from a cup of salt water while a belt was buckled round the waist of the initiate. Members would wear special trousers known as *libas al-futuwwa*. After induction, members would pass through various internal hierarchies.[1]

Some mystic groups, concerned with extending their hospitality, fraternity, and protection to the needy, incorporated the *futuwwa* model, as did religious and warrior groups such as the *al-murabitun*, who undertook the defence of the Islamic frontiers against invaders.[2] In addition to these groups, which seem to have adopted fully the *futuwwa* model, we find other groups – such as the Sufi mystics and craft and trade guildsmen – whose links, while close, remain obscure (Breebart 1961).

The *futuwwa* model was also adopted by rebellious groups in the Muslim world. These consisted mainly of the poor and illiterate urban masses such as the *'ayyar*[3] (vagrants, outlaws) of Baghdad and the *zu'ar*[4] (scoundrels) of Cairo and Damascus. The activities of the *'ayyar* ranged from plundering to resistance to the governing authorities. They protected the poor strata of society, and, in times of weak government, set up their own courts to regulate the lives both of the *fityan* and the weak. The activities of the *zu'ar* included criminal assassinations, theft and pillaging, as well as leading and participating in mass protests against food shortages and high prices.

By the eighteenth, but possibly as early as the sixteenth century, the *futuwwa* model had been adopted by groups variously referred to as *shuttar, 'ayaq, 'asab,* or *ru'asa' al-'asab.* We do not know if these different labels stand for different groups or are synonymous for one. However, the perhaps interchangeable uses of the labels in early epic literature give us a picture of the character traits associated with the *futuwwa* prototype. In these he is depicted as being generous, courageous, and possessing *muru'a* (manliness). He is also, in Egyptian epics, noted for his cleverness, cunning, sense of humour, and verbal skill.[5]

Craftiness and a sense of humour are obviously not from the pre-Islamic core values of the *futuwwa* and are apparently an Egyptian addition. For example, in the ballads honouring the legendary figure of Ali al-Zaybak al-Misri (see note 5), he was lauded for his courage and unswerving sense of justice, but also for his cunning and the tricks he played upon his teachers to get what he wanted. As an adult he is portrayed as a hero who revolted against the rule of different secular authorities but whose loyalty to the Muslim Caliph, God's deputy on earth, was never questioned.

In Cairo the *futuwwat* adopted these same attributes for themselves, and as the informal leaders of their quarters, frequently placed themselves in opposition to ruling groups, especially when these latter were non-indigenous, such as the Mamluks or Ottomans. For example, Sheikh al-Kafrawi, one of the religious scholars (*'ulema*) opposed the Mamluk elite on several occasions, but they could not harm him because 'he was married to the daughter of Mu'allam Daras, the butcher of al-Hussiniyya; thus he enjoyed the protection of the people of the quarter, the *zu'ar* and the *shuttar*' (al-Jabarti 1958, p. 200). Thus some of these groups were so reputed for their strength and boldness that they were able to intimidate parts of the ruling elite. They were associated not only with the people of their quarters but also with the indigenous population (*awlad-al-balad,* pl. of *ibn al-balad*) of the city as a whole (El-Messiri 1970).

The ruling elite, whether Mamluk, Turk, or otherwise, constituted a privileged stratum that exploited the urban population. The collaboration of the *futuwwa* with elements of this population was effective in stopping many unjust measures such as high taxes, arbitrary arrests, or official plundering of towns, villages or quarters. In one instance of plundering, for example, the *zu'ar* rallied the people of the quarters, and, led by Sheikh al-Dardiri, in turn threatened to plunder the homes of the ruling elite. Fearing precisely that, the Mamluks promised the mob that all the spoils would be returned to them and that a sort of jury would be appointed to investigate the perpetrators of the original abuses. One of the latter, when reproached for his deeds by the Mamluk Governor, declared: 'We are all plunderers – you, Ibrahim Bey (the Governor) plunder, Murad Bey (another Governor) plunders, and I plunder too' (al-Jabarti 1958, p.136).

When the ruling elite was foreign and non-Muslim, the revolt of the masses was intensified because it became a religious as well as a 'national' cause. Resistance to the French was not limited to the Ottoman and Mamluk soldiery but took the form of two major popular uprisings in 1798 and 1800. In view of the new weaponry that the French used in Egypt, and the ignorance of the masses of their firepower, one can appreciate the bravery of the people of al-Hussiniyya in confronting Napoleon's troops:

Many of the *ghawgha* (mob) united and proclaimed *al-jihad* (holy war), and the *hasharat al-Hussiniyya* (the insects of al-Hussiniyya) and the *zu'ar* of the quarter of al-Barraniyya. They shouted 'God save Islam'. They proceeded to the house of the judge and were followed by another thousand or more like them (i.e., *zu'ar*) ... When the French learned of their gathering, an officer and his troops proceeded to their quarters, but the *zu'ar* were fortified behind barricades, and they killed several soldiers and prevented them from entering ... The French shelled the quarters that lay around (the university-mosque) al-Azhar. The people of the quarters were alarmed, for they never before had seen such missiles, and ran away. As for the people of al-Hussiniyya and al-Atuf, they went on fighting until their gunpowder was exhausted, while the *al-frinj* (the French) fired on them constantly. (Finally) having exhausted their arms and unable to continue, they left their positions to the French. (al-Jabarti 1958, pp. 273-4.)

Such incidents indicate the role of these groups and the unity they achieved in times of political crisis. Their leadership of the quarters in collaboration with religious leaders was particularly effective. In 1805 this collaboration was sufficient to bring about the downfall of Tahar Pasha, the Turkish Governor of Egypt, and the accession to that position of Muhammed Ali (1805-49). But it would seem that the coalition of *futuwwa* and *'ulema* became inoperative thereafter. Indeed, by the middle of the nineteenth century one no longer hears of resistance movements spanning several quarters, but rather of influential personages, including *futuwwat*, operating within quarters. While documentary evidence is scarce, one may nonetheless deduce something of the role the *futuwwat* played within the quarters or *harat*.[6] In many ways these were social entities as well as physical and geographical units, and their inhabitants were often set off from those of neighbouring *harat* by ethnic, religious, or occupational characteristics. To some degree interests among *harat* were conflicting, and it was in the context of defending those interests that the nineteenth-century *futuwwa* exercised his role as protector. In all historical periods, however, one may assume that his contacts with the inhabitants of the neighbourhood were intimate and founded on face-to-face relations.

The futuwwa in the twentieth century

In recent times, one finds the *futuwwa* seeking to establish himself within his neighbourhood as the paragon of all those virtues and qualities that most citizens of old Cairo would like in some measure to claim as their own. Foremost among these qualities, and of paramount importance to the image of the *futuwwa*, is physical strength. Many of the nicknames of famous *futuwwa* refer to this quality: 'Urabi, drawn from the famous Egyptian Nationalist hero of 1879-81; *al-fahl al-kabir*, the big animal; *zalat*, the stone; *al-Husan*, the horse. The *futuwwat*, even the women among them, are physically imposing. For example, 'Aziza al-Fahla was described by those who knew her as follows:

I saw 'Aziza al-Fahla who was at the top of all the *futuwwat* of al-Migharbilin. A giant lady who possessed extraordinary strength. Around her arms were tons of gold (i.e. bracelets). One blow from her hand was enough to knock any man to the ground. A blow with her head would split a stone. She was married to a man called *al-fahl al-kabir*, the big animal. He used to support his wife in any quarrel, but this was rare because 'Aziza was always capable of gaining victory alone. By becoming one of 'Aziza's follower, I learned my first lesson in *fatwana* (i.e. the brave deeds of the *futuwwa*). (al-Miligi 1970, p.13)

But strength must be accompanied by bravery. The young man 'Abdoun, an admirer of a *futuwwa* known as al-Dukma, set out to cultivate those characteristics that would permit him to join al-Dukma's clique of supporters. Thus was he advised: 'Be careful, don't get near him with this mien, this odor, and this oily garment. Be like pure water and try your luck.' It was also said to him 'our *futuwwa* loves beauty and purity and is unique in the series of our *futuwwat*.'

'Abdoun was convinced that way to al-Dukma was easy. Thus he went to the public bath to change his skin in the tub, prepared a new *galabiyya* (loose, ankle-length garment) and *bulgha* (slippers). While thus busy renewing himself, one of his friends asked, 'What is it 'Abdoun, are you thinking of marriage?' 'Abdoun told him his secret, but his friend said, 'Cleanliness alone doesn't interest al-Dukma; he loves tales.'

'Abdoun's secret became known, and everyone knew that he was preparing himself for *al-fatwana*. Several took the initiative to advise him, one of them saying: 'Cleanliness is important, tales are important, but for al-Dukma bravery is more important than both.'

'Bravery?'

'Yes, also be careful not to arouse his jealousy for otherwise he will be angry rather than pleased (with you).'

'How can I compromise between the one and the other?'

Another person said, 'Strength is also important; you have to prove your strength, you have to prove that you are capable of striking the final blow and enduring them however hard they may be. At the same time, you have to prove to him that your strength is not comparable to his.' (Mahfuz 1972, p. 4)

This passage refers not only to the basic characteristics of *fatwana* but, as well, to the process by which one might set about to achieve it.

The *futuwwa* of the *ibn al-balad* type is usually recruited from the people of the sub-quarter, the *hitta*, a very intimate unit where all are neighbours. He is generally employed in local trades such as butcher, coffee-shop owner, dealer in food-stuffs, cart owner, or scrap merchant. Mu'allam Yussuf, a *futuwwa* of the 1920s who later wrote his memoirs, refers to his upbringing in these terms:

I was born in the streets of al-Hussiniyya. My father and mother dwelt in *harat-al-husr*. I was brought up among lovers of abuse and scorners of school education. They were the advocates of education by the meat-cleaver. In fact most of the inhabitants of al-Hussiniyya are butchers who kill and skin but of course don't read and write. My father, who owns a butcher shop, sent me to the *kuttab*.[7] For three years I attended the *kuttab* only by continual spanking. I left the *kuttab* after learning just how to write my name and read two lines in the newspaper in an hour or two. My father used to tell me, why bother about the *kuttab*, are you going to be a government employee, or an *abu-katoo* (avocat/lawyer), or catch a wolf by the tail? What you need is a couple of calves and a shop, and God will take care of the rest. I submitted to God's wish and took off the tarbouch[8] and put on the turban, changed my shoes for slippers and became a *balady* (local) lad ... I joined a clique, and we used to go every night to a wine shop, or ghorza (hashish party). (al-Hagg Yussuf 1924, p. 3)

Part of the social identity of the *futuwwa* relates to the network of activities he is involved in. The *futuwwa* in his *hitta* is mainly conceived of as the protector of the neighbourhood against rival *futuwwat* or any other outside opponents. Most of the problems the people bring to the *futuwwa* relate to work situations, or those that emerge from the traditional style of life and the values attached to it. Typically, people interacted on a personal basis with no formal contracts, bills, or receipts. In these arrangements a man was tied by his tongue, that is bound by what he had said. In this way if someone had borrowed money from his neighbour without receipt and refused to pay it back or denied that he had borrowed it, the *futuwwa*, after investigation, could force him to return the money. Some clients may take commodities, promising to pay later, and then continually postpone payment or refuse it altogether; the merchant would then seek help from the *futuwwa*. The *futuwwa* might even end a dispute by paying what was at issue himself.

The *futuwwa* would also look after the welfare of the community as a whole. For example, he would protect the *hitta* from thieves, or help supply the *hitta* with scarce commodities, such as oil or kerosene, to spare the people from black market prices. In the economic crisis of 1942, a certain *futuwwa* used to procure the kerosene allotment of his whole *hitta*, protect it during delivery, and then distribute it equally throughout the *hitta* without taking any fee.

The *futuwwat* have also been engaged in safeguarding public morality and the reputations of the local inhabitants, especially those of the women. In the 1930s, in quarters known for prostitution, such as al-Ezbekiyya, the local protectors were referred to insultingly by outsiders as the '*futuwwat* of females'.

Charity to the poor was and is an important attribute of the *futuwwa* and one of the basic values that confers prestige and fame. Wealth in itself does not make one popular, but rather what one does with it, how much one spends on the poor, on others, or how much one spends to feed others. For instance, a *futuwwa* was known for his generosity and was said to have an 'open house' (*bait maftuh*) in which large amounts of food were cooked for those who needed to be fed. The amount of food prepared is a value in itself because it is often used as an index of hospitality and hence of prestige. The roots of this practice lie in the 'good old days' when good families cooked considerable amounts of food daily, well beyond their needs, so that anyone was welcomed to their table at any time. From the above it is clear that the *futuwwat* work in financially rewarding jobs that set them above the average wage-earner and which allow them to be generous. 'Aziza al-Fahla, the most renowned *futuwwa* in al-Migharbilin, worked as a dealer in food stuffs such as cheese, eggs, fruits, vegetables, and beans. From this she earned enough to enable her to buy about eight houses in the *hitta*, a coffee-shop and several other shops. Similarly, the earnings of the butchers and coffee-shop owners were such that they could afford to be more generous than most.

One of the *futuwwa*'s most clearly-defined duties is that of protector of his people during ceremonial occasions such as marriages and circumcisions. Part of the marriage ceremony consists in a procession, or *zaffa*, in which many of the male residents of the *hitta* gather. In the 1920s, if the *zaffa* of the bridegroom moved from one quarter to another, it could proceed only with the permission of the *futuwwat* of that *hara*. Anyone in the locality sponsoring a ceremony would usually seek the protection of the *futuwwat* of the *hara* to safeguard the ceremony from rival *futuwwat*, or any other trouble-makers, or to guard the ceremony from the depredations of the local *futuwwa* himself were he to have been neglected by his clients. It is common, even now, that weddings occasion quarrels in the quarters of old Cairo. Rival *futuwwat* usually seek such occasions to express their animosity, and the gathering of the people of one neighbourhood in that of another often leads to friction. Protection by the *futuwwa* is thus essential for the continuity and orderliness of the ceremony. At the same time, the *futuwwa*'s ability as an attacker and defender is established and adds to his reputation.

As a leader, the *futuwwa* does not work alone. His prestige in the *hitta* depends upon the number of his supporters. The *futuwwa* is usually identified as someone who has *'azwa* (from *'aza* meaning to trace back). Strictly speaking *'azwa* means having the support of one's ancestry, but for the *futuwwa* *'azwa* refers to the number of his living supporters. The potential supporters come from various categories that are referred to as 'followers' (*atb'a*), 'boys' or 'lads' (*subyan*), a clique (*shilla*), and 'those who stand for you' (*mahasib* and *mashadid*).[9] A common threat or challenge today is: 'I will beat you and those who stand for you!' Thus it was that part of 'Aziza al-Fahla's strength lay in the fact that she had ten strong brothers, a strong husband, about thirty men who worked for her, 'boys' in food merchandise, a clique of women sellers who accompanied her in the market and were her *mahasib*, and finally all the people of the *hitta* who were potential *mashadid*. It was common to find several of the prestigious *futuwwat* in businesses that involved a large number of apprentices, his *subyan* of 'boys', who were simultaneously a major source of support. Being a *futuwwa* was and is not a negligible business, and it was occasionally profitable, but profits and prosperity came from the profession itself rather than from the *futuwwa*'s extra-professional role as protector and strong-arm.

The *futuwwat* within and among different localities are in constant competition and conflict to assert their supremacy, their quarrels taking on the proportions of feuds. To end a feud between two equally-renowned *futuwwat* is difficult because any appeal for reconciliation would be answered by the saying 'we are *gada'an* (tough and brave) and men do not give up their revenge'.[10] In a quarrel it is expected that a *futuwwa* will beat and be beaten by others. But to be attacked and run away, or not hit back, would identify a *futuwwa* as a 'woman' (*mara'*) which is the most humiliating insult he could receive. Reconciliation of rival *futuwwat* is done as diplomatically as possible to lessen the tension between the parties and the shame of the loser. The most important thing is to preserve the honour and manliness of each and to assert that they are both *gada'an*.

It is also common that the *futuwwa* is in more or less constant conflict with the local authorities. His fights, for instance, frequently lead to the voluntary or involuntary 'closing of shops' in the *hitta* as shopowners want to keep themselves and their merchandise out of harm's way. Entire streets or quarters may close down in anticipation of or during a brawl. When a renowned *futuwwa* starts a fight, moreover, the number of shops that close is an index of his prestige and power; therefore if compliance is not spontaneous, he will, in the interests of his own reputation, have to force their shutters down. While the local authorities treat these as illegal acts, the *futuwwa* sees them as legitimate expressions of *gada'ana* and bravery.

If someone acts improperly in the *hitta*, the *futuwwa* may take it upon himself to correct that behaviour. If the police intervene in the matter, the *futuwwa* is likely to take on the police. In some instances of particularly brutal police intervention, the *futuwwat* have responded by attacking the police station and the policemen. The result is that *futuwwat* are frequently taken into custody and imprisoned. However there is no stigma attached to being jailed, and the *futuwwat* proclaim that they are not criminals but *gada'an*, and that 'prison is for the *gada'an*'. Correspondingly they consider the authorities weak, corrupt, and easily fooled and thus contrive to outwit the authorities and their systems. Al-Hag Yussuf, in his memoirs, describes an incident in which he escaped six months' imprisonment after having wounded and beaten up a couple of men in a quarrel:

While walking with the policeman to prison, I planned to run away. To put the policeman at ease, I started giving him one cigarette after another, and then I told him what a scandal it was for a *futuwwa* like me to walk like a prisoner with handcuffs, so I called a coach and we rode in it. In the coach I disjoined the handcuffs with a coin with which I could pry the iron. In front of a coffee-shop, I asked the coachman to stop. The policeman asked why we were stopping. I said 'just to take care of you for your help (meaning to get him some money)'. The policeman's face relaxed, and I left him in this state and went home. Do you know why I escaped? Afraid of prison? Never. I just wanted to prove to them (the government) that they are stupid.

This anecdote highlights the fact that in all his actions the *futuwwa* depends not only on his strength but also on his intelligence and craftiness.

The opposition of the *futuwwa* to officialdom is intensified when the authorities are foreign. The means of opposition vary however. The *futuwwat* in opposing one another rely mainly on their personal merits of strength and skill in fighting, particularly in the use of clubs, knives and swords. But in the face of authorities with overwhelming means of coercion at their disposal, the *futuwwat* must rely on deception. During the British occupation of Egypt (1882-1954), the *futuwwat*, assisted by the people of their quarters, resisted the British by such acts as throwing hot water on them, killing drunken soldiers at night, and digging holes in the paths of soldiers and covering them with straw. The *futuwwat* exploited British ignorance of local customs. For example, during a periodic search for weapons the British came across a sword in the house of 'Aziza al-Fahla. They were about to arrest her when she explained that the sword was not a weapon but a symbol that she used in the *zar*, or ceremonies of ritual exorcism. The British accepted this explanation, although swords have no place in such ceremonies.

In their resistance to the British authorities there is no indication of group action in which the *futuwwat* of different localities united with the people of the quarters in the manner of the *zu'ar* in the eighteenth century in their resistance to the French. Rather, resistance in the twentieth century took the form of individual, patriotic acts on the part of the *futuwwat*. 'Aziza al-Fahla, for example, used to lure rural migrants away from British employment during the Second World War by offering them higher salaries. She used also to attack and beat those whom she suspected of collaboration with the British.

In general, the political awareness of the *futuwwat* was not as sophisticated as that of the educated classes. The cooperated with explicitly nationalist groups, such as the students, because they found the students to be brave young men willing to stand up to the British. al-Hag Yussuf in his memoirs recalls the 1919 uprising:

I was walking in al-Hussiniyya when I met a large group of *effendi* (gentleman) students and religious students (from al-Azhar) who were shouting and demonstrating. In asking about the reason for the clamour, they said the British had imprisoned Said Pasha (the Prime Minister). I asked who was Said Pasha. They said he is asking the British to leave Egypt, but they put him in prison. I said he is then a *gada'*, and immediately I joined the demonstration. To tell you the truth I discovered that these students are real men. Among them were daring ones who just threw themselves upon the British to fight them. I and my clique joined the students, and when the British tried to capture one of them, we tried by all our means to release him.

The baltagi

The other polar type that is associated with the role of the *futuwwa* is the *baltagi*, the thug or tough. The *baltagi* might be from the locality, or from outside, but he is not closely associated with the people of the *hitta*. The *baltagi* shares with the *futuwwa* physical strength and skill in fighting. Achieving these core qualities and hence the identity, *al-fatwana* becomes for the *baltagi* a source of profit or a crude expression of power. The sorts of activities in which he engages are different from the *futuwwa* of the *ibn al-balad* model. He is not associated with the protection of the interests of the *hitta*. On the contrary, he abuses the people of the *hitta*, by taking ransom on certain commodities that they sell, or simply taking goods that he wants without payment. In other cases, he is ready to sell his skill and will accept payment to beat someone up, wreck a ceremony, or close a shop or club. He does not abide by the norms and values of the people, and his leadership is imposed upon the quarter by exploitation, force, and fear. In the following description of one of these *baltagi* by an inhabitant of the *hara*, one can discern this relationship:

Go'los Dananiri is a dangerous *futuwwa* and one of the most effective in the *hara*. He sits in the coffee-house like a mountain, or leads his procession like a huge building. I look at him breathless, but my father grabs me by the hand saying, 'walk straight on, are you crazy?' I ask my father, 'Is he stronger than 'Antara?' He replies, smiling, ''Antara is a legend, but this one is real and God help us.'

His voice is only heard raging, storming or screaming, and always insulting. He addresses his friends by 'that s.o.b.', he curses religion while going or coming back from prayer. He is never seen smiling even when he is receiving protection money or listening to flattery. In all, he doesn't differentiate between the owner of the *wikala* (i.e., a wealthy merchant) and Hamuda the pimp. In the presence of the notables of the *hara*, he breaks wind or displays his genitals.

A merchant may be unable to pay his protection money and asks for a week's respite but is refused; and the man is forced to remain at home with the 'harem' until he is relieved of his financial crisis.

The school principal punishes the son of one of his clients, so he blocks his way back from school and orders him to go home naked. The principal pleads for forgiveness, entreating earnestly with the names of God and the Prophet, but Go'los, sulky and hot-headed, waits for his orders to be obeyed. The principal, in tears, is forced to take off his clothes piece by piece. He tries to stop when there is nothing left besides his underwear, but Dananiri roars, the man shivers and takes them off, covers his genitals with his hands and runs back home followed by the gang's laughter. He disdains established tradition, he doesn't refrain from obliging a person to divorce his wife in order to marry him. He marries and divorces several times, and no-one dares marry one of his divorced wives. They are left to face life as lonely beggars and prostitutes.

He falls sick and stays in bed for a week. A fortune-teller tells him that his illness is a result of the curses of the people of the *hara*. So when he recovers, he orders the people not to celebrate the (feast of) Bayram — even visiting the tombs is forbidden. During the days of the feast, the *hara* is empty, the shops closed, and the houses silent as if in mourning. (Mahfuz 1974, p.4)

At the same time the *baltagi*'s reputation for brutality protects the *hitta* from outsiders: he, at once, abuses the people of the *hitta* and protects them from the abuse of others:

... he also terrifies the neighbouring *harat* and smashes the *futuwwat* of al-Hussiniyya, al-'Otuf, and al'Darasa. Hence the bridegroom's *zaffa* would proceed from our *hara* without protection and people would avoid our footsteps to protect themselves from the strongman's rage. (Mahfuz 1974, p. 4)

The *baltagi*, too, measures his strength by the number of his supporters, but supporters of a different breed. The *baltagi* might have a core group of *subyan*, but they, instead of being workmen or apprentices, or having an honourable craft (*san'a*), would be jobless (*suy'a*). His clique of *mahasib* and *mashadid* would be mainly other *baltagi futuwwat* and rarely people from the *hara*. Among the *futuwwat*, the *baltagi* would be ranked as 'a traitor who is paid', that is one who takes protection money.

There is good evidence that in the 1920s, 1930s and 1940s it was common for the *baltagi* to dominate a given locality or perhaps a specific grouping. These latter in some instances consisted of belly-dancers or prostitutes who were obliged to buy the *baltagi*'s protection. Some of these men were powerful enough to close off their geographic areas to the police. Although there are still isolated examples of this today, particularly in those quarters around al-Batiniyya and al-Ghuri known for drug trade, the extent of their influence is generally fairly restricted. One hears of them most frequently in relation to their protection functions in the 'gypsy' markets operating illegally in the streets of Cairo and consisting mostly of unlicensed tradesmen. At various times, *baltagis* have physically resisted police attempts to disperse these markets. Impressive confrontations between them and the police took place on Muski Street, in a housing development in Mataria, and near al-Ghuri, all in 1974.

Conclusion

In conclusion we find that the role of the *futuwwa* in the informal power structures of the urban masses is that of protector against the formal power of the State. This role has placed him in direct confrontation with various ruling elites. In turn, the urban masses have distinguished themselves from these elites (at least) since the eighteenth century by appropriating to themselves the characteristics associated with *ibn al-balad*. The elites returned the favour by referring pejoratively to the masses as animals (*al-awbash*) or rabble (*ghawgha*). Historians referred to popular movements as directionless and chaotic, but participants in them identified themselves, in folktales and ballads, as heroes, capable of changing rulers and of avenging those who suffered injustice.

Indeed these movements were not completely chaotic, and by acts of violence, sabotage, rioting, or even passive resistance, they did achieve some limited success in minimising the abuses and exploitation of the authorities. In this sense, Cairo's popular rebellions belong to the classical archaic, pre-political movements described by Hobsbawm (1971, p.110):

The mob may be defined as the movement of all classes of the urban poor for the achievement of economic or political changes by direct action – that is by riot or rebellion – but as a movement, which was yet inspired by no specific ideology, or if it found expression for its aspiration at all, in terms of traditionalism and conservatism.

Although the mob of Cairo had no lasting ideological allegiance it was nevertheless capable of mobilising behind leaders who were reformist, such as the religious leaders (*'ulema*). Even then, though they might be capable of changing a ruler, they did not seek to change the political or social order. Moreover, from the time of Mohammed Ali (1805-49), historical sources are silent as to the participation of the *futuwwat* in revolts or movements such as the 1919 uprising. Rather we hear of individual patriotic acts, a reflection, perhaps, of a strongly-centralised government after 1882, coupled with the systematic effort after 1919 to disarm all self-appointed leaders.

The *futuwwa*'s role at the beginning of the twentieth century is achieved by certain personal qualities that cannot be transferred or inherited. The role is rooted in the specific rights and duties that he asserts or must perform. How he maintains his dominance in any given locality differs widely. As *ibn al-balad*, the *futuwwa* is a working man, occupied mainly in traditional and profitable jobs that require several apprentices. He is not formally educated and adheres to the traditional style of life. The *futuwwa*'s resources differ in degree but not in kind from those of his supporters, i.e., the people of the *hitta*. He simply acquires more of what they have or would like to have. Thus even his physical strength is not unique because most of the young *awlad al-balad* would include physical strength as part of their attributes. The *futuwwa* is pre-eminent; he is the strongest and the bravest. The major issue is what he does with his strength. A strong man who abuses his power for his own interests is not a real *futuwwa*, he is a traitor. A real *futuwwa* is one who uses his strength to protect those in need. Accordingly, whatever assets he has should be shared. His relation with the people of the *hitta* is reciprocal. He provides them with tangible goods as well as protection, and in return he receives non-tangible benefits such as prestige and status. His dominance in the *hitta* is based not on brute force but on authority and quasi-institutionalised rights and duties. In contrast, the *baltagi*'s leadership is based on power, and he asserts his dominance by sheer force. His relation with the *hitta* is one· of avoidance rather than reciprocation, and his protectees change their status from client to victim.

As a protector, the *futuwwa* is not alone in his locality. Other potential protectors or informal leaders include the *ibn al-balad* himself, who, although not necessarily a skilled fighter, may be a merchant, craftsman, or shop owner, and with some advantage in financial resources is prepared to undertake leadership functions. The *'ulema* of the *hara* are potential protectors as well, but how effective their role has been since the beginning of the twentieth century is moot. It seems that unless they were financially well off their leadership was limited. In all instances, however, accompanying the broad changes in the composition and occupational structure of urban society in the last fifty years, has been a profound transformation of the bases of protection. The personalised and individualistic style of the *futuwwa* has been partially overwhelmed by more anonymous groupings associated with factories, the sprawling public bureaucracy, or associations based on social level and wealth.

Within the *hara* both the social milieu and the protection functions that the *futuwwa* undertakes have changed considerably. Successive waves of rural migrants, especially during and since the Second World War, have swamped some of the older quarters of Cairo. In place of the relative homogeneity that existed prior to the twentieth century, one may today find side by side in any neighbourhood a mixture of upper Egyptians (*Sa'idis*), lower, Delta Egyptians (*bahrawis*), people from the oases, and the original Cairenes, the *awlad al-balad*. The co-existence of these different groups, with different life styles and occupations leads, minimally, to a fair degree of social distance among the component parts of the neighbourhood and sometimes to open conflict. One must add to this two other factors. The first is the enormous overcrowding now prevailing in old Cairo with all the tensions that that produces. The second is the general overall decline in the standard of living for many strata of these quarters. It is now common to hear the local inhabitants comment that the *futuwwa* is merely someone who can make ends meet for himself but not much more. This suggests that there is no longer any margin for his requisite generosity in a situation where resources are so limited. With the increased heterogeneity of the population, combined with its sheer size, it is extremely difficult for the *futuwwa* to establish his reputation and to enjoy the trust of all the residents of his neighbourhood. He tends to be lost in the crowd and his potential services overwhelmed by the extent of the crowd's needs.

The processes of rapid social change, and to some extent social breakdown, may give us clues as to the gradual decline of the *futuwwa* of the *ibn al-balad* type and the prevalence of the *baltagi*. On the other hand, the increasing intervention of the state in terms of policing and the maintenance of local order, along with the extension of a wide variety of welfare services, have narrowed the scope of the activities of the *futuwwa*. The destruction of the old guild system as industrialisation and industrial unions took root also has deprived the *futuwwa* of one of his traditional constituencies. At the same time the new context favours the activities of the *baltagi*. In increasingly conflictful situations he can market his strength to any of the contenders, and his non-adherence to any particular group becomes an asset rather than a liability. He may become a crucial figure in a broad range of urban, quasi- or totally illicit activities involving prostitution, trade in hashish and other narcotics, and growing black market trade in foodstuffs and building materials, or, as we have noted, the protection of unlicensed tradesmen. It is probably going too far to say that the *baltagi* is a growing phenomenon; it may just appear that way in a relative sense given the decline in prominence of the *futuwwa* of the *ibn al-balad* variety.

Since the French invaded Egypt in 1789, Cairo has grown from some 200,000 inhabitants to over six million today. The role of the *futuwwa*, in one form or another, survived this phenomenal growth but has hardly emerged as a thriving form of leadership and patronage. While the *baltagi* has prospered in a relative sense, his role has evolved so rapidly that it is very difficult to establish his linkages with older forms of the *futuwwa*. Still, institutional substitutes for the functions performed by the *futuwwat'* of all varieties have not firmly rooted themselves in the poorer quarters of Cairo, and until they do it is likely that the values associated with the *futuwwa*, if not the role itself, will be kept alive.

NOTES

Data for this paper were compiled from primary sources of history, folk ballads, autobiographical literature, short stories, as well as field research and interviews of *futuwwat*, conducted by the author.

1.   The literature on the internal structure, ceremonies and ritual of the *futuwwa* is sparse until the time of the 'Abbasid Caliph Nasr al-Din Allah (1180-1225 A.D.). He sponsored a group of *futuwwa* in his court and encouraged the ruling circles to join it. See Jawad et al. (1958).

2.   For example the al-Ahdath in Asia Minor who were described by Ibn Battuta in the fourteenth century as a brotherhood whose members (*fityan*) lived together in a kind of monastary (*zawiya*) under a superior called *akhi*. They lived in scattered towns, united by their sense of fraternity. They were hospitable to strangers but ruthless in their opposition to tyrannical governors and their followers. See C. van Arendonk, 'Futuwwa', *Encyclopaedia of Islam*, p.124. See also on the *murabitun* and other frontier warriors or Sufi groups associated with the *futuwwa*, Hassanain Fu'ad (1959), p.9.

3.   The *'ayyar* were most powerful in Baghdad from the ninth to the twelfth centuries and had special troops known as the *'awiniyya* who were responsible for the welfare of the weak and the poor (Hassanain Fu'ad 1959, pp. 10, 12).

4.   Organised gangs of young men in the city. This label was used for the first time in the fifteenth century, and they dressed with distinctive shoulder robes and a hair style known as *qar'ani* (Lapidus 1967, p. 154).

5.   In Egyptian folklore there is a collection of tales known as *al-siyar*, relating the lives of heros such as Abu Zaid al-Hilali and al-Zahir Baybars. The 'Sirat 'Ali al-Zaybak', which is a section of *The Thousand and One Nights*, is another of these biographies whose setting is Cairo.

6.   *hara*, pl. *harat*; in old Cairo this refers to a main street off of which are a number of small lanes or allies. During the Fatimid period the *hara* constituted a major subdivision of the city of which there were fifteen. Over the centuries the number increased so that by the time the French arrived in 1798 there were 53 *harat*. The French reorganised these into eight sub-divisions (*thumn*) whose basic contours have been maintained until the present time (Abu-Lughod 1971).

7.   *al-kuttab* is the traditional school for learning the Qur'an and how to read and write.

8.   A tarboush, more commonly known as a fez, is a red felt headcover used mainly by the so-called *effendi* class of western-educated businessmen, professionals and bureaucrats. *Effendi* is the opposite of *baladi* which refers to the uneducated masses.

9.   *mashadid* is a label which came from the term *mashad,* i.e. the buckling on of the devotee's belt. Ali Mubarrak (1880), p.84, refers to this kind of follower in some of Cairo's quarters in the late nineteenth century.

10. *gada'an*, referring to young manhood, was a term applied in one instance to a group in Cairo at the beginning of the twentieth century who so excelled in their fighting that the police stayed well clear of them (Ahmad Amin 1953, p.134).

REFERENCES

Abu-Lughod, J. (1971) *Cairo: 1001 Years of the City Victorious*. Princeton.

Amin, A. (1953) *Qamus al-'Adat wa al-Taqalid wa al-Ta'abir al-misriyya*. Cairo.

Breebart, D.A. (1961) *The Development and Structure of the Turkish Futuwwa Guilds*. unpub. PhD dissertation, Princeton University.

El-Messiri, Sawsan (1970) 'The concept of *Ibn al-Balad*', unpub. Master's Thesis in Anthropology, American University in Cairo.

Fu'ad, Hassanain (1959) *Kitab al-Futuwwa*. Cairo.

Hobsbawm, E.J. (1971) *Primitive Rebels*. Manchester.

Jabarti, Abd al-Rahman al- (1958) *'Aja'ib al-Athar fi al-Tarajim wa al-Akhbar*. Cairo.

Jawad, M. et al. (1958) *Kitab al-Futuwwa of Ibn al-Mimar*. Baghdad.

Lapidus, I.M. (1967) *Muslim Cities in the Later Middle Ages*. Cambridge, Mass.

Mahfuz, N. (1972) 'Hikayat Haratna', *al-Ahram*, July 29.

Miligi, Mahmud al- (1970) 'Mahmud al-Miligi and Talk of his Memoirs', *al-Akhbar*, Dec. 10.

Mubarak, Ali (1880) *al-Khitat al-Tawfiqiyya al-Jadida*. vol. II. Cairo.

Yussuf, al-Mu'allam al-Hag (1924) 'Mudhakkirat futuwwa', *Lisan al-Sha'b. 1.*

Clement Henry Moore

Clientelist ideology and political change: Fictitious networks in Egypt and Tunisia

Whose hypothesis of which networks?

On June 27, 1970, the bi-annual assembly of Destour Socialist Party cadres of the Tunisian Sahel overwhelmingly reelected as general secretary of the Committee of Coordination for the governorate of Sousse a man whom higher party authorities had apparently forbidden to run.[1] The elections were rerun on July 19 to replace him. Earlier he had refused to testify against Ahmed ben Salah at the special trial in which the former planning minister was convicted of high treason and sentenced to ten years of hard labour. How, though, if he was clearly a Ben Salah supporter, had he been reelected in June? Was it not the peasants of Ouardanine, in the Sahel, who had precipitated Ben Salah's removal in 1969 by making violent demonstrations against his compulsory cooperatives? Even if important personalities opposed to Ben Salah had encouraged these incidents, did the fallen minister command such widespread support among Sahel party leaders that, after his downfall, they would re-elect his known supporter?

Was the incumbent secretary in fact part of a Ben Salah patron-client network? It is true that he came from the same village as a former governor who had been so politically identified with Ben Salah as to be brought to trial and given a suspended sentence. It was also true that before the Ben Salah era, the secretary had been president of the village cell when the governor had been assistant secretary of the Committee of Coordination. But subsequently, the latter governed Sfax, not Sousse, and had no direct responsibility for the political affairs of his home province. It is extremely unlikely that he could have engineered the secretary's original election, an action which, moreover, would not have been in character. At most, his word might have helped clear the secretary with higher party authorities, though the secretary must have been well known, given the Sahelian origins of so many of the Tunisian top elite and their continuous contacts with their home villages.[2]

I was given a second interpretation of the troubled elections by a principal supporter of Ben Salah four years after the event. Two members of Bourguiba's Political Bureau, including a minister who came from Ouardanine, were trying to put 'their' man in office. It must be remembered that at this time the fourteen members of the Bureau were Bourguiba's appointees, not elected in their own right. Since a national party congress was scheduled for the autumn of 1970, the leaders needed grass-roots support. The incumbent secretary gathered a large majority of the votes because he was opposing this clan's bid to gain control of the Sahel's party machinery.

This interpretation may appear plausible. The two Political Bureau members could easily have been vying with other Political Bureau members from the Sahel for control of their home base, and hence any orders to exclude the incumbent from re-election in June may have been ambiguous. Moreover, a patron-client network can easily be traced. The new candidate was a veteran party militant, apparently politically inactive since independence, but from the key village of Ouardanine. His family and that of the minister were linked by marriage, and further bound by the help the latter had provided in setting up several of the former's members in petty trade (Moore 1965, p.138). The relationship was not altogether one-sided, for the villagers' resistance against the French in the early 1950s had probably helped the political career of both the minister and his brother, the General Prosecutor of the Republic. Again in 1969, the villagers' demonstration against Ben Salah was surely not unrelated to the minister's promotion of September 8, 1969, from postal affairs to agriculture. The minister's brother subsequently presided over Ben Salah's trial.

But why, then, on this second interpretation, did Bourguiba on September 9, 1970, postpone the scheduled congress, claiming 'I cannot run the risk of having it infested with troublemakers who may be behaving themselves while awaiting the right time to throw off their masks' (Amor 1973). Publicly Bourguiba was projecting the continuing survival of a Ben Salah network in the party, and events like the initial re-election of the secretary of Sousse's Committee of Coordination could be cited as evidence. Yet my informant, who had definitely been in a position to know the facts and who, four years afterwards, had no interest in hiding them, dismissed Bourguiba's projection as mere propaganda. If, indeed, the alleged network were strong enough one year after Ben Salah's downfall to make a party congress problematic, then it becomes difficult to explain how he fell in the first place. During the intervening year new elections had been held in party cells throughout the Republic, and Ben Salah's principal supporters at higher levels had been removed from political life. On the assumption that a network endured, it would surely have been sufficiently strong a year earlier to have neutralised the intrigues in the presidential entourage which led Bourguiba to reverse policies he had totally backed for seven years.

The real 'troublemakers' turned out, in fact, to be none other than

Bourguiba's interior and defence ministers, two influential politicians from Tunis who were spearheading efforts to strengthen party institutions at the expense of the presidency, so as to prevent future cases of political misjudgment. In return for their support against Ben Salah, whom one of the ministers had publicly attacked in 1968 but opposed bringing to trial in 1970, Bourguiba gave them carte blanche to lead public discussions of the future of the regime and the restructuring of what they agreed should remain a one-party system. These discussions perhaps convinced Bourguiba that he would not be able to dominate a party congress held on schedule, in 1970. As it turned out, even after changing party directors and dismissing his minister of the interior, he was unable to prevent these 'liberals' from dominating the proceedings a year later.

A third and probably correct interpretation, then, of the Sousse Committee of Coordination elections, is that Bourguiba was seeking pretexts for containing the liberals, just after giving them the green light by speaking on June 8, 1970, of the country's need for institutions to supplement a president whose judgment was not always infallible.[3] It is probable that the party director (who was a liberal) permitted the incumbent secretary to run for re-election the first time. The minister from Ouardanine, however, would then have had little trouble convincing Bourguiba of the need to re-run the elections. Whether either the minister or the president believed in the existence of a Ben Salah network is immaterial. It could be used by a variety of politicians on the Political Bureau to postpone the national congress and thereby neutralise the liberals. It was only after 1971, once the Tunis liberals had been eliminated from national politics, that rivalry among Sahel politicians on the Political Bureau would develop and hence that clientelist explanations of local politics, like the one provided by my informant, would become plausible. His interpretation made retroactive the rivalry which surfaced in the spring of 1974 between the prime minister and his deputy minister and also made the unlikely assumption that the latter's relationship with the minister from Ouardanine (who had once been with Ben Salah) was a solid and enduring one.

The political theory of clientelism

In the Tunisian context clientelism was obviously a propaganda weapon used by everybody to label and discredit his opponents. But most of all it was used by Bourguiba, along with tribalism and even riots after soccer matches,[4] to signify the country's political immaturity, backwardness and hence its continuing need of his political instruction.

Clientelism, it will be argued here, is a concept that has travelled too fast too easily from anthropological peripheries to developing polities. What is one to make of Keith Legg's and René Lemarchand's statement, for instance, that 'intervening socio-economic changes may fundamentally alter the original basis of patronage and yet have relatively little effect on the clientelistic underpinnings of the regime'? Or that clientelism 'may reappear embedded within the bureaucratic structures of governments which have extensively penetrated society'? (Lemarchand and Legg 1972, pp. 159 and 163).

The new 'ism' seems to be everywhere. It is supposed to 'shape' political systems (Schmidt 1974, p. 425), explain who gets where in politics, how goods get allocated, and, more basically, define the real units of political activity underlying formal political parties and interest groups which native politicians copied from foreign model but could not really adapt to the local scene. The underlying patron-client relationships may have an additional attraction in the eyes of the beholder. They can serve to unmask the natives' ideological utterances by pointing to the networks they serve to hold together. Thus the disjunction between theory and practice so evident in most Third World declarations has a rational explanation. Among politically underdeveloped natives, politics can be reduced to the interplay of patron-client networks. This intellectual step is somewhat analogous to Arthur Bentley's reduction in 1908 of the American political process to an interplay of interest groups. And just as the focus upon interest groups was originally an ideological reflection of the Muckrakers' Movement, so the new clientelism reveals in Morocco at least, that corruption 'has displaced and dwarfed all other forms of politics' (Waterbury 1974, p. 534). What more fun can a new generation disenchanted with 'developing' polities hope for?

But what goes in Morocco does not necessarily travel to other new states. Eric Wolf says 'patron-client relationships operate in markedly different ways', but it is not clear what happens when 'the institutional framework is extensive and the ties between multiple sponsors and multiple clients diffuse and cross-cutting'. Such a description fits Egyptian bureaucracy but no longer quite corresponds to the paradigm of clientelism elaborated by Landé (1973), Scott (1972) and Lemarchand and Legg (1972). The paradigm calls for each client to have only one intermediate patron at the same time – client monogamy. The relationship is supposed to be asymmetrical, that is, the terms of trade favour the patrons, even though alternative patrons should be potentially available. The relationship is typically multiplex, and that is, servicing more than one specific need of the client, and overladen with sentiments of loyalty and responsibility which make the adverse terms of trade acceptable, indeed not too closely calculated.

Now this paradigm, which may characterise landlords and tenant farmers in some societies,[5] gets stretched in two ways when it is applied to developing (or underdeveloping) political systems. First, the patron-client relationships have to be pyramidded into networks linking national leaders to, say, the tenant farmers. Without pyramidding – and the emphasis in the literature is very definitely on the vertical linkages rather than upon horizontal ones between patron-clients at intermediary levels – clientelism could hardly perform the brokerage or integrative functions its enthusiasts sometimes claim for it, much less maintain an entire system through some sort of balance or conflict among its parts. Secondly, the quality of the relationships is usually admitted to change with modernisation. Client monogamy gives way to a sort of successive monogamy akin to polygamy. The scope of exchanges becomes less multiplex, and affective ties become more instrumental. Indeed, even the terms of trade may change, becoming less asymmetrical as patrons rely more on their 'second-order' resources of bureaucratic office or political influence than upon the old standbys of wealth and special wisdom. Scott adds that patron-client clusters within a given network will become more differentiated, with the bureaucrat's following coming primarily from his agency, etc., and that the networks will cover society with less density than in traditional times (Scott 1972, pp. 106-7). But what, then, remains of the paradigm? Can we still speak of patron-client *networks*, in essence hierarchical, under the new conditions which encourage polygamy? When there are changes along each dimension defining the syndrome, what is left of the syndrome? When do quantitative changes – for one can speak of 'more' or 'less' affectivity, multiplexity, density, durability, differentiation, and proportion of first to second-order resources – lead to qualitative differences?

It seems plausible to assume that the types of resources available to potential patrons will condition the other variables associated with the syndrome. Specifically, the lower the proportion of first to second-order resources, the less likely it will be that patron-client ties are dense, durable, undifferentiated, and characterised by a high degree of affectivity and multiplexity. A crude indicator of the degree to which potential resources have become second-order in any given society is the percentage of GDP expended by its government, including the public sector and public authorities. Table 1 presents these data for selected Mediterranean countries. Our indicator admittedly may exaggerate the degree to which the governments of major petroleum-producing countries, such as Iran, Iraq, and Algeria, control their economies. It may also underestimate the *de facto* control exercised by other regimes over ostensibly private agricultural or commercial property. Table 1 nevertheless offers a starting point for a comparative analysis of clientelistic relationships among Mediterranean countries.

At the extremes, the differences are striking between Egypt or Tunisia and Lebanon. We might expect that 'clientelism' offers a reasonably good description of the politics of countries like Lebanon, where government is relatively small. It may be significant that the Lebanese – unlike the Egyptians – have words in colloquial Arabic for

Table 1. General government expenditures as a percentage of Gross Domestic Product at factor cost (1970)*

Egypt	55.7
Iran	51.6
Iraq	44.2
Algeria	42.8 (1969)
Tunisia	40.7
Syria	37.9 (1971 est.)
France	37.4
Italy	35.5
Greece	27.6 (1969)
Morocco	25.6
Spain	19.7
Turkey	18.1
Lebanon	14.3 (1969)

* Total government budgets, including public monopolies, public sector investments, and operating expenditures of public authorities are included, whenever possible, but the variety of sources used makes it unlikely that the resulting percentages are strictly comparable.

Sources: United Nations Economic Commission for Africa, Summaries of Economic Data for Algeria, Egypt, Morocco, and Tunisia; UN *Yearbook of National Accounts Statistics* 1972; *The Middle East and North Africa*, 1969-70 (Europa Publications); OECD National Accounts 1960-70; statistical yearbooks of Iraq and Syria.

a clique (*asbah*), a criminal gang (*asabah*), and a clientele (*zilm*) that they readily employ to describe networks of notables and their followers. The clientelist politics of Lebanon have been well documented in two essays in this volume (Khalaf, Johnson). Public policy there indeed seems reducible to the interplay of private interests aggregated by patron-client networks.

But what about countries at the other end of the spectrum, such as Egypt or Tunisia, where government is relatively large? In these societies, if our assumption about the effects of different types of resources is correct, patron-client ties may no longer fit the paradigm. It will be argued here, firstly, that big government tends to undermine the asymmetrical dependence of clients upon patrons posited by the anthropological model. Secondly, reliance upon the model may, as our Tunisian case study suggested, lead the observer to accept without question the propaganda about dense networks which in fact do not exist. Thirdly, political forces are not reducible, for purposes of analysis, to patron-client networks in these countries where traditional asymmetries have been eroded. In neither Tunisia nor Egypt, despite evident differences between these polities, are political decisions reducible to an interplay between the presidential patron and his clients, together with their personal followings.

Personal dependence

It may be assumed that middle and upper-level bureaucrats and politicians operate in a climate of relatively scarce personal resources and opportunities in both Tunisia and Egypt. In Egypt the ratio is probably even more adverse than in Tunisia between the supply of educated personnel and that of jobs commensurate with their abilities. In a climate of such scarcity virtually everyone needs as many patrons as possible; certainly personal connections are vital to any bureaucrat who wishes to beat the stultifying seniority system. But the principal vehicle of protection for these vulnerable Egyptians is neither a gang nor a clientele, as in Lebanon, but rather the *shilla* (p. *shillal*), which is literally a circle of friends, without any hierarchical connotations. Bureaucrats who manage to beat the system cannot be considered personal retainers or 'clients' of their administrative superiors or any other single patron. The *shilla* does not work by hierarchy or presuppose the informal but binding asymmetries that tie client to patron.

The typical pattern is as follows. The son of one of Egypt's most important contractors becomes undersecretary of a ministry at an incredibly early age because the minister happens in normal times to be the contractor's principal design consultant. When the minister returns to his professional practice, the son naturally stays on because the job carries automatic tenure. In the mid-sixties, because of so many such deals, the Ministry of Industry was carrying 28 undersecretaries, and the only way Aziz Sidky could eliminate them, when he returned as minister in 1968, was to promote them. Table 2 indicates the extent to which the bureaucracy under Nasser was bloated with top ranking jobs (though the adverse ratio of supply to demand increased during this period). The actual work load is unrelated to the number of such jobs, as many of them were political sinecures. The contractor's son was not likely to be worked by the minister's successor, but he still received his salary. So also two professional diplomats purged in 1972 for making anti-Soviet remarks at a seminar held at *al-Ahram* kept rank and salary without assignments for a year. Was some 'patron' protecting them? The influential editor of *al-Ahram* lost his job for objecting to Egypt's pro-American foreign policy in the wake of the October War, but meanwhile one of the two diplomats had become foreign minister.

The beneficiary of a *shilla* may often need only a one-shot pay-off to be boosted beyond the normal confines of bureaucratic seniority. But once in orbit he is likely, if he wishes to avoid early paid retirement (without entertainment allowances), to require a succession of patrons to reach the President. (It is said that Nasser personally vetted the appointments of all public sector company managers, but it is unlikely that he alone, even with the help of or under pressure from

Table 2. Numbers of Egyptian civilian officials in government and the public sector (excluding companies), 1962-72

	1962-3	*1966-7*	*1971-2*	*Percentage increase 1962-72*
Top officials (grade 1 and above)	967	1,544	1,905	97
Grades 2 and 3	9,897		20,433	106
Specialised jobs	71,661	103,587	137,814	92
Technical jobs	126,090	161,031	288,044	128
Administrative and organisational	13,671	14,862	25,281	85
Clerical	63,451	76,011	85,928	35
Total*	770,312	1,035,747	1,290,538	68
(Total Work Force)				(20)

* The total number of jobs is not the sum of the preceding, some of which overlap and all of which, except the clerical jobs, are relatively high-ranking and well paying.

Source: Mohammed Sbihi al-Atribi, 'The overgrowth of bureaucrats within the past ten years', *al-Tali'a*, October, 1972, 72-5.

Marshal Amer, recruited them all). Take the following career, which must remain anonymous because it has probably not yet ended. In 1959 our subject, a young university lecturer, was unable to complete his fourth academic year teaching in Baghdad because President Qassim cracked down on the Baath and repatriated Egyptian technical assistants. Cairo University no longer had an opening for him, but Zakariyah Mohieddine, the patron of overseas operations for, and subsequently against the Baath, was probably already taking an interest in our subject's career. It is possible that he intervened with Egypt's first atomic energy commission to obtain for his former agent an administrative position in applied research. Definitely the Mohieddine connection helped post our man abroad four years later as a cultural attaché (to organise Egyptian students against the Baath). It also propelled him into his next job, undersecretary in a ministry headed by Prime Minister Mohieddine's brother-in-law. But this minister was less fortunate than most: he lasted only as long as his patron's cabinet survived – less than a year. Meanwhile, however, our undersecretary avoided being temporarily 'parked' in his sinecure by latching on to Ali Sabry's bandwagon and helping him reform the universities. Though Mohieddine and Sabry were bitter rivals by this time, the undersecretary successfully jumped *shillal*, so to speak. But with the defeat of 1967, university reform became a dead issue, and so Sabry sent his loyal 'client' to the Arab Socialist Union, which he had been attempting to build up as a power base since 1965, first against

Marshal Amer, and subsequently, in a sense, against Nasser himself. When, in 1969, Nasser purged Sabry to deter the Russians from meddling in internal Egyptian politics, our subject proved his capacity for political survival. He had meanwhile developed a close relationship with the ASU's new general secretary, Anwar Sadat. When, after succeeding Nasser, the new president consolidated his power by liquidating Sabry's network, most of which was concentrated in the ASU's 'secret organisation', our subject became a minister. And though his ministry was abolished in a cabinet reshuffle within less than a year, he retained his rank in a new academic post, a relatively safe position at a time when Sadat's was insecure. It proved an effective springboard to a top office in an international agency.

Such personal odysseys are not uncommon in Egyptian politics; they are the mark of a successful politician. Note that the ostensible client remains his own man, dependent not on any one patron but only on the system. Neither Mohieddine, Sabry, nor even Sadat could 'buy' our subject because their favours, second-order resources, were one-shot affairs. Top officials retain their salaries even after they are retired. In 1973, according to a leading member of parliament, 154 individuals were receiving salaries as vice-ministers, and over 200 were receiving ministerial pay (and allowances). Their security undermines the sort of asymmetry required of the patron-client paradigm. To be sure, these officials may also, as in Morocco, be involved in illicit deals, but they seem less vulnerable to blackmail than their Moroccan colleagues because corruption is less centralised than in King Hassan's system. If corruption is as pervasive in Egypt as in Morocco, it works laterally, paralleling the structure of the *shilla*, rather than vertically, as indicated by a patron-client structure. The president is unable to control lucrative exchanges between top government and public sector officials, because the structure is too immense, the *shillal* too interwoven, for any single man, however pure and disinterested, to control it without relying on a staff that is equally penetrated with *shillal*.

The *shilla* is not a permanent group, nor need it be. It may last just long enough to promote one official, or provide him a villa at the expense of the public sector in exchange for protection. Any individual may have as many alternatives as his friends multiplied by their friends can provide, as long as they have the time to form a friendly circle, meeting occasionally although not always together, to cement their mutual transactions. Durable *shillal* are generally the furthest removed from power, homogeneous, centred perhaps on classmates or colleagues at work in uncompetitive positions. Robert Springborg documents one case of five classmates, functionaries in the Ministry of Local Government, who slowly worked their way up to grade two by sharing their contacts and experiences. But to move further, they would need to join less homogeneous *shillal* (Springborg 1974). Most effective are those that link the strategic offices of a variety of ministries, public authorities, and public sector companies, especially in lucrative areas such as contracting. But these will be volatile.

Hypothetical networks

Patron-client networks are supposed to permeate society, thus linking centre to periphery and performing functions of mediation and social integration that interest groups are alleged to do in more organised societies. When a patron at the centre gains or loses wealth or office, reverberations are therefore likely further down the line. Conversely, as Gellner has suggested of independent Morocco, local dissidence may be testing the strength of a central politician's network (Gellner 1972). But these relationships are not visible in either Tunisia or Egypt.

Instead, as we have seen, at least one Tunisian network was a political fiction. Concerned, in fact, over the adverse foreign publicity his authoritarian regime was receiving by 1973, Bourguiba further exaggerated the dangers of Planning Minister Ben Salah's alleged plotting four years earlier. He claimed that his minister, believing Bourguiba to be on his death bed, had arranged for his officials in the cooperatives to take over the party (Speech, Aug. 1, 1973). But in 1970, much of the political elite, including the liberals and the incumbent prime minister, had not wanted Ben Salah to go on trial at all, and only six of his supporters were indicted, of whom five were convicted. If, among them, the ex-director of the Cooperative Union was one of two actually jailed, he was not accused then of plotting to take over the party.[6] Another indication of the flimsiness of Ben Salah's network, once Bourguiba withdrew his support, was the composition of the new Committees of Coordination. For Tunis only 5 out of 25 members were changed by June, 1970; in Sfax, where one of the Ben Salah Seven had been governor, only 6 out of twenty were changed.[7] In each election there were more than twice as many candidates as posts to fill, and electors from the cells had themselves undergone re-election beforehand. No wonder Bourguiba could subsequently complain to the liberal party director that he had not adequately purged the party of Ben Salah supporters – on the assumption of a dense network!

So also in Egypt, while *shillal* seem omnipresent, networks are evanescent. Too many cross-cutting possibilities virtually preclude fixed vertical linkages, much less ties at one remove. 'Clientelism' in the sense of appointments from above, for instance, was endemic in the ASU but could rarely guarantee the client's loyalty. As a close observer of local Egyptian politics points out, power struggles at that level were discontinuous with those at regional and national levels (Harik 1973, pp. 87-8, 98-105). Until 1965, the locally elected officers reflected the balance of forces within the village but operated in an organisational vacuum. According to Nasser's alter-ego, 'The facade of the political organisation rises, represented by the Socialist Union, but its nervous system still has to be completed'.[8] What was needed was a vanguard. At first, Nasser's philosophy of the new revolution was to have each of his close collaborators find a few friends who would in turn find friends, etcetera, all of whom would constitute the vanguard.[9] Eventually, however, he adopted Ali Sabry's suggestion of building the vanguard as he had once organised the Free Officers, clandestinely. The 'Secret Organisation' founded in 1966 grew to over 1500 by the time Sadat smashed it in 1971.

Secrecy had the advantage, perhaps, of protecting the anointed militants from *shillal* that might otherwise have diverted their attention from building a socialist society. Nasser's efforts to stay informed suggest he was not always told whom Sabry recruited. After the June defeat, the latter probably retained the largest disciplined network outside the army, although Amer's suicide made it no longer in Nasser's interests to retain such a strong civilian counterweight. Secrecy had another principal advantage for Ali Sabry. It meant that the offices he bestowed on his 'clients' were not readily convertible to administrative posts under other patrons. He sometimes promoted people Nasser purged, but any client who switched loyalties would have to trade on his overt rank and office.

It would seem, however, that many did so, once Sadat arrested the principals (along with those who had spied against them for Nasser). His 'correction' of the Revolution put less than a hundred under arrest, and most of them were released in a matter of weeks. Some members of the Secret Organisation, coopted either personally by Sabry or by a close collaborator, retained positions even as minister. It may have been in Sadat's interest, unlike Bourguiba confronting Ben Salah, to minimise the degree to which the Secret Organisation had penetrated society. Certainly there were considerably more than a hundred people who feared for their careers and freedom when the president announced the 'correction'. Still, such disintegration of five years of organisational effort suggests that the networks had little cohesion. It would take considerably more research to estimate their density, by examining the impact Sadat's consolidation of power had upon the composition of various elected bodies. In the professional syndicates, for instance, the percentages of new officers varied from 85 to 38 in 1971, and turnover may be a rough measure of the density of Sabry's network (Moore, forthcoming).

Political forces

When patron-client networks are not in fact dense, then on a clientelist view of politics the followings of prominent personalities are bound to be weak and disorganised. Clientelism may further assume that their public appeals are usually reducible to private (patron-client) relationships. On this view ideological pronouncements are not intended to educate publics or guide public policy so much as to divert attention from the other ties binding clients to their patrons. Low literacy rates, controlled mass media, and other limits to freedom of speech and association in both Tunisia and Egypt may be considered evidence, too, that political leaders lack access to a large public. The way followings tend to evaporate when leaders are suppressed may further suggest that the followers, at least, are politically inconsistent. Political forces, then, on this view can always be reduced to small groups of individuals – severed in theory as well as practice from broader constituencies.

Or so, at least, Bourguiba tried to argue, to explain away the liberal current of opinion which prevailed at the Destour Socialist Party's congress held at Monastir in October, 1971. At the time Bourguiba did not dare castigate Ahmed Mestiri and his allies for dominating the congress; in fact he told the delegates the final day that Mestiri might one day be president of the Republic (speech, Oct. 14, 1971). But three months later he accused him of packing the congress, and the following year, after first attacking some of his colleagues for actions committed two decades earlier, he singled out the liberal leader as a 'subversive element' (speeches, Jan. 12, 1972 and May 7, 1973).

In actual fact Mestiri was chief of the 'liberals' only in the sense that he was the principal spokesman for a coherent set of ideas about the role of the party in Tunisia's one-party system. He advocated freedom of expression within the party, free elections at all levels, and the institutionalisation of its deliberations so that they might have a genuine impact upon government policies. At Monastir debate had focussed on whether the Political Bureau should be elected by the congress or designated by Bourguiba. The liberals offered as a compromise resolution that the Central Committee elected by the congress should in turn elect the Political Bureau. Despite opposition from the president's entourage, the motion carried, and the liberals also prevailed concerning the selection of Bourguiba's successor in the event that the president could not complete his term of office. In the elections to the Central Committee Bahi Ladgham (the prime minister whom Bourguiba had recently dismissed) and Ahmed Mestiri received the most votes, while the incumbent prime minister got almost 20 per cent fewer. The congress represented a clearcut victory for Mestiri and his allies – so much so that Bourguiba not only ignored its resolutions but tried to discredit the congress.

The way to discredit it was to explain away its decisions as the work of Mestiri and a few followers, a 'clan' or clientele. But how could this clan have possibly packed the congress? Bourguiba had dismissed Mestiri as minister of the interior one month before the congress, and his principal ally, the defense minister, had lost his post as party director the previous year. While Mestiri nominally presided over the commission created in 1970 to restructure the party, Bourguiba had slipped other members on to the commission to neutralise him and, moreover, had appointed a party director opposed to Mestiri to organise the congress. Bourguiba subsequently accused Mestiri of packing it with sympathetic observers, but one of the latter's colleagues indicated to me that the organisers had tried to tamper with the votes of almost one-fifth of the 1070 delegates.[10]

The simplest explanation of the liberals' success at Monastir is that their ideas reflected those of a large majority of party cadres, and that no faction of national politicians had been able either to preselect the delegates or to control their voting. An official survey of the party's 998 cells taken in 1970 had indicated considerable sentiment in favour of free elections at all levels inside the party. Two hundred ninety-two cells expressed this view on their own initiative in answering the open-ended questionnaire.[11] Extensive public discussion further articulated it during the summer of 1970. Mestiri and his allies had no need of personal networks at Monastir. Patron-client ties might even have been counter-productive. Coming from Tunis, Mestiri might have projected a regionalist image if he had attempted to mobilise personal networks.

A clientelist view of politics would not have predicted the ground-swell of support for the liberals at Monastir, and it would probably underestimate the latent support for their views in 1974. In the intervening three years Mestiri, after losing his ministry, was excluded from the party and eventually removed from parliament. Resigning in solidarity, the defense minister discouraged subsequent feelers about returning to office. In Tunis the biannual elections for the city's Committee of Coordination had to be postponed for a couple of years. On the other hand, ministers who had sided with the liberals in 1971 and resigned from their posts subsequently sought Bourguiba's pardon and returned to office. One militant liberal even accepted office shortly after Bourguiba violated the procedures agreed at Monastir for electing his Political Bureau. He subsequently returned to the liberal fold after being sacked for voicing protest inside the party against an arbitrary expansion of the Central Committee. His political fluctuations illustrate the fluidity of a Mestiri 'clan'. By 1974 it appeared to be a handful of individuals, none of whom could be counted on as unconditionally loyal to the others.

But I would still argue that the 'liberalism' articulated by Mestiri represents a significant force in Tunisian politics, in that these views coincide with those of a majority of party cadres whenever the latter are permitted to express themselves freely. The cadres are ageing, and the party enjoys little support among educated Tunisians who have come of political age since independence. Consequently the future of the Tunisian single-party system is not assured.[12] The liberals, moreover, are too aware of the party's weaknesses to remain confident that the party might provide an institutional framework for political expression. But they represent party orthodoxy and thus retain a virtual constituency, however eroded and disorganised it may appear, which Bourguiba most probably takes into account in his political calculations.

In Egypt, too, though political life is less structured than in Tunisia's forty-year-old party, it is still not quite reducible to the evanescent *shillal*. Most audiences may be less politicised than Tunisian party cadres, but, even apart from workers and students, some virtual constituencies can be identified. In 1972, for instance, anti-Soviet feeling among Egyptian army officers was running high. There is no evidence that the minister of defence, whom Sadat had appointed in May 1971, had been able to develop a clientele comparable to that of Marshal Amer before 1967. But he achieved considerable popularity by making nationalist, implicitly anti-Soviet speeches to his men. The strength of his virtual constituency emboldened a *shilla* of retired conservatives to write an anti-Soviet letter to President Sadat, although none of its members seems to have been in direct contact with the defence minister. Sadat shrewdly dismissed the army's 20,000 Soviet advisers, the focus of his officers' discontent, before sacking his minister.

Even the ASU seemed after 1965 to be discovering and developing a constituency which transcended the cliques of politicians at the top centering around Ali Sabry and Sami Sharaf. The Youth Organisation, ideological institutes, and production committees in large public enterprises were training new cadres to subject the gigantic state bureaucracy to political control and enlarge its social bases. Their socialist ideology, lacking the intellectual rigour of Marxism-Leninism (except among certain Communists who joined the ASU after disbanding their parties in 1965), admitted a variety of interpretations, but a general tendency was evident. Agrarian reform was to be extended, workers were to have more say in management, and 'workers and peasants' were to be redefined so as to ensure more effective representation of their interests. The lengths after 1967 to which Nasser went to neutralise the ASU – temporarily disbanding the youth organisation, eliminating the ideological institutes, limiting the roles of the production committees, permitting landowners 50 rather than an expected 25 feddans, reorganising agricultural co-operatives to exclude illiterate leaders, depriving ASU leaders of ministerial responsibilities, encouraging Sharaf and Heykal to oppose the ASU leadership, and finally purging Sabry – suggest that the virtual constituency, no longer counter-balanced by Marshal Amer's clientele, was becoming too influential to suit the president.

Evidently the ASU, which ensured Sadat's succession to Nasser, constituted an even greater threat to the new president. Indeed, by May 1971 Sadat rightly feared that Sabry, invoking the supremacy of the ASU over the state, intended to become Sadat's Nasser. Sadat therefore had to neutralise his rival while avoiding a head-on confrontation with Sabry's constituency. He did so first by arresting Sabry and then accusing some of his allies of conspiracy against the president. Much was made of the family ties connecting the alleged conspirators, despite the fact that Nasser had earlier pitted two of the principals, Sami Sharaf and Sha'rawi Goma'a, against Sabry.[13] For Sadat and his supporters, at least, the principle of ASU supremacy was reduced to the interests of a *shilla*, not a constituency.

While such reduction may appear more plausible than analogous efforts of Bourguiba to reduce Tunisian liberalism, Egyptian as well as Tunisian rulers must take virtual constituencies into account. Even on a strictly clientelist view of the relationships between Nasser or Sadat and their respective lieutenants, the patron's principal resource was his authority, unquestioned as long as he was considered legitimate. By whom and by what criteria? On a strictly clientelist view only the core of clients counts, and indeed most people, especially in semi-literate societies, are unlikely to raise questions of political obligation. But there is a certain circularity in arguing that clients alone accept presidential authority and thus remain clients. Legitimation rests on broader constituencies, though they are not necessarily organised. It may even be immaterial whether a client actually believes in his patron's claim to rule, as long as he believes that politically critical constituencies do. Thus the interests and shared values of wider communities have to be smuggled back into any analysis of presidential calculations, if the leader seeks legitimacy. Of course rulers may temporarily retain their authority without legitimacy, but the cost of preserving the asymmetries of clientelistic relationships seems to be centralised corruption, as in Morocco, if not terror, Idi Amin style.

In Tunisia as well as Egypt, however, the constituencies which either support or threaten legitimacy remain, for the most part, unorganised and 'virtual'. Only at the Monastir Congress, for instance, did the liberal constituency postulated and articulated by Mestiri manifest itself. In retrospect, however, Bourguiba's gambits in 1970 to delay the congress can be interpreted as indicating his anticipation, too, of such a constituency. In fact his initial tactic in 1970 for regaining authority, which his illnesses coupled with the Ben Salah affair had eroded, was to appeal to this constituency. Similarly, when Nasser in 1966 finally came out in favour of 'scientific socialism', he was not just indicating his support for Ali Sabry but also appealing to a constituency in the making. His political choices were constrained by his need to conciliate its interests and values with those of Marshal Amer's officers, without allowing either to paralyse a new managerial class from running the public sector. One curious result of his efforts to square the circle was the Committee to Liquidate Feudalism, presided over by Amer, to carry out an ostensibly leftist campaign with the help of military tribunals which finally sabotaged it.

It is not always easy for a ruler to cast aside or ignore the interests of a virtual constituency he has helped to create, even if it is not sufficiently organised to exercise obvious pressure. To retain his authority, he will require alternative constituencies, as Bourguiba demonstrated in 1970-1 by building up both organised labour and private enterprise to counter liberal party orthodoxy. So also in Egypt, Sadat sought the support of an upper middle class of managers and administrators. In place of 'scientific socialism', he called for 'science and faith' to erect the modern state. While the slogan lacks the clearcut connotations of Mestiri's liberalism or even Sabry's socialism, it was translated into a number of policies favouring the new urban elite. Sadat's decisions to desequestrate property, liberalise the importing of luxury goods, and restore to office judges purged by Nasser did more than satisfy a few *shillal*; they were designed to ensure the loyalty of Egypt's administrative establishment even before Sadat had built up a personal clientele within it. But unlike Bourguiba or Nasser, who had acquired a fund of support and legitimacy for their earlier accomplishments, Sadat remained in dire straits until the October War made him a hero. Strikes at Helwan in August, 1971, signalling the continued vitality of the socialist constituency, coupled with student demonstrations in 1972 and 1973, had seriously eroded his authority.

Foreign constituencies, which are neither 'virtual' nor unorganised, may also enhance or undermine a ruler's authority. The less institutionalised, hence predictable, a country's domestic constituencies, the more prominently foreign ones are likely to weigh in its domestic politics. The Russian presence in Egypt after 1967 diminished Nasser's authority in two ways. Comparable to the British presence before 1952, it jeopardised his nationalist credentials. By supporting the new socialist constituency, it limited Nasser's latitude to shift alliances at home. Conversely, his acceptance of Saudi and Kuwaiti aid after 1967 may be related to more conservative domestic policies though there was also the more immediate need, after Amer's demise, to find counterweights to the ASU. In 1969, Nasser purged Sabry – whose ties to the Russians the President had earlier forged quite deliberately – as a signal against Soviet involvement in internal Egyptian affairs, but he did not thereby eliminate Russian influence; ironically, he was subsequently pressured into reinstating Sabry. On a clientelist reading Sabry would be the principal political force whereas in fact it was the Russians. Whether or not he was their client, he had become a symbol of their presence. Buying off foreign politicians, on the other hand, probably works only in societies where a sense of national community is extremely low, or when the service purchased is either marginal to the interests and values of any constituency or congruent with those of a dominant one. The Russians gambled not on Sabry but that his socialist constituency could become dominant.

Conclusion

Neither Tunisia nor Egypt has evolved the strong political institutions which would render active and visible the virtual constituencies to which actors appeal for support and legitimacy. Politics is consequently to some extent a shadow play in which clients may be ordered, like Ali Sabry, to represent a constituency, and later be purged for their efforts. But an exclusive preoccupation with the shadows would leave us, like Plato's cave-dwellers, without an appreciation of what animates them.

The more heavily bureaucracy weighs upon society, the more likely it is that vertical patron-client networks give way to horizontal *shillal*. In Egypt the *shillal* tend to be serviced primarily by governmental rather than private resources, and corruption appears to be extensive yet decentralised. While a strong leader like Nasser can attempt to control it by mobilising alternative constituencies, mobilisation from above is likely to be ineffectual. As bureaucracy becomes heavier, it is likely to become more corrupt, especially near the top, in the absence of effective political coordination and supervision. Thus state socialism, Egyptian style, may increase disparities between the haves and the have-nots even while undermining traditional patron-client relationships based on first-order resources. Extensive corruption, in turn, may release the resources needed to feed new networks which link the public sector with private enterprise. It does not follow, however, that these networks will be based on private enterprise, despite recent talk in Egypt of 'opening up' the economy. The new Egyptian patrons, even and perhaps especially when they become ministers, remain highly vulnerable and dependent upon *shillal* to retain their influence, without which their business empires would collapse.

The *shillal* Sadat has done so much to cultivate since he came to power – and understandably so, to grasp the hydra-headed administration and consolidate his power – cannot substitute for the more formal political organisations needed to articulate and dampen social pressures. If patron-client networks are supposed to 'integrate' society and prevent class conflict, *shillal* certainly cannot. Consequently Sadat faces choices about the direction of political change in Egypt that no combination of *shillal* can really circumscribe. He may permit the new public sector entrepreneurs and their friends to convert their second-order resources into private property by liberalising the economy and dismantling the public sector – but at the risk of igniting class conflict. He may tolerate the status quo – but at the risk that corruption becomes so salient as to endanger his newly won legitimacy. Or he may try to replay Nasser's game of mobilising the socialist constituency – but at the risk that Egypt goes broke for lack of foreign investment.

Bureaucracy and corruption have weighed less heavily on Tunisia than on Egypt. The Ben Salah purge terminated Tunisia's 'pyramidal structure' of agricultural cooperatives before they could take hold, and the subsequent government released to private ownership substantial amounts of settler land, public industry, and foreign and domestic commerce. Consequently Tunisia seems already to have chosen the first of the alternatives outlined above, and indeed the conversion of influence into property is already visible in the hills above Gamarth blanketed since 1972 by sumptuous villas. Such a choice, however, will not have been explained by clientelistic analyses.

There is a concluding irony. Strong political institutions explain in part why various reductions of political forces to clientelist relations were so unconvincing in Tunisia. But the recent demise of the liberals seems to have fatally undermined these institutions. Moreover, the sharp reversal of Ben Salah's policies may ultimately be translated into a drastic reduction of the proportion of GDP expended by government. Might Tunisia then become a Lebanon in which clientelist analysis would regain full validity?

NOTES

1. Amor (1973) makes the point that the incumbent secretary had been forbidden to run for office. But since a new party director took over in Tunis only four days before the elections, the lines of authority may have been confused.

2. Of the 96 top officials studied by the Centre de Recherches et d'Etudes sur les Sociétés Méditerranéennes, 25 per cent came from the Sahel. See the Centre's *La Formation des élites politiques maghrébines* (Paris 1973), p.187.

3. The relevant portions of this important speech are published by the *Annuaire de l'Afrique du Nord*, 1970 (Paris, 1971), p. 865.

4. See Bourguiba's speeches (Secretariat of Information, Tunis) of July 24, 1971, especially pp. 13-16; February 24, 1973; March 13, 1973; and May 7, 1973.

5. Lande (1973), p.119, argues that tenants seek patrons when land is scarce, but that 'compulsory clientage' may occur when labour is scarce relative to land.

6. The parliamentary commission which first investigated the case did, however, describe the cooperatives as 'a pyramidal edifice on a national scale duplicating the party and national organisations, and even certain administrations'. See *L'Annuaire de l'Afrique du Nord*, 1970, p. 856. Ben Salah's former chef de cabinet, who became party director in late 1968, brought only one new assistant with him into the party's central offices. Fifteen of the old staff were released, but on orders of the prime minister, not Ben Salah, and for budgetary rather politican reasons.

7. Interview, 8 June 1970, with a member of Party Director Hassib ben Ammar's staff.

8. Cited by Gerard Duprat, *Révolution et autogestion rurale en Algérie* (Paris 1973), p.188.

9. See the minutes of the meeting between Nasser and his principal subordinates reported in *al-Tali'a*, March 1965, pp. 9-26.

10. Only 878 delegates voted, out of a total of 1070. This fact was cited by my informant to substantiate his allegations. He claimed that some delegates had been deprived of their ballots but that he had foiled the organisers' attempt to use them.

11. Destour Socialist Party, Political Bureau, *General Results of the Consultation of Destour Cells Concerning Political, Organizational, Economic, Social Matters*, mimeo. 3 pp., n.d. (Arabic).

12. In his speech of October 6, 1973, p.7, Bourguiba voiced concern over the absence of any membership statistics in his party director's official report.

13. Thus the Minister of Communications, while owing his position to Sharaf, was married to Ali Sabry's niece. Goma'a and the Ministers of Housing and Electricity were married to sisters. One of the Minister of Electricity's brothers, moreover, was married to Goma'a's daughter. Sharaf's wife was indirectly related (through the Foreign Minister, whom Sadat spared) to the Minister of War, and one of her very close friends was the wife of the Minister of Transport. A political anthropologist, however, might trace similar connections among almost any random sample of leading Egyptian politicians – beginning with those friendly antagonists, Nasser and Amer, a brother of the former having married a daughter of the latter just one year before the principals' final break.

REFERENCES

Amor, Abdelfattah (1973) *La Régime politique de la Tunisie*, Thèse de Doctorat en Droit, Université de Droit, d'Economie et des Sciences Sociales de Paris.

Gellner, E. (1972) 'Patterns of rural rebellion in Morocco during the early years of independence', in E. Gellner and C. Micaud (eds), *Arabs and Berbers*, London, 361-74.

Harik, I. (1973) 'The single party as a subordinate movement: The case of Egypt', *World Politics* XXVI, no.1.

Lande, C.H. (1973) 'Networks and groups in Southeast Asia: Some observations on the group theory of politics', *American Political Science Review* LXVII, no.1 (March), 103-27.

Lemarchand, R. and Legg, K. (1972) 'Political clientelism and development: A preliminary analysis', *Comparative Politics* 4, no.2 (January), 149-78.

Moore, C.H. (1965) *Tunisia Since Independence*. Berkeley.

Moore, C.H. (forthcoming) 'Professional syndicates in contemporary Egypt: The "containment" of the new middle class', *American Journal of Arabic Studies*.

Schmidt, S.W. (1974) 'Bureaucrats as modernizing brokers? Clientelism in Columbia', *Comparative Politics* 6, no. 3 (April).

Scott, J.C. (1972) 'Patron-client politics and political change in Southeast Asia', *American Political Science Review* LXVI, no.1 (March), 68-90.

Springborg, R. (1974) *The Ties that Bind: Political Association and Policy-Making in Egypt*, PhD Dissertation, Political Science, Stanford University.

Waterbury, J. (1973) 'Endemic and planned corruption in a monarchical regime', *World Politics* XXV, no.4 (July), 533-55.

Emrys Lloyd Peters

Patronage in Cyrenaica

The terms patron and client have come to be used widely in social anthropological literature, especially in the accounts of Mediterranean peoples. Virtually every country bordering on the Mediterranean is reported to have patron-client relationships of one sort or another. Also, these relationships have been reported to occur much further afield, in Europe, middle America, and even as far afield as the Arctic (Wolf 1966; Paine 1971). The spread is likely to continue until patron-client relationships will become universal phenomena, appearing in increasing varieties and entering into increasingly disparate sets of relationships. The rapidity of the spread is largely due to the use of the concepts as descriptive labels. Consequently, when comparison is undertaken the reference is to actions, in the rawness of their unanalysed state, and the immediacy of likeness is accepted as social anthropological comparability. The glib use of the terms among anthropologists – and to a lesser extent among political theorists – has proceeded to the point where the patron has become synonymous with a person who seeks to maximise his personal gain by chicanery, and the client becomes an object of commiseration (see e.g. Boissevain 1974; Kenny 1961). An attempt will be made to restore a measure of exactitude to the meanings to be given to the twin concepts of patrons and clients by considering the case of the bedouin of Cyrenaica.[1]

Among the bedouin several different sorts of statuses can be readily identified: *Hurr* (freeborn), *Marabtin* (clients), *Laff* (grafts), *Khut* (agnates), *Jar* (neighbour), *Nail* (a person in sanctuary), *Daif* (guest), to mention only some of them. Only the first two of these constitute a patron-client relationship. Common to all six statuses are certain – albeit different – forms of dependence and protection. Mair gives as a minimum definition of a patron-client relationship: 'a relationship of dependence not based on kinship, and formally entered into by an act of deliberate choice' (1961, p.315). While accepting that kinship excludes the relationship, and that in it there is a component of choice – both matters to be raised later – the importance, and particularly the priority given to dependence is rejected. For dependence of one sort or another occurs in practically all sets of social relationships, and, therefore, lacks all discriminatory usefulness; the same remark applies to protection. A definition, the terms of which subsume aspects of a wide range of discrete relationships, is in danger of becoming so vacuous that it degenerates – as the term 'exchange' has done in the hands of some writers – to become equivalent to saying that it is 'a social relationship'.

Bedouin themselves distinguish between patrons and clients by referring to descent, those able to claim, successfully, descent from the founding ancestress of the nine main tribes being referred to as *Hurr* (freeborn), and those unable to do this being referred to as *Marabtin* (tied). Fustel de Coulanges attaches considerable importance to this kind of genealogical distinction, and saw this as a device for keeping the relationship permanently fixed.[2] Genealogical origin is of consequence to the bedouin in the sense that it is their cultural mode of drawing the distinction, of rough and ready categorisation of people for purposes of contemporary identification, and for explaining how patron-client relationships come about. They are also aware that the relationship can and has been reversed. Their genealogies, however, are related intimately to a wide field of contemporary social relations, between individuals and groups, and just as they have been altered in the past, so too they continue to be rearranged to comprehend population shifts, status alterations and so on. Elsewhere (Peters 1960, 1968) I have written at length about the significance of bedouin genealogies, and for this reason there is little point in recounting the details here. Suffice it to say that 'the genealogical basis of the distinction must be relegated to the position of a fact of bedouin thinking about their relationships, shorn of the primacy they grant to it', which makes it 'only peripherally important', in the present context, as a cultural emblem of status.[3]

The distinction between patrons and clients 'was manifest', for Fustel de Coulanges, in their relation to property. The proprietor was patron. Whatever enjoyment of this property might be accorded him 'le client ne peut jamais devenir proprietaire' (Fustel de Coulanges 1870, p.272). For the relationship, I would give proprietary rights in property analytical priority over all else. This statement, as it stands, is not saying much; nor is there a great deal of refinement in specifying landed property, since the latter takes on many forms. The land of Cyrenaica – outside the few areas where it has a value as real estate[4] – becomes significant as an asset when it is sufficiently watered to permit the cultivation of a catch-crop, when the wells on it contain water to provide for the needs of human beings and animals, and when the rains give pastures for animals to graze. The climatic conditions in Cyrenaica are such that these optimum conditions occur whimsically. In a given year they may appear in several localities, but miss many others, and the distribution of localities experiencing these optimum or deficient conditions varies from year to year. Thus, although landed property remains fixed, its value as an asset for use in social relationships is characteristically unstable.

Various means are employed by the bedouin for reducing the effects of the instability, but they are left with the reality which faces men, during the course of a life history, that there will be times when these means are inadequate to prevent more demands being made on resources than can be met by them. Now, were proprietary rights so distributed that all males in the population held them, and that these males were all immobilised by them, in the sense that they all were tied to particular parcels of land, then dire economic crises would become a chronic condition of their lives. Moreover, since the surpluses accumulating where conditions were at their optimum could not be shifted into areas of deficiencies, a considerable wastage of surplus resources would occur, since optimum conditions were not being fully utilised. The bedouin manner of dealing with the difficulty is to withhold proprietary rights from a small percentage of the population.

Bereft of proprietary rights, the men composing this small percentage also lack the tie to land which immobilises the proprietors. Therefore, when pressures on local resources mount to the point of crisis, they can, and do, move out of a deficiency situation to take up the surpluses accruing elsewhere. Briefly, the way in which this mobility is patterned is as follows. A well, with the strip of territory, is owned as a bundle of equal rights by a corporation of agnates. Each such corporation carries with it a small number of clients – about 10% of its total population – who do not possess proprietary rights to natural resources anywhere in the country. When they are accepted by a corporation, it is because its members have granted their supplication for the use of natural resources, and when they are told they must leave, they repeat their supplications to another corporation. It must be stressed that patrons do not tell their clients to move before they have tried all means available to retain them. They use affinal connections to gain access to the resources of others, for watering their animals and for growing some barley each year. A 'debt' link might serve the purpose of relief in extremity. Barley can be stored for up to five years, and since a year of good winter rain on the fertile soils enables the bedouin to reap bumper crops, storage is an important means for planning to meet a few years of crop deficiency. Nevertheless, about every twenty to thirty years or more, patrons are compelled to move their clients for economic reasons only. Loth as the patrons are to do this, I have, in fact, been present when they have had to tell clients that they must leave. Thus, each year a small number of clients become detached from patrons, with whom they have been resident for a long period, to become attached to new ones, sometimes the enemies of those they have left.

Bearing in mind that political status is anchored in proprietary rights to land (Fustel de Coulanges 1870, p.273), that the defence of this land and its extension by aggression is the responsibility of the members of the land-owning corporation, then it becomes evident that clients can never mature to full political status. This does not mean that they are debarred from all political activities. They are often as interested as are its full members in maintaining the integrity of a corporate group's natural resources, they fight with them, they are slain alongside them, they exploit water and cultivable land with them, and they work together in maintaining wells and tending animals. But they are not answerable to others for their actions; the right to assume responsibility and its attendant accountability, is denied them. They can prosper economically to become wealthier in animals than their patrons, but they cannot convert this wealth into political relationships for the purpose of power advancement.

When clients 'commend' or 'entrust' themselves, as Bloch (1961, p.150) expresses the act, they abdicate certain social statuses wholly to the exclusive care of their patrons. In the areas of social relationships captured by these defined statuses they lack any standing. In others they enjoy a standing similar to their patrons. They are not members of lineage corporations to which their patrons belong, and for this reason they are excluded from proprietary rights to natural resources. Patrons do not inherit land and water as individuals, but membership of lineage corporations *ipso facto* confers on them proprietary rights to both. Animal wealth and animal products, however, are the proprietary possessions of patrons and clients alike, inherited by their heirs severally, and used by both without interference by either. Managerial rights in animals are nevertheless limited for clients, since where they pasture them, in which flocks or herds they place them, are the prerogatives of patrons; even if, in practice, clients might sometimes decide these issues, they do so only with the good grace of their patrons. Secondly, clients do not wholly surrender their right to control the selection of spouses. The marriage bars recognised by patrons are those recognised by all Muslims, clients included. In practice, it is most unlikely that a client would seek the daughter of a prominent patron as his wife, but a small percentage of clients do marry the daughters of patrons, and patrons take the daughters of clients as wives, although only to a limited extent. Thirdly, clients do not suffer any religious or ritual disabilities by virtue of their status: the spiritual well-being of clients does not depend on patrons permitting them to be participants. Religion is not the patrimony of patrons; it is the birthright of all Muslims, whatever their status. Nor is the intercession of saints reserved for patrons. Clients have the same ease of access to the tombs of saints as do patrons. Finally, the field of kinship relationships is beyond the purview of patron-client relationships. This is not to say that patrons and clients who are conjoined by affinity, and the consanguineous relationships which flow from it, are not affected by them in their social relationships: they certainly are, and, in turn, these connections might well significantly affect the development and progress of peoples' relationships as patrons and clients. The texture of the relationships might alter, but the individuals concerned remain patrons and clients. For the social relationships between kin, whether they be patrons or clients, are governed by jural rules and moral precepts which are quite distinct from those in patron-client relationships and are not subsumed under these. That is to say, when kinship relationships are to be seen operating within the nucleus of patron-client relationships they do so contingently, not intrinsically. The same rules govern the inheritance of animal and domestic wealth, the inheritance of social positions, the marital duties between spouses, the precepts of father-son, mother's brother-sister's son relationships and so on, whether these operate within or outside the context of patron-client relationships. The view of patron-client relationships as analogous to or modelled on the kinship relationship is, for these reasons, dangerously misleading.[5]

The exact social relationships obtaining between a particular lineage corporation of patrons and its attached clients varies with the local circumstances. This flexibility is provided for in that there is the understanding that a moral relationship exists between the two. Badian makes much of this.[6] Writing about Roman patron-client relationships, which, even when 'the institution appears in a highly developed form' it remains 'still in that penumbra and inescapable custom that is not quite law – or is more than law', he states: 'In fact, *clientela* is not (in origin or development) a simple relationship, but at all historical times a name for a bundle of relationships united by the element of a permanent (or at least long-term) *fides* ... ' (Badian 1958, p.10; Peters 1968, p.167). While admitting that 'modern historians, lawyers and philologists are still arguing about it' (the state of being *in fide*), Badian's estimation of its meaning is that 'it implies trust, and therefore trustworthiness: it is a term of moral obligation and of moral judgment, with the religious implications that such terms often have' (Badian 1958, pp. 2, 10). He deals carefully with inheritance, power, political standing and prestige, both secular and religious punishment, voting, diplomatic status, military authority, and so on. This variety of sets he then parcels together and wraps them round with the moral bond, *fides*. Precedence of this sort given to what is a strand in a bundle of relationships is quite unwarranted – for the trust, moral obligation and judgment in the patron-client relationship occurs in very many relationships, often giving them their tone or style, but seldom characterising them sociologically.

Among bedouin camel herders there is a clear moral component in their patron-client relationship. All patrons vow that they are prepared to defend their clients with their lives, and clients substantiate the claim: the war, during the early 1860s, between two of the country's most powerful tribes, alleged to have been precipitated by a gross insult to a client, is given as an example *par excellence* of the behaviour expected of patrons. The same willingness to leap to the defence of a client or to afford him protection is equally enthusiastically proclaimed in the case of the *Jar* (temporary neighbour), the *Daif* (guest) and the *Nazil* (fugitive) – anyone, in fact, sharing local residence, for however long or short a duration, whether the person concerned be a visiting client, a visiting patron, or one of the most distinguished sheikhs in the land.

Reciprocally, clients are expected to assist in the defence of their patrons' homeland (*Watan*), to join in hostilities and to protect a patron from assault. Patrons sometimes speak contemptuously of clients because, lacking full membership of the lineage corporation, they are not jurally compelled to engage in any of these risks, but can opt to offer a 'fee' instead. It is said, also, that clients are required to offer or to give a 'fee' *Sadaqa* (a word with many meanings, including the sacrifice offered to God), consisting of animals, fleeces or barley, whenever asked by their patrons. The requests made for such *Sadaqat* that I knew of came only from one or two of the more indigent patrons, and an old man of ninety, nicknamed 'Funeral', because he made a lifelong habit of attending funerals at which he could always eat well. Clients help patrons in many ways, with entertainment, with labour and with animal products: but patrons do likewise to clients and among themselves.

The moral content in patron-client relationships is a function of the residential pattern, which throws people of both statuses together in the same camp or camps as neighbours. In the rough and tumble of everyday life patrons and clients are indistinguishable in dress, habitation or modes of behaviour, and it is in this sense of communion between human beings that the moral bond is strengthened, weakened, is allowed to prosper or wither. It is never a matter of wealthy patrons holding poor clients in thrall, dispensing contractually precise bits and pieces of morality to commiserable clients. Consequently the significance of the moral bond varies as widely as the vast number of local communities there are with patrons and clients living together. Therefore the *fides* part of the relationship, always present in one of its multiple forms, cannot be given the analytical priority ascribed to it by Badian – a catalysis of all sets of relationships which are caught up in it – but must be relegated to the place of an attribute, which commonly occurs in combination with it.

Potestas, 'a coercive power of the same nature as *patria potestas*' (see Badian 1958, pp. 2, 3, 10, 160, 164; Fustel de Coulanges 1870, pp. 100-3, 270-1; Peters 1968, pp. 179-83) is another element singled out by students of Roman history as important in the position of the patron. Roman clients contributed to the power of a patron, because 'the number of a man's clients showed the trust placed in his *fides*, which was at all times considered one of the main attributes of a gentleman',[7] and for a Roman seeking a public career ' ... there was the reputation they gave him: for power, in Rome, was indissolubly linked with standing and prestige, and these were advertised by the foreign *clientelae* as much as by the attendance of Roman clients' (see Badian 1958, p.163; Fustel de Coulanges 1870, p.274). Disregarding the carelessness of bringing together *patria potestas* and the *potestas* of the patron as of the same nature,[8] the suggestion that clientage is an aspect of the power of patrons to which it can add and from which it can detract is illuminative of bedouin data.

A lineage corporation which lacks attached clients is said to be of doubtful origin. Clients help make a corporate group into a group of patrons, and not merely a group of agnates. In order to establish freeborn descent beyond doubt clients are necessary, since, although clients might include people of *Laff* (grafts) origin among their numbers, clients cannot be clients to other clients in any circumstance. They are a mark of true 'noble' status.[9] Secondly, it is a fact that the larger and more powerful corporate groups include many clients, and, if hearsay evidence is correct, these clients have been decisive in past armed combats. It is as fighters that they have assisted the power ambitions of patrons, although their numbers serve as an 'advertisement' of prestige. Patrons do not, however, boast the number of their clients: on the contrary, their boast is to be able to say that certain valourous deeds were performed, or domination achieved without their aid. Their presence in a corporate group is none the less indicative of political power. The number is no indication of the trust clients put in the *fides* of their patrons: I have known the latter to deal with them shabbily in certain circumstances. It is the ability to carry clients that is of significance here, for this in turn implies strength and diversity of resources possessed by patrons. Since resources in any locality in the territories of camel herding bedouin are unstable from year to year, sufficient stability can be injected into the economy of a corporate group to permit population expansion (of any kind) by having preferential access to the resources of like groups. Access of this kind is only available where the right connections have been created to facilitate it. A sheikh[10] seeking to expand his span of power must first dominate his own corporate group by thrusting differentiation into an otherwise politically undifferentiated group of agnates, and control the means of bringing this about. Further expansion of power is to be achieved by differentiating among the like corporate groups in a general area, to make some of them close allies, contributing economic and manpower resources. The number of clients does not show the trust placed in the *fides* of patrons; it shows the strength, extent and durability of the resources and connections dominated by a sheikh. Clients enlarge the puissance of a sheikh, but his power is measured by the span of a structure he has built. Where they are present clients constitute a segment in a sheikh's power structure. Some sheikhs have matured to positions of power with very few clients, or even none, to lift them in their ascent.

A major advantage which clients present to a seeker after power is the possibility of rapidly increasing the population directly under his control. There are obvious limitations to attempts to entice clients away from other groups: the local resources must be sufficient to meet the needs that a sudden increase of population stimulates, or else they will depart summarily; these increased needs must be met also during periods of local deficiencies; the receiving corporate group must be strong enough numerically not to have to face the threat of domination, *de facto* if not *de jure*, by their clients. For these reasons clients are fractionised into small groups, so that groups sharing the same ethnic name live in small clusters throughout the land. These small groups are not interlocked. Consequently the main device for building a structure for large and enduring group formations is missing.[11]

Before venturing to note some of the changes which have had marked effects on the bedouin patron-client relationships it is necessary now to summarise the main points of this case, so that the import of changes will be better understood. These main points, in order of analytic priority, are as follows:

1.   At the core of the relationships are the proprietary rights, held by patrons, in landed property (including water resources). Exclusiveness in rights to land places in the hands of patrons monopolistic control of the most important single asset. It is important in the sense that it affects a wider range of social relationships than any other critical element.

In Cyrenaica the basic resource is land. It need not be in all patron-client relationships. Some essential resource there must be, and it should approximate, at least, in its social significance, to that of land, as in the bedouin case. The client must also have urgent need for the resource possessed by the patron, and this need does not arise if it is generally and easily available. The resource must be sought after, and this condition materialises only when the needed resource is possessed in an exclusive right of some kind.

2.   Proprietary rights in landed property and political status go hand in hand in Cyrenaica. A client can become wealthy in animals and reap abundant harvests of grain, but until he is able to move out of his status category, he will always suffer the disability of being unable to control the means of making wealth and of sustaining it. While clients are debarred from proprietary rights in land they can never aspire to leadership of corporate groups, to command the group in which these rights are vested.

3.   Just as the client's relationship to land debars him from full political maturity, so too he is denied full jural status. Clearly, although he is enabled by his patron's acceptance of his supplication to enjoy managerial rights in cultivation and animal husbandry, he has no jural status with regard to proprietorship. It follows that,

although he is free to assist in its defence against any attempt at aggrandisement, he cannot take the initiative nor carry jural responsibility, since proprietorship is not his to defend or to expand. Further, since he is not one of an agnatic group of proprietors the client is not subject to the same jural constraints as are patrons. Thus although the client might kill in vengeance for a patron, pay blood-money in greater measure than any of his patrons, contribute more substantially to funeral and wedding feasts than any of them, and give a large bride-wealth donation to facilitate the marriage arrangements of patrons, these are obligatory for the latter, whereas, if the client does not give in these circumstances, he has not defaulted because, without the impositions of membership to constrain him, he cannot be held accountable.

4. The relationship has durability. This it has in two senses. As between particular patrons and clients it is likely to endure over a long period of time. Indeed the *fides* in the relationship is inconsequential unless it is allowed the time to grow in the intimacy of relations of co-residence. For, while patrons have the right to command clients to leave – and clients, for that matter, have the right to go if they consider that their attachment to a particular corporate group is unsuitable – sufficient latitude is available to meet exigencies on a seasonal basis before the extremity of a prolonged deficiency in crop and animal products occurs, forcing patrons to slough off part of a corporate group's total population by detaching clients. Secondly, there is perpetuity in the relationship in that it is to be found everywhere among camel herding bedouin, and it is transmittable. The death of a client does not alter the status of his son, even though the latter might have inherited riches in animal wealth. Were he to leave his deceased father's patron the only option open to him would be to attach himself to another patron group.

5. Patronage is an important part of power, particularly so in this bedouin case since clients are always present in the total population included in the span of a man's power, the more so the greater the span. The sheikh whose power is restricted to a small camp of five to ten tents might not include any clients within his following, and their influence on his career is, therefore, indirect. Sheikhs who exert power over corporate groups or the few whose span of power arches over several such groups count, in their followings, scores and hundreds of clients respectively. It would be erroneous to equate patronage with power; it is present as a segment in the structure of power, but just as the ability of a man of power to bend affines to his will is effected through one kind of jurality and through a different kind in his dealings with patrilineal relations, so too the contraints he is able to bring to bear on clients are unlike those he can clamp on to his fellow agnates.

6.   Clients in Cyrenaica cannot opt to be either clients or patrons. In this sense, choice is absent from the relationships. They can, however, choose particular patrons. Choice of this sort is critical since it can be used as a threat to thwart power ambitions, possibly to reduce the availability of surplus in animal products, or to deny patrons the many kinds of services they perform for them.

7.   Clients are dispersed in small numbers among patron groups. In the bedouin case, this dispersal disables clients from nucleating into large groups with the potential to articulate with like groups – an important consideration, because otherwise a local growth in the number of attached clients would always be a threat to their patrons' agnatic corporation.

8.   The *fides* aspect of the relationship, covering as it does the protection of the client and his reciprocal return of services, is a function of propinquity not of the relationship proper. Nevertheless, in bedouin notions it is highly estimated, and affords them one of many opportunities to boast of their honour, integrity and manliness.

9.   The genealogical separateness of patrons and clients was given first in this analysis simply because this is the means employed by the bedouin when making the distinction. Claims to lineage nobility (in this context) serve to express the status distinction, little else.

10. Many and varied social relationships lie outside the range of the patron-client relationship. The more important of these are as follows:
    (a)   Mobile property, including animals and chattels (like tents, the expensive horses' saddles, valuables, women's silver ornaments) is not in the exclusive control of patrons: clients have precisely the same rights to this.
    (b)   Kinship is excluded from the relationship, since it is operative independently, even though behaviour relating to what for the sake of brevity might be called kinship behaviour impinges upon it.
    (c)   Neither inheritance rules nor practice, as far as they relate to mobile property, are dependent on a person being a patron or a client.
    (d)   With regard to proprietary rights in land a client has no jural status, but this disability does not enlarge to capture all his jural statuses: his status as father, his jural obligations to his children, to his wife, the right to divorce, to guardianship and so on are all free of the juridical constraints of the patron-client relationship.
    (e)   For a man to marry, whether he is a patron or client, three minimum conditions must be satisfied: consent, witness and a statement of the wealth to pass in a prescribed fashion

between the parties. Marriage between patrons and client women, a client marrying a patron's daughter, has different social consequences to marriage within the two categories; and the distribution of these four kinds of marriage is obviously reflected in the configurations of marriage patterns. But the kind of marriage a client makes is a matter of choice for him: he cannot be coerced nor threatened by patrons to give his daughters to men of their choosing, nor to receive as wives women they have selected.

(f)   Finally, patrons do not own Allah. Religion does not mark the difference.[12]

Many writers on patronage insist on stressing inequality, the dominance of the patron and subordination of the client. There is this in Cyrenaica, but it is situational. Thus, in animals a client might be substantially wealthier than his wealthiest patron, his horse adorned with the best finery, and so on. Other clients might be poor, but not in their positions as clients. The bedouin who had by far the largest number of camels, as far as I was able to observe, was a client, and in this wealth he exceeded the combined camel wealth of all the men of his patron corporate group; but he did not have proprietary rights in land. Lest it be thought, however, that these latter rights are so ubiquitous in their effect on social relationship as to leave clients deprived in a general sense, the corrective of appreciating that proprietary rights fix groups of men to it must be added. Thus, in extremity, clients must move and their agnatic group of patrons remain. But the move takes clients to surplus resources, while their erstwhile patrons are still suffering scarcity. Therefore, the notion of dominance and subordination as a general characteristic of the patron-client relationship is inappropriate. The relation is one of symbiosis, in the proper meaning of the term.

It is not suggested that patronage, wherever it appears, should contain all the characteristics which compose the bedouin bundle of relations, still less that they should merit the same analytic weighting as that given to them here. For example, the dispersal of clients is of importance in Cyrenaica, meriting perhaps greater weighting than it has received; but dispersal of this kind might be of little consequence elsewhere. Similarly bedouin patrons are assembled in agnatically constituted corporate groups, and just as they own land as a collectivity, their relationships with clients are similarly ordered. Patrons need not form a group elsewhere for the relationship to appear. There is no reason why a single patron should not have the same kind of relationship with either individual clients or groups of them. Indeed, powerful sheikhs of corporate groups approximate to the position of single patrons, in a *de facto* sense, among the bedouin. Thirdly, the emblematic use of descent, as adopted by the bedouin, to designate status and give the relationship its *raison d'etre*, need not appear in that particular genealogical form (a somewhat specialised one anyway), or the emblem could appear in a different guise altogether. Finally, while the prime resource in the bedouin case is land, its essence as a property is that its value changes because it has the potential to produce surpluses and to create deficiencies, thus serving to attract and drive away people. Partly for these reasons it is very difficult to divide land and water on an individual basis. Instead they are shared among a group of agnates as and when the land is wet enough for cultivating, the wells have water in them, and pasturage is available. Elsewhere, the prime resource need not necessarily be land, certainly not with the peculiarities which characterise its value among the bedouin. But whatever the resource possessed by patrons it should be of a prime order in social relationships, and the exclusivity that comes of land being vested in an agnatic corporate group among bedouin should also appear, no doubt in a different form, conceptualised differently, elsewhere.[13]

The details of the bedouin case are derived from data on conditions obtaining among the camel herding bedouin. In other parts of the country they are radically different. On the higher plateau area (altitudes range up to about 2500 ft.) in the north, the rain-fall is much more regular in its annual appearances, the quantities are larger, much of the rain falls on limestone to gush out, when it reaches an impermeable layer, as a series of springs. Bumper crops of barley are unknown (about an eighteen fold return is rated as very good on the plateau, compared with over a hundred fold in the south), but then the deficiencies are much more marginal (in a year of poor condition the return drops to about ten fold on the plateau, in the south either a crop is not sown or it is too poor to reap), and only a little below subsistence needs. According to bedouin evidence, prior to the advent of the Italians in 1911, patrons had their attached clients, much as described for the camel herding bedouin. Part of Italian policy was to get rid of this status distinction. Agostini, a fine scholar with a deep interest in bedouin history and social organisation, wrote, probably quite genuinely, of the need to eradicate 'little by little' 'the ancient social disparity' (1922-3, p.31).

The Italians affected clients in two ways. In areas which came under their effective jurisdiction, wells and land were taken over by the state for use by their colonial settlers and what remained of these were made public. Secondly they recognised bedouin sheiks of their own choosing and paid them a regular income. It is not suggested that clients, as a category of people, deserted to the Italians to exploit whatever advantages there were to be wrung out of the colonial regime: the fact that some clients were given paid political recognition was enough to re-order certain social relationships, particularly those relating to positions of power. The effects of these two measures persisted beyond the end of Italian colonial rule, and continue to be at the root of discord to this day.

On the southern, and more particularly the western side of the high plateau, the topography, climate and vegetation combine to produce a major ecological divide, conspicuous in its sharpness. Those areas lying to the north and east are sufficiently well endowed ecologically to support cattle, and, along with them, goats. Immediately south of the divide, the increasing aridity impoverishes the vegetation making it possible only for camels and sheep, with relatively small numbers of goats, to be kept there. In the area of this divide, there were some powerful water points, and although the Italians did not colonise the area with settlers, they took these wells and the land in the immediate vicinity into public ownership. Residing in this area were mixed groups of clients and patrons, most of the patrons, apparently, to the north of the divide. Sheikhs were appointed from both categories, and they were given an income, albeit a small one. Genealogical evidence suggests that marriage links, in the past, had straddled the divide, with obvious mutual benefit to the people living on either side. After the advent of the Italians the clients were given political recognition, and, while they did not come to be proprietors in land immediately, their rights to natural resources, although only in a limited geographical area, were at least the same as those of patrons. A client could not become a sheikh, and added to whatever value his paternity had conferred on his daughter previously was political desirability: a 'patron' sheikh, living some twenty miles south of the divide, married the daughter of a 'client' sheikh living to the north of it, and two of his sons have married close relatives of their mother.[14] During recent years fundamental changes have occurred. Means for conserving water on a fairly extensive scale, made possible by the vast oil royalties Libya now receives, have wrought an economic transformation in the area. Where previously barley was the only crop grown, and there was always doubt whether this could be sown each year, there is now a diversity of crops, including tomatoes, potatoes, eggplant, onions, olives and, experimentally as yet, oranges and almonds. Economic diversity, the spread of individual ownership of land beyond the previous limits of publicly owned land, and government edicts relating to the status of the inhabitants have brought about an almost total reconfiguration of social relationships. As early as the late 1940s changes in both the plateau area and the area of ecological transition were evident, and none of these were more dramatic than in political relationships. Patrons and clients were both given the vote, and in the first parliamentary election in 1950 clients were in a position to tip the result one way or another in some constituencies. On the plateau, the *mustashar* (a sort of tribal adviser to the government) of one of the larger tribes (total population in the region of 20,000 souls) was a sheikh of known client origin who owned his own land and well, who had established himself under the Italians, who had received recognition under the British, and who, by the time the country was moving towards independence in 1950, was in favour with the new officialdom, and its head, the ex-king. In the transitional area, once of the prominent sheikhs was a client, an upstart was linked to him affinally, and other clients were being acknowledged as sheikhs. As to be expected, this transitional area was in a state of political turbulence during the late forties, most of it generated by conflicting claims to land and water rights. The disputes were so severe that they sometimes developed into fighting with arms. In both areas the words for patrons and clients are still used, but nowadays they are used only for abuse and insult, and the aspersion is cast at a client or a patron indiscriminately. Retention of words as part of a vocabulary does not necessarily mean that concepts related to them persist, nor that they continue to express a modified form of a previous relationship. The patron-client relationship, in these two areas, has not changed its form. It has gone.

ACKNOWLEDGMENTS

I wish to thank Mr K. Abi Habib, Dr D. Turton and Dr R. Werbner for the stimulus of the conversation I have had with them on the subject of patronage. I am also grateful to Dr Werbner for correcting the manuscript.

NOTES

1.   The data used in this analysis are based on 27 months fieldwork carried out among the bedouin prior to the discovery of oil. Remarks made about subsequent periods are separately cited. The bedouin case has been dealt with more fully in Peters (1968).

2.   See Fustel de Coulanges (1870), pp. 271, 272. I suspect that the priority he gave to the genealogical distinction is due to the fact that, writing about history, his only evidence was documentary. If he had had my privilege of being able to talk to the people about whom one writes, he would have been the first to relegate the significance of the distinction to its proper peripheral place.

3.   See Peters (1968) pp. 172, 173. Davis (1974), p.2, uncharacteristically misunderstands the significance I ascribe to descent.

4.   Save in the capital and the few small towns, the real estate value of land in Cyrenaica, before the discovery of oil, was inconsequential. After oil royalties increased dramatically during the early sixties, the value of land as real estate soon increased, and real estate became more widespread.

5.   Mair (1961) unlike many who have made it an important part of patronage, quite correctly excludes it.

6.   See Badian (1958), p.1. I am most grateful to Dr J. Davis for drawing my attention to this work despite the fact that our estimations of it differ.

7.   See Badian (1958), p.10. This was not the reason at all, as Badian demonstrates himself in Chapter 7.

8.   Among the bedouin, *patria potestas* did not extend to landed property, which was vested in a corporate group, and not in men as individuals.

9.   The term noble is used here to denote nobility of descent only, and not to refer to the material trappings associated with the nobility in Western Europe.

10.   The word sheikh has different meanings in various parts of the Arab world. Here it refers to a man of power, only.

11.   Fustel de Coulanges (1870, p. 259) was quick to see the importance of clients being able to form groups.

12. I am not dealing with holy men in this article, not because I am 'unwilling' as Davis (1974, p. 8) states. Their position is so different as to merit separate treatment.

13. While I am prepared to evaluate resources other than land as containing a potential significance akin to it, I doubt whether any resource has affected such a range of social relationships as profoundly as land has done, until now, in most societies. See Engels (1940), and Wittfogel (1957), Chapter 7.

14. I am grateful to Mr Subhi Gannous, who has been conducting research recently in this transitional area, for this information.

REFERENCES

Agostini, E. de (1922-3) *Le popolazioni della Cirenaica.* Benghazi.

Badian, E. (1958) *Foreign Clientelae.* Oxford.

Bloch, M. (1961) *Feudal Society.* London.

Boissevain, J. (1974) *Friends of Friends.* Oxford.

Bujra, A.S. (1971) *The Politics of Stratification.* Oxford.

Buxton, J. (1958) 'The Mandari of the Southern Sudan', in J. Middleton & D. Tait (eds), *Tribes Without Rulers.* London.

Campbell, J.K. (1964) *Honour, Family and Patronage.* Oxford.

Chapman, C.G. (1973) *Milocca, A Sicilian Village.* London.

Davis, J. (1974) *Patronage.* Mimeographed paper for Conference on Changing Forms of Patronage In Mediterranean Society. Rome.

Engels, F. (1940) *The Origin of the Family, Private Property and the State.* London.

Fustel de Coulanges, N.D. (1870) *La Cité antique.* Paris.

Ganshof, F.L. (1952) *Feudalism.* London.

Goody, J. (1962) *Death, Property and the Ancestors.* London.

Kenny, M. (1961) *A Spanish Tapestry.* London.

La Fontaine, J.S. (1975) 'The mother's brother as patron', *Archiv. Europ. Sociol.* XVI.

Lewis, I.M. (1961) *A Pastoral Democracy.* London.

Mair, Lucy (1961) 'Clientship in East Africa', *Cahiers d'Etudes Africaines,* 2, no.6.

Maquet, J.J. (1961) *The Premise of Inequality in Ruanda.* London.

Mayer, A.C. (1967) 'Patrons and brokers: Rural leadership in four overseas Indian communities'. In M. Freedman (ed.), *Social Organisation.* London.

Nadel, S.F. (1942) *A Black Byzantium.* London.

Oberg, K. (1961) 'The kingdom of Ankole in Uganda', in M. Fortes and E.E. Evans-Pritchard (eds), *African Political Systems.* London.

Paine, R. (1971) 'A theory of patronage and brokerage', in R. Paine (ed.), *Patrons and Brokers in the East Arctic.* Toronto.

Peters, E.L. (1960) 'The proliferation of segments in the lineage of the Bedouin in Cyrenaica', *J.R.A.I.* 90.

Peters, E.L. (1963) 'Aspects of rank and status among Muslims in a Lebanese village', in J. Pitt-Rivers (ed.), *Mediterranean Countrymen.* The Hague.

Peters, E.L. (1968) 'The tied and the free', in J. Peristiany (ed.), *Contributions to Mediterranean Sociology.* The Hague.

Peters, E.L. (1972) 'Shifts in power in a Lebanese village', in R. Antoun and I. Harik (eds), *Rural Politics and Social Change in the Middle East.* Bloomington, Indiana.

Peters, E.L. (1975) 'Aspects of affinity', in J. Peristiany (ed.), *Mediterranean Family Structures.* London.

Pitt-Rivers, J.A. (1954) *The People of the Sierra.* London.

Savarese, E. (1928) *La terra della Cirenaica.* Benghazi.

Smith, M.G. (1974) *Corporations and Society.* London.

Srinivas, M.N. (1955) 'The social system of a Mysore village', in M. Marriott (ed.), *Village India.* Chicago.

Stenning, D.J. (1959) *Savannah Nomads.* London.

Suleiman, M.W. (1967) *Political Parties in Lebanon.* New York.

Wittfogel, K.A. (1957) *Oriental Despotism.* New Haven.

Wolf, E.R. (1966) 'Kinship, friendship, and patron-client relations in complex societies', in M. Banton (ed.), *The Social Anthropology of Complex Societies*. London.

Bruno Etienne

Clientelism in Algeria

The distinctiveness of Algeria today consists of two factors; first, that there is frequent confusion, or at least parallelism, between the different forms of blood descent and the rules that regulate these forms, and the various manifestations of clientelism; second, that the colonial presence of France re-enforced both blood descent and clientelism while changing the patterns through which they manifest themselves. There has thus emerged a sort of autochthonous clientelism parallel to another evoked by the colonial presence. In the same vein, the independent, modernising Algerian state seems confronted with the same type of resistance as the colonial state. Today, clientelism could either erode the modern state apparatus or serve, conversely, to diffuse a new rationality.

We propose to examine the following hypothesis. Clientelism in Algeria is a mechanism promoting the integration into the fabric of national life of a marginal and peripheral population having its own system of values. This integration is imposed by another population (the elite which dominates the nation state) which seeks to extend its own system of values all the while invoking and utilising that of the marginal population. In this manner the elite re-enforces its own power, but the very success of the operation implies the disappearance of the technique itself, to the profit of new systems of relations. It goes without saying that this is not the sole technique of integration available to the elite, for beyond the means of coercion, the state has a quasi-monopoly over the symbols of religious and nationalist ideology.

To support this hypothesis, we shall develop two notions:

1. Why is there co-existence of different forms of clientele? The answer depends, on the one hand, on the difficult distinction between clientele and blood descent, protection (*al-wala*) and clan-feeling (*al-'asabiyya*), and, on the other, on the definition of new clienteles, such as the Army of National Liberation (ALN) and the single party (The Front for National Liberation: FLN) in its post-resistance role.

2. What is the functional capacity of clientelism at the present time? As indicated above, the answer to this question lies in the distinction

between the conquest of the state apparatus by the ethos of clientelism as opposed to the imposition of a new rationality mediated by existing forms of clientelism.

1. Co-existence of several forms of clientele in Algeria

Clientelism or patronage imply relations of inequality that maintain the power of the patron, that lead to the distribution of goods and services to the clients, and that protect the latter from the threats of the central government (known in the past and pejoratively today as the *makhzen*), rival patrons, and the environment. Most often clientelism is an overlay of the general phenomenon of patrilinear groups or other horizontal groups such as religious brotherhoods or tribal alliances. In this respect the problem becomes particularly complex, for, theoretically there are no differences in status among brothers who share the same blood or their status as Muslims.

There are considerable difficulties in utilising clientelism as an approach to the understanding of Algerian society, because the exact nature of the social relations that dominated Algeria at the time of the French conquest are not yet fully understood. If one judges what transpires in Algeria after 1830 by what we know of similar changes in Morocco and Tunisia, the least that one can say is that the arrival of the French brought a halt to an important process of change. But beyond that, various authors advance very divergent opinions. (Vatin 1974, pp. 68, 97). A conclusion that seems indisputable is that the feudal elements, the warrior aristocracy (*jawwad*), the putative descendants of the Prophet (*shurafa*), and the 'marabouts' who led the religious brotherhoods all experienced dramatic alterations in the roles they played in society. The quasi-disappearance of these groups, or their subservience to the colonising power, favoured the passage of an entire segment of the colonised society to clandestinity. For the colonial authorities, only the bonds of blood descent appeared important, and they were sustained in this view by various ethnographers and the native affairs officers (*officiers des affaires indigènes*). This explains in large measure the extensive studies on this subject, particularly as regards the Berber areas and their systems of segmentary organisation (Favret 1966, 1968). At the same time, it makes difficult the distinction between clientele and patrilinear groupings, at least before the colonial system itself caused the emergence of new solidarities based on resistance to its presence.

It is clear that pre-colonial Algeria, like all other monotheistic and patrilinear Mediterranean societies, was familiar with and practiced a classic form of patronage. In a society that tended toward autarky, or at least toward local subsistence and auto-consumption, the bulk of commercial transactions took place through barter, money and certain consumer goods playing the role of the common denominator of value and not as instruments of speculation, even when the accumulation of goods and movable assets took place (in the form of jewelry in particular). Relations both in production and exchange were personal, direct, and specific; from which flows the importance of the trade in honour and prestige, the pacts of association and protection which, in the absence of a labour market and investment capital, assured the circulation of goods and services (Bourdieu 1963). The most striking example was the generalisation of the *touiza* (collective labour or corvée) throughout the Algerian countryside. But clientelistic pacts existed also in the cities. One finds proof of this, even today, in private houses that contain a room reserved for the receptions of the patron (*al-wali*). At the same time, it should be noted that along the perimeters of the large cities a tendency toward the privatisation of land was established before the French conquest (Valensi 1969).

It is obvious that in this context the concepts of work, of time, and of production that came with the colonial society amount to aggression. Like all that was characterised by economic rationality and speculation, the institution of credit was poorly grasped and led to usury in its various local forms (*rahniya, tsenia*).[1] Solidarity and mutual self-help normally prevailed where the trade in honour was still of importance.[2] Within this context credit, or any other reciprocal obligation, was founded on mutual confidence but did not preclude a certain level of mutual suspicion. In effect, restitution or the counter-gift being deferred to a later date, the future, and with it, risk, entered into the relation. Within the trade in honour, the obligation to reciprocate is imposed by personal loyalty, the guarantees residing not in wealth but in the man who disposes of it. Credit in the market place, by contrast, is based on the financial reliability of the borrower. Finally, a gift establishes a supra-economic link between two parties, the counter-gift being already 'present' in the interhuman relation upon which it confers solemnity. Credit, on the other hand, pre-supposes the total depersonalisation of relations between contracting parties and a purely abstract view of the future. Thus two radically different conceptions of transaction, and of the most fundamental human and economic values, the one founded on prestige and honour, the other on interest and careful calculation, came to oppose one another.[3]

All this leads to a permanent ambiguity: basic exchanges are simultaneously calculated within narrow interests that are not acknowledged, and within the norms of generosity which are openly proclaimed. Economic motives are always dissimulated beneath a veil of fraternity, loyalty or prestige. The logic of the gift, of mutual self-help and of the pact of honour is a means to overcome or cover up crass calculations of interest. The gift, like credit, entails the obligation to give back more, but the obligation of honour, as imperative as it may be, remains tacit. The counter-gift, being deferred, is a 'generous' exchange that tends to mask a closely calculated transaction. All this occurs as if this society had ingeniously invented means to deny economic acts and relations their strictly economic sense by accentuating their symbolic function and significance.

To the extent that this impression is accurate, it has been facilitated by the fact that Algerian society, after several centuries, had perfected a model of human relations that raised the competition in honour to the level of a fundamental activity. The sense of honour (*al-nif*) is a motor-force of behaviour (Bourdieu 1972, p.15). It subsumes a broad play of ostentatious consumption and allocation that marks one's group status. Several techniques are used in combination, but, in the final analysis, they all revolve about social standing and nearly always are based on matrimonial strategies. These techniques can be summarised as follows:

— hold others simultaneously in a network of honour and of compromise
— pay nothing oneself, but rather exchange, and not only material goods
— have others do for you what you could do yourself

The Algerian of 1830 was enclosed in a complex network of alliances, blood relations, tribal and religious groupings. Thus, when Abdel-Qader (who fought against the French between 1830 and 1844) undertook to mobilise all Algerians in resistance to the French, he was confronted with such obstacles that he was forced to break certain groups that did not fight at his side (Nadir 1972). The colonising force, for its part, manipulated social dissensions, playing off religious brotherhoods and tribes one against another. Some brotherhoods, such as the Tijaniyya, still pay today the price of their earlier collaboration. However the French colonial authorities did not immediately seize the importance of the parallel networks that they came to use more or less efficiently. For, as is always the case in a process of conquest, where the rules of group behaviour differed too greatly from its own norms, the conquering power concluded that there were simply no rules. It was only with advances in colonial ethnology that the complex mechanisms of Algerian society were grasped and that the opportunity to exploit certain of these rules to diffuse the colonialist ideology became manifest.

At the same time, however, certain elements of the society withdrew in upon themselves, and Algeria entered a long phase of clandestinity and resistance – of reserve (*kitman*) and refusal. This favoured a sort of 'interior migration' that re-enforced oral and fraternal relations and set the stage for the creation of a counter-culture and a counter-strategy that led to the final outbreak of armed resistance on November 1, 1954. It was essentially with regard to Europeans that the principle of dissimulation took on importance, while the colonial situation, followed by the war, contributed to the attenuation of particularistic feelings and the stimulation of a national consciousness.[4]

France created and put in place a broad array of local notables (*qu'ids*, *bachaghas*, etc.), even 'feudalists',[5] whose complicity with the regime could be easily manipulated. In effect, colonisation led to a redistribution of alliances, and, above all, their transformation into political clienteles. According to some reports prepared by native affairs officers entire extended 'families', sometimes comprising as many as 8,000 votes, could be led to vote for one of their number designated by the administration (Berge 1953, p.12; Vatin 1974, p.263). In other words, having destroyed certain social structures – for example the large tribes by policies of cantonment and the sale of tribal pasturage, or the brotherhoods through the sale of *habous* (known elsewhere in the Islamic world as *waqf*, or religious mortmain property) land – the colonial authorities remade and put to use certain of these structures. Concomitantly, certain traditional techniques changed in nature: the *habous* became a means employed by the urban bourgeoisie to evade laws regulating private property or to bring under private ownership tribal lands and undivided properties. Likewise, communal labour (the *touiza*) was gradually displaced by new contracts under which each of the parties contributed what he had: a draft-animal, a plow, seed, or labour. Such a contractual association deprived the *touiza* of its benevolent and reciprocal nature. The mode of production was thus profoundly modified by the impact of colonisation. Even the saintly cults and the brotherhoods lost both their lands and their clientele and were obliged to cooperate with the administration. Little by little the religious cults were put on public subsidy. Finally, it should be emphasised that a number of Algerians, educated in French schools and imbued with French culture, acquired sufficient power to rival that of the traditional bourgeois families. The prestige of the civil service permitted many urbanites to accommodate themselves to the French presence. But the practice of this kind of collaborative clientelism proved irreparably damaging to its adepts during the war of liberation. This was especially the case for prominent Algerian families, some of which, like that of that of the Bachagha Boualem, controlled a major armed force and an important piece of territory. Such powerful clients created the new symbolism of their good fortune; when a new *qa'id* (local administrator) was appointed, the ceremony known as *haqq al-burnus* entailed the offering to the new appointee of three *burnus* (a long woollen cloak with hood) one blue, one white and one red!

What is striking in the Algeria of the inter-war years is, over and above the destructive impact of the colonial regime, the capacity for survival of the society's basic structures.[6] One must note that it was ethnocentric themes that led to the mobilisation of the masses. Poverty, rural solidarity, sermons in the mosques, wandering pilgrims, bards and story-tellers, were the catalytic agents at the level of the family. The arguments of the old (in Algerian dialect,

synonymous with the wise, but in fact the leaders of the patrilineages;
Sanson 1969) represent an important guarantee of the basic order by
their inherent stability and continuity. The new order, introduced by
the colonial administration, appeared to be disorder, even if the 'old
turbans' occasionally were able to manipulate both the old and the
new orders to their advantage.

The basic, operational objectives of national liberation masked the
real problems of the country. But one could only reflect upon oneself
after the war. Many Algerians, however, broke with local interests
and familial considerations to join the *maquis*, i.e., the ALN, itself a
new grouping, but one that relied upon traditional methods of
recruitment.[7] We have personally consulted certain registers compiled
by the secretaries of the *wilayat* (the ALN operated within zones each
one of which was known as a *wilaya*: today the term is used to
designate a province governed by a *wali* or governor) during the war
of liberation. For each *katiba* (the equivalent of a platoon) whose
territorial sphere fluctuated with control of the terrain, its real source
of strength was a certain number of hamlets (*douar*; generally
containing one or more patrilinear descent groups). These provided
shelter and refuge, protection, food, but also a contingent of men. The
registers also contained information on those men who had not joined
the ALN as a proportion of the number of 'guns' potentially available
from each *douar*, and, at least as far as we have been able to determine,
a balance was maintained between those who were in the *maquis* and
those who worked more or less with the colonial authorities (*harkis*,
mukhaznis, or watchmen). These procedures emphasised the principle
that one can never be sure of anyone but one's brother or cousin. But
in this context, it was necessary that debts occasioned by murder be
handled informally and within the system. This is apparent from the
entries in the registries:

— X has a brother in *katiba* Y
— X participated in such and such operation
— X performed the following service, etc. ...

Obviously, however, when a grouping becomes overly
collaborationist, as was the case in several parts of the Aurès that J.
Servier describes in all his works, blood vengeance (*riqba*) is rigorously
applied, often with the knife (*bousaadi*) rather than a modern firearm.
The slitting of one's throat is a precise, social, ritual act.

Nonetheless, the war was the cause of the emergence of new forms
of clientelism after the winning of independence. The former *mujahidin*
(freedom fighters, but also the Islamic term that designates those who
fight for Islam and Allah) came to constitute an important pressure
group, a rambling clan founded on the legitimacy of having taken up
arms, but one that merits the label of clientele in only an equivocal
sense for it finds itself between the single party, the FLN, the former
ALN which has little rapport with the modern army (The ANP), and
local group or clan feeling (*al-'asabiyya*). In a certain sense, these

brothers in combat were less adept at extricating themselves from this limbo than the migrant workers in France who integrated themselves in the partisan movements, either with the Etoile Nord-Africaine (a workers' movement of the inter-war period, based in France and led by Messali Hadj) or with various labour unions, thus leading them ultimately to totally new forms of solidarity. This gap in experience and roles can be explained by two historical phenomena. The first is that the Front of National Liberation (the FLN) was never a real political party even if it described itself in those terms. It was, and is to some extent, an assemblage of men and ideological currents among which the sole point in common was action and the commitment to independence. The second phenomenon resides in the fact that after independence in 1962 it was not the former maquisards (*mujahidin*) of the interior who acceded to power,[8] but rather the politicians, regrouped in sanctuaries outside Algeria, and their allies drawn from among competent technocrats (CRESM 1972, 1973a and b).

It is precisely this situation, comprising an ideological vacuum and the isolation of the technocratic cadres, that in our view is the cause of the resurgence of clientelism in Algeria. In the absence of plausible processes of social transition, advanced by the state apparatus, the way is clear for the activation of the traditional system which operates from south to north, at once geographically from the countryside (the *bled*) towards the capital and politically from the local to the national.

How does contemporary Algeria utilise this original system of clientelism that made such an important contribution to the resistence between 1954 and 1962? First of all, in denying its existence, because the official credo offers the nation state against all ethnocentric groupings: extended families, tribes, brotherhoods, etc. The nation state is, a priori, ethnophobic, even ethnodestructive. Nonetheless, and on a temporary basis, the state still prefers to employ the original system of clientelism, for there still exist too many groups (not always of basic importance) that it can ill afford to ignore. Over time, the state will try systematically to break these groups, even though it may, in the process, create new ones. After the trying experiences of *wilayism*, in which the military regions of the resistance tended to become rival fiefdoms led by local war-lord patrons, and the crisis involving the provisional government in 1962, the regime preferred to isolate the major leaders of the armed struggle and to create new cadres, trained in institutes such as the National Administration School (ENA), who would be faithful to the State apparatus rather than to a former patron from the *wilaya*.

2. The functional capacity of clientelism in independent Algeria

The manifestations of clientelism that have emerged in independent Algeria may function in two very different senses which are but the two faces of the same phenomenon. They may, on the one hand, absorb the state appartus, or, on the other, serve to impose the new rationality advanced by the nation state. As it exists at present, the system is capably of distributing the goods and services that the state monopolises, but it is still too early, after ten years of independence, to say in whose interests this capability actually works. Thus one can only describe the system and offer a few hypotheses.

The manner in which patronage is used by the administration has been significantly shaped by the legacy of French bureaucratic practice. Within the administration, many processes are conducted in French, while the requests submitted by various individuals, particularly from the countryside, are in Arabic, which presents major semantic difficulties of accurate rendering from Arabic and Berber dialects (Kabyle, Chawia/Zenete, etc.). As a result, the possession of the means of communication with the administrative hierarchy (in the direction commune-prefecture-capital) is a fundamental element of a particular social status that binds the possessor more to the national bureaucratic arena of Algiers than to the local society. The key personages are, then, those who belong to two worlds, either by birth, or because of joint membership in the party (FLN) and the administration, or as a result of their legitimacy as former resistants. On occasion, they might oppose a local notable who had succeeded in surviving the colonial era, either by passive resistance or by compromise. In many ways, however, the bureaucrats have become the new notability. The intermediary elites possess a precious capital; they know how the system works. Many drew their experience from the pre-independence era, like the civil servants of the Lacoste period, followed by those that benefited from the 1958 *ordonnance*, who moved into privileged positions with the departure of the French civil servants in 1962.

How to make the state machine work is a problem that every revolutionary movement must face once the years of violent action are over. In Algeria, France left an administration emptied of its upper-level cadres, but one that had already accustomed the Algerians to a certain type or style of administrative practice. The departure of the Europeans in 1962 created a void at every level of society, and despite the re-entry of several categories of Algerians,[9] the same phenomenon occurred throughout the administration. The status of the lower level bureaucrats was inflated as a result of the departure of French administrators, and, in contrast to the resistants (the *mujahiddin*), they knew how the state apparatus worked. Thus, it was necessary not only to retain them (in fact, there were other solutions but that they were not chosen poses the problem of the ideology of the FLN), but, moreover, to indulge them and to offer them a social standing of considerable prestige even though it was clearly recognised that their nationalist resistance or loyalty to the revolution was newly-acquired and tied to their social ascension. The crux of the debate revolved about the choice between technically competent (but politically questionable) personnel,[10] or incompetent militants. The Charter of Algiers (adopted by the FLN in 1964) analysed perfectly the new situation of this fringe of the Algerian population, francophone for the most part, and destined to become the bureaucracy of the state, and even its basic support. Since 1965 (and the overthrow of Ben Bella by Boumedienne) this group has multiplied its alliances with other segments of the population that gravitate about positions of power and authority: the military, and subsequently the new property-owners, the speculative activities of 1962-3 having permitted the indigenous bourgeoise, restricted by the colonial regime, to resurface.

This bureaucracy has varying relations with its environment, depending on whether it is acting locally or in Algiers. Locally, clientelism allows certain civil servants to integrate themselves within their sphere of jurisdiction, because, in return, they allow the poor and the powerless to find a place in the administrative machine. But in the capital, Algiers, it is more a question of clans within the administration and the power structure, which confront one another over questions of patrons, that is, questions of personality and recent history rather than over points of doctrinal debate. This juxtaposition of levels fosters conflictful relations, for the two worlds do not share the same rationale, and the users of the administrative system participate neither in its functioning nor in its control.

This system favours, in contradiction with its own ethic, transactions and inter-relations, that, in the absence of institutionalised channels, can only be founded on patronage, influence, affectivity, and discrimination. There should be no suggestion in all this that we propose to explain all that goes on in Algerian society by the persistence of personal relations handed down from traditional society, but often one has the impression that certain administrative services constitute veritable opposed segments, imbued with *cousinage* (blood ties) interwoven with the legitimacy of the various coteries that emerged out of the war (such as 'Boussouf's boys', the 'Oujda Group', the Kabyles, the veterans of Willaya I and their role in the Zbiri attempt to overthrow Boumedienne in 1967, etc.).

When we note that those who have recourse to the bureaucracy and the bureaucrats themselves obey two different rationalities, that does not necessarily mean that they are of different cultures, but rather that for one (the bureaucrat) there is cultural interference. His Europocentrism leads him to expect a certain number of services from the state that he does not think will be of the same significance to the others, the ethnocentrists. But it is these same services that he utilises as exchange resources in the ethnocentric system. This means that in one sense the state appears as a manipulable instrument of local power, particularly in those instances where the local 'ethic' absorbs it. On the other hand, the too-rapid expansion of the central bureaucracy has rendered illusory attempts at decentralisation that seek to revivify the grass-roots, generally with abundant reference to historical precedent.[11] In reality, the governer (the *wali*) is the strongest, and the local councils (the *jema'a*) no longer have much significance.

The Europocentrists opted for what one might call the Jacobin model of the state because they were incapable – culturally insusceptible – of conceiving of anything else but the French system. The initial attempts to create something outside this framework, particularly as regards self-managed farms and factories, were ultimately ruined by public sector companies and state capitalism. Moreover, these Jacobins were well aware, having lived through the era of *wilayism*,[12] that locally-based traditional power centres could easily reconstitute themselves. The three years of disorder that characterised the Ben Bella period (July 1962-June 1965) confirmed the validity of their views. The construction of a powerful state apparatus was accepted as the most pressing and important objective. There was no need to worry unduly about formal legalism, for the paraphernalia of modern legal systems would have been relatively inapplicable in the Algerian countryside. Furthermore, what the rural population expects from the administration has little to do with Weberian norms, such as equal treatment, regularised work habits, public service, etc.

It is incontestable that in Algeria administrative success, like all other forms of social ascension, entails basic obligations towards one's family, and, if one is of rural origins, towards the 'home town' people in general. In this sense, education is indeed an investment in a system in which anyone who earns a salary – from civil servants to army veterans or worker-migrants – remits part of his earnings to his people in the *bled*. In this context, the bureaucrat posted to a middle-size rural town is better able to master the administrative system than his low-ranking counterpart in the capital. The former mediates between the Jacobinism of the state apparatus, the law, the particular agency for which he works (with all the accompanying signs of bureaucratic status: printed matter, telephones, travel pay etc.); and the people who express themselves in some dialect or other, and whose needs must be translated into the correct papers, forms, certificates, all duly stamped and signed. All of which constitute symbols of this quiet violence that is imposed upon everyone by these same intermediary elites. At these strategic thresholds, the 'republic of cousins' is fully operative, trading in protection against vulnerability and access against obstructionism.

It is scarcely surprising that *wala* (clientelistic pacts) work in both directions as well, whether it is to obtain something from the state apparatus or to escape it. This process can be seen through a few examples. To establish one's civil status (*état civil*, entailing an identity card) frequently requires immersion in a complicated bureaucratic routine and always the services of a scribe/translator. It is preferable, therefore, to underdeclare those newly-born to a family, especially daughters, or to substitute identity among young children. There comes a moment when an official of the civil registries has to 'fix things up'. Moreover, the eight years of war in Algeria led to the proliferation of irregular situations; papers were lost, destroyed, falsified, and so forth. None the less, the state demands various kinds of documentary proof before delivering desired services. For instance, certain benefits may be drawn by those that can prove their membership in the FLN or ALN before 1962, but that in turn requires locally validated certification. This gives rise, in the absence of documentation, to sworn testimony. Recourse to the testimony of bona fide resistants reinforces the hagiography of the maquis, and, at the same time, tends to introduce into the framework of nationalist legitimacy an increasingly large group of persons who had hitherto been excluded. Inclusion, and the material benefits that flow therefrom, is achieved through the genesis of new patronage links.

The various allocations available through the system can be more positive. For example agricultural credit has frequently been distributed according to criteria that are not always economic, and even today, as the agrarian revolution takes hold, final legal attribution of parcels of land is not always determined by need or militancy. It must be noted that Algerian television has reproduced the symbolism of the system marvelously: the president himself has set the example by presiding over the first distributions of 'agrarian revolution' lands. After him came the turn of ministers, then the military commanders of local garrisons, then the governors and assistant governors – and finally local representatives of the FLN and the Popular Communal Assemblies (APC). But the symbolic celebration is always the same. A broad podium with the people assembled beneath it; the name of someone who is to receive land is announced, and he goes to the podium to receive from the hands of one of the above-mentioned dignitaries, the legal act of proprietary rights. The *fellah* (peasant) sees in all this the local personage who arranged his acquisition of land, and the person – perhaps one and the same – who handed over to him the official state papers.

The tandem of distributions and postponements can, at the same time, act as a barrier or an opening. A specific example might be the policy of sedentarising nomads. The state offers a steady water supply and schools for the children. A well-placed civil servant, for example in charge of irrigation at *douar* X, can reinforce the 'traditional' system if clan Y (*farqa*) so desires, or sap it, if clan X no longer wishes to safeguard its way of life. In either case, the civil servant can do favours for the local populations, and, in this hypothetical example, control the marketing of rugs woven by local women that will be destined for the shops of Algiers. Whatever his profit level, he is performing a favour, a service. If one day there are elections, he will surely be deputy from that region, for, unlike in the past, the services he has performed cannot be compensated for with the traditional variety of counter-gifts. Overcoming the growing disparity between what administrative patrons are able to provide, and the proportionately declining value of services that non-administrative clients are able to return, is the basic challenge to the patronage systems that have emerged in independent Algeria.

The clearly-expressed will of Algerian authorities to make of the country a sort of Mediterranean Japan is embodied in concrete but not always consistent policies. Modernisation and integration are not always compatible. State centralisation is at once a conscious choice and part of the French heritage, but it is in contradiction with counter-tendencies of decentralisation embodied in the Popular Communal Assemblies and the Popular Provincial Assemblies. Socialism, after all, can be seen to be in direct conflict with religion, but both officially co-exist in contemporary Algeria. In order to modernise, and 'civilise', the Algerian state opted for a combination of nationalisation and moralisation. The Algerian, rendered relatively passive by the colonial regime, has internalised this mix fairly well. This is all the more possible in that the revolutionary and *étatiste* legitimacy of the regime is sufficient in and of itself to sustain its own goals, and in that any system that is able to maintain itself for any length of time succeeds. Of course, modernisation is more evident along the coast while moralisation has been reserved for the countryside. For this juxtaposition to operate, the state had to cultivate intermediary elites. There is no denying that the team in power has been fairly pragmatic in its use of the state apparatus. The regime has allowed clan spirit to flourish wherever a rational solution could not be imposed.

Such solutions are impractical, as we have already noted, in the interstices of the confrontation between the Jacobin state and the bed-rock of Algerian society. The form, but not always the content, of the colonial administrative heritage has been retained. That the content is different stems from the fact that those who make the basic decisions differ in cultural background from those who apply them and from those who must submit to them. French administrative practice would assume that the low-ranking civil servants of Algeria share the same culture as their superiors, but the latter are an amalgam of rural, former resistants, with but the rudiments of a modern education and a group of highly-trained, westernised technocrats. The amalgam itself, with all its subtle distortions and innovations, gives rise to what is called in Algeria 'specific socialism'.

If we add to all this the fact that there exists, theoretically, a parallel administration embodied in the party, it is easy to understand the intricacies of this 'rationality' which impinges upon urbanites in a different manner than the rural dwellers, and likewise upon men and women, upon the educated and the illiterate, etc. There is in Algeria a discontinuity between the former elites and structures and the new political elites that, in fact, never intended to maintain links with a past that was regarded as out-moded. For the moment, the regime is letting things 'take their course'. It is well-known, for instance, that frequently it is the local committees of the villages that handle the essential matters of justice and supervise public behaviour. The formal system of courts and judges is distant and quasi-absent. The erosion of the Jacobin model does not occur without friction, and any local conflict may be raised to the system of justice provided by the state, or settled within the groups involved. In the first instance, one is inclined to concur in the hypothesis advanced by Charnay with regard to the colonial period; that what actually is brought to court is but the tip of the iceberg, while the 'out-of-court settlements' are ten times more frequent. Rare are those who are willing to transgress group norms. Marginal groups may well try, however, and one may single out for particular attention in this respect urban women.[13] Moreover, it has been proven time and again that modern tribunals are not immune to ethnocentrist judgements. Formal jurisprudence is not necessarily a source of law in Algeria. The judgments of the Supreme Court, for instance, are not all published, and the 'family code', affecting all aspects of personal status, is still under wraps. There is a real contradiction, then, between ideal law – be it Koranic or *étatiste* – and customary law (*'urf*). Anything having to do with the family remains within the province of local authorities and the family itself. The government (*al-hukuma*) is Algiers, them, over there. ... The presence of the party and the communal assemblies has not upset the functioning of local, particularistic networks.[14] If this state of affairs can be viewed as a function of scarce administrative staffing, it is more difficult to understand why the central authorities tolerate current administrative practice (cf. Leca 1971, p.228). Perhaps it is a question of ideological weakness and the regime's incapacity to mobilise the urban masses, that is, those who are theoretically the least poorly socialised to the values of the new order. Perhaps also, because these same authorities could put themselves in considerable danger by an over-hasty effort to impose new administrative structures and to integrate local elites into the state system.

Within this context, special attention must be paid to marriage strategies which are more or less consciously planned among the members of the urban bourgeoisie. To our knowledge there is no study of this phenomenon currently available.[15] It is, however, a good indicator of the emergence of a class that employs to its benefit a 'parochial' or 'particularistic' technique. The class itself is founded on, for the most part, state officialdom, still relatively young (the average age of the Council of the Revolution is 40 years: 1974), and blocking the way to a growing mass of younger civil servants produced by the expanding educational system. This gives rise, once again, to a situation in which the dominant group seeks to protect its own position and to create links of dependency with aspirant groups through the assertion of blood and clientelistic ties. Favours that move both horizontally and vertically in these linkages include state-owned cars, villas, trips abroad, scholarships, administrative short-cuts, etc.

The 'ruling class' (*classe dirigeante*) does not own the means of production. To adopt a term that is in vogue, it is above all a technostructure. It controls strategic knowledge and the decision-making system. The most precious thing in Algeria that it can allocate is the opportunity to economise one's energy – not in the sense of doing nothing, for the high-ranking bureaucrats work very hard – but to be able to make others assume the real drudgery. As we indicated above, this permits one to control others, to avoid doing things for oneself, and to pay nothing. A bureaucrat in Algeria is not rich because he earns a lot, but because he pays nothing: a home, a servant, an automobile, travel, and so forth, are part of the perquisites of his job. By contrast, the poor are those who lose a day's wages in administrative red-tape, looking for a bottle of cooking gas, an inner tube for their motorbike, potatoes, and, in some quarters of Algiers, even water.

Conclusions: from patronage to dependence

Algeria's declared intention to develop rapidly, especially through the expansion of heavy industry, would entail sharp breaks with the past. The traditional society is undergoing profound changes as it urbanises. Rural migrants in Europe and Algeria's coastal cities learn, often with pain, that there are other types of relations than those that they have heretofore known. In the process they become people apart. As workers, technicians or students, they are not only privileged in the sense that they are the objects of the official solicitude of the state, but they also learn of a new rationality and new forms of solidarity. The emergent working class, for example, is in constant contact with foreign labour unions, attuned to a new order of material and professional concerns, and initiated into direct communications with managerial hierarchies.

In a general manner, then, the old system of values, patterns of distribution, and ties of blood solidarity are called into question, and with them the very foundations of the regime's political power. How does the regime keep itself afloat? Neither through the party nor any other institutions for their role has been negligible. Part of the answer lies in the creation of a dependent corps of middle-range functionaries, who, because of their technical competence, have been able to prise themselves loose from ethnocentric linkages. At the same time, the members of this corps, particularly the engineers, are thrust into the role of patron by those without privileges in a society undergoing severe dislocation. The bureaucrat becomes a new notable to the extent that he manipulates access to the distribution of desired goods and services monopolised by the state.

The ruling elite, upon whom the bureaucrats are entirely dependent, thus benefits from a source of support that assures it considerable room for manoeuvre. This in turn permits the elite to fill the role – and perhaps to play it consciously – of transmission belt, or even of bridgehead, of the world capitalist system. It seems apparent that there is a liaison, if not a causal link, between the pattern of social stratification that one observes in Algiers, as well as the attitudes, practices and ideology of the consumerist strata, and the domestic and foreign economic options of the regime. In short we are talking of the dependency of Algerian society upon its various international partners. But even here Algeria offers an original formula. Denying the logic of its own ideology, claiming in the name of the fraternity of Islam to be immune to class struggle, Algeria urges the other states of the Third World to elevate their conflicts to the level of the developed vs. the developing nations and thus to break their dependence on foreign technology and markets.

We have, then, the following hierarchy: the decision-makers, by training and preference, adhere to western models. They rely for support upon a bureaucratic corps whose loyalty is exchanged against the high value the regime places upon their technical competence. The bureaucratic groups, however, resort to ethnocentric techniques in making the administration work mainly because the civil society is undergoing a series of severe dislocations. Because of its almost total control over the major elements of the distributive process, the regime has made the following gamble. Even if it allows intermediate power groups to develop, to which it occasionally delegates real power, this over the long haul will favour the processes of political integration which can only be ethnodestructive. For some time however, it will be the intermediaries that master the distribution of state allocations. It will only be as a result of the gradual reduction in the advantages they draw from the services they render that the relations of clientage will change. It is precisely this that is happening. Against a backdrop of overall social change, the kinds of services the bureaucrat can deliver far outweigh the advantages he can expect in return. Ethnocentrism may no longer have significant pay-offs, and the Jacobin state, with its developmentalist ideology and close links with foreign sources of technology and capital, may gradually move toward the 'rational' integration of Algerian society.

NOTES

1. These terms refer to traditional mortgages (Charnay 1964, pp. 187 ff.).
2. For instance, the practice known as *tawsah*, or reciprocal participation in the expenses of feasts and celebrations. See Charnay (1964), p.226.
3. That they were opposed does not mean that they did not co-exist. There were market forces operative even before 1830, including the need of some tribesmen to borrow from the rich in order to plant wheat or buy sheep. The terms of

reimbursement were well understood by both parties. Honour and economic calculation operated together.

4.   This is still evident today in the popular songs and tales recited by the *meddah* in public squares and markets. They combine the splendour of the Islamic past, the acts of the Prophet, mythic and real heros, and the *maquisards*.

5.   This involves Muslim landowners favoured by the colonial regime. The laws of the late nineteenth century allowed some native owners to acquire title to certain parcels of 'undivided' lands. Subsequently these owners became, in some ways, 'feudalists', but this term, like that of the feudal mode of production, must be used with caution with respect to Algeria.

6.   What is more important than the social destruction itself is the varying nature of the dislocations according to whether or not they occurred in tribal areas, cities, or affected particular patterns of property. These variations gave rise to new groups and new solidarities.

7.   This debate is well represented in the film 'Le Vent des Aurès'. The hero leaves his family in the middle of the harvest, even though the obligations of the *touiza* have not been fulfilled.

8.   The statistics published by the civil service show that the *mujahiddin* are concentrated in the lower echelons. Aside from the bureaucracy, they were rewarded primarily with licenses to sell cigarettes, drinks, or drive taxis. In effect, the *mujahiddin* have replaced the former orderlies of the bureaucracy, the *chaouchs*, who were themselves mostly veterans of the First World War and the mainstay of the colonial administration. The new arrivals fill exactly the same functions with the same efficiency and the same inadequacies.

9.   Those who had been displaced in pacification centres, prisoners, members of the ALN in Tunisia and Morocco, worker migrants, etc.

10. In the first years of independence the politically suspect were those who had collaborated with the French or who had been reticent in their attitude toward the FLN: after 1970 they would be those considered insufficiently 'socialist'.

11. Among the themes of all the documents of the revolution is consistent reference to a pre-colonial Algeria with which independent Algeria asserts its continuity. These references occur with more or less precision in the Charter of Agrarian Reform, the Communal Charter, the Charter of the Wilayas, etc. The Communal Charter adopted in 1966 argues that long before 1830 local organisation was a reality. The village asembly (*jema'a*) represented the *douar* in all its activities. What the Charter fails to note is that these *jema'as* functioned for the most part in the absence of the control and supervision of a central state authority. It was one of the principal goals of the Emir Abdelqader to wed the myriad of local powers with some sort of centralised control, and his efforts to do so have been faithfully chronicled and serialised in the FLN newspaper *al-Moujahid*. He created eight *khalifalik*, sub-divided in *aghalik*, and he tried to impose a corps of bureaucrats to run them.

12. The principal manifestations of *wilayism* after 1962 consisted of the Kabyle uprising of 1963, led by Ait Ahmad Hoceine; and Mohand ou al-Hajj, followed in 1964 by that of Chibani, who was executed, and then by Zbiri in 1967, supported by the former chiefs of Wilaya I. In each instance it was local loyalty of a quasi-familial kind that permitted certain of these chiefs to raise armed support, even though their proclaimed political goals varied; Ait Ahmad, for example, was far more 'socialist' than Colonel Zbiri.

13. Women who refuse to 'play by the rules' of tradition, become marginal much more frequently than men. They have no alternative but to integrate themselves in the modern system. If women in general are somewhat outside the links of clientage it is because they are frequently the object of clientelist arrangements. Those who go to the cities and undertake advanced studies do not easily accept the deals made over their heads.

14. The Communal Assembles are frequently equated in the popular mind with the *Sections Administratives Specialisées*, set up in the latter years of French domination and

charged with programmes for rural development. The equation is thus APC = SAS, symbolising how Algerian state intervention is perceived as an exogenous element.

15. Various surveys carried out by AARDES in the Wilaya of Algiers do furnish some evidence. In 1962-3, in the euphoria of independence, there were many civil marriages concluded at the *mairie* in Algiers, while in the period 1972-4 practically all marriages were concluded before the Muslim *qadi*. It would seem that the families have reasserted their control over the marriage contract.

REFERENCES

Berge, M.G. (1953) *Caids et élus en Algérie*, Archives CHEAM, Paris (26/10/53).

Bourdieu, P. (1963) *Sociologie de l'Algérie*. Paris.

Bourdieu, P. (1972) 'Le sens de l'honneur', in *Esquisse d'une Théorie de la pratique*. Genève-Paris.

Charnay, J.-P. (1964) *La Vie Musulmane en Algérie d'après la jurisprudence de la première moitié du XXe siècle*. Paris.

CRESM (Centre de Recherche et d'Etudes sur les Sociétés Méditerranéennes) (1972) *Elites, pouvoir, et legitimité au Maghreb*. Aix-en-Provence.

CRESM (1973a) *La Formation des élites politiques maghrébines*. Paris.

CRESM (1973b) *Elites, pouvoir, et légitimité au Maghreb*. Paris.

Favret, J. (1966) 'La segmentarité au Maghreb', *l'Homme*, 105-11.

Favret, J. (1968) 'Rélations de dependance et manipulation de la violence en Kabylie', *l'Homme* (Oct.-Dec.) 18-43.

Leca, J. (1971) 'Administration locale et pouvoir politique en Algérie', *l'Annuaire de l'Afrique du Nord* X, Aix-en-Provence.

Nadir, A. (1972) 'Les ordres réligieux et la conquête française', *Révue Algérienne des Sciences Juridiques, Politiques, Economiques, et Sociales*, 819-72.

Sanson, R.P. (1969) *Monde rural et monde urbain*. Algiers, Secrétariat Social.

Valensi, L. (1969) *Le Maghreb avant la prise d'Alger*. Paris.

Vatin, J.C. (1974) *L'Algérie politique, histoire et société*. Paris.

Kenneth Brown

Changing forms of patronage in a Moroccan city

In the literature on Muslim cities, the structures of urban societies
have largely been discussed in terms of formal categories, such as
extended families, neighbourhoods or quarters, occupational guilds,
schools of law, Sufi brotherhoods, ruling elites, notables and masses.
In reading about these cities one rarely has the sense of real
individuals and groups of people interacting in everyday situations or
at moments of crisis.[1] During the course of my research on the social
history of the city of Salé in Morocco, I came to the conclusion that
the familiar formal categories in the earlier literature on urban social
structure had little explanatory value. The information that I had
gathered suggested a different sort of analysis: the social composition
of the population looked at over time seemed generally loose and
malleable. Relations among individuals and the structuring of groups
formed a pattern of fragile, shifting factions and alliances. Social
relations could best be conceived of as 'networks', in the metaphorical
sense used by Radcliffe-Brown (1952, p.190), or as 'individual-
centred coalitions that tended to take the form of patron-client
relations', a typology so defined by Wolf (1966).

Salé in 1967, when I completed my research, was becoming a sort of
dormitory suburb for the capital of Rabat across the Bou Regreg
river, and part of an urban sprawl from Casablanca to Kenitra. Its
population had grown to well over 100,000, and probably more than
half had migrated from the countryside and lacked any social roots in
the city. Yet a generation earlier, in the 1930s, its inhabitants had
numbered less than 30,000, and, it was said, most people had known
one another on a face-to-face basis, and had been somehow interrelated
by a degree of kinship or friendship. There was still a solid kernel of
Slawis (Salétins) in the 1960s, many of whom were tied together by
descent, marriage, or common experiences and values. As they put it,
Salé had been and to some extent still was bound together, everything
and everyone flowed together.[2]

The documentary sources and the oral traditions concerning Salé's
past suggested that a good part of its population had, indeed, been
linked together, but that within the larger community smaller groups
of people had been allied as patrons and clients. These alliances had
made possible particular kinds of activities at different periods of

Moroccan history. Clientelism in Morocco, as in all complex societies, has been a constant attribute, but the type of vertical power relations implied by this concept have changed over time and in respect to the structure of the state.[3] This can be seen in the case of Salé by a consideration of such alliances over three centuries.

In the discussion to follow, I explain the nature of clientage in Salé by applying that concept to the social relations which are expressed in texts and by informants according to their own idioms. These idioms are in turn considered in some detail. I do this by presenting examples of events or situations during the eighteenth, nineteenth and twentieth centuries. These have been chosen to illustrate the changing modality and significance of patron-client relations over time and within differing political contexts in Morocco.

During the centuries under discussion Salé's population has increased in number dramatically, especially over the past fifty years. At the same time, it has since the last century become more directly dominated by the central power and authority of the state. In the first example from the eighteenth century, its population was around 10,000 and for a while it was a sort of city-state with a relatively high degree of local autonomy. In the second example, early in the nineteenth century, it still could, if the need arose, provide its own self-defence. Two examples from the nineteenth century, when the population numbered some 15,000, show how the city had become an adjunct of the Makhzen, or central state authority, with a privileged position in a patrimonial bureacratic system. Patron-client ties remained significant but they depended upon government support. In the final examples, when Salé was flooded by migrants and largely proletariatised, clientelism seemed to have a different, more limited and less effective role.

I

During most of the seventeenth century, Morocco had been divided up into autonomous territorial and political principalities, including the city-state of Salé. Only with the rise of the Alawite dynasty, and particularly its fourth sultan Mulay Isma'il (1672-1727), did the country become reunified (Laroui 1970, p.253). Isma'il's power and authority were based on armed force – the slave-army of 'Abid al-Bukhari that he formed, and his religious prestige as a descendent of the prophet. Salé was brought to heel by these soldiers. The sultan had a large garrison stationed close by.

When Isma'il died in 1727 a thirty year period of disorder ensued in Morocco. His successor, Mulay 'Abd Allah, was deposed five times and during his reign there was poverty and a return to decentralisation. In many places, the slave-army acted without discipline, sometimes causing havoc. One of Salé's historians describes the continuous and widespread unrest and fear during which the Slawis were repeatedly humiliated by the 'Abids. This situation precipitated a rebellion in Salé, and a renewed period of local independence for about thirty years.

The man who led the rebellion, 'Abd al-Haqq Fannish, is described as one of the leaders of Salé.[4] One day after irrigating the vineyards in his gardens outside of the city, he came upon a soldier who was carrying off to the garrison a woman from Salé. According to the story, when she screamed at Fannish that he lacked any sense of honour and manliness, he killed the soldier. Then, afraid of the governor of the city and of the 'Abid soldiers, he proceeded to gather a group of his friends who would stand by him and were courageous. They went to the governor's house, reported what had happened and placed him under arrest. Then Fannish gathered equipment and arms to expel the soldiers from their garrison. The latter meanwhile had taken fright and fled during the night. After destroying the garrison, Fannish and his men took control of the city and established his governorship. According to one local historian, Fannish accomplished this with his 'supporters'. Another states that he ruled independently over the city with his 'kinsmen' and 'group' (Nasiri 1894, IV, p.103; Dukkali n.d., p.36).

Fannish and his followers maintained authority in Salé for some thirty years, until he was apprehended by Sultan Muhammad III (1757-1790). His demise resulted from his having killed one of the notables of the city, apparently a member of the illustrious Znibar family. Supporters of Znibar went to the Sultan who succeeded in having Fannish brought to him at his court in Meknes. After having heard the accusations, the Sultan delivered Fannish over to the supporters of Znibar so that they might have revenge. But they refused to spill his blood. The Sultan then had Fannish killed and ordered the confiscation of all wealth belonging to the Governor and his family, the sale of their property and their banishment from the city. Yet, as the historian an-Nasiri reminds us, within a generation the Fannish family had been allowed to return to Salé and were again rich and influential.

This episode has been retold at some length because it permits an analysis of the social relations in the alliance that formed around Fannish. His followers are variously referred to as his friends, supporters, kinsmen, and group. It is clear that to some degree common descent is of importance: thus his brother's support and punishment by death, and the confiscation of the family's property and their banishment from the city. Salé's historians interpret the episode as a calamity that struck the 'people of his (Fannish's) House', and underline the conflict with another family of notables – the Znibars. Furthermore a poem is quoted to show that at least one of the Znibars, and probably more, had been forced into exile in Rabat because of 'the ordeal that had struck his "clan" (*Qabila*) at the hands of the governor' (Brown 1971, p.68).

The idioms of 'house' and 'clan' are fairly common in Arabic historiography, but I think that too much has been made of these terms by Western scholars. This is not to deny the importance of the idiom in our documentation. Indeed, the material from Salé implies the importance of family groups, and their solidarity and strength. It is part of the urban ideology. Thus, for example, a special broken plural form appears in texts and in speech to refer to the totality of a family grouping: *al-Fanansha* (the Fannishs), *al-Znabra* (the Znibars), *al-Ma'ana* (the Ma'ninus), etc., as well as the forms *awlad* X, or *bayt* Y (the sons of X, or the house of Y). At least one street in the city is named in this way – *darb Ma'ana* – with the implication that at sometime in the past the Ma'ninu family, in its totality, occupied all or most of its houses. Moreover, in discussions, people sometimes claimed that family solidarities had until the recent past been the dominant feature of social organisation.

The ideals of family solidarity were, insofar as I have been able to ascertain from texts and interviews, never realised. The Slawis expressed what Ibn Khaldun in his discussion of urban social structure has called, with little charity, the 'delusion' of nobility: 'Isolated inhabitants of cities can have a "House" only in a metaphorical sense.' Prestige does not depend on family descent: it belongs to those groups which are feared and can make others obey them. Those without power 'cannot sway anyone's opinions, and their own opinions are not sought' (Ibn Khaldun 1958, Vol.1, pp. 273 ff.).

Fannish was obviously a man of power. Salé's historians show that his followers were composed of a variety of allies. The most important term used to characterise a body of followers, and one which has enjoyed great currency in Moroccan historiographical writing is that of *'asabiyya*. It is usually translated as 'group feeling', and is one of the key concepts in the political theory of Ibn Khaldun (Ibn Khaldun 1958, Vol. 1, LXXVII; and Mahdi 1964, p.196). It has seldom been noticed that Ibn Khaldun carefully distinguishes between the 'group feeling' of 'bedouins', i.e. 'primitive' or non-urban peoples, and inhabitants of cities. In its pure form, group feeling 'results only from (blood) relationship or something corresponding to it'. It is shared by kinsmen, but also by those in a relationship of clientage (*al-wala'*) and alliance (*al-hilf*). It results from the feeling of shame that a person experiences when one of his neighbours, relatives or affines of any degree of kinship is humiliated. The relationship between a master and his client is as close as that of people of common descent, for both lead to mutual assistance and affection.

For Ibn Khaldun, the inhabitants of cities have group feeling, but their social relations and associations are weaker than those based on common descent. Townsmen are drawn together by affinal ties and eventually individual groups are constituted; their interactions are marked by the same kind of friendship or hostility that one finds among tribes. When a dynasty weakens, townsmen have to manage their own affairs and protect themselves – people separate into higher and lower classes. Everyone competes with one another, trying to attract followers (*al-atba'*) such as clients (*al-mawali*), partisans (*ash-shiya'*) and allies (*al-ahlaf*). They spend whatever they possess on the rabble and the mob. Everybody forms a group with his fellows, and one of them achieves superiority' (Ibn Khaldun 1958, Vol. II, p. 302).

Moroccan historians use the term 'group feeling' in this sense when they discuss urban situations, that is to say forms of solidarity within groups of townsmen. Thus Nasiri, who uses the term to designate Fannish's followers, also employs the same concept to describe a revolt in Fez during the reign of Sultan Sulayman (1792-1822). He relates that when the people of Fez rebelled against the governor and sought to remove him, a group of followers sided with the governor so that authority in the city became divided and fighting ensued (Nasiri 1894, IV, p.154). Another historian from Salé describes a similar situation, without however employing the same term. When Sulayman died in 1822 and Sultan 'Abd al-Rahman acceded to power, the rural people living outside the city cut off the trade routes and raided the caravans. The governor of Salé lacked the power to control the brigands; one of the city's notables who had ties with the rural people and the urban lower classes gathered a group of some two hundred riflemen, attacked and arrested the brigands and recovered the goods and animals that they had stolen (Dukkali, n.d., p.38).

In the examples that I have cited from the eighteenth and early nineteenth centuries, urban factions competed for power in the city and did sometimes gain independent control over it. These factions were, I suggest, composed of followers tied to a leader by transactional relations. They were recruited personally in situations of conflict over honour or control of resources, mainly according to principles of patronage (cf. Boissevain 1974, pp.19-22). In Salé, patrilineal kinship groups existed in name only; they offered no effective means for political action. A family name to which some degree of nobility or prestige might be ascribed at best offered a potential social and political asset. A man would proclaim his family identity proudly, intending to give others the impression that he belonged to a powerful and influential house. Yet, in practice, the crucial social relationships in the city – those connected with wealth and power – were based on ties of mutual interest and interdependence, sometimes reinforced by marriage links, and almost never based on consanguinity.

The elite of the city were not leaders of powerful cohesive families, although some blood relatives might ally themselves for particular purposes. Positions of power belonged to men who controlled or could call upon a large number of supporters – what I propose to call a group of clients. In using the term client, I mean to include both the general English usage, viz., a dependent, one who is under the protection or patronage of another, and the common features of most of the definitions suggested by recent writings by social scientists: a specific type of dyadic relation involving (1) asymmetry, that is the unequal power and status of actors, (2) reciprocity, that is a self-regulating form of interpersonal exchange, and (3) informality, that is a relationship which is particularistic and private (cf. Kaufman 1974).

Moroccan colloquial Arabic is replete with terms that describe relations among patrons and clients involving protection, defence, confidence, and alliance. Yet the most important of these terms has been *suhba*. A man's *sahb* (pl. *shab*) was friend, companion, comrade, associate, accomplice and, depending on context, patron or client. Thus, for example, a Jewish merchant from Salé described the workings of itinerant commerce in the countryside before the protectorate: 'Everyone had his friends (*shab*), including the Muslims. If he had no protection (*mizrag*), he could not budge. If you lacked protection, if someone did not know you, you were unable to move'.

These informal relationships, which permeated the urban society of Salé, bound together townsmen of different religions and linked the city with its hinterland and sometimes with other cities. The larger factions and coalitions that have been described in Salé were based on such relationships. The formation of these larger groups, centred around powerful individuals and held together by links of patronage, depended on the relative weakness of the central government and the strength of local autonomy. Once Salé lost all vestiges of its independence, that is from the 1830s onwards, the larger factions and coalitions ceased to exist. Patron-client relations became more fragile and were restricted to small, competing groups which depended on the protection of the Makhzen.

II

The types of men now to be referred to as patrons were those individuals in Salé who during the half century between 1880 and 1930 served as high government functionaries – governors, customs officials, judges, etc. At that time Fez, Tetuan, Rabat and Salé enjoyed the reputation of being the centres of urban culture in Morocco. The major source of income of the state came from customs duties. To administer its finances the central government began to recruit from these cities most of the personnel necessary for the expanding bureaucracy. As a result, educated Slawis not only filled official positions in the city itself, but at the sultan's court and to a fairly large extent throughout the empire, as well. A handful of men from the city managed to gain the appointments for most of the others, and this was accomplished by means of personal networks of patron-client relations.

Several examples will illustrate the process involved. The biography of Nasiri describes how he began and furthered his career in the administration under the auspices of his teacher, friend, and later father-in-law, the head judge of the city (Brown 1972, p.127). Because his patron rose in rank and influence, his own situation improved significantly. Their relations were complex and changed over time: first that of student and teacher, then father and son-in-law, and later they became companions. The judge took him along on his travels to other cities, introduced him into the ruling circles of the country, and secured for him appointments, first in the administration of pious endowments in Salé, and later as a customs official in various port cities. In return, Nasiri was expected to assist and support his benefactor whenever called upon to do so.

Another personage from Salé who may be taken as an illustration of a patron was 'Abd Allah Bin Sa'id, who succeeded his father as governor at the age of twenty-nine and held office from 1892 until 1905. Born of wealth and power, Bin Sa'id established a network of alliances (mainly by means of his uncles and their wives' fathers and brothers) with a small group of the city's most influential men. He spent most of his tenure in office on missions for the palace, and at the same time served as customs agent at Tangier and later as assistant to Torres, the old and ailing vizier, in whose absence he received Kaiser William II in 1905. Because of his influence in government during the thirteen years of his governorship, over forty Slawis owed him their appointments as customs officials, notaries and even artillerymen, throughout the port cities of Morocco. As in the case of the judge, some of those to whom he extended his patronage also became his kinsmen through marriage. Thus, for example, the governor of Casablanca, arrested and deported for opposing the French invasion of 1907, originated from Salé and had had his career furthered by his patron and kinsman, Bin Sa'id. Eventually, Bin Sa'id lost his governorship because the *qadi* (Islamic judge) attempted to prosecute his personal secretary. The governor protected his client, gave him sanctuary in his house, and refused to deliver him over to the *qadi*. The two officials with their respective supporters could not resolve the dispute; neither group had the power to impose its will on the other. Eventually both individuals presented their cases to the sultan who decided to exile each of them to different corners of the empire. Bin Sa'id was soon in good graces again and sent on an official mission to Tangier. Later he managed to become a German protegé, a gamble which cost him dearly when the French established a protectorate over the country several years later.

A final illustration of what may be called 'patronage *manqué*' is the career of Bil Amin Znibar, a prosperous merchant and government official. His grandfather had been governor of Salé. His father, a wealthy wholesale merchant and customs agent, had married four wives, all daughters of influential figures in the city, and had taken at least an equal number of concubines. Most of the twelve surviving children from these unions had married into the families of prominent local men. Bil Amin had himself wed the sister of someone who later became assistant governor and then administrator of pious endowments, and their relationship became subsequently strengthened by the marriage of his widowed sister to the latter. In time, Bil Amin amassed a considerable fortune by dealing in Manchester cottons (and becoming a British protegé in the process), and later by holding various governmental appointments, rising from customs agent in Larache to Minister of Finance. His career was apparently marred by only one setback – the refusal by the palace to accept his bid to become governor of Salé. He failed, despite his readiness to pay the price demanded by the palace, because he had not sufficient local support. The government would not appoint as local officials those who lacked the backing of a sufficient number of important clients in the city.

Bil Amin's inability to mobilise supporters was a result of an excess of conscientiousness, his extreme rectitude as an official and refusal to comply with current practices of patronage. To the consternation and bitterness of many people in Salé, only one Slawi had served in his cabinet. Moreover, as informants were quick to observe, he had made the mistake of entrusting all of his local affairs to a single individual. His failure to share the benefits of his favourable situation with others did not win him any friends. Indeed, as people pointed out, he had lacked the qualities of generosity expected by a patron to the extent that when his only local client died, he had lacked the means to leave his children any inheritance. Local townsmen were incensed by the miserliness of Bil Amin towards a devoted client, and also no doubt because the individual concerned had been highly respected and loved for his piety. The general feeling of reproach in the town was sufficient to constrain Bil Amin to donate two houses to the sons of the deceased.

III

These cases show that the actual or potential patrons in nineteenth and early twentieth century Salé were wealthy and powerful government officials. To understand the nature of patronage relations within the city, it is necessary to consider the state system, and its political and economic organisation. The Sharifian government of Morocco, or Makhzen, both before the protectorates and afterwards, fits Weber's definition of a patrimonial administration (Weber 1947; Bendix 1962, p.334). Mardin has shown a similar fit in his discussion of the Ottoman Empire, where competition for membership in the patrimonial bureaucracy was more important than the mechanisms of the market in determining the distribution of wealth and power (Mardin 1969, pp. 209, 247). In Morocco it is difficult to separate such competition from market processes, for the bureaucracy and commerce often overlapped. Appointments to official posts did not carry fixed salaries, and the government failed to control the incomes generated by its officials, especially in the case of customs agents, but also in regard to governorships, judgeships, etc. Merchants and *ulama* (religious savants) – not always easily separable categories – had favoured access to administrative positions, and these allowed them to increase or establish important economic interests in trade. Indeed, during the nineteenth century, customs agents came to control most of the export-import trade and as a result became the 'bankers of the Makhzen' (Aubin 1904, pp. 186-7). In my view it would be clearly misleading to conceive of these notables as a group of individuals who shared a common class-consciousness. The elite of each of the main cities were socially entrenched in the communities in which they lived.

In theory, appointments to official administrative posts – ministers, customs agents, governors, judges, market inspectors, administrators of pious endowments, preachers, prayer leaders of Friday mosques and even mosque teachers – emanated directly from the sultan. In practice, recruitment resulted from decisions taken by government officials at one of many levels, and usually on the recommendation or intervention of an official or trusted individual from the same city as the appointed individual. All of these appointments were ratified by decree of the sultan.

These decrees, issued from the head of state and bearing the stamp of the sultan, conferred some honour or favour on its recipient.[5] They formalised official appointments, and might also be used to accord various kinds of privilege, e.g. ownership or use of government property, revenues from the tomb of a saint or the lodge of a religious order, exemptions from duties or taxes, etc. Privileges stipulated by decree normally applied only to the beneficiaries, but could be explicitly hereditary. Often the heirs of a beneficiary had the decree renewed. Appointment to an office by decree was both an investiture and a prescriptive right to the all-embracing favour of the sultan. Thus, for example, in 1894, the new sultan 'Abd al-'Aziz renewed the appointment of Salé's governor by a 'Decree of Honour and Respect', a kind of *titre de dignité*.[6] In addition to granting the governor 'honour and respect', it freed him from obligations to serve in the army or pay taxes in consideration of services that he and his forefathers had rendered to the Makhzen, and it guaranteed the same privileges to his children, in-laws, and paternal cousins.

The fates and fortunes of these officials and beneficiaries depended on the reigning sultan and his government; the bureaucracy was built on patronage, a hierarchy of clientelism based in various locales, with the Makhzen at the apex. The decree represented a kind of contract between the palace and individual members of what may broadly.be termed the elite: office and honour were bestowed in exchange for loyalty and support. Just how much wealth moved upwards in these transactions, the price for the office and the 'membership dues', remain in our present state of knowledge unknown, as do the material calculations involved in reaping the benefits from office. In Salé, economic exchanges were involved in these relations, but there was a good deal more to them. The Slawi officials enjoyed close personal ties with the palace, held favoured positions incommensurate with their wealth, and provided a constituency safely within the fold of the Makhzen. We find sultans entrusting some of their sons for education to certain individuals in the city, sending their concubines to pasture there, and generally acting with greater familiarity in regard to Salé's notables than with those from most other places.[7]

The special relationship between the Makhzen and the notables, particularly the officials, helped the latter to maintain their power and influence within the city. And it allowed them to attract and reward their clients and supporters. Officials distributed largesse (and thereby redistributed wealth), arranged administrative appointments, employed people and interceded in external and local affairs on behalf of their clients. These officials were generally in competition with one another for power, wealth and prestige, and they did not enjoy anything approaching a secure 'tenure of contract'. The conflicts and tensions in contemporary Moroccan politics, the elite behaviour and characteristics described by Waterbury, closely resemble the competition between patronage groups in nineteenth century Salé.[8] Officials' positions depended on their maintaining favour within the Makhzen, and on the longevity and good graces of their patrons and friends at court. To lose one's patron almost certainly meant dismissal from office, and probably the loss of honour, perhaps property and conceivably one's life. In Salé, when an official was promoted or dismissed, his clients generally shared his fate.

IV

As a corrective to the tendency in much of recent political anthropology, and especially in the literature on patronage, to ignore the structures and institutions of politics and to focus instead on decision-making, strategies of alternatives, networks and social fields – the 'processual approach' – I have focused on the wider political system in which they have existed (cf. Swartz et al. 1966, introduction). In the first case looked at, this meant a consideration of the city's local autonomy. In the second case, it was necessary to show that the city was dominated by the central government.

To complement the wider context of state power, it is useful to focus on small-scale politics, the actual ways in which patron-client relations worked and the functions that they fulfilled within the city itself. During the nineteenth and early twentieth centuries, Salé's 'patrons' were those leaders who competed for power, wealth and influence by vying for access to the state's privileges. All men had clients to a greater or lesser degree. The political importance of a man within the local context was judged by the size and quality of his 'entourage'. Those who were attached to a leader did not all act as his servants, but they had the courtier's gift of being acceptable and did perform services for him. They were his 'mates' – habitual companions who enlivened and shared his table, made his evenings pass quickly, carried out errands and delicate matters for him, acted in complicity with him, and perhaps conspired with, aided and abetted him.

It was considered self-evident that a leader needed companions for these purposes; and the predominant social ethic placed a high value on companionship – a man of honour should never go anywhere alone or eat alone. A man's status was demonstrated by the size of his suite and the clearest demonstration of this was in the number of people whom he voluntarily fed. Commensality established more obviously than any other activity the bonds of patronage amongst men; one could justifiably assert to the Slawis: 'Tell me with whom you eat, and I will tell you who you are!' Ties of patronage manifested themselves in the 'heroic virtues' – loyalty, honour, and hospitality. Social reputation depended on and manifested itself in generosity in the distribution of food in one's house and around one's table. Clients counted on material benefits, on food and gifts of various kinds to begin with, and on indirect assistance and protection in the public world and under the eyes of other people. In return, a patron would be expected at some time to make demands upon his clients which would be satisfied.

The discussion of reciprocity in patron-client relations by Paine (1971), drawing on the work of Barth and Sahlins, is useful and relevant in this regard. Generosity is expressed by general reciprocity through gifts. What characterises a patron is that he establishes a diffuse obligation to reciprocate, and that by converting his resources into influence, he is able to create a body of followers. His condition for the continuation of his largesse is that prestations by clients also be generalised and determined by him: 'Ultimately, what distinguishes the patron from his client is that only values of the patron's choosing are circulated in their relationship. Further the client demonstrates to his patron and others his acceptance of the value which the patron has chosen for circulation between them; herein lies the "loyalty" and "dependence" for which the client is rewarded' (Paine 1971, p.15).

In the Moroccan context, the explanatory value of Paine's view has severe limitations, and would lead to an overly systematised and basically mechanistic image of the complex and nuanced links amongst individuals. In a general sense, the patronage relationships that I have described fit into a pattern of general reciprocity. However, it is not the case that the values in circulation are always chosen by the patron. Status differences among clients vary significantly over time, and so does the degree of loyalty and dependence vis-à-vis the patron. A diversity of interests and resources adhere to patron-client relations, and the transactions involved defy precise definitions. To be sure, the documentation and souvenirs presented in oral information are only suggestive and incomplete. However, contemporary material from Salé indicates the complexity and variety of interests, resources and transactions involved in relations of clientage.

V

A bookshop which I frequented in the course of my field research in the 1960s served as an informal meeting place for about ten elderly men between the ages of sixty and seventy who were prominent in Salé. All of them at one time or another had held official positions in the administration. A few had served in the pre-colonial bureaucracy, others had been employed by the protectorate, and at least one of them had worked high up in a government ministry since independence in 1956. These men had been friends and companions for decades, and had often shared social and political interests. They formed a kind of interlocking 'old boy' network which had extensive ramifications within the old urban population (that is, those families present in the city before 1930). There were gradations of status among them which had altered over the years. At different moments in time, one or another of them had the status of a patron in regard to the others, and that continued to be the case. Changing personal conditions in regard to fortune, employment, age, family responsibilities, place of domicile, ambition, and chance had affected the configuration of their relations in various ways over the decades. The patron amongst them at any given moment had at hand more resources and influence than the others, and he used these to further the interests of his friends and to maintain their support for his interests. This informal group had no fixed membership, nor continuity over time, but it had re-emerged periodically in various combinations. None of the men was related to another by descent; each of them belonged to a family whose name was highly reputed and whose members were in some cases numerous; several were closely related through marriage, and all of them could probably trace some distant affinal tie. But there was in their relationships no discernible pattern of kith and kin. They were in their own view tied together solely by the links of friendship. To be sure, all were notables in the city, but they were a small minority from within that group. Each of them had in his own right an extensive network that included relatives and friends dependent on and loyal to him. The pattern of their inter-relations can best be summed up by the expression 'wheels within wheels'.

These men were still involved in important dealings. Although their activities had no doubt generally diminished in scope and significance in respect to earlier times, these were not elders waiting out their days in reminiscences and small-talk. The bookshop in which they congregated, coming and going throughout the day, was a bourse of information – collected, sifted, and disseminated through them. The information exchanged touched upon economic, social and political matters of utmost importance. Their particular expertise was in the domain of law: the procedures of marriage, divorce, inheritance and the buying and selling of property. Some of them actually worked on a part-time basis as notaries in the court, all had a precise knowledge of real estate values and in most cases significant interests in property, and most of them had a hand in the politics of marriage. There was a continual flow of people in the shop to confer with these individuals, but they alone made it their headquarters. They carried with them a good deal of precious information which they had gathered elsewhere from their individual social networks.

I was struck in observing the interactions of these bookshop patrons by the following characteristics:

1. the familiarity, respect and civility they showed to one another, born of constant frequentation over a long period of time, and indeed what seemed to me an exaggerated use of politeness and decorum towards one another;

2. their intellectual awareness of the contemporary world and general erudition concerning the past, and their intimate knowledge of people and things, within the city and, to a lesser extent, countrywide. The essential function of these gatherings was clearly the *exchange of information* – a crucial factor in most situations in which I observed patronage relations.

In Salé, and I believe that one can generalise about Morocco in this regard, to cope with everyday contingencies, to settle petty or significant matters, to defend oneself, to get ahead in the world, has usually demanded knowledge of people. This means knowing how to get to the right person at the right place and time. The Slawis said that human affairs were regulated through *ma'rifa* – '*intuitus personal*'[9] and through *ttisal* – perhaps best expressed by the French concept of *piston* or American expressions like 'pull' and 'clout'. The implications of the terms are clear: relations with the appropriate individuals are precious resources, because the doings and dealings of this world only fall within one's grasp by mediation and hence depend on effective intermediaries.

These were not straightforward contractual relations in regard to specifically defined areas and for limited purposes. To request the mediation of someone was to enter into a broad relationship of reciprocity and solidarity over an undefined and general area of life and interests. In the older sociological vocabulary, these were relationships of *Gemeinschaft*, rather than *Gesellschaft*. The mediator granted a request and in the process became a potential patron. The ties established thereby were at once political and moral, and they were imbued with and clothed in sentiments of trust, fidelity and honour.

Such ties of patronage among people in Salé extended both into the Jewish community and the rural countryside. In regard to the Jewish community, most leaders allied themselves as clients with leading

Muslim personalities in the city, and they, in turn, acted as patrons to individual co-religionists within the Jewish quarter. It may be the case, however, that in distinction to the Muslims, they maintained more cross-cutting ties with their co-religionists in other cities. The rural *qa'ids* (local appointed officials) likewise acted as patrons in their own areas and some of them strengthened their ties in the city by entering into marriage alliances with urban patrons or clients.

It is extremely difficult to assess the stability or continuity of patron-client relations in Salé under various conditions and over time. The rises and falls in individual careers affected a man's ability to attract followers or attach himself to influential personalities. Fluidity in social relations and a relatively high degree of social mobility caused shifts in alignments among individuals. But the pattern of clientage remained widespread, constant and durable, as long as the city maintained its homogeneity and the political system of the state retained its main characteristic – that of a patrimonial bureaucracy.

VI

The political circumstances of Morocco since 1912 have altered to some extent the characteristics of the governmental system, and the process of socio-economic change during this century has also affected the scope and significance of clientage. Colonialism, nationalism and intense political struggles since independence have undermined some of the old bonds of loyalty and encouraged the formation of new ones. The French protectorate attempted to govern under the guise of indirect rule by using the traditional Moroccan state bureaucratic structure – the sultanate and the Makhzen. But colonialism in Morocco, as elsewhere, awakened opposition and eventually resistance by sections of the urban population, and eventually by the palace itself. Clientele relations continued to play an important role in social, economic and political life; at the same time divisions between 'haves' and 'have-nots', between collaborators and nationalists, between old and young, expressed themselves in a new pattern of social groupings. In Salé, these groups took the forms of a nationalist movement, emergent socio-economic classes, and political parties. It is beyond the scope of this paper to enter into these developments in detail, but it is important to note the tension that existed in the city since the 1930s between ties of loyalty to individuals, on the one hand, and patriotic, class, or political allegiances, on the other hand. In regard to Salé, it is instructive to look at the parliamentary elections of 1963 in order to better understand how these tensions were resolved in a situation marked by rapid urbanisation.

In an excellent journalistic account of Morocco written in 1958, the authors noted that urban politics was made up of men rather than ideas (Lacouture 1958, p.127). The elections held in Salé in 1963 do not entirely support this view. To be sure, three leaders of national stature, representing the principal political parties, originated from Salé. The Istiqlal party was led by Bubkar Qadiri, and many of the city's old elite supported him and his party. In the communal elections of 1960, the Istiqlal had received almost 84 percent of the total vote of some 22,500, and those elected from the party list included many of the city's most prominent personalities. The local leader from the radical UNFP, was (Union Nationale des Forces Populaires) was Abderrahim Bouabid, while the candidate of the PDI (Parti Democratic de l'Indépendance) was Hmed Ma'aninu.

All three men were seasoned veterans in the nationalist movement, well-known throughout the country, and highly placed in the echelons of their respective parties. Qadiri had been a leader in the nationalist struggle in Salé from an early period, and had established and maintained the most important school in the city. His prestige and connections both local and national were extensive, and most Slawis with a modern Arabic education had been his pupils. Ma'aninu had a similar background, but enjoyed a lesser degree of influence and contacts. Both men had widespread ties of kinship and friendship in Salé and could expect to capitalise on them in the elections. Bouabid also had deep roots in Salé, as well as the lustre of having played an important role in the nationalist movement and in the Aix-les-Bains talks. He was, moreover, a highly educated man, a barrister-at-law trained in France, and completely at home in European culture. He lacked, however, local ties commensurate with those of the other two men.

When the UNFP met to work out their strategy only two weeks before the elections, it was felt that Salé might well be lost to the Istiqlal because of the status of Qadiri in the city, and the clientage that he could command. Moreover, Bouabid is said to have been extremely reluctant to oppose his former teacher, a man to whom he still felt a bond of loyalty. On the other hand he had also lived and was known in Kenitra, a city whose proletarian image more closely fitted the party ideology. Therefore, the executive committee decided that Bouabid should forego the elections in Salé, and instead present himself as a candidate in the workers' city of Kenitra where he was likely to win. The choice of an UNFP candidate for Salé continued to preoccupy the party. After much deliberation, the executive committee decided upon a relatively unknown young solicitor, Mehdi Alawi, who had recently completed his studies in France and returned to Salé. Although a native Slawi, Alawi had few local ties and was not identified with any patronage group. It was hoped, however, that this might prove advantageous, and that the subtlety involved in choosing a candidate whose name was Alawi, to represent a party that wanted to undermine the power of the Alawite dynasty, would not be lost on the electors.[10]

To the great surprise of almost everyone, and not least the UNFP, Alawi won the seat for Salé. Qadiri and Ma'aninu had mobilised their supporters largely by means of informal clientele networks, using in most cases the old method of holding meetings in the private homes of their closest followers. The UNFP, in contrast, had adopted the strategy of large public rallies, held in open squares within and outside the city and addressed by Alawi and the national leaders of the party. The UNFP strategy proved more effective, because it had taken account of the changing social composition of the city. The total population of Salé had increased dramatically in recent years and by 1963 numbered well over 100,000. Most of its demographic growth had been a consequence of large-scale rural migration (Naciri 1963, p.44). Probably less than one-quarter of the voting population had social roots in Salé, and the rest remained, on the whole, uninvolved in local networks of patronage. These newcomers, largely unknown by the 'true' Slawis, were simply called 'outsiders' in the local idiom.

It was these 'outsiders' who provided Alawi's margin of victory. The UNFP reached these people, many of whom lived outside the walls of the city in new quarters and in shanty-towns, through public rallies and by mobilising a large number of youngsters – some of them sons of the town's elite and students of the other candidates. These youngsters canvassed the poor quarters and helped turn out the vote that proved the margin of victory for the UNFP.

This election shows, it seems to me, that the Slawi politicians had failed to realise that ties of clientage could not determine the results of the election process in the city. The Istiqlal lost Salé because their patronage system was not sufficiently widespread. The UNFP won the city, to their surprise, because mass politics had become effective. Neither party, it should be noted, had moulded a political machine based on patronage and able to mobilise a majority of the electors.

The situation in Salé, to be sure, contrasts with what some have argued is the more general pattern of urban Moroccan politics. Thus, in Fez, the Istiqlal with the passive support of the monarchy was able through its clients (the heads of quarters) to mobilise the city's votes in their favour. In the context of Fez, according to this argument, the new middle class that had gained influence in the Istiqlal still represented the old families – the old bourgeoisie. The traditional pattern of patronage controlled by the Istiqlal ('the subtle play of alliances and exchanges of services of the bourgeois dynasties') had allowed it to win the election, and thereby helped the monarchy to continue to control the administration and the economy and abandoned to it the exercise of political power (Marais 1973, p.173).

The case in Salé differed considerably. The Istiqlal was tied to the old bourgeoisie, but it cannot be said to have represented a new middle class, nor to have had the active backing of the palace. The election results may be interpreted as an indication of the ways in which personalistic ties in urban Morocco are giving way to rationalised and depersonalised forms of organisation. But such a formulation is likely to lend credence to the rather too glib premises of a traditionalism-into-modernity interpretation of social change. A more modest and convincing argument can be made along the following lines: traditional urban elites in some of Morocco's cities have proven unable to maintain or extend their ties of patronage, or to hold on to or incorporate the younger generation, despite their continued access to the resources and passive support of the palace and its bureaucracy. In Salé, a sufficient number of voting citizens, beyond the reach of patronage networks, could be mobilised so as to win the elections for a political party which had, in comparison to the other parties, the least amount of resources to distribute. Public rallies were politically effective, and private meetings were not. The young, politicised and often educated members of the party – the 'moderns' – were able to capitalise successfully on the migrant vote by means of their enthusiasm, propaganda, and contagious conviction in regard to the party's position on the socio-economic and political issues at stake. The majority of the urban population now lay outside the reach of old or new ties of clientage.

Conclusion

An examination of patron-client relations in Salé over the past two centuries, by focusing on a series of historically distinct examples, shows that the functions of such relations can best be understood within the varying contexts of the wider state system. In the eighteenth century, Salé was, during a limited period, a relatively homogeneous and autonomous political entity. Various urban groups competed for power, and the ties that bound individuals together in these groups were based on patronage. The city was composed of factions led by powerful individuals who gave protection to their followers in exchange for support. Thus, one man – Fannish – gained effective control within the city and ruled over it independently for a generation. Fifty years later, again during a period of crisis, a local leader, Znibar, could in a similar manner mobilise his following from amongst the lower classes and people from the countryside in order to defend the city against outside threats.

By the late nineteenth century, patron-client relations had begun to function in a different way. There was no longer any possibility of local independence through the control over the city by extensive factions. Those who had influence depended for it on their ties with the central government. Their clients could hope to better their situations through the grace of their patrons, but all were incorporated into a centralised patrimonial bureaucracy. Local conflicts could no longer be settled without recourse to the Makhzen.

During the twentieth century, local groups bound by ties of patronage continued to fulfil significant roles. The regulation of most affairs still needed the assistance of intermediaries, and local patrons maintained a hold over most matters touching upon family and property law. But in regard to large-scale political issues, clientèle groups were no longer effective. The parliamentary elections of 1963 give evidence of the failure of patron-client ties to influence the results significantly.

In the absence of free elections since 1963, it is difficult to judge the possible effectiveness of patronage within the wider arena of politics. The monopolisation of power by the state and its administration has no doubt strengthened the usefulness of maintaining ties of patronage, especially among the elite. The majority of the population also remains dependent on the protection and help of the more influential and those ready to serve as intermediaries. However, it appears that most inhabitants of Salé today are excluded from such relations. It seems unlikely that a return to democratic life, as far as Salé is concerned, would create a new system of patronage, at least in the short run. In a highly heterogeneous population now numbering more than 150,000 mass politics shaped by ideological and class identities would, I think, prove more important than personalistic ties. This is, of course, arguable, and the combination of class interests and patron-client ties may not prove mutually exclusive.

NOTES

1. For a critical evaluation of these earlier studies, and examples of successful efforts to bring Muslim cities to life, see the works of Lapidus (1967) and Hourani and Stern (eds), 1970.
2. The metaphor used to describe these interconnections was the *noria*: 'Each cup (on the water-wheel) emptied into another cup, everything emptied into everything else'.
3. Kaufman (1974), following on Lemarchand and Legg, emphasises the importance of delineating different types of clientelism in respect to the formal systems in which they exist. I am suggesting that a similar distinction is necessary when considering one society as it changes over time.
4. '*min zu'ama' sala.*' Cf. ad-Dukkali (n.d.:36). Fannish was of renegade origin. His brother was later apprehended by Sultan 'Abd Allah who before killing him reminded him that like his father he was one of the renegade slaves (*'uluj*) of the Alawite dynasty.
5. This decree or *zahir* (pronounced *dahir* in Morocco) was the equivalent of the Persian *firman*.
6. *zahir al-ihtiram wa'l-taqdir*. A copy of this particular decree is reproduced in Brown (in press).
7. The four *hadara* cities whose notables enjoyed special relations with the Makhzen, and from which most of the recruitment for the late nineteenth century bureaucracy was drawn, were Fez, Tetuan, Rabat and Salé.
8. Waterbury (1970, pp. 3 ff.). His use of the segmentary model is, however, open to serious criticism.
9. A translation suggested by Berque's discussion of North African cities: 'Toujours *l'intuitus personal*, les relations d'homme à homme, les mêmes bases, et les mêmes echappées du culture citadaine' (1959), p.27).
10. One of the slogans of the UNFP – 'no prostration from now on' (*la ruku' ba'd al-yawm*) – was an obvious attack against the monarchy and its religious legitimation. When proclaimed by an Alawi (a 'cousin' of the king), it may have been, as some Slawis have claimed, especially effective. On the elections, in general, cf. Waterbury (1970, pp. 260 ff.).

REFERENCES

Aubin, E. (1904) *Le Maroc d'aujourd'hui*. Paris.

Bendix, R. (1962) *Max Weber: An Intellectual Portrait*. Garden City.

Berque, J. (1959) 'Médinas, villeneuves et bidonvilles', *Cahiers de Tunisie* 21-2, 5-42.

Boissevain, J. (1974) *Friends of Friends*. London.

Brown, K. (1971) 'An urban view of Moroccan history: Salé, 1000-1800', *Hespéris-Tamuda* XII, 5-106.

Brown, K. (1972) 'Profile of a nineteenth-century Moroccan scholar', in N. Keddie (ed.) *Scholars, Saints and Sufis*. Berkeley.

Brown, K. (in press) *Moroccan Townsmen: Tradition and Change in a Muslim City*. Manchester.

Dukkali, M. (n.d.) *Al-ithaf al-wajiz*. Ms. D 1320. Rabat, Archives Générales.

Hourani, A.H. and Stern, S.M. (eds) (1970) *The Islamic City*. Oxford.

Ibn Khaldun (1958) *The Muqaddimah: An Introduction to History*. Translated by F. Rosenthal. New York.

Ibn Khaldun (1950) *An Arab Philosophy of History*. Selections translated by C. Issawi. London.

Kaufman, R.R. (1974) 'The patron-client concept and macro-politics: Prospects and problems', *Comparative Studies of Society and History* 16, no.3, 284-308.

Lacouture, J. and S. (1958) *Le Maroc à l'épreuve*. Paris.

Lapidus, I.M. (1967) *Muslim Cities in the Later Middle Ages*. Cambridge, Mass.

Laroui, A. (1970) *L'Histoire du Maghreb: Un essai de synthèse*. Paris.

Mahdi, M. (1964) *Ibn Khaldun's Philosophy of History*. Chicago.

Marais, O. (1973) 'Sociologie politique de Fès', *Revue de l'Occident musulman et de la Méditerranée* (Mélanges Le Tourneau) 15-16, 169-74.

Mardin, S. (1969) 'Power, civil society and culture in the Ottoman empire', *Comparative Studies in Society and History* 11, 258-81.

Naciri, M. (1963) 'Salé: Etude de géographie urbaine', *Revue de Géographie du Maroc* 3-4, 11-82.

Nasiri, A. (1894) *Kitab al-istiqsa fi akhbar al-maghrib al-aqsa*. Cairo.

Paine, R. (ed.) (1971) *Patrons and Brokers in the East Artic*. St. John's, Newfoundland.

Radcliffe-Brown, A.R. (1952) *Structure and Function in Primitive Society*. London.

Swartz, M.J., V.W. Turner, and A. Tuden (eds) (1966) *Political Anthropology*. Chicago.

Waterbury, J. (1970) *The Commander of the Faithful*. New York.

Weber, M. (1947) 'Gerontocracy, patriarchalism and patrimonial authority', in T. Parsons (ed.), *The Theory of Social and Economic Organisation*. New York.

Weber, M. (1958) *From Max Weber: Essays in Sociology*. Translated, edited and with an introduction by H.H. Gerth and C. Wright Mills. New York.

Weber, M. (1962) *The City*. Translated and edited by D. Martindale and G. Neuwirth. New York.

Wolf, E.R. (1966) 'Kinship, friendship, and patron-client relations in complex Societies', in M. Banton (ed.), *The Social Anthropology of Complex Societies*. London.

John Waterbury

An attempt to put patrons and clients in their place

The concept of patronage and patron-client relations offers all the analytic frustrations common to most attempts at categorising social action and human motivation. One cannot advance irrefutable, generally accepted criteria by which to establish what patronage is and when (not to mention how) it has become something else. In short there is little consensus as to what should and should not be considered an aspect or manifestation of patronage.[1] Likewise there are widely varying views of the analytic power of the concept, ranging from those who contend that patronage is no more than a simple descriptive device encompassing one kind of inter-personal relations, without *explaining* anything about them, to those who consider the concept a powerful analytic tool seminal to the understanding and explanation of the use of power in human society.

The debate over inclusivity, exclusivity and analytic utility can probably be resolved only by individual scholars according to their own research priorities, working hypotheses, and ideological outlooks. The essays collected within this volume have advanced our knowledge of the points at issue in the debate. In what follows, no attempt shall be made to touch upon all these issues, but rather I shall confine myself to a brief discussion of those points which seem most sharply to divide us or about which we are manifestly unsure. This is not meant to be a summary or distillation of the many questions raised by the contributors in writing or in discussion. It is, instead, my own perhaps arbitrary selection and assessment of those elements of patronage relations through whose understanding we may be able to bring the phenomenon into sharper focus.

There are several elements that act in combination to constitute a patron-client relationship, and there is some agreement on what these elements are. The problem is to know which are most crucial or, by contrast, simply ancillary to the relationship, how they mix, and when one may speak of patronage networks or even of patronage systems. The most fundamental characteristic of patron-client relations is that they are asymmetrical, one party being demonstrably more powerful or prestigious than the other. But one may immediately pose a question that can be asked of all other elements of the relationship: how disproportionate must the power of the dominant party be to qualify, or conversely not qualify as that of a patron? The difficulty does not lie in dealing with extremely asymmetrical cases but rather with those in which the parties may be quite close in the power at their disposal.

The problem is compounded if the patron wields power in only one sphere of activity, let us say bestowing a specific kind of bureaucratic favour or advancing credit, but has no control over his client in other spheres. How dependent must the client be upon his patron? Must subordination affect all aspects of his life, or may his dependency be functionally specific? Anticipating my own conclusion to questions of this kind, perhaps the most useful way of coping with them is to avoid dealing in thresholds or absolute levels, and, instead treat each element as a variable that can be present to a greater or lesser degree.

For instance, it has been argued that a true patron must have monopolistic control over some scarce or desired resource, generally land, and thereby be in a position to manage access to it among his clients.[2] This argument would preclude consideration of instances in which more than one, if not several patrons, seek at one another's expense to corner the market on some desired resource, such as jobs, and in which prospective clients may have a choice of patrons. Such situations are quite common. Local landowners may manipulate the terms of tenancy competitively to hold their client tenant farmers. Party machines can monopolise public patronage only if they sweep the elections, and even then their hold may last no longer than the period between elections. In brief, does the introduction of competitiveness into the patronage arena, and the attendant watering-down of monopoly control render the relationship something other than that between patron and client?

An equally difficult element to treat is that of durability. It is frequently proposed that patron-client relations must be fairly durable although it is seldom specified with any precision how long-lasting or resilient the links must be. Common sense would suggest that if clientelism is measured by the degree of dependency of the client upon the patron, there must be a minimum life-span to the relationship, short of which it becomes a simple exchange of favours. Patrons may have a vested interest in prolonging the relationship, for its continuation means that the fundamental asymmetry in power, and hence the patron's status, is being maintained. However legitimate they consider their dependent status, clients are far more likely to terminate a relationship if some alternative means for achieving their ends becomes available. Part of the patron's strategy must be to preclude such possibilities, but to the extent that patronage arenas become competitive, relations with clients will be to varying degrees fragile and of short duration. This may be most pronounced in those situations in which the major trade between the weak and the powerful consists in votes and political support in exchange for administrative favours or protection from bureaucratic action. While it may be the case that any patronage link (or patronage 'dyad') is short lived, one may still speak plausibly of enduring patronage or patronage 'systems' if the only alternative for the parties is to recreate the same kind of relations with other patrons.

Far more slippery is the problem of relations that lie dormant for extended periods of time. A favour rendered at a given point in time may not be called in for years and neither party may have a clear idea of what is expected of the other nor when obligations fall due. Yet as long as the account is open and disproportionate power lies in the hands of one party, then a patronage relation can be said to exist.

Durability itself may vary with the affective or contractual nature of the link. Clearly patrons who exert some sort of emotional or moral hold over their clients can expect more stable and enduring relations with them, minimising the possibility of other patrons enticing away their wards through simple material promises. But as patronage links become less diffuse and more specific in purpose, hard-nosed calculations of reciprocity may come to displace affective loyalty. This may mean in some instances that relations become more coercive, with the patron imposing his own terms on unwilling but generally helpless clients. The case would seem to be otherwise, however, in increasingly urban societies with large interventionist bureaucracies that force all citizens to come to terms with them. This context encourages the emergence of competing patron-brokers whose links to their clients may be contractual, renegotiable, and unstable.

Patrons and clients must exchange something, and explicitly or implicitly they maintain accounts. But it is moot whether or not there are any general rules or guide lines as to how the terms of reciprocity are determined. Certainly the relative power of the partners will shape the exchange although not always in the same direction. A local landlord, controlling both a large latifundia and a body of landless peasants, may be able to extract terms of exchange from his clients approaching serfdom. His disproportionate strength leads to a heavy imbalance in the terms of reciprocity in his favour. By contrast, a patron controlling bureaucratic favours may be victimised by his own power, unable to extract from his clients anything commensurate with the services he has rendered. These two examples merely testify to the difficulties one encounters in trying to generalise about reciprocity between patrons and clients. Much depends on the sphere of activity of the partners. The ward-heeler wants votes in exchange for his solicitude; the landowner wants labour, produce, physical support, and perhaps votes; the labour-recruiter requires docility from those who get the jobs; the bureaucrat may try to clientelise other bureaucrats or interest groups with which he deals in order to consolidate his position within the administration. Clients, for their part, will bargain for as much of whatever vital resource it is that binds them to their patron: land or access to land, jobs or job security, credit, support in disaster, protection from the government, access to schools, hospitals and so forth. Finally exchanges, like the relationship itself, may be diffuse, multiplex, involving deference, physical support, gifts, labour in return for the paternalistic involvement of the patron in all aspects of the client's life; or they may be single-purpose, specific and quasi-contractual. A client with a wide range of specific needs may need several patrons.

To sum up, patronage relations provide discriminatory access to desired goods. The desired good may simply be to be left alone or protected from a worse fate than is one's own already,[3] or it may be of a more positive nature consisting in material rewards or strategic resources. Access is governed by a patron who may have varying degrees of control over the resource. There are, of course, never enough rewards or available resources to satisfy potential demand. The nature of the resource, the number of people who seek it, the degree of the patron's control over it (does he share it with other patrons?) will determine the strength of his links to his clients and the degree of their dependency upon him. Degrees of monopoly and durability will tend to vary together. On the other hand, the moral content of the relationship, the asymmetry in power between parties, and the nature of their exchanges may all vary independently. Disproportionate power, for instance, need not entail monopolistic control, morally sanctioned subservience, nor durable relations. However one measures monopoly, asymmetry, durability, affective content, specificity or multiplexity, and the terms of reciprocity, these variables taken in combination are surely requisite to any attempt to identify manifestations of patronage. The strength of specific links can be estimated by assessing the strength or weakness of their constituent parts.

Patron-clientele networks may be seen as strategies for the maintenance or aggrandisement of power on the part of the patrons, and of coping and survival on the part of the clients. They are probably never the sole strategies available. It is in this sense that it may be generally misleading to depict any political or distributive system as being dominated by patronage. Patronage indeed may play a prominent role in the distribution of goods and power within a political system, but it can neither be seen as the system itself nor explain fully how the system operates. If one is ultimately concerned with the analysis of social cleavages, economic distribution, and the concentration of political power, then single-minded attention to patronage will produce only one facet of the system.

In short it is difficult to imagine situations in which it could be said that patronage analysis would be the only fruitful approach to their understanding. It is too easy to forget that the categorisations social scientists apply to human activities are only abstract constructs, and that the actors themselves seldom categorise their own actions.

Patrons and clients may, and probably do, engage in a wide range of interactions revolving about family, peers, work place, recreation, workshop, etc., aspects of which we, the outside observers, single out for attention as manifestations of patronage, or class, or exploitation, or alienation, and so forth.

With this in mind, it becomes easier to understand that one may frequently find given individuals employing a number of seemingly incompatible strategies simultaneously or *seriatim*. It has been argued in some of the contributions to this volume that patronage networks are in direct contradiction to the formation of strategies based on 'horizontal' or class linkages where all those sharing about the same amount of power tend to act together. Patronage brings together parties of widely disparate degrees of power and thus stresses vertical linkages. All this is perfectly true, in the abstract and even empirically, but it may also be the case that a client, or patron, may on occasion stress action through patronage linkages, and on others through class linkages. A worker may have been recruited by a village 'boss' to whom he owes his job and his fidelity, but that does not preclude his joining a union which may from time to time call upon him to engage in some form of class action. A relatively powerless person may find it possible to achieve certain of his ends through a straightforward assault on the bureaucracy in which he presents himself on an equal footing with all other citizens, or through interest groups, or perhaps through some sort of corporate or ethnic group. In societies in which there are marked disparities in wealth and power, one may expect to find an oscillation between short, frequently violent manifestations of class conflict and longer periods in which corporate and patronage linkages are reasserted.

Inevitably, it is asked whether or not patronage is a 'good' thing. Is it 'functional'? Answers to these questions can only come in light of one's ideological preferences. If one believes that classless societies in which power and wealth are evenly distributed are utopian nonsense, then a good case can be made for the positive, 'integrative' functions of patronage which mitigate class cleavages and social conflict and link the powerless to the larger system. An unheeding aristocracy and an unapproachable bureaucracy could deny any real access to the powerless, while patronage evokes the *oblige* of the powerful and the need to perform on the part of the bureaucrats. This view is widely held and occasionally is extended to vigorous defence of bureaucratic corruption or other forms of self-serving activities on the part of public officials (Leff 1964). In a different vein Hirschman (1973, p.556) has speculated on the impact of income inequalities in the process of economic growth and come to the conclusion that some societies are better adapted than others to sustain these disparities.[4]

Members of traditional societies are typically tied to each other by a dense network of obligations that are both mutual and flexible: it is none too clear what it is that is owed nor when it falls due. Hence, when some members of such a society advance, their obligations are apt to expand, and many of those who remain behind expect to be benefited in due course and in some measure as a result of their pre-existing, if imprecise, claims on the former.

On the other hand, patronage networks not only thwart organisation along class lines, but promote privileged, discriminatory access to scarce goods, at the expense of universalistic criteria. Patronage thus lies equally in the path of Weberian universalistic bureaucracy and Marxian class consciousness. It is precisely because Weberian or Marxian philosophies have shaped the symbols of legitimacy in so many Mediterranean societies (Lebanon is a notable exception) that patronage politics have been stubbornly denied official legitimacy. If one adds to this situations in which the patrons identify with one another and in fact form a class of the wealthy and the powerful, but in which the clients are dependent, subservient, and divided, then it is not difficult to conclude that patronage is not only a manifestation of class domination but crucial to its continued maintenance. On these grounds, patronage would surely have to be condemned. Still, both its supporters and detractors have ample scope for empiric investigations of the validity of their normative judgments.

It is tempting at times to see patronage everywhere. Power is always unequally distributed, people use their power advantages and others have to cope with their weakness. Occasionally patronage would seem to have become a residual category for any kind of power game that is not played out according to universalistic, class, ethnic or corporate group criteria. Perhaps more important is the need to identify when patronage relations have become something else. An example from Morocco may help clarify the problem. In Moroccan cities migrants from a small cluster of southern, Berber tribes have, over the years, developed quasi-monopolistic control over grocery and other forms of retail trade as well as over wholesale trade in foodstuffs. Within the ascriptive framework of tribal identity, powerful wholesalers have 'patronised' their less powerful co-tribesmen through the extension of credit and inventory for their shops. Credit-worthiness is based to a large extent on tribal and lineage referrants rather than upon business acumen. No one outside the group gets access to credit nor to valued commodities such as tea or sugar which are vital for any grocery enterprise. Here we have asymmetrical power relations, discriminatory access to scarce goods, durable links founded on recurrent need, a quasi-monopolistic form of resource control among a *group* of patrons (although some competition among them), and an underlying sentiment of moral commitment founded on tribal identity. The system, and it is that, supplies the weak and the up-and-coming with the means for survival while ensuring for the patrons not only their continued dominance but a kin-based framework for applying sanctions to those who violate commercial transactions – i.e. those who fail to pay their debts (Wolf 1966, p.10).

So far so good except that the system seems to be changing rapidly and thereby becoming something else. One may speculate as follows. The commercial networks of the tribesmen have been saturated and there is little room for further expansion. Yet would-be grocers continue to seek access to credit and inventory. There are too many tribal claimants. The wholesalers must choose carefully among them, and that choice may continue to be based on close kinship or friendship at the expense of purely rationalistic considerations. On the other hand it is clear that increasingly the wholesalers demand collateral for loans from their co-tribesmen, a thing unheard of in the past. Thus, the relationship comes to resemble a straightforward commercial transaction with 'objective' criteria of credit-worthiness coming into play. The kin-based system of sanctions has begun to lose its relevance, and it should become possible for non-tribesmen, with adequate credit ratings, to break in. Once that happens the crucial element of discriminatory access on the basis of non-universalistic or non-rational criteria is destroyed and hence, in my view, the underpinning of this particular manifestation of patronage. It is replaced by familiar commercial networks for the financing of retail and wholesale trade (Waterbury 1973).

Analytic problems of a similar order are raised by the notion of groups as clients. A good case can be made for ethnic groups, religious minorities, interest groups, and even nations standing as clients in relation to some more powerful entity. Gellner has documented the manipulation of entire tribes by political patrons, and Khalaf has rightly noted that religious sects in nineteenth-century Lebanon became the clients of foreign powers (Gellner 1962, Khalaf, this volume). Joseph LaPalombara has argued forcefully that Italian interest groups stand in relation to the bureaucracy as clients (*clientela*) and that there is a sort of group interaction with the administration based on 'political kinship' that he refers to as *parentela* (La Palombara 1964, chs 8 and 9). This approach must be handled with care for it may be difficult to distinguish aggregates of clients from what is normally referred to as interest groups or their activities from simple lobbying. Another problem is that of measuring degrees of asymmetry in power between clients and patrons when the client groups, qua groups, are fairly powerful. Moreover, the fact that one or both parties to the relationship may be a group, minimises personal, face-to-face relations for most of the groups' members, and such intimate contacts are generally considered to be an integral part of patronage networks.

The state and its administrative apparatus can be seen as a patron in the abstract. In most countries the public bureaucracy has great power over the lives of average citizens. It may award various services on a discriminatory basis to clients whose recurrent needs ensure a stable relationship. However, in any given instance the disbursing patron may not be the same. Individual bureaucrats, moving from post to post, broker the services of the anonymous patron, the state, to their own advantage. The state controls first order resources, and its civil servants manipulate access to them. The careers of administrative patron-brokers may have little to do with their clients among the citizenry (unless they happen to be powerful interest groups which may treat certain civil servants as *their* clients) and far more to do with the relations they build with other bureaucrats. Unlike party politicians, the administrative patron-broker cannot bargain for advantage on the basis of the numerical strength of his clientele. Promotion will rather depend on strategically placed support in the administration itself. In this sense there may be no patrons and clients but rather cronies who enjoy shifting fortunes but concert to help one another along according to their strengths of the moment. Cronyism, however, based on links between co-equals, is not patronage. Power advantages are generally too short-lived to provide the minimal durability that patronage would require. However, if a bureaucratic figure is able to consolidate his hold on some sector of the administration he may well be able to act as a patron and to build a clientele.[5] In any event the modern bureaucratic state is by no means incompatible with patronage, and in certain circumstances the extent of patronage will vary directly with the extent of bureaucratic intervention.

It is the need to know how patronage varies in degree and kind from one system to another that leads us to another important set of questions. It is indisputable that all political systems or arenas manifest some forms of patronage, but on intuitive grounds most of us probably have the feeling that some systems are more patronage-prone than others. If there is empiric validity to these intuitions, can we explain the variations? At a very broad and simplistic level – but one that is not always taken into consideration – I think that we can.

The crucial variable to my mind is real or perceived vulnerability. Patronage is after all a means of protection both for the weak and for the politically powerful and hence the politically exposed. One may posit that resort to patronage mechanisms will be the more pronounced where the weak are disproportionately weak, the strong disproportionately strong, and formal, alternative mechanisms for protecting citizens – laws, court systems, police, procedural rules of the game, etc. – remain embryonic, manipulable or perhaps imbued with little or no legitimacy. For analytic purposes one could argue that Jimmy Hoffa of the Teamsters Union, or the late Adam Clayton Powell, congressional representative of Harlem, were patrons within their respective constituencies. However, the relations they maintained with their constituents are of an entirely different order from those between a union leader or politician in a country with a vast sea of unemployed, per capita incomes in the $200-$300 range, widespread illiteracy and a powerful interventionist bureaucracy. The American (or Northern European) worker or ghetto-dweller has more financial security, more room for manoeuvre, and much greater latitude in chosing alternative strategies than his counterparts of the southern, eastern, and, to a lesser degree, northern shores of the Mediterranean. So too the patron's role is utterly different in the two contexts. The rules of the game in the 'west' are (at least up until the middle '70s) relatively well understood and tolerated, if not endorsed, by most citizens.

It may be, as several authors have argued (Foster 1965, Silverman 1968, Scott 1968) that in many societies people perceive available resources as being fixed, and thus competition for them is seen as a dangerous and potentially destructive exercise. For the weak, the goal may not be so much to improve one's lot but rather to keep it from becoming worse. The powerful may spend a great deal of effort in dissimulating their power, for the ostentatious aggradisement of power, in a 'zero-sum' context, cannot fail to arouse the jealousy, fear, and counter-action of other patrons apprehensive of the erosion of their own power-base. Patron and client alike may play a very cautious, defensive game seeking to minimise their own vulnerability. Relative prosperity and relative abundance should wreak havoc with these relations, for the individual perception of vulnerability and helplessness will diminish proportionately. New patrons may emerge without destroying the old. The weak and the powerful may both play to maximise advantage rather than to ward off disaster. Both may pursue alternate strategies to the neglect of patronage links.

Vulnerability, of course, varies not only in degree but also in kind. This point is particularly relevant for the societies of the Mediterranean. In the pre-industrial, predominantly agrarian history of the area we encounter what we might call traditional forms of vulnerability. These would consist in a combination of environmental factors and 'predatory' government, all beyond the control of the people themselves. Rain, drought, soil erosion, soil quality, pests, locusts, disease, etc. were elements to which the rural world had to submit but could in no way predict, no less control. Added to this were central authorities whose primary if not sole representatives were the tax collector and army recruitor.[6] The individual peasant's best hope was to minimise the damage, and to do so he would combine hard work, magic or saintly intercession, fatalism, and patronage. The patron would help him through the bad years and keep the government off his back. The patrons themselves would use a combination of material assets, predominantly land, and the size or quality of their clientele to protect their material advantage and to obtain for themselves or their underlings privileged positions in the government apparatus.

What has happened in many Mediterranean societies, and others throughout the world, is that traditional forms of vulnerability have been traded in, although not entirely, for the vulnerabilities of 'modernisation'. The constant factor historically has been continued material scarcity of the most severe kind. Let us focus our attention on two elements generally considered inherent in 'modernisation', the growth of large-scale market economies and of pervasive bureaucratic structures. If these elements are introduced into societies where the bulk of the population lives in or slightly above what we could objectively identify as poverty, then 'modernisation' might entail no more than a change in the terms of subsistence and vulnerability.

In talking of market economies, I do not mean those exclusively of a capitalistic nature, but those in which there are broad networks for the exchange of goods and in which producers supply specific commodities for exchange rather than for auto-consumption. Transactions are carried out in money and pricing is determined either by market forces or the state. Technological advances may have brought the environment under some sort of control, but the producer is now at the mercy of pricing mechanisms beyond his control. The cost of inputs such as seed, fertilisers, pesticides, irrigation pumps, electricity, gasoline, mechanical implements and so forth may well be fixed by the state. Even if the market is allowed to operate freely to determine prices, they will either reflect the high cost of imported goods or the high costs of locally-manufactured products. Likewise the state, or an even more remote force, world markets, will determine the price at which primary produce is marketed. Consolidating the new vulnerability is the recurrent, vital need for credit to finance the next crop. This too may be meted out on a discriminatory basis by the state or at exorbitant interest rates determined by supply and demand. What is important to remember is that, by virtue of the nature of the development process, vital resources and inputs are in chronically short supply and most producers will never be able to have enough of them to prosper. Their goal is to negotiate access to resources in order to assure a sufficient supply to keep from going under from one year to the next. This is a fertile context for patron-client networks in which the patrons increasingly become the brokers and middlemen who trade in access to first order resources.

Credit, within the general context of scarcity, becomes a fundamental element in generating new links of dependency and clientage. Capital, like everything else, is in very short supply and collateral may have to be calculated according to several non-economic measures such a political loyalty, voluntary labour, deference or unspecified future services. Borrowing need not imply lasting relationships, and today's borrower may be tomorrow's lender or both simultaneously. Nonetheless because credit is a recurrent and critical need in 'modernising' but poor societies, opportunities for patronage are proportionately vast.

The vulnerabilities of modernisation are by no means confined to the rural world. In several societies around the shores of the Mediterranean the state has come, for all intents and purposes, to determine the cost of all the factors of production in nearly all economic spheres. Mandatory pricing, wage regulation, import duties and import licensing, public industries, public credit agencies and investment bodies allow the state to intervene directly or indirectly in every aspect of production. Not only can it control pricing mechanisms but it also comes to administer a range of services that few citizens could or would do without. Education, public health, transportation, public sector employment, trade licenses, import licenses, building permits, commercial licensing, passports, birth certificates, criminal records, pensions, social security all form a part of the vast array of benefits that the state, through its agents, can grant or deny to the citizens. And the fundamental point, once again, is that, in the absence of prosperity, even under the best of circumstances, not everyone can benefit from them even if they are so entitled. A selection process must emerge, and it is frequently discriminatory. One implement at the state's disposal that is of extraordinary importance in making and breaking the patrons themselves is the state's control over the allocation of hard currency. Nothing is in shorter supply than hard currency, for the outlays for capital goods and consumer goods importations always outstrip the export capacity (leaving aside the oil-rich) of the developing countries. Who gets access to these limited funds and what is imported become matters for fierce competition. The patrons of hard currency allocation are figures of great power.

Perhaps we may give some tangibility to all these generalisations if we take the mundane example of a taxi-driver in Cairo. Cairo is a city of seven million inhabitants where only about 1.5 million have any kind of remunerative employment. The great bulk of the city's population has to struggle to eke out an existence. Much of the work force is illiterate, recently arrived or only one generation removed from the countryside. Steady work itself is the scarce factor. People make do as scavengers, paper gatherers, push-cart merchants, vegetable haulers, carriers, pushers, pimps, car watchers and a myriad of other parasite trades. A man who can become a taxi-driver can move up a notch. He need not be literate and it can be empirically verified that knowing how to drive is not requisite. All the terms of the taxi trade are controlled by the state and every element in it is in short supply. Locally-produced cabs are sold at high cost and after years of waiting. Imported vehicles, until recently, were exorbitantly expensive due to high import duties. Spare parts and tires, mostly imported, have been very expensive when they could be found at all. Further, the state sets the base fare (which in the event, has not changed since 1952), the price of gasoline, safety standards, licensing procedures, inspection of meters, etc. To break in requires capital, well-placed friends or both. The pattern is increasingly for upper-echelon bureaucrats and police and army officers with the right connections to constitute fleets and hire drivers whom they can trust not to abuse their vehicles. The drivers pocket one fourth of the fares. Fleet-owners and taxi-drivers come to constitute patron-client networks, based on privileged access to a scarce means of livelihood. The relationship may, as in Morocco, change into something far more contractual and anonymous, but the overall economic context is conducive to the regeneration of such relations.

What of the governments themselves and the nature of elite competition? In the traditional period, governments may have been predatory but their legitimacy was seldom questioned. But the twentieth-century states of the Mediterranean have experienced and continue to experience acute conflicts, often violent, over the symbols of legitimacy. In many instances not only the rules of the game, but the political system itself are disputed. One need not belabour this point, but the stakes of the Mediterranean game are high. The higher up in the political world one moves the more dangerous it becomes. Politicians face hard decisions, and if they choose in error they may pay a high price. We do not ask 'What after Tito or Bourguiba?' in the same sense as 'What after Wilson, Ford, or Giscard?' When we ask 'Can Sadat survive, or Karamanlis, or Costa Gomes?', we are merely reflecting the general impression that these heads of state are faced with systemic challenges that require either the right choices or the leader's downfall. All those close to the summit must also make their choices and they are equally risk-laden. There are no absolute guarantees against the future, but a strategic or impressive clientele and a well-constructed alliance of cronies is a good hedge. Political vulnerability encourages such defence strategies.

Taking all the above factors into account, it can be argued that material, bureaucratic, and political vulnerabilities are maximised in the so-called developing countries with low standards of living, constant conflict over the symbols of legitimacy and the rules of the game, and marked inequalities in the distribution of scarce resources. Moreover, those other characteristics associated with patronage – asymmetrical power relations, durability, monopolistic control of resources, moral underpinnings, and multiplexity – will be most evident where vulnerability is most salient. The manifestation of patronage in these situations is more pronounced than in societies where prosperity, political concensus of sorts and more manageable distribution problems have opened up new strategies for the weak and the strong. In the poorer societies patronage helps obscure and disorient class alignments and to perpetuate the power advantage of the dominant groups by the conscious cultivation of vulnerability and dependency. As the more prosperous societies of the Mediterranean come under the growing threat of economic collapse in the face of rising energy costs, we may be able to assess with greater certainty the relations between scarcity, vulnerability and patronage.

One may conclude from the above that for the concept of patronage to become something more than a residual category or a phenomenon so ubiquitous as to deprive it of any analytic utility, it is important to join the examination of any of its discrete manifestations with that of the general politico-economic context in which it is found. It is this context that can 'explain' the characteristics of patronage networks rather than the other way around. Resource availability, resource and income distribution, social stratification, market processes, administrative behaviour, and channels for political representation must be generally understood in order to determine what range of strategies is open to the weak and powerful. Once this is known, then patronage can be situated among these strategies and the attempt to weigh its constituent parts begun.

NOTES

1.   We are, of course, not without definitions. One of the most useful attempts at synthesising various definitions is that of Hall (1974). *The International Encyclopaedia of the Social Sciences* (Crower, Collins and MacMillan Inc., N.Y. 1968) has no separate entry for either client or patron/patronage, including the latter as an aspect of 'paternalism' (Vol. 11, pp. 475-6). In *A Dictionary of the Social Sciences* (ed. Gould and Kolb, Tavistock, London, 1964), Hugh Bone treats patronage almost exclusively from the point of view of the distribution of spoils, jobs, and favours, generally from a public source, pp. 486-7. The authors of the essays in this volume have all set down their own working definitions.

2.   This proposition poses a logical dilemma. If the patron has a monopoly over a scarce and *vital* resource, then anyone who needs access to it must become a client. But clientage is based on discriminatory or differential access to the resources the patron controls; some get it and others don't. Exclusion from the resource would lead to a non-relationship, for the prospective client would have to leave the patron's arena in order to survive. On the other hand if everyone is a client one wonders how long the patron can maintain his monopoly before the clients come to sense their shared interests.

3.   This may take the extreme form of creating a need for protection where none existed before. The Mafia in the US became proficient in the technique whereby a patron forces people into a client relationship and then protects them against himself for a fee.

4.   In a different but equally positive vein, see Lemarchand (1972), pp. 68-90. On this and many of the other questions discussed in this essay, see Kaufman (1974), pp. 284-308.

5.   Algeria provides good examples of both groups. President Boumedienne's Oujda Group consists (or consisted) of his cronies. His Minister of Industry and Petroleum Affairs, Abdessalm Belaid, has held his post for over a decade and has clearly become a patron.

6.   One of a myriad of examples would be that of the reign of Mohammed Ali (1805-49) in Egypt who raised labour corvées of as many as 300,000 in a single year – i.e., about 10 percent of the population at that time – to dig and clean the irrigation canals. In 1819, as many as 100,000 may have died during the corvée over a ten-month period. See Rivlin (1961), esp. Chapter 12.

REFERENCES

Foster, G. (1965) 'Peasant society and the image of the limited good', *American Anthropologist* 67, no. 2.

Gellner, E. (1962) 'Patterns of rural rebellion in Morocco: Tribes as minorities', *European Journal of Sociology* 3, no. 2.

Hall, A. (1974) 'Patron-client relations', *Journal of Peasant Studies*, 1, no. 4, 506-8.

Hirschman, A.O. (1973) 'The changing tolerance for income inequality in the course of economic development', *Quarterly Journal of Economics* 87, no. 4, 544-66.

Kaufman, R. (1974) 'The patron-client concept and macro-politics', *Comparative Studies in Society and History* 16, no. 3, 284-308.

LaPalombara, J. (1964) *Interest Groups in Italian Politics*. Princeton.

Leff, N. (1964) 'Economic development through bureaucratic corruption', *American Behavioural Scientist* 8, 8-15.

Lemarchand, R. (1972) 'Political clientelism and ethnicity in tropical Africa', *American Political Science Review* LXVI, no. 1, 68-90.

Rivlin, H. (1961) *The Agricultural Policy of Mohammed Ali in Egypt*. Cambridge, Mass.

Scott, J.C. (1968) *Political Ideology in Malaysia: Beliefs of an Elite*. Yale.

Silverman, S.F. (1968) 'Agricultural organisation, social structure and values in Italy: Amoral familism reconsidered', *American Anthropologist* 70, no. 1, 1-20.

Waterbury, J. (1973) *North for the Trade: The Life and Times of a Berber Merchant*. Berkeley.

Wolf, E. (1966) 'Kinship, friendship and patron-client relations in complex societies', in M. Banton (ed.), *The Social Anthropology of Complex Societies*. London.

Index of Authors

General Index